The grandiose Maya ruins at Cobá are beside a beautiful _____ jungle. See chapter 5.
© Hollenbeck Photography.

Abundant coral reefs and stunning tropical fish make Cozumel a popular snorkeling destination. See chapter 4. © R. Rocha Filho/Image Bank.

The walled Maya city of Tulum is an easy excursion from Cancún. See chapter 5.
© Jose Fuste Raga/Stock Market.

Cancún's sparkling blue shoreline and luxury resorts draw scores of visitors. © M.C. Price/Viesti Associates, Inc.

A beachfront resort in Cancún. See chapter 3. © *Cosmo Condina/Tony Stone Images.*

A Chaac-Mool statue at the Maya ruins of Chichén-Itzá. See chapter 6.
© Bob Krist Photography.

A giant Olmec head on display at the Parque Museo de la Venta in Villahermosa. See chapter 7. © M. Timothy O'Keefe Photography.

Frommer's®

Cancún, Cozumel & the Yucatán

2004

by David Baird & Lynne Bairstow

Here's what the critics say about Frommer's:

"Amazingly easy to use. Very portable, very complete."
—*Booklist*

"Detailed, accurate, and easy-to-read information for all price ranges."
—*Glamour Magazine*

"Hotel information is close to encyclopedic."
—*Des Moines Sunday Register*

"Frommer's Guides have a way of giving you a real feel for a place."
—*Knight Ridder Newspapers*

WILEY

Wiley Publishing, Inc.

Published by:

Wiley Publishing, Inc.

111 River St.
Hoboken, NJ 07030

ISBN 0-7645-3735-0
ISSN 1064-1416

Editors: Marie Morris and Kelly Regan
Production Editor: Suzanna R. Thompson
Cartographer: John Decamillis
Photo Editor: Richard Fox
Production by Wiley Indianapolis Composition Services

Front cover photo: Cancún's Hotel Zone
Back cover photo: Cenote Dzitnup, near Valladolid

For information on our other products and services or to obtain technical support, please contact our Customer Care Department within the U.S. at 800-762-2974, outside the U.S. at 317-572-3993 or fax 317-572-4002.

Wiley also publishes its books in a variety of electronic formats. Some content that appears in print may not be available in electronic formats.

Manufactured in the United States of America

5   4   3

Contents

Appendix B: Useful Terms & Phrases   285

Index   291

List of Maps

Acknowledgments

Thanks to Claudia Hurtado Valenzuela for her work on the Riviera Maya chapter.
—David Baird

Many thanks to all of the many people who helped me gather the information, tips, and treasures that have made their way into this book. I am especially grateful for the assistance of Claudia Velo, whose tireless work helped to ensure the information in this book is correct, and for her valuable ideas and contributions.
—Lynne Bairstow

An Invitation to the Reader

In researching this book, we discovered many wonderful places—hotels, restaurants, shops, and more. We're sure you'll find others. Please tell us about them, so we can share the information with your fellow travelers in upcoming editions. If you were disappointed with a recommendation, we'd love to know that, too. Please write to:

Frommer's Cancún, Cozumel & the Yucatán 2004
Wiley Publishing, Inc. • 111 River St. • Hoboken, NJ 07030

An Additional Note

Please be advised that travel information is subject to change at any time—and this is especially true of prices. We therefore suggest that you write or call ahead for confirmation when making your travel plans. The authors, editors, and publisher cannot be held responsible for the experiences of readers while traveling. Your safety is important to us, however, so we encourage you to stay alert and be aware of your surroundings. Keep a close eye on cameras, purses, and wallets, all favorite targets of thieves and pickpockets.

About the Authors

David Baird is a writer, editor, and translator who doesn't much like writing about himself in the third person (too close to being an obituary). Texan by birth, Mexican by disposition, he has lived several years in different parts of Mexico following his interests, which include food, drink, and the afternoon siesta. Now based in Austin, Texas, he spends as much time in Mexico as possible. At home, his hobbies include painting, scraping, mowing, patching dry wall, and extemporaneous engineering.

For **Lynne Bairstow**, Mexico has become more home than her native United States. After living in Puerto Vallarta for most of the past 11 years, she's developed an appreciation and a true love of this country and its complex, colorful culture. Her travel articles on Mexico have appeared in the *New York Times,* the *San Francisco Chronicle,* the *Los Angeles Times, Frommer's Budget Travel* magazine, and *Alaska Airlines Magazine.* In 2000, Lynne was awarded the Pluma de Plata, a top honor granted by the Mexican government to foreign writers, for her work in the Frommer's guidebook to Puerto Vallarta.

Other Great Guides for Your Trip:

Frommer's Mexico
Frommer's Portable Cancún
Mexico's Beach Resorts For Dummies

Frommer's Star Ratings, Icons & Abbreviations

Every hotel, restaurant, and attraction listing in this guide has been ranked for quality, value, service, amenities, and special features using a **star-rating system.** In country, state, and regional guides, we also rate towns and regions to help you narrow down your choices and budget your time accordingly. Hotels and restaurants are rated on a scale of zero (recommended) to three stars (exceptional). Attractions, shopping, nightlife, towns, and regions are rated according to the following scale: zero stars (recommended), one star (highly recommended), two stars (very highly recommended), and three stars (must-see).

In addition to the star-rating system, we also use **seven feature icons** that point you to the great deals, in-the-know advice, and unique experiences that separate travelers from tourists. Throughout the book, look for:

Finds	Special finds—those places only insiders know about
Fun Fact	Fun facts—details that make travelers more informed and their trips more fun
Kids	Best bets for kids, and advice for the whole family
Moments	Special moments—those experiences that memories are made of
Overrated	Places or experiences not worth your time or money
Tips	Insider tips—great ways to save time and money
Value	Great values—where to get the best deals

The following **abbreviations** are used for credit cards:

AE	American Express	DISC	Discover	V	Visa
DC	Diners Club	MC	MasterCard		

Frommers.com

Now that you have the guidebook to a great trip, visit our website at **www.frommers.com** for travel information on more than 3,000 destinations. With features updated regularly, we give you instant access to the most current trip-planning information available. At Frommers.com, you'll also find the best prices on airfares, accommodations, and car rentals—and you can even book travel online through our travel booking partners. At Frommers.com, you'll also find the following:

- Online updates to our most popular guidebooks
- Vacation sweepstakes and contest giveaways
- Newsletter highlighting the hottest travel trends
- Online travel message boards with featured travel discussions

What's New in Cancún, Cozumel & the Yucatán

Despite the uncertain travel environment worldwide, Mexico tourism remains strong. During 2002, more than 19.7 million international visitors arrived, a decrease of less than 1% from the previous year. Many tourists from the U.S. and Canada, who in the past might have gone to Europe, are making their way to Mexico. The U.S. remains Mexico's main market, representing 88.2% of international arrivals. The peso has declined against the dollar (about 20%) while the euro has risen, making Mexico cheaper and Europe more expensive for Americans, Brits, and Canadians. And the present political climate has changed perceptions of Mexico. Before terrorism became a major concern for travelers, many perceived Mexico as a riskier destination than Europe; today, the reverse is the case. Still, the economic slowdown is keeping many at home, and this means that there are still deals to be found in Mexico.

Politically and socially, Mexico remains stable. Like the U.S., it is experiencing economic hard times. A common expression heard here is, "When America sneezes, Mexico gets the flu." There are growing signs of discontent with NAFTA, an issue that will probably not go away until the economy turns around. President Vicente Fox will have his hands full trying to convince his fellow citizens that he has Mexico on the right track by tying its interests more closely to the U.S., while at the same time showing them that he isn't kowtowing to Washington.

Tourists will find good value, thanks to the favorable exchange rate. But they will also have to spend a little more here and there. For example, the Instituto Nacional de Antropología e Historia (INAH), the agency that overseas the administration of museums and archaeological sites, has ended its policy of allowing tourists free admission on Sunday.

According to the U.S. Department of Transportation, travel to Mexico currently accounts for one-third of the total number of U.S. residents traveling abroad. With its "Closer than Ever" ad campaign, Mexico is positioned as one of the few destinations outside of the United States that offers North American travelers proximity, security, and a welcoming atmosphere.

Here is a quick rundown on what else is new and noteworthy in Cancún, Cozumel, and the Yucatán:

PLANNING YOUR TRIP Most hotels in Mexico—with the exception of places that receive little foreign tourism—quote prices in U.S. dollars. Thus, currency fluctuations are unlikely to affect the prices at most hotels. Prices in this book (which are always given in U.S. dollars) have been converted to U.S. dollars at 10 pesos to the dollar.

CANCUN For complete information on Cancún, see chapter 3. **Pleasant Holidays** is boosting service into

Cancún aboard scheduled nonstop ATA Airlines flights. The round-trip service leaves from both Los Angeles and San Francisco.

Attractions   The first Jack Nicklaus Signature Golf Course in the Cancún area has opened at the Moon Palace Golf Resort (www.palaceresorts.com), along the Riviera Maya. Two additional PGA courses are planned for the area just north of Cancún in the next 2 years.

Magic Sky (© 998/885-1720) offers panoramic helicopter tours of Cancún and the surrounding areas, with day and evening flights available. Tours to the ruins and flights south along the Riviera Maya are also an option, as are customized tours. A 25-minute ride over the Cancún Hotel Zone costs $120.

Another option for taking in the view from above is in the new rotating sightseeing tower, **La Torre Cancún,** at the El Embarcadero marina (www.el embarcadero.com). Also recently opened at El Embarcadero is the **House of Mexican Folk Art,** a museum featuring colorful folk art, including traditional masks, regional costumes, Virgin of Guadalupe images, toys, musical instruments, and more. Admission is $5 per person, $3 for children ages 5 to 11. Open daily from 9am to 9pm.

After Dark Bulldog Café has replaced the once-dominant disco Christine. The atmosphere is now much more casual, and the music is pure dance.

ISLA MUJERES   For complete information, see chapter 4.

Among the most newsworthy of Mexico's unique inns is the recently opened **Secreto.** A stylish enclave in this otherwise funky village, it's on a secluded cove on the northern end of the island, close to the activity of "downtown" Isla.

Avalon Resorts has opened the 144-room **Avalon Reef Club** (© 888/ 497-4325; www.avalonresorts.net), an all-inclusive resort at the northern tip of the island.

THE RIVIERA MAYA   For complete information on this region, see chapter 5.

Puerto Morelos & Environs   There are now four luxury spa resorts near Puerto Morelos. Each offers a different angle on how to pamper its guests, with "pamper" being the operative word.

Playa del Carmen   New restaurants and new hotels add variety to this destination, which keeps growing at an astonishing rate.

Costa Maya   Highway work continues between Bacalar and Limones and between Limones and Majahual. It slows the trip from Tulum to Chetumal by about 30 to 60 minutes.

Río Bec Ruins   Becán suffered damage from Hurricane Isidore, and access to certain buildings and the inner chambers has been restricted until the buildings can be made structurally sound.

MERIDA, CHICHEN ITZA & THE MAYA INTERIOR   For complete information on this region, see chapter 6.

Mérida   The only signs left from the extensive damage caused by Hurricane Isidore are the missing trees. In **Uaymitún,** the observation tower for viewing flamingos remains closed for repairs.

CHIAPAS   Archaeologists continue work on Structure 13 at **Palenque,** where they are trying to excavate subterranean chambers. Rancho Esmeralda, a small ecolodge near Ocosingo, is no longer open, having been invaded by peasants from a nearby village. See chapter 7.

1

The Best of Cancún, Cozumel & the Yucatán

The Yucatán Peninsula welcomes more visitors than any other part of Mexico. Its tremendous variety attracts every kind of traveler with an unequaled mix of sophisticated resorts, rustic inns, ancient Maya culture, exquisite beaches, and exhilarating adventures. Between the two of us, we've logged thousands of miles crisscrossing the peninsula, and these are our personal favorites—the best places to go, the best restaurants, the best hotels, and must-see, one-of-a-kind experiences.

1 The Best Beach Vacations

- **Cancún:** Essentially one long ribbon of white sand bordering aquamarine water, Cancún has one of Mexico's most beautifully situated beaches. If you want tropical drinks brought to you while you lounge in the sand, this is the vacation for you. Though Cancún has a reputation as a bustling, modern megaresort, it's also a great place for exploring Caribbean reefs, tranquil lagoons, and the surrounding jungle. The most tranquil waters and beaches on Cancún Island are those at the northern tip, facing the Bahía de Mujeres. See chapter 3.

- **Isla Mujeres:** If laid-back is what you're after, this idyllic island offers peaceful, small-town beach life at its best. Most accommodations are smaller, inexpensive inns, with a few unique, luxurious places tossed in. Bike—or take a golf cart—around the island to explore rocky coves and sandy beaches, or focus your tanning efforts on the wide beachfront of Playa Norte. Here you'll find calm waters and *palapa* restaurants, where you can have fresh-caught

fish for lunch. You're close to great diving and snorkeling just offshore, as well as Isla Contoy National Park, which features great bird life and its own dramatic, uninhabited beach. If all that tranquility starts to get to you, you're only a ferry ride away from the action in Cancún. See chapter 4.

- **Cozumel:** It may not have big, sandy beaches, but Cozumel has that island feel going for it. The water on the sheltered western shore is so calm it's like swimming in an aquarium. Cozumel is perfect for those who spend more time in the water than on land and like it calm and clear. See chapter 4.

- **Playa del Carmen:** This is one of our absolute favorite Mexican beach vacations. Stylish and hip, Playa del Carmen offers a beautiful beach and an eclectic assortment of inns, B&Bs, and cabañas. Activity centers on the small but excellent selection of restaurants, clubs, sidewalk cafes, and funky shops that run the length of pedestrian-only Avenida 5. You're also close to the coast's major attractions, including

Mexico

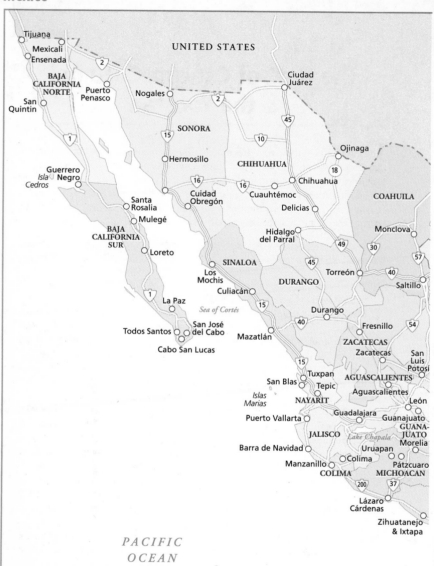

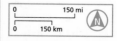

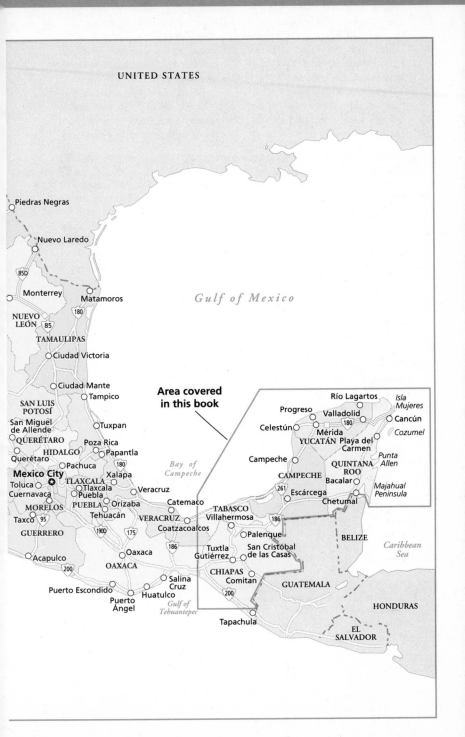

Tulum, *cenote* (sinkholes or natural wells) diving, and Cozumel Island (just 30 min. away by ferry). Enjoy it while it's a manageable size. See chapter 5.

- **Tulum:** Fronting some of the best beaches on the entire coast, Tulum's small *palapa* hotels offer guests a little slice of paradise far from crowds and megaresorts. The bustling town lies inland; at the coast, things are quiet and will remain so because all these hotels are small and must generate their own electricity. If you can pull yourself away from the beach, nearby are ruins to explore and a vast nature preserve. See chapter 5.

2 The Best Cultural Experiences

- **Streets and Park Entertainment** (Mérida): Few cities have so vibrant a street scene as Mérida. Throughout the week you can catch music and dance performances in plazas about the city, and on Sunday, Mérida really gets going—streets are closed off, food stalls spring up everywhere, and you can enjoy a book fair, a flea market, comedy acts, band concerts, and dance groups. At night, the main plaza is the place to be: People dance to mambos and rumbas in the street in front of the town hall. See chapter 6.

- **Exploring the Inland Yucatán Peninsula:** Travelers who venture only to the Yucatán's resorts and cities miss the tidy inland villages, where women wear colorful embroidered dresses and life seems to proceed as though the modern world (except highways) didn't exist. The adventure of seeing newly uncovered ruins, deep in jungle settings, is not to be missed. See chapter 5.

- **San Cristóbal de las Casas:** The city of San Cristóbal is a living museum, with 16th-century colonial architecture and pre-Hispanic native influences. The highland Maya live in surrounding villages and arrive daily in town wearing colorful handmade clothing. The villages are a window into another world, giving visitors a glimpse of traditional Indian dress, religious customs, churches, and ceremonies. See chapter 7.

- **Regional Cuisine:** A trip to the Yucatán allows for a culinary tour of some of Mexico's finest foods. Don't miss specialties such as *pollo* or *cochinita pibil* (chicken or pork in savory *achiote* sauce), great seafood dishes, the many styles of *tamal* found throughout Chiapas and the Yucatán, and Caribbean-influenced foods such as fried bananas, black beans, and yucca root. For a glossary of popular regional dishes, see Appendix B.

3 The Best Archaeological Sites

- **Calakmul:** Of the many elegantly built Maya cities of the Río Bec area in the lower Yucatán, Calakmul is the broadest in scope and design. It's also one of the hardest to get to—about 48km (30 miles) from the Guatemalan border and completely surrounded in jungle (actually, the Calakmul Biological Reserve). Calakmul is a walled city with the tallest pyramid in the Yucatán—a city whose primary inhabitants are the trees that populate the plazas. Go now, while it remains infrequently visited. See "The Río Bec Ruin Route," in chapter 5.

- **Tulum:** Some dismiss Tulum as less important than other ruins in the Yucatán Peninsula, but this seaside Maya fortress is still inspiring. The sight of its crumbling stone walls against the stark contrast of the clear turquoise ocean just beyond is extraordinary. See "Tulum," in chapter 5.
- **Uxmal:** No matter how many times I see Uxmal, the splendor of its stone carvings inspires awe. A stone rattlesnake undulates across the facade of the Nunnery complex, and 103 masks of Chaac—the rain god—project from the Governor's Palace. See "The Ruins of Uxmal," in chapter 6.
- **Chichén Itzá:** Stand beside the giant serpent head at the foot of the El Castillo pyramid and marvel at the architects and astronomers who positioned the building so precisely that shadow and sunlight form a serpent's body slithering from peak to the earth at each equinox (Mar 21 and Sept 21). See "The Ruins of Chichén Itzá," in chapter 6.
- **Palenque:** The ancient builders of these now-ruined structures carved histories in stone that scholars are only now able to decipher. Imagine the magnificent ceremony in A.D. 683 when King Pacal was buried below ground in a secret pyramidal tomb—unspoiled until its discovery in 1952. See "Palenque," in chapter 7.

4 The Best Active Vacations

- **Scuba Diving in Cozumel and along the Yucatán's Caribbean coast:** The coral reefs off the island, Mexico's premier diving destination, are among the top five dive spots in the world. The Yucatán's coastal reef, part of the second-largest reef system in the world, affords excellent diving all along the coast. Especially beautiful is the Chinchorro Reef, lying 20 miles offshore from Majahual or Xcalak. Diving from Isla Mujeres is also quite spectacular. See chapters 4 and 5.
- **Fly-fishing off the Punta Allen Peninsula:** Serious anglers will enjoy the challenge of fly-fishing the saltwater flats and lagoons of Ascención Bay, near Punta Allen. See "Tulum, Punta Allen & Sian Ka'an," in chapter 5.
- *Cenote* **Diving on the Yucatán Mainland:** Dive into the clear depths of the Yucatán's *cenotes* for an interesting twist on underwater exploration. The Maya considered the *cenotes* sacred—and their vivid colors indeed seem otherworldly.
Most are located between Playa del Carmen and Tulum, and dive shops in these areas regularly run trips for experienced divers. For recommended dive shops, see "Cozumel," in chapter 4, and "Playa del Carmen" and "South of Playa del Carmen to Tulum," in chapter 5.
- **An Excursion to Bonampak, Yaxchilán, and the Usumacinta River:** Bonampak and Yaxchilán—two remote, jungle-surrounded Maya sites along the Usumacinta River—are now accessible by car and motorboat. The experience could well be the highlight of any trip. See "Road Trips from San Cristóbal," in chapter 7.
- **Birding:** The Yucatán Peninsula, Tabasco, and Chiapas are an ornithological paradise, with hundreds of species awaiting the birder's gaze and list. One very special place is Isla Contoy, with more than 70 species of birds as well as a host of marine and animal life. See p. 101, chapter 6, and chapter 7.

5 The Best Places to Get Away from It All

- **Isla Mujeres:** If there's one island in Mexico that guarantees a respite from stress, it's Isla Mujeres. You'll find an ample selection of hotels and restaurants, and they're as laid-back as their patrons. Here life moves along in pure *mañana* mode. Visitors stretch out and doze beneath shady palms or languidly stroll about. For many, the best part about this getaway is that it's comfortably close to Cancún's international airport, as well as shopping and dining, should you choose to reconnect. See "Isla Mujeres," in chapter 4.

- **The Yucatán's Riviera Maya:** Away from the busy resort of Cancún, a string of quiet getaways, including Capitán Lafitte, KaiLuum, Paamul, Punta Bete, and a portion of Xpu-ha, offer tranquility on beautiful beaches at low prices. See "North of Playa del Carmen to the Puerto Morelos Area" and "South of Playa del Carmen to Tulum," in chapter 5.

- **Tulum:** Near the Tulum ruins, about two dozen beachside *palapa* inns offer some of the most peaceful getaways in the country. This stretch just might offer the best sandy beaches on the entire coast.

Life here among the birds and coconut palms is decidedly unhurried. See "Tulum," in chapter 5.

- **Rancho Encantado Cottage Resort** (Lago Bacalar; © 800/505-MAYA in the U.S. or 983/831-0037; www.encantado.com): The attractive *casitas* are the place to unwind at this resort, where hammocks stretch between trees. The hotel is on the shores of placid Lago (Lake) Bacalar, south of Cancún near Chetumal, and there's nothing around for miles. But if you want adventure, you can head out to the lake in a kayak, follow a birding trail, or take an excursion to Belize and the intriguing nearby Maya ruins on the Río Bec ruin route. See p. 161.

- **Eco Paraíso Xixim** (Celestún; © 988/916-2100; www.mex online.com/eco-paraiso.htm): In these crowded times, space is a luxury that's getting harder to come by. Space is precisely what makes this place so great: Fifteen bungalows dot 5km (3 miles) of beach bordering a coconut plantation. Throw in a good restaurant, a pool, and a couple of hammocks, and you have that rare combination of comfort and isolation. See p. 195.

6 The Best Museums

- **Museo de la Isla de Cozumel** (Cozumel): More than something to do on a rainy day, this well-done museum is worth a visit any time. It unveils the island's past in an informative way not found anywhere else. There's a good bookstore on the first floor and a rooftop restaurant overlooking the *malecón* (boardwalk) and the Caribbean. See p. 116.

- **Museo de la Cultura Maya** (Chetumal): This modern museum, one of the best in the country, explores

Maya archaeology, architecture, history, and mythology. It has interactive exhibits and a glass floor that allows visitors to walk above replicas of Maya sites. See p. 163.

- **Museo Regional de Antropología** (Mérida): Housed in the Palacio Cantón, one of the most beautiful 19th-century mansions in the city, this museum showcases area archaeology and anthropological studies in handsome exhibits. See p. 184.

- **Museo Regional de Antropología Carlos Pellicer Cámara** (Villahermosa): This anthropology museum addresses Mexican history in the form of objects found at archaeological sites, with particular emphasis on the pre-Hispanic peoples of the Gulf Coast region. See p. 232.
- **Parque–Museo la Venta** (Villahermosa): The Olmec, considered Mexico's mother culture, are the subject of this park/museum, which features the magnificent stone remains that were removed from the La Venta site not far away. Stroll through a jungle setting where tropical birds alight, and savor the giant carved stone heads of the mysterious Olmec. See p. 233.

7 The Best Shopping

Some tips on bargaining: Although haggling over prices in markets is expected and part of the fun, don't try to browbeat the vendor or bad-mouth the goods. Vendors won't bargain with people they consider disrespectful unless they are desperate to make a sale. Be insistent but friendly.

- **Resort Wear in Cancún:** Resort clothing—especially if you can find a sale—can be a bargain here. And the selection may be wider than what's available at home. Almost every mall on the island contains trendy boutiques that specialize in locally designed and imported clothing. See "Shopping," in chapter 3.
- **Duty Free in Cancún:** If you're looking for European perfume, fine watches, or other imported goods, you'll find the prices in Cancún's duty-free shops (at the major malls on the island and in downtown Cancún) hard to beat. See "Shopping," in chapter 3.
- **Precious Gemstones in Isla Mujeres:** Isla Mujeres, also a duty-free zone, offers an impressive selection of both precious stones and superb craftsmen who can make jewelry designs to order. See "Isla Mujeres," in chapter 4.

- **Avenida 5, Playa del Carmen:** Once Playa del Carmen was considered a shopping wasteland. All that has changed, though: Today, the pedestrian-only Avenida 5 abounds with small boutiques selling batik clothing and fabric, Guatemalan textiles, Mexican dance masks, premium tequilas, Cuban cigars, and decorative pottery from Mexico's best pottery-making villages. See "Playa del Carmen," in chapter 5.
- **Mérida:** This is *the* marketplace for the Yucatán—the best place to buy hammocks, *guayaberas,* Panama hats, and Yucatecan *huipiles.* See "Exploring Mérida," in chapter 6.
- **San Cristóbal de las Casas:** Deep in the heart of the Maya highlands, San Cristóbal has shops, open plazas, and markets that feature the distinctive waist-loomed wool and cotton textiles of the region, as well as leather shoes, handsomely crude pottery, and Guatemalan textiles. Highland Maya Indians sell direct to tourists from their armloads of textiles, dolls, and attractive miniature likenesses of Subcomandante Marcos—complete with ski masks. See "San Cristóbal de las Casas," in chapter 7.

8 The Hottest Nightlife

Although, as expected, Cancún is home to much of the Yucatán's nightlife, that resort city isn't the only place to have a good time after dark.

Along the Caribbean coast, beachside dance floors with live bands and extended "happy hours" in seaside bars dominate the nightlife. Here are some favorite hot spots, from live music in hotel lobby bars to hip techno dance clubs.

- **Coco Bongo, Carlos 'n' Charlie's, La Boom & Dady'O:** These Cancún bars all offer good drinks, hot music, and great dance floors. **Mango Tango** is a top spot for live Cuban and Caribbean rhythms in Cancún. See p. 77.
- **Forum by the Sea:** Here's one place that has it all: The newest of the seaside entertainment centers in Cancún has a dazzling array of dance clubs, sports bars, fast food, and fine dining, with shops open late as well. You'll find plenty of familiar names here, including the Hard Rock Cafe and Rainforest Cafe. It's also the home of Cancún's hottest club, **Coco Bongo,** which can—and does—regularly pack in up to 3,000 revelers. See p. 88.
- **The Lobby Lounge:** Located in Cancún's luxurious Ritz-Carlton Hotel, this is the most elegant evening spot on the island. Romantic live music, a selection of fine cigars, and more than 120 premium tequilas (plus tastings) allow you to savor the spirit of Mexico. See p. 88.
- **San Cristóbal de las Casas:** This city, small though it may be, has a live-music scene that can't be beat for fun and atmosphere. The bars and clubs are all within walking distance, and they're a real bargain. See "San Cristóbal de las Casas," on p. 244.
- **Avenida 5, Playa del Carmen:** Stroll along the lively, pedestrian-only Avenida 5 to find the bar that's right for you. With live music venues, tequila bars, sports bars, and cafes, you're sure to find something to fit your mood. See p. 137.

9 The Most Luxurious Hotels

- **Le Méridien Cancún Resort & Spa** (Cancún; ✆ 800/543-4300 in the U.S. or 998/881-2200; www.meridiencancun.com.mx): This is the most intimate of the luxury hotels in Cancún, with an understated sense of highly personalized service. Most notable is its 4,546 sq. m (15,000 sq. ft.) Spa del Mar. See p. 68.
- **Ritz-Carlton Hotel** (Cancún; ✆ 800/241-3333 in the U.S. or 998/885-0808; www.ritzcarlton.com): Thick carpets, sparkling glass and brass, and rich mahogany surround guests at this hotel, which clearly sets the standard for luxury in Cancún. The service is impeccable, leaving guests with an overall sense of pampered relaxation. See p. 69.
- **Presidente InterContinental Cozumel** (Cozumel; ✆ 800/327-0200 in the U.S. or 987/872-9500; www.cozumel.intercontinental.com): Surrounded by shady palms, this hotel also has the best beach on the island, right in front of Paraíso Reef. Favorite rooms are the deluxe beachfront units with spacious patios and direct access to the beach—you can even order romantic in-room dining on the patios, complete with a trio to serenade you. See p. 120.
- **Ikal del Mar** (N of Playa del Carmen; ✆ 888/230-7330 in the U.S.): Small, secluded, and private, Ikal del Mar offers extraordinary personal service and spa treatments. Rooms spread out through the jungle, and there's a

beautiful seaside pool and restaurant. See p. 141.

- **Maroma** (N of Playa del Carmen; © **866/454-9351** in the U.S.): You cannot ask for a better setting for a resort than this beautiful stretch of Caribbean coast with palm trees and manicured gardens. You begin to relax before you even take the first sip of your welcome cocktail. Service is very attentive, and the rooms are large and luxurious. See p. 142.

- **Paraíso de la Bonita** (N of Playa del Carmen; © **800/327-0200** in the U.S.): Operated by InterContinental Hotels, this resort has a super-equipped spa based on the elaborate system of thalassotherapy. The guest rooms are elaborate creations, and the hotel provides all kinds of service. It has three pools and an immaculately kept beach. See p. 142.

10 The Best Budget Inns

- **Cancún Inn El Patio** (Cancún City; © **998/884-3500**; www.cancun-suites.com): This European-style inn welcomes many guests for repeat or long-term stays. Each room is tastefully decorated, and all surround a plant-filled courtyard. Special packages combine Spanish lessons and accommodations. It's an oasis of cultured hospitality in one of Mexico's most commercial beach resorts. See p. 73.

- **Treetops** (Playa del Carmen; © **984/873-0351**; www.treetops hotel.com): An economical, quiet hotel steps from both the beach and Avenida 5, Treetops could easily get by on its location alone. But the owners have gone out of their way to create a distinctive lodging with plenty of amenities. The hotel has its very own *cenote* and piece of shady jungle, making it a lovely place to relax after a trying day of strolling the beach and wandering the village streets. See p. 134.

- **Villa Catarina Rooms & Cabañas** (Playa del Carmen; © **984/873-0970**): These stylishly rustic rooms nestle in a garden of tall palms, flowering trees, and singing birds. Just a block from the wide beach and tranquil Caribbean, it's also a short walk from the action of Avenida 5. See p. 134.

- **Casa San Juan** (Mérida; © **999/923-6823**; www.casasanjuan. com): This B&B, in a colonial house in Mérida's historic district, is the perfect combination of comfort and character at a great price. The guest rooms in the original building evoke an earlier time, while the modern rooms in back are quite large and border a lovely patio. See p. 189.

- **Hotel Dolores Alba** (Mérida; © **999/928-5650**; www.dolores alba.com): The new rooms offer all the comforts at a rate that other hotels in this category can't match. Add to this the new pool and large sunning area, and I call it a bargain. See p. 189.

11 The Best Unique Inns

- **Hotel Villa Rolandi Gourmet & Beach Club** (Isla Mujeres; © **998/877-0700**; www.rolandi. com): In addition to being steps

away from an exquisite private cove, a tranquil infinity pool, and Isla's finest dining, this intimate inn also pampers guests with every conceivable in-room amenity. Each unit even has a private Jacuzzi on the balcony and a shower that converts into a steam room. See p. 103.

- **Hotel Jungla Caribe** (Playa del Carmen; ✆ **984/873-0650;** www.jungla-caribe.com): In a town filled with exceptional inns, this one's a standout. The eclectic decor combines neoclassical details with a decidedly tropical touch. The rooms and suites surround a stylish courtyard, restaurant, and pool. You couldn't be better located—1 block from the beach, with an entrance on happening Avenida 5. See p. 133.

- **Deseo Hotel + Lounge** (Playa del Carmen; ✆ **984/879-3620**): Perhaps it should be Hotel = Lounge. That might be an overstatement, but the lounge is at the center of everything, making Deseo the perfect fit for outgoing types who are into an alternative lodging experience. Enjoy a cocktail at the bar or on one of the large daybeds and chill to the modern lounge music. See p. 132.

- **Cuzan Guest House** (Punta Allen Peninsula; ✆ **983/834-0358;** www.flyfishmx.com): Getting to the isolated lobster-fishing village of Punta Allen is half the adventure. Then you can retreat to one of the thatched-roof cottages, swing in a hammock, dine on lobster and stone crabs, and absolutely forget there's an outside world. There are no phones, televisions, or newspapers, and "town" is 56km (35 miles) away. Nature trips and fly-fishing are readily arranged. See p. 154.

- **Casa Mexilio Guest House** (Mérida; ✆ **800/538-6802** in the U.S. or 999/928-2505; www.mexicoholiday.com): An imaginative arrangement of rooms around a courtyard features a pool surrounded by a riot of tropical vegetation. The rooms are divided among different levels for privacy and are connected by stairs and catwalks. Breakfast here provides an extra incentive for getting out of bed. See p. 188.

- **Casa Na-Bolom** (San Cristóbal de las Casas; ✆ **967/678-1418**): This unique house-museum is terrific for anthropology buffs. Built as a seminary in 1891, it was transformed into the headquarters of two anthropologists. The 12 guest rooms, named for surrounding villages, are decorated with local objects and textiles; all rooms have fireplaces and private bathrooms, and the room rate includes breakfast. See p. 250.

12 The Best Restaurants

Best doesn't necessarily mean most luxurious. Although some of the restaurants listed here are fancy affairs, others are simple places to get fine, authentic Yucatecan cuisine.

- **Aioli** (Cancún; ✆ **998/881-2225**): Simply exquisite French and Mediterranean gourmet specialties served in a warm and cozy country French setting, at the hotel Le Méridien. For quality and exceptional service, it's Cancún's best value in fine dining. See p. 75.

- **La Dolce Vita** (Cancún; ✆ **998/885-0150**): A longtime favorite, La Dolce Vita remains untouched by newer arrivals. It continues to draw diners with such blissful dishes as green tagliolini with lobster medallions, veal with morels, and fresh salmon with cream sauce, all served (at night) to the sound of live jazz music. See p. 76.

- **Zazil Ha** (Isla Mujeres; © **998/ 877-0279**): Its doesn't get more relaxed and casual than Zazil Ha, with its sandy floor beneath thatched *palapas* and palms. This is the place for island atmosphere and well-prepared food. Along with its signature seafood and Caribbean cuisine, this restaurant continues to prove that vegetarian cuisine can be both artfully and tastefully prepared. It also offers special menus for those participating in yoga retreats on the island. See p. 107.

- **Cabaña del Pescador** (Cozumel; no phone): If you want an ideally seasoned, succulent lobster dinner, Cabaña del Pescador (Lobster House) is the place. If you want anything else, you're out of luck— lobster dinner, expertly prepared, is all it serves. When you've achieved perfection, why bother with anything else? See p. 121.

- **Prima** (Cozumel; © **987/872-4242**): The Italian food here is fresh, fresh, fresh—from the hydroponically grown vegetables

to the pasta and garlic bread. And it's all prepared after you walk in, most of it by owner Albert Domínguez, who concocts unforgettable shrimp fettuccine with pesto, crab ravioli with cream sauce, and crisp house salad in a chilled bowl. See p. 122.

- **Media Luna** (Playa del Carmen; © **984/873-0526**): The inviting atmosphere of this sidewalk cafe on Avenida 5 is enough to lure you in. The expertly executed and innovative menu, together with great prices, makes it one of the top choices on the Caribbean coast. See p. 136.

- **La Pigua** (Campeche; © **981/ 811-3365**): Campeche's regional specialty is seafood, and nowhere else will you find seafood like this. Mexican caviar, coconut-battered shrimp, and chiles stuffed with shark are just a few of the unique specialties. Thinking about La Pigua's pompano in a fine green herb sauce makes me want to start checking flight schedules. See p. 215.

2

Planning Your Trip to the Yucatán

A little planning can make the difference between a good trip and a great trip. When should you go? What's the best way to get there? How much should you plan on spending? What festivals or special events will occur during your visit? What safety or health precautions should you take? We'll answer these and other questions in this chapter. In addition to these basics, I highly recommend taking a little time to learn about the culture and traditions of Mexico and the Yucatán. It can make the difference between simply getting away for a few days and truly adding cultural understanding to your trip. See Appendix A for more details.

1 The Region at a Glance

Travelers to the peninsula have an opportunity to see pre-Hispanic ruins—such as **Chichén Itzá, Uxmal,** and **Tulum**—and the living descendants of the cultures that built them, as well as the ultimate in resort Mexico: **Cancún.** The peninsula borders the dull aquamarine Gulf of Mexico on the west and north, and the clear blue Caribbean Sea on the east. It covers almost 134,400 sq. km (84,000 sq. miles), with nearly 1,600km (1,000 miles) of shoreline. Underground rivers and natural wells called *cenotes* are a peculiar feature of this region.

Lovely rock-walled Maya villages and crumbling *henequén* haciendas dot the interior of the peninsula. The placid interior contrasts with the hub-bub of the Caribbean coast. From Cancún south to **Chetumal,** the jungle coastline is spotted with all kinds of development, from posh to budget. It also boasts an enormous array of wildlife, including hundreds of species of birds. The Gulf Coast beaches, while good enough, don't compare to those on the Caribbean. National parks near **Celestún** and **Río Lagartos** on the Gulf Coast are home to amazing flocks of flamingos.

To present the Maya world in its entirety, this book also covers the states of **Tabasco** and **Chiapas.** The Gulf Coast state of Tabasco was once home to the Olmec, the mother culture of Mesoamerica. At Villahermosa's Parque–Museo La Venta, you can see the impressive 40-ton carved rock heads that the Olmec left behind.

San Cristóbal de las Casas, in Chiapas, inhabits cooler, greener mountains, and is more in the mold of a provincial colonial town. Approaching San Cristóbal from any direction, you see small plots of corn tended by colorfully clad Maya. The surrounding villages are home to many craftspeople, from woodcarvers to potters to weavers. In the eastern lowland jungles of Chiapas lie the classic Maya ruins of **Palenque.** Deeper into the interior, for those willing to make the trek, are **Yaxchilán** and **Bonampak.**

Destination Yucatán: Red Alert Checklist

- Has the **U.S. State Department** (http://travel.state.gov/travel_ warnings.html) issued any travel advisories regarding Chiapas or other parts of the region?
- Do you have your passport? Did you pack insect repellent? Sun-block? A hat? A sweater or jacket?
- Do you need to book tour, restaurant, or travel reservations in advance?
- Did you make sure attractions and activities that interest you are operating? Some attractions, such as seasonal nature tours, sell out quickly. (Mexico is considered at low risk for a terrorist attack; few event schedule changes or building closings have been instituted.)
- If you purchased traveler's checks, have you recorded the check numbers and stored the documentation separately from the checks?
- Do you know your daily ATM withdrawal limit?
- Do you have your credit card personal identification numbers (PINs)?
- If you have an E-ticket, do you have documentation?
- Do you know the address and phone number of your country's embassy?

2 Visitor Information

SOURCES OF INFORMATION

The **Mexico Hot Line** (© 800/44-MEXICO) is an excellent source for general information; you can request brochures about the country and get answers to the most commonly asked questions.

The official source is the site of Mexico's Tourism Promotion Council, www.visitmexico.com. An independent site sanctioned by Mexico's Ministry of Tourism, www.allmexicohotels. com, has information about hotels in the region. The **U.S. State Department** (© 202/647-5225; http://travel. state.gov) offers a **Consular Information Sheet** about Mexico (http://travel. state.gov/mexico.html), with safety, medical, driving, and general travel information gleaned from reports by its offices in Mexico. You can also request the Consular Information Sheet by fax (© 202/647-3000). Visit **http://travel.state.gov/travel_ warnings.html** for other Consular Information sheets and warnings; and **http://travel.state.gov/tips_mexico. html** for *Tips for Travelers to Mexico*.

Another source is the Department of State's background notes series. Visit the State Department home page at **www.state.gov/travel**.

The **Centers for Disease Control and Prevention Hot Line** (© 800/ 311-3435 or 404/639-3534; www.cdc. gov) is a source of medical information for travelers to Mexico and else-where. For travelers to Mexico and Central America, the number with recorded messages is © **877/FYI-TRIP**. The toll-free fax number for requesting information is © 888/232-3299. Information available by fax is also available at **www.cdc.gov/travel**. Here, you'll also find links to health resources for people traveling with children or with special needs, as well as tips on safe food and water. The U.S. State Department offers medical information for Americans traveling

The Yucatán Peninsula

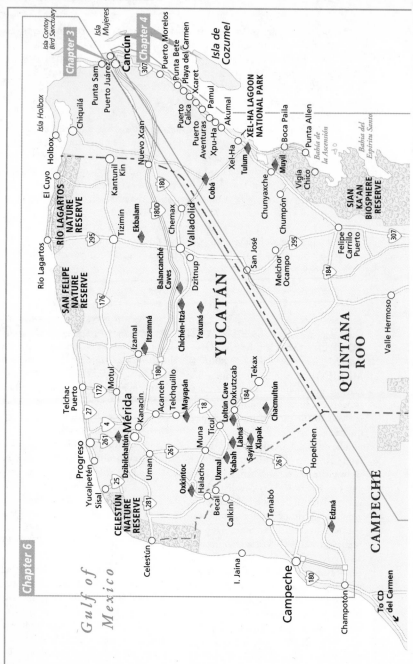

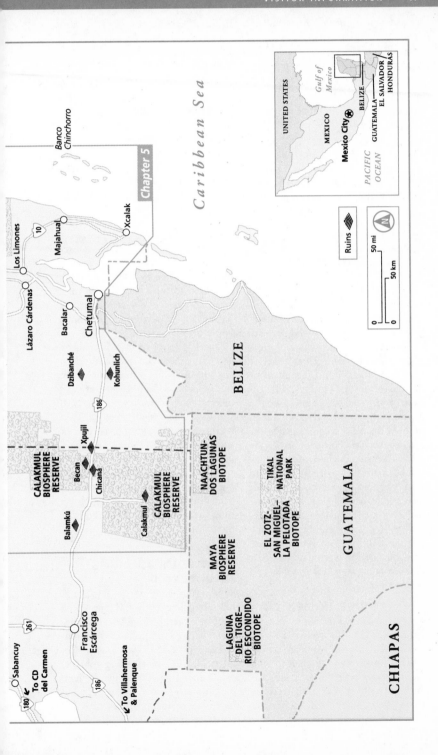

abroad and a list of air ambulance services at **http://travel.state.gov/medical.html**.

MEXICAN GOVERNMENT TOURIST BOARD   The board has offices in major North American cities, in addition to the main office in Mexico City (© **55/5203-1103**).

U.S.: Chicago (© **312/606-9252**); Houston (© **713/772-2581**, ext. 105, or 713/772-3819); Los Angeles (© **213/351-2069;** fax 213/351-2074); Miami (© **305/718-4095**); and New York (© **212/821-0304**

or 212/821-0322). The Mexican Embassy is at 1911 Pennsylvania Ave. NW, Washington, DC 20005 (© **202/728-1750**).

Canada: 1 Place Ville-Marie, Suite 1931, Montréal, QUE, H3B 2C3 (© **514/871-1052**); 2 Bloor St. W., Suite 1502, Toronto, ON, M4W 3E2 (© **416/925-0704**); 999 W. Hastings, Suite 1110, Vancouver, BC, V6C 2W2 (© **604/669-2845**). Embassy office: 1500-45 O'Connor St., Ottawa, ON, K1P 1A4 (© **613/233-8988;** fax 613/235-9123).

3 Entry Requirements & Customs

ENTRY REQUIREMENTS

All travelers to Mexico are required to present **proof of citizenship,** such as an original birth certificate with a raised seal, a valid passport, or naturalization papers. Those using a birth certificate should also have current photo identification such as a driver's license or official ID. If the last name on the birth certificate is different from your current name, bring a photo identification card *and* legal proof of the name change, such as the original marriage license or certificate. *Note:* Photocopies are *not* acceptable.

The best ID is a passport. Safeguard your passport in an inconspicuous, inaccessible place like a money belt and keep a copy of the critical pages with your passport number in a separate place. If you lose your passport, visit the nearest consulate of your native country as soon as possible for a replacement.

ONCE YOU'RE IN MEXICO

You must carry a **Mexican Tourist Permit (FMT),** the equivalent of a tourist visa, which Mexican border officials issue, free of charge, after proof of citizenship is accepted. Airlines generally provide the necessary forms aboard your flight to Mexico. The FMT is more important than a

passport in Mexico, so guard it carefully. If you lose it, you may not be permitted to leave the country until you can replace it—a bureaucratic hassle that can take anywhere from a few hours to a week.

The FMT can be issued for up to 180 days. Sometimes officials don't ask but just stamp a time limit, so be sure to say "6 months," or at least twice as long as you intend to stay. If you decide to extend your stay, you may request that additional time be added to your FMT from an official immigration office in Mexico.

Note: Children under age 18 traveling without parents or with only one parent must have a notarized letter from the absent parent(s) authorizing the travel.

CUSTOMS
WHAT YOU CAN BRING INTO MEXICO

When you enter Mexico, Customs officials will be tolerant as long as you have no illegal drugs or firearms. You're allowed to bring in two cartons of cigarettes or 50 cigars, plus a kilogram (2.2 lb.) of smoking tobacco; two 1-liter bottles of wine or hard liquor; and 12 rolls of film. A laptop computer, camera equipment, and sports equipment that could feasibly

Tabasco & Chiapas

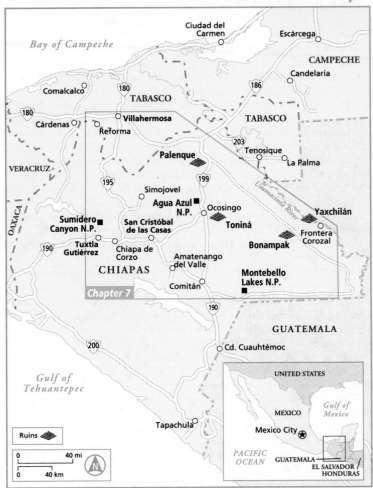

be used during your stay are also allowed. The underlying guideline is: Don't bring anything that looks as if it's meant to be resold in Mexico.

WHAT YOU CAN TAKE HOME

Returning **U.S. citizens** who have been away for at least 48 hours are allowed to bring back, once every 30 days, $800 worth of merchandise duty-free. You'll be charged a flat rate of 4% duty on the next $1,000 worth of purchases. Be sure to have your receipts handy. On mailed gifts, the duty-free limit is $100. You cannot bring fresh foodstuffs into the United States; tinned foods are allowed. For specifics on what you can bring back, download the invaluable free pamphlet *Know Before You Go* from **www. customs.gov**. (Click "Traveler Information," then "Know Before You Go.") Or contact the **U.S. Customs Service,** 1300 Pennsylvania Ave. NW, Washington, DC 20229 (✆ **877/287- 8867**) and request the pamphlet.

Tips **A Few Words About Prices**

The peso's value continues to fluctuate—at press time, it was roughly 10 pesos to the dollar. Prices in this book (which are always given in U.S. dollars) have been converted to U.S. dollars at 10 pesos to the dollar. Most hotels in Mexico—with the exception of places that receive little foreign tourism—quote prices in U.S. dollars. Thus, currency fluctuations are unlikely to affect prices at most hotels.

Mexico imposes a **value-added tax** of 15% (*Impuesto de Valor Agregado,* or *IVA,* pronounced "ee-bah") on almost everything, including restaurant meals, bus tickets, and souvenirs. Exceptions are Cancún and Cozumel, where the IVA is 10%; as ports of entry, they receive a break on taxes. Hotels charge the usual 15% IVA, plus a locally administered bed tax of 2% to 2.5% (in many but not all areas), for a total of 17% to 17.5%. In Cancún and Cozumel, hotels charge the 10% IVA plus 2% room tax. The prices quoted by hotels and restaurants will not necessarily include IVA. You may find that upper-end properties (3 stars and above) quote prices without IVA included, while less expensive hotels include IVA in their quotes. Always ask to see a printed price sheet, and always ask if the tax is included.

For a clear summary of **Canadian** rules, request the booklet *I Declare* from the **Canada Customs and Revenue Agency** (© 800/461-9999 in Canada, or 204/983-3500; www.ccra-adrc.gc.ca). Canada allows citizens a $750 exemption, and you're allowed to bring back duty-free one carton of cigarettes, one can of tobacco, 40 imperial ounces of liquor, and 50 cigars. In addition, you're allowed to mail gifts to Canada valued at less than $60 a day, provided they're unsolicited and don't contain alcohol or tobacco (write on the package "Unsolicited gift, under $60 value"). Declare all valuables on the Y-38 form before departure from Canada, including serial numbers of items you already own, such as expensive cameras. Note: The $750 exemption can only be used once a year and only after an absence of 7 days.

U.K. citizens returning from a non-E.U. country have a customs allowance of 200 cigarettes; 50 cigars; 250g of smoking tobacco; 2 liters of still table wine; 1 liter of spirits or strong liqueurs (over 22% volume); 2 liters of fortified wine, sparkling wine or other liqueurs; 60cc (ml) of perfume; 250cc (ml) of toilet water; and £145 worth of all other goods, including gifts and souvenirs. People under 17 cannot have the tobacco or alcohol allowance. For more information, contact **HM Customs & Excise** (© 0845/010-9000 or 020/8929-0152 from outside the U.K.; www.hmce.gov.uk).

The duty-free allowance in **Australia** is $400 or, for those under 18, $200. Citizens can bring in 250 cigarettes or 250 grams of loose tobacco, and 1,125ml of alcohol. If you're returning with valuables you already own, such as foreign-made cameras, file form B263. A helpful brochure, available from Australian consulates or Customs offices, is *Know Before You Go.* For more information, contact the **Australian Customs Services** (© 1300/363-263; www.customs.gov.au).

The duty-free allowance for **New Zealand** is $700. Citizens over 17 can bring in 200 cigarettes, or 50 cigars, or 250 grams of tobacco (or a mixture of all 3 if their combined weight doesn't exceed 250g); plus 4.5 liters of wine and beer, or 1.125 liters of liquor. New Zealand currency does not carry import or export restrictions. Fill out a certificate of export, listing the valuables you are taking out of the country; that way, you can bring them back without paying duty. A free pamphlet available at New Zealand consulates and Customs offices, *New Zealand Customs Guide for Travelers, Notice no. 4,* answers most questions. For more information, contact **New Zealand Customs,** The Customhouse, 17–21 Whitmore St., Box 2218, Wellington (© **04/473-6099** or 0800/428-786; www.customs.govt.nz).

GOING THROUGH CUSTOMS

Mexican Customs inspection has been streamlined. At most points of entry, tourists are requested to press a button in front of what looks like a traffic signal, which alternates on touch between red and green. Green light and you go through without inspection; red light and your luggage or car may be inspected. If you have an unusual amount of luggage or an oversized piece, you may be subject to inspection anyway.

4 Money

CURRENCY

The currency in Mexico is the Mexican **peso.** Paper currency comes in denominations of 20, 50, 100, 200, and 500 pesos. Coins come in denominations of 1, 2, 5, 10, and 20 pesos, and 20 and 50 **centavos** (100 centavos = 1 peso). The current exchange rate for the U.S. dollar is around 10 pesos to the dollar; at that rate, an item that costs 10 pesos would be equivalent to US$1.

Getting **change** continues to be a problem in Mexico. Small-denomination bills and coins are hard to come by, so start collecting them early in your trip. Shopkeepers everywhere always seem to be out of change and small bills; that's doubly true in markets.

Many establishments that deal with tourists, especially in coastal resort areas, quote prices in dollars. To avoid confusion, they use the abbreviations "Dlls." for dollars and "M.N." (*moneda nacional,* or national currency) for pesos.

EXCHANGING MONEY

The rate of exchange fluctuates a tiny bit daily, so you probably are better off not exchanging too much of your currency at once. Don't forget, however, to have enough pesos to carry you over a weekend or a Mexican holiday, when banks are closed. In general, avoid carrying the U.S. $100 bill, the bill most commonly counterfeited in Mexico and therefore the most difficult to exchange, especially in smaller towns. Because small bills and coins in pesos are hard to come by in Mexico, the $1 bill is very useful for tipping. A tip of U.S. coins, which cannot be exchanged into Mexican currency, is of no value to the service provider.

The bottom line on exchanging money: Ask first, and shop around. Banks generally pay the top rates.

Exchange houses (*casas de cambio*) are generally more convenient than banks because they have more locations and longer hours; the rate of exchange may be the same as at a bank or slightly lower. Before leaving a bank

Money Matters

The **universal currency sign ($)** is used to indicate pesos in Mexico. The use of this symbol in this book, however, denotes U.S. currency.

or exchange-house window, count your change in front of the teller before the next client steps up.

Large airports have currency-exchange counters that often stay open whenever flights are operating. Though convenient, they generally do not offer the most favorable rates.

A hotel's exchange desk commonly pays less favorable rates than banks; however, when the currency is in a state of flux, higher-priced hotels are known to pay *higher* rates than banks, in an effort to attract dollars. It pays to shop around, but in almost all cases, you receive a better rate by changing money first, then paying, rather than by paying with dollars.

BANKS & ATMS

Banks in Mexico are rapidly expanding and improving services. Hours tend to be weekdays from 9am until 5pm, with some open for at least a half day on Saturday. In larger resorts and cities, they can generally accommodate the exchange of dollars (which used to stop at noon) anytime during business hours. Some, but not all, banks charge a service fee of about 1% to exchange traveler's checks. However, most purchases can be paid for directly with traveler's checks at the stated exchange rate of the establishment. Don't even bother with personal checks drawn on a U.S. bank—the bank will wait for your check to clear, which can take weeks, before giving you your money.

Travelers to Mexico can also easily withdraw money from **ATMs** in most major cities and resort areas. Although the U.S. State Department has an advisory against using ATMs in Mexico for safety reasons, it pertains primarily to Mexico City. If you take the usual precautions during daylight hours, this is a convenient and practical way to obtain local funds in most other Mexican towns and resorts. Universal bank cards (such as the Cirrus and PLUS systems) can be used. This is a convenient way to withdraw money and avoid carrying too much with you at any time, and the exchange rate is generally more favorable than that at a currency house. Most ATMs offer Spanish/English menus and dispense pesos, but some offer the option of withdrawing dollars. Be sure to check your daily withdrawal limit before you depart, and ask your bank whether you need a new personal ID number. Also keep in mind that many banks impose a fee every time a card is used at a different bank's ATM, and that fee can be higher for international transactions (up to $5 or more) than for domestic ones. For Cirrus locations abroad, check ⓒ **800/424-7787** or www.mastercard.com. For PLUS outlets abroad, call ⓒ **800/843-7587** or go to www.visa.com.

TRAVELER'S CHECKS

Traveler's checks denominated in dollars are readily accepted nearly everywhere, but they can be difficult to cash on a weekend or holiday or in an out-of-the-way place. Their best value is in ease of replacement in case of theft.

If you carry traveler's checks, be sure to keep a record of their serial numbers separate from the checks in the event that they are stolen or lost. You'll get a refund faster if you know the numbers.

You can get American Express traveler's checks over the phone by calling ⓒ **800/221-7282;** Amex gold and platinum cardholders who use this number are exempt from the 1% fee. AAA members can obtain checks without a fee at some AAA offices. **Visa** offers traveler's checks at Citibank locations nationwide, as well as at several other banks. The service charge ranges between 1.5% and 2%. Call ⓒ **800/732-1322** for information. **MasterCard** also offers traveler's checks. Call ⓒ **800/223-9920** for a location near you.

Tips **Dear Visa: I'm Off to Cancún!**

Some credit card companies recommend that you notify them of any impending trip abroad so that they don't become suspicious and block your charges when the card is used numerous times in a foreign destination. Even if you don't call your credit card company in advance, you can always call the toll-free emergency number (see "Fast Facts," later in this chapter) if a charge is refused—a good reason to carry the phone number with you. But perhaps the most important lesson is to carry more than one card on your trip; if one card doesn't work for any number of reasons, you'll have a backup.

CREDIT CARDS

Visa, MasterCard, and American Express are the most accepted cards. However, many establishments do not take American Express. You'll be able to charge most hotel, restaurant, and store purchases, as well as almost all airline tickets, on your credit card. You can get cash advances of several hundred dollars on your card, but there may be a wait of 20 minutes to 2 hours. You generally can't charge gasoline purchases in Mexico.

Credit card charges will be made in pesos and then converted into dollars by the bank issuing the credit card. Generally you receive a favorable bank rate when paying by credit card. Your credit card company will likely charge a commission (1% or 2%) on every foreign purchase you make, but don't sweat this small stuff; for most purchases, you'll still get the best deal with credit cards when you factor in things like ATM fees and higher traveler's check exchange rates. However, be aware that some establishments add a 5% to 7% surcharge when you pay with a credit card. This is especially true when using American Express. Also, many times, advertised discounts do not apply when you pay with a credit card.

For tips and telephone numbers to call if your wallet is stolen or lost, go to "Lost & Found" in "Fast Facts," later in this chapter.

5 When to Go

SEASONS

High season in the Yucatán begins around December 20 and continues to Easter. This is the best time for calm, warm weather; snorkeling, diving, and fishing (the calmer weather means clearer and more predictable seas); and for visiting the ruins that dot the interior of the peninsula. Book well in advance if you plan to be in Cancún around the holidays.

Low season begins the day after Easter and continues to mid-December; during low season, prices may drop 20% to 50%. In Cancún and along the Riviera Maya, demand by European visitors is creating a summer high season, with hotel rates approaching those charged in the winter months.

Generally speaking, Mexico's **dry season** runs from November to April, with the **rainy season** stretching from May to October. It isn't a problem if you're staying close to the beaches, but for those bent on road-tripping to Chichén Itzá, Uxmal, or other sites, temperatures and humidity in the interior can be downright stifling from May to July. Later in the rainy season, the frequency of **tropical storms** and **hurricanes** increases; such storms, of course, can put a crimp in your vacation. But they can lower temperatures, making climbing ruins a real joy, accompanied by cool air and a slight wind. November is especially ideal for Yucatán travels. Cancún, Cozumel, and Isla Mujeres also have a rainy season from November to January, when northern storms hit. This usually means diving visibility is diminished—and conditions may prevent boats from even going out.

Villahermosa is sultry and humid all the time. San Cristóbal de las Casas, at an elevation of 2,152m (7,100 ft.), is much cooler than the lowlands and is downright cold in winter.

YUCATAN CALENDAR OF FESTIVALS & SPECIAL EVENTS

Note: All banks and official public offices in Mexico close on national holidays.

January

New Year's Day (Año Nuevo). National holiday. Perhaps the quietest day in all of Mexico; most people stay home or visit church. All businesses close. In traditional indigenous communities, new tribal leaders are inaugurated with colorful ceremonies rooted in the pre-Hispanic past. January 1.

Three Kings Day (Día de Reyes). Nationwide. Commemorates the Three Kings bringing gifts to the Christ Child. On this day, children receive presents, much like the traditional gift-giving that accompanies Christmas in the United States. Friends and families gather to share the *Rosca de Reyes,* a special cake. Inside the cake is a small doll representing the Christ Child; whoever receives the doll in his or her piece must host a tamales-and-*atole* party the next month. January 6.

February

Candlemas (Día de la Candelaria). Nationwide. Music, dances, processions, food, and other festivities lead up to a blessing of seed and candles in a ceremony that mixes pre-Hispanic and European traditions marking the end of winter. Those who attended the Three Kings Day celebration reunite to share *atole* and tamales at a party hosted by the recipient of the doll found in the *Rosca.* February 2.

Constitution Day (Día de la Constitución). National holiday. Celebration in honor of the signing of the constitution that currently governs Mexico, signed in 1917 as a result of the revolutionary war of 1910. This holiday is celebrated with small parades. February 5.

Carnaval. This celebration takes place over the 3 days preceding Ash Wednesday and the beginning of Lent. It is celebrated with special gusto in Cozumel, where it resembles Mardi Gras in New Orleans, with a festive atmosphere and parades. Transportation and hotels are packed, so it's best to make reservations well in advance and arrive a couple of days before the celebrations begin.

Ash Wednesday. The start of Lent and a time of abstinence, this is a day of reverence nationwide, but some towns honor it with folk dancing and fairs.

March

Benito Juárez's Birthday. National holiday. Small hometown celebrations crop up countrywide. March 21.

Spring Equinox, Chichén Itzá. On the first day of spring, the Temple of Kukulkán—Chichén Itzá's main pyramid—aligns with the sun, and the shadow of the plumed serpent moves slowly from the top of the building down. When the shadow reaches the bottom, the body joins the carved stone snake's head at the base of the pyramid. According to ancient legend, at the moment that the serpent is whole, the earth is fertilized to ensure a bountiful growing season. Visitors come from around the world to marvel at this sight, so advance arrangements are advisable. March 21. (The shadow can be seen Mar 19–23.) Elsewhere, the equinox is celebrated with festivals and celebrations to welcome spring in the custom of the ancient Mexicans, with dances and prayers to the elements and the four cardinal points, to renew their energy for the year. It's customary to wear white with a red ribbon.

April

Holy Week. This celebrates the last week in the life of Christ from Palm Sunday to Easter Sunday with somber religious processions almost nightly, spoofing of Judas, and reenactments of specific biblical events, plus food and craft fairs. Businesses close during this traditional week of Mexican national vacations.

If you plan on traveling to or around Mexico during Holy Week, make your reservations early. Airline seats on flights into and out of the country will be reserved months in advance. Buses to almost anywhere in Mexico will be full, so try arriving on the Wednesday or Thursday before Good Friday. The week following Easter is also a traditional vacation period.

May

Labor Day. National holiday. Workers' parades take place countrywide, and everything closes. May 1.

Holy Cross Day (Día de la Santa Cruz). Workers place a cross on top of unfinished buildings and celebrate with food, bands, folk dancing, and fireworks around the work site. May 3.

Cinco de Mayo. National holiday. This holiday celebrates the defeat of the French at the Battle of Puebla. May 5.

Feast of San Isidro. The patron saint of farmers is honored with a blessing of seeds and work animals. May 15.

Cancún Jazz Festival. For dates and schedule information, check ℂ **800/ 44-MEXICO** or www.gocancun. com.

June

Navy Day (Día de la Marina). All coastal towns celebrate with naval parades and fireworks. June 1.

Corpus Christi. Nationwide. The day honors the Body of Christ (the Eucharist) with religious processions, Masses, and food. Dates vary.

Día de San Pedro (St. Peter and St. Paul's Day). Nationwide. Celebrated wherever St. Peter is the patron saint, this holiday honors anyone named Pedro or Peter. June 29.

August

Assumption of the Virgin Mary. This is celebrated throughout the country with special Masses and in some places with processions. August 20 to 22.

September

Independence Day. This day of parades, picnics, and family reunions throughout the country celebrates Mexico's independence from Spain. At 11pm on September 15, the president of Mexico gives the famous independence *grito* (shout) from the National Palace in Mexico City, and local mayors do the same in every town and municipality all over Mexico. On September 16, every city and town conducts a parade in which both government and civilians display their pride in being Mexican. For these celebrations, all important government buildings are draped in the national colors—red, green, and white—and the towns blaze with lights. September 15 to 16; September 16 is a national holiday.

Fall Equinox, Chichén Itzá. The same shadow play that occurs during the spring equinox repeats at the fall equinox. September 21 to 22.

October

Día de la Raza ("Ethnicity Day" or Columbus Day). This commemorates the fusion of the Spanish and Mexican peoples. October 12.

November

Day of the Dead. What's commonly called the Day of the Dead is actually 2 days: All Saints' Day, honoring saints and deceased children, and All Souls' Day, honoring deceased adults. Relatives gather at cemeteries countrywide, carrying candles and food, and often spend the night beside the graves of loved ones. Weeks before, bakers begin producing bread formed in the shape of mummies or round loaves decorated with bread "bones." Decorated sugar skulls emblazoned with glittery names are sold everywhere. Many days ahead, homes and churches erect special altars laden with Day of the Dead bread, fruit, flowers, candles, favorite foods, and photographs of saints and of the deceased. On the two nights, children dress in costumes and masks, often carrying through the streets mock coffins and pumpkin lanterns, into which they expect money will be dropped. November 1 to 2; November 1 is a national holiday.

Revolution Day. National holiday. This commemorates the start of the Mexican Revolution in 1910 with parades, speeches, rodeos, and patriotic events. November 20.

December

Feast of the Virgin of Guadalupe. Throughout the country, religious processions, street fairs, dancing, fireworks, and Masses honor the patroness of Mexico. This is one of Mexico's most moving and beautiful displays of traditional culture. The Virgin of Guadalupe appeared to a young man, Juan Diego, in December 1531, on a hill near Mexico City. He convinced the bishop that he had seen the apparition by revealing his cloak, upon which the Virgin was emblazoned. It's customary for children to dress up as Juan Diego, wearing mustaches and red bandanas. One of the most famous and elaborate celebrations takes place at the Basílica of Guadalupe, north of Mexico City, where the Virgin appeared. Every village celebrates this day, though, often with processions of children carrying banners of the Virgin and with *charreadas* (rodeos), bicycle races, dancing, and fireworks. December 12.

Christmas Posadas. On each of the 9 nights before Christmas, it's customary to reenact the Holy Family's search for an inn, with door-to-door candlelit processions in cities and villages nationwide. These are also hosted by most businesses and community organizations, taking the place of the northern tradition of a Christmas party. December 15 to 24.

Christmas. Mexicans extend this celebration and often leave their jobs beginning 2 weeks before Christmas all the way through New Year's Day. Many businesses close, and resorts and hotels fill up. Significant celebrations take place on December 24.

New Year's Eve. As in the rest of the world, New Year's Eve in Mexico is celebrated with parties, fireworks, and plenty of noise. December 31.

6 Travel Insurance

Check your existing insurance policies and credit-card coverage before you buy travel insurance. You may already be covered for lost luggage, cancelled tickets, or medical expenses. The cost of travel insurance varies widely, depending on the cost and length of your trip, your age and health, and the type of trip you're taking.

If you'll be driving in Mexico, see "Getting Around: By Car," later in this chapter, for information on **collision and damage** and **personal accident insurance.**

TRIP-CANCELLATION INSURANCE Trip-cancellation insurance helps you get your money back if you have to back out of a trip, if you have to go home early, or if your travel supplier goes bankrupt. Allowed reasons for cancellation can range from sickness to natural disasters to the State Department's declaring your destination unsafe for travel. (Insurers usually won't cover vague fears, though, as many travelers discovered who tried to cancel their trips in late 2001 because they were wary of flying.) In this unstable world, trip-cancellation insurance is a good buy if you're getting tickets well in advance—who knows what the state of the world, or of your airline, will be in 9 months? Insurance policy details vary, so read the fine print—and especially make sure that your airline or cruise line is on the list of carriers covered in case of bankruptcy. For information, contact one of the following insurers: **Access America** (© 866/807-3982; www.accessamerica.com); **Travel Guard International** (© 800/826-4919; www.travelguard.com); **Travel Insured International** (© 800/243-3174; www.travelinsured.com); and **Travelex Insurance Services** (© 888/457-4602; www.travelex-insurance.com).

MEDICAL INSURANCE Most health insurance policies cover you if you get sick away from home—but check, particularly if you're insured by an HMO. With the exception of certain HMOs and Medicare/Medicaid, your medical insurance should cover medical treatment—even hospital care—overseas. However, most out-of-country hospitals make you pay your bills up front, and send you a refund after you've returned home and filed the necessary paperwork. And in a worst-case scenario, there's the high cost of emergency evacuation. If you require additional medical insurance, try **MEDEX International** (© 800/527-0218 or 410/453-6300; www.medexassist.com) or **Travel Assistance International** (© 800/821-2828; www.travelassistance.com; for general information on services, call the company's Worldwide Assistance Services, Inc., at © **800/777-8710**).

LOST-LUGGAGE INSURANCE On domestic flights, checked baggage is covered up to $2,500 per ticketed passenger. On international flights (including U.S. portions of international trips), baggage is limited to approximately $9.05 per pound, up to approximately $635 per checked bag. If you plan to check items more valuable than the standard liability, see if your valuables are covered by your homeowner's policy, get baggage insurance as part of your comprehensive travel-insurance package, or buy Travel Guard's "BagTrak" product. Don't buy insurance at the airport, where it's usually overpriced. Be sure to take any valuables or irreplaceable items with you in your carry-on luggage, because airline policies don't cover many valuables (including books, money, and electronics).

If your luggage is lost, immediately file a lost-luggage claim at the airport, detailing the contents. For most airlines, you must report delayed, damaged, or lost baggage within 4 hours of arrival. The airlines are required to deliver luggage, once found, directly to your house or destination free of charge.

Keep in mind that in these uncertain times, insurers no longer cover some airlines, cruise lines, and tour operators. *The bottom line:* Always, always check the fine print before you sign; more and more policies have built-in exclusions and restrictions that may leave you out in the cold if something goes awry.

7 Health & Safety

STAYING HEALTHY
COMMON AILMENTS
HIGH-ALTITUDE HAZARDS
Travelers to certain regions of Mexico occasionally experience **elevation sickness,** which results from the relative lack of oxygen and the decrease in barometric pressure that characterizes high elevations (more than 1,515m/ 5,000 ft.). Symptoms include shortness of breath, fatigue, headache, insomnia, and even nausea. Mexico City is at 2,121m (7,000 ft.) above sea level, as are a number of other central and southern cities, such as San Cristóbal de las Casas (even higher than Mexico City). At high elevations, it takes about 10 days to acquire the extra red blood corpuscles you need to adjust to the scarcity of oxygen. To help your body acclimate, drink plenty of fluids, avoid alcoholic beverages, and don't overexert yourself during the first few days. If you have heart or lung problems, talk to your doctor before going above 2,424m (8,000 ft.).

BUGS, BITES & OTHER WILDLIFE CONCERNS
Mosquitoes and **gnats** are prevalent along the coast and in the Yucatán lowlands. Insect repellent *(repelente contra insectos)* is a must, and it's not always available in Mexico. If you'll be in these areas and are prone to bites, bring along a repellent that contains the active ingredient DEET. Avon's Skin So Soft also works extremely well. Another good remedy to keep the mosquitoes away is to mix citronella essential oil with basil, clove, and lavender essential oils. If you're sensitive to bites, pick up some antihistamine cream from a drugstore at home.

Most readers won't ever see a scorpion *(alacrán)*. But if one stings you, go immediately to a doctor. In Mexico you can buy scorpion toxin antidote at any drugstore. It is an injection and it costs around $25. This is a good idea if you plan to camp in a remote area where medical assistance can be several hours away.

MORE SERIOUS DISEASES
You shouldn't be overly concerned about tropical diseases if you stay on the normal tourist routes and don't eat street food. However, both dengue fever and cholera have appeared in Mexico in recent years. Talk to your doctor or to a medical specialist in tropical diseases about precautions you should take. You can also get medical bulletins from the U.S. State Department and the Centers for Disease Control (see "Visitor Information," earlier). You can protect yourself

---

Tips Over-the-Counter Drugs in Mexico

Antibiotics and other drugs that you'd need a prescription to buy in the States are available over the counter in Mexican pharmacies. Mexican pharmacies also carry a limited selection of common over-the-counter cold, sinus, and allergy remedies.

by taking some simple precautions: Watch what you eat and drink; don't swim in stagnant water (ponds, slow-moving rivers, or wells); and avoid mosquito bites by covering up, using repellent, and sleeping under netting. The most dangerous areas seem to be on Mexico's west coast, away from the big resorts, which are relatively safe.

WHAT TO DO IF YOU GET SICK AWAY FROM HOME

In most cases, your existing health plan will provide the coverage you need. But double-check; you may want to buy **travel medical insurance** instead. (See the section on insurance, above.) Bring your insurance ID card with you when you travel.

If you suffer from a chronic illness, consult your doctor before you depart. For conditions like epilepsy, diabetes, or heart problems, wear a **Medic Alert Identification Tag** (✆ **800/825-3785**; www.medicalert.org), which will immediately alert doctors to your condition and give them access to your records through Medic Alert's 24-hour hot line.

Pack **prescription medications** in your carry-on luggage, and carry them in their original containers, with pharmacy labels—otherwise they won't make it through airport security. Also bring along copies of your prescriptions in case you lose your pills or run out. Don't forget an extra pair of contact lenses or prescription glasses. Carry the generic name of prescription medicines, in case a local pharmacist is unfamiliar with the brand name.

Contact the **International Association for Medical Assistance to Travelers** (✆ **716/754-4883** or 416/652-0137; www.iamat.org) for tips on travel and health concerns in Mexico and lists of local English-speaking doctors. The United States **Centers for Disease Control and Prevention** (✆ **800/311-3435**; www.cdc.gov)

provides up-to-date information on necessary vaccines and health hazards by region or country. Any foreign consulate can provide a list of area doctors who speak English. If you get sick, consider asking your hotel concierge to recommend a local doctor—even his or her own. You can also try the emergency room at a local hospital; many have walk-in clinics for emergency cases that are not life-threatening. You may not get immediate attention, but you won't pay the high price of an emergency room visit.

EMERGENCY EVACUATION In extreme medical emergencies, a service from the United States will fly people to American hospitals. **Global Lifeline** (✆ **888/554-9729**, or 01-800/305-9400 in Mexico) is a 24-hour air ambulance. Other companies also offer air evacuation service; for a list, refer to the U.S. State Department website, http://travel.state.gov/medical.html.

STAYING SAFE
CRIME

I have lived and traveled in Mexico for over a decade, have never had any serious trouble, and rarely feel suspicious of anyone or any situation. You will probably feel physically safer in most Mexican cities and villages than in any comparable place at home. However, crime in Mexico has received attention in the North American press over the past several years. Many feel this unfairly exaggerates the real dangers, but it should be noted that crime, including taxi robberies, kidnappings, and highway carjackings, is on the rise. The most severe problems have been concentrated in Mexico City, where even long-time foreign residents will attest to the overall lack of security. Isolated incidents have also occurred in Cancún, Ixtapa, Baja, and even traditionally tranquil Puerto Escondido. Check the U.S. State Department advisory before you travel for any notable "hot spots." See "Visitor Information," earlier, for information on the latest **U.S. State Department advisories.**

Precautions are necessary, but travelers should be realistic. Common sense is essential. You can generally trust people whom you approach for help or directions—but be wary of anyone who approaches you offering the same. The more insistent the person is, the more cautious you should be. The crime rate is, on the whole, much lower in Mexico than in most parts of the United States, and the nature of crimes in general is less violent—most crime is motivated by robbery or jealousy. Random, violent, or serial crime is essentially unheard of in Mexico. You are much more likely to meet kind and helpful Mexicans than you are to encounter those set on thievery and deceit.

See also "Emergencies" under "Fast Facts," later in this chapter.

BRIBES & SCAMS

As is the case around the world, there are the occasional bribes and scams in Mexico, targeted at people believed to be naive—i.e., the telltale tourist. For years Mexico was known as a place where bribes—called *mordidas* (bites)—were expected; however, the country is rapidly changing. Frequently, offering a bribe today, especially to a police officer, is considered an insult, and it can land you in deeper trouble.

If you believe a **bribe** is being requested, here are a few tips on dealing with the situation. Even if you speak Spanish, don't utter a word of it to Mexican officials. That way you'll appear innocent, all while understanding every word.

When you are crossing the border, should the person who inspects your car ask for a tip, you can ignore this request—but understand that the official may suddenly decide that a complete search of your belongings is in

order. If faced with a situation where you feel you're being asked for a *propina* (literally, "tip"; colloquially, "bribe"), how much should you offer? Usually $3 to $5 or the equivalent in pesos will do the trick. Many tourists have the impression that everything works better in Mexico if you "tip"; however, in reality, this only perpetuates the *mordida* attitude. If you are pleased with a service, feel free to tip, but you shouldn't tip simply to attempt to get away with something illegal or inappropriate, whether it is crossing the border without having your car inspected or not getting a ticket that's deserved. There's a number to **report irregularities with Customs officials** (© **800/001-4800** in Mexico). Your call will go to the office of the Comptroller and Administrative Development Secretariat (SECODAM); most employees there do not speak English. Be sure you have some basic information—such as the name of the person who requested a bribe or acted in a rude manner, as well as the place, time, and day of the event.

Whatever you do, **avoid impoliteness;** under no circumstances should you insult a Latin American official. Extreme politeness, even in the face of adversity, rules Mexico. In Mexico, *gringos* have a reputation for being loud and demanding. By adopting the local custom of excessive courtesy, you'll have greater success in negotiations of any kind. Stand your ground, but do it politely.

As you travel in Mexico, you may encounter several types of **scams,** which are typical throughout the world. One involves some kind of a **distraction** or feigned commotion. While your attention is diverted, a pickpocket makes a grab for your wallet. In another common scam, an **unaccompanied child** pretends to be lost and frightened and takes your hand for safety. Meanwhile the child or an accomplice plunders your

Tips Treating and Avoiding Digestive Trouble

It's called "travelers' diarrhea" or *turista*, the Spanish word for "tourist": persistent diarrhea, often accompanied by fever, nausea, and vomiting, that used to attack many travelers to Mexico. (Some in the U.S. call this "Montezuma's revenge," but you won't hear it called that in Mexico.) Widespread improvements in infrastructure, sanitation, and education have practically eliminated this ailment, especially in well-developed resort areas. Most travelers make a habit of drinking only bottled water, which also helps to protect against unfamiliar bacteria. In resort areas, and generally throughout Mexico, only purified ice is used. If you do come down with this ailment, nothing beats Pepto-Bismol, readily available in Mexico. Imodium is also available in Mexico and is used by many travelers for a quick fix. A good high-potency (or "therapeutic") vitamin supplement and even extra vitamin C can help; yogurt is good for healthy digestion.

Because dehydration can quickly become life-threatening, the Public Health Service advises that you be careful to replace fluids and electrolytes (potassium, sodium, and the like) during a bout of diarrhea. Drink Pedialyte, a rehydration solution available at most Mexican pharmacies, or natural fruit juice, such as guava or apple (stay away from orange juice, which has laxative properties), with a pinch of salt added.

How to Prevent It: The U.S. Public Health Service recommends the following measures for preventing travelers' diarrhea: **Drink only purified water** (boiled water, canned or bottled beverages, beer, or wine). **Choose food carefully.** In general, avoid salads (except in 1st-class restaurants), uncooked vegetables, undercooked protein, and unpasteurized milk or milk products, including cheese. Choose food that is freshly cooked and still hot. In addition, something as simple as **clean hands** can go a long way toward preventing *turista*.

---

pockets. A third involves **confusing currency.** A shoeshine boy, street musician, guide, or other individual might offer you a service for a price that seems reasonable—in pesos. When it comes time to pay, he or she tells you the price is in dollars, not pesos, and becomes very hostile if payment is not made. Be very clear on the price and currency when services are involved.

8 Specialized Travel Resources

FAMILY TRAVEL

Children are considered the national treasure of Mexico, and Mexicans will warmly welcome and cater to your children. Many parents were reluctant to bring young children into Mexico in the past, primarily due to health concerns, but I can't think of a better place to introduce children to the exciting adventure of exploring a different culture. Cancún is one of the best destinations. Hotels can often arrange for a babysitter.

Before leaving, ask your doctor which medications to take along. Disposable diapers cost about the same in

Mexico but are of poorer quality. You can get Huggies Supreme and Pampers identical to the ones sold in the United States, but at a higher price. Many stores sell Gerber's baby foods. Dry cereals, powdered formulas, baby bottles, and purified water are easily available in midsize and large cities or resorts.

Cribs may present a problem; only the largest and most luxurious hotels provide them. However, rollaway beds are often available. Child seats or high chairs at restaurants are common.

Consider bringing your own car seat; they are not readily available for rent in Mexico.

Throughout this book, the "Kids" icon distinguishes attractions, hotels, restaurants, and other destinations that are particularly attractive and accommodating to children and families.

You can find good family-oriented vacation advice on the Internet from sites like the **Family Travel Network** (www.familytravelnetwork.com); **Traveling Internationally with Your Kids** (www.travelwithyourkids.com); and **Family Travel Files** (www.the familytravelfiles.com).

How to Take Great Trips with Your Kids (The Harvard Common Press) is full of good general advice that can apply to travel anywhere.

TRAVELERS WITH DISABILITIES

Mexico may seem like one giant obstacle course to travelers in wheelchairs or on crutches. At airports, you may encounter steep stairs before finding a well-hidden elevator or escalator—if one exists. Airlines will often arrange wheelchair assistance to the baggage area. Porters are generally available to help with luggage at airports and large bus stations, once you've cleared baggage claim.

Mexican airports are upgrading their services, but it is not uncommon

to board from a remote position, meaning you either descend stairs to a bus that ferries you to the plane, which you board by climbing stairs, or you walk across the tarmac to your plane and ascend the stairs. Deplaning presents the same problem in reverse.

Escalators (and there aren't many in the country) are often out of order. Stairs without handrails abound. Few restrooms are equipped for travelers with disabilities; when one is available, access to it may be through a narrow passage that won't accommodate a wheelchair or a person on crutches. Many deluxe hotels (the most expensive) now have rooms with bathrooms for people with disabilities. Those traveling on a budget should stick with one-story hotels or hotels with elevators. Even so, there will probably still be obstacles somewhere. Generally speaking, no matter where you are, someone will lend a hand, although you may have to ask for it.

One exception is Puerto Vallarta, which has recently renovated the majority of its downtown sidewalks and plazas with ramps that accommodate wheelchairs. A local disabled citizen deserves the credit for this impressive task—hopefully setting the stage for greater accessibility in other towns and resorts.

Organizations that offer assistance to disabled travelers include **Access Adventures** (© 716/889-9096); **Accessible Journeys** (© 800/ TINGLES or 610/521-0339; www. disabilitytravel.com); the **Moss Rehab Hospital** www.mossresourcenet.org), which provides a library of accessible-travel resources online; and the **Society for Accessible Travel and Hospitality** (© 212/447-7284; www. sath.org; annual membership fees: $45 adults, $30 seniors and students), which offers a wealth of travel resources for all types of disabilities.

SENIOR TRAVEL

Mexico is a popular country for retirees. For decades, North Americans have been living indefinitely in Mexico by returning to the border and re-crossing with a new tourist permit every 6 months. Mexican immigration officials have caught on, and now limit the maximum time in the country to 6 months within any year. This is to encourage even partial residents to acquire proper documentation.

Some of the most popular places for long-term stays are Guadalajara, Lake Chapala, Ajijic, and Puerto Vallarta, all in the state of Jalisco; San Miguel de Allende and Guanajuato in Guanajuato state; Cuernavaca in Morelos; Alamos in Sinaloa; and to a lesser extent Manzanillo in Colima and Morelia in Michoacán. But crowds don't necessarily indicate the only good places: Oaxaca, Querétaro, Puebla, Tepoztlán, and Valle de Bravo have much to offer, even though Americans have yet to collect there in large numbers.

AIM (Apdo. Postal 31–70, 45050 Guadalajara, Jalisco) is a well-written, informative newsletter for prospective retirees. Issues have evaluated retirement in Aguascalientes, Puebla, San Cristóbal de las Casas, Puerto Angel, Puerto Escondido and Huatulco, Oaxaca, Taxco, Tepic, Manzanillo, Melaque, and Barra de Navidad. Subscriptions are $18 to the United States and $21 to Canada. Back issues are three for $5.

Sanborn Tours, 2015 S. 10th St., Post Office Drawer 519, McAllen, TX 78505-0519 (© **800/395-8482**), offers a "Retire in Mexico" orientation tour.

Recommended publications offering travel resources and discounts for seniors include: the quarterly magazine *Travel 50 & Beyond* (www.travel 50andbeyond.com); *Travel Unlimited: Uncommon Adventures for the Mature Traveler* (Avalon); *101 Tips for Mature Travelers,* available from Grand Circle Travel (© **800/221-2610** or 617/350-7500; www.gct. com); *The 50+ Traveler's Guidebook* (St. Martin's Press); and *Unbelievably Good Deals and Great Adventures That You Absolutely Can't Get Unless You're Over 50* (McGraw-Hill).

GAY & LESBIAN TRAVELERS

Mexico is a conservative country, with deeply rooted Catholic religious traditions. Public displays of same-sex affection are rare and still considered shocking for men, especially outside of urban or resort areas. Women in Mexico frequently walk hand in hand, but anything more would cross the boundary of acceptability. However, gay and lesbian travelers are generally treated with respect and should not experience any harassment, assuming

---

Tips Advice for Female Travelers

As a female traveling alone, I can tell you firsthand that I feel safer traveling in Mexico than in the United States. But I use the same common-sense precautions I use anywhere else in the world and am alert to what's going on around me.

Mexicans in general, and men in particular, are nosy about single travelers, especially women. If a taxi driver or anyone else with whom you don't want to become friendly asks about your marital status, family, and so forth, my advice is to make up a set of answers (regardless of the truth): "I'm married, traveling with friends, and I have three children." Saying you are single and traveling alone may send the wrong message.

they give the appropriate regard to local culture and customs.

The **International Gay & Lesbian Travel Association** (© **800/448-8550** or 954/776-2626; www.iglta. org) is the trade association for the gay and lesbian travel industry, and offers an online directory of gay and lesbian-friendly travel businesses; go to the website and click "Members."

STUDENT TRAVEL

Because Mexicans consider higher education more a luxury than a birthright, there is no formal network of student discounts and programs. Most Mexican students travel with their families rather than with other students, so student discount cards are not commonly recognized.

However, more hostels have entered the student travel scene. The **Mexican Youth Hostel Network,** or Red Mexicana de Albergues Juveniles (www.remaj.com), offers a list of hostels that meet international standards in Mexico City, Cuernavaca and surrounding areas, Oaxaca, and Veracruz. The **Mexican Youth Hostel Association,** or Asociación Mexicana de Albergues Juveniles (www.hostels.com.mx) offers a list of hostels in Cancún, Playa del Carmen, Tulum, Uxmal, Palenque, Mexico City, Zacatecas, Guanajuato, and Puerto Escondido.

9 Planning Your Trip Online

SURFING FOR AIRFARES

The "big three" online travel agencies, **Expedia.com, Travelocity.com,** and **Orbitz.com,** sell most of the air tickets bought on the Internet. (Canadian travelers should try expedia.ca and Travelocity.ca; U.K. residents can go to expedia.co.uk and opodo.co.uk.) Each has different business deals with the airlines and may offer different fares on the same flights, so it's wise to shop around.

But don't fire your travel agent just yet. Although online booking sites offer tips and hard data to help you bargain shop, they cannot offer the hard-earned experience that makes a seasoned, reliable travel agent an invaluable resource.

Of the smaller travel agency websites, **SideStep** (www.sidestep.com) has gotten the best reviews from Frommer's authors. It's a browser add-on that purports to "search 140 sites at once," but in reality only beats competitors' fares as often as other sites do.

Also remember to check **airline websites,** especially for low-fare carriers such as Southwest, JetBlue, AirTran, WestJet, or Ryanair, whose fares are often misreported by or missing from travel agency websites. Even with major airlines, you can often shave a few bucks from a fare by booking directly through the airline and avoiding a travel agency's fee. But you'll get these discounts only by **booking online:** Most airlines now offer online-only fares that even their phone agents know nothing about. For the websites of airlines that fly to and from your destination, see "Getting There," later in this chapter.

If you're willing to give up some control over your flight details, use an **opaque fare service** like **Priceline** (www.priceline.com; www.priceline.co.uk for Europeans) or **Hotwire** (www.hotwire.com). Both offer rock-bottom prices in exchange for travel on a "mystery airline" at a mysterious time of day, often with a mysterious change of planes en route. The mystery airlines are all major, well-known carriers. But your chances of getting a 6am or 11pm flight are pretty high. Hotwire tells you flight prices before you buy; Priceline usually has better deals than Hotwire, but you have to play their "name our price" game. If you're new at this, the helpful folks at

Tips   **Frommers.com: The Complete Travel Resource**

For an excellent travel-planning resource, we highly recommend **Frommers.com** (www.frommers.com). You'll find the travel tips, reviews, monthly vacation giveaways, and online-booking capabilities thoroughly indispensable. Among the special features are our popular **Message Boards,** where Frommer's readers post queries and share advice (sometimes even our authors show up to answer questions); **Frommers.com Newsletter,** for the latest travel bargains and inside travel secrets; and the **Frommer's Destinations Section,** where you'll get expert travel tips, hotel and dining recommendations, and advice on the sights to see for more than 3,000 destinations around the globe. When your research is done, the **Online Reservations System** (www.frommers.com/book_a_trip) takes you to favorite sites for booking your vacation at affordable prices.

BiddingForTravel (www.biddingfortravel.com) do a good job of demystifying Priceline's prices.

For much more about airfares and savvy air-travel tips and advice, pick up a copy of *Frommer's Fly Safe, Fly Smart* (Wiley Publishing, Inc.).

SURFING FOR HOTELS

Shopping online for hotels is much easier in the U.S., Canada, and certain parts of Europe than it is in the rest of the world. Of the "big three" sites, **Expedia** may be the best choice, thanks to its long list of special deals. **Travelocity** runs a close second. Hotel specialist sites **hotels.com** and **hotel discounts.com** are also reliable. An excellent free program, **TravelAxe** (www.travelaxe.net), can help you search multiple hotel sites at once, even ones you may never have heard of.

Priceline and Hotwire are even better for hotels than for airfares; with both, you're allowed to pick the neighborhood and quality level of your hotel before offering up your money. Priceline's hotel product even covers Europe and Asia, though it's much better at getting five-star lodging for three-star prices than at finding anything at the bottom of the scale. *Note:* Hotwire overrates its hotels by one star—what Hotwire calls a four-star is a three-star anywhere else.

SURFING FOR RENTAL CARS

For booking rental cars online, the best deals are usually at rental-car company websites, although all the major online travel agencies also offer rental-car reservations services. Priceline and Hotwire work well for rental cars, too; the only "mystery" is which major rental company you get, and for most travelers the difference between Hertz, Avis, and Budget is negligible.

10 The 21st-Century Traveler

INTERNET ACCESS AWAY FROM HOME

Travelers have any number of ways to check their e-mail and tap into the Internet on the road. Of course, using your own laptop—or even a PDA or electronic organizer with a modem—gives you the most flexibility, though dialing long-distance to the United States or Canada from Mexico can be costly. A better option is to gain access to your e-mail and even your office computer from cybercafes.

WITHOUT YOUR OWN COMPUTER

It's hard nowadays to find a city or town in Mexico that *doesn't* have a few cybercafes. The "Fast Facts" sections in this book list cybercafes in major destinations. Although there's no definitive directory of cybercafes—these are independent businesses, after all—three places to start looking are **www. cybercaptive.com**, **www.netcafe guide.com**, and **www.cybercafe.com**.

Hotels that cater to business travelers often have **in-room dataports** and **business centers,** but the charges can be exorbitant.

To retrieve your e-mail, ask your **Internet service provider (ISP)** if it has a Web-based interface tied to your existing e-mail account. If your ISP doesn't have such an interface, you can use the free **mail2web** service (www. mail2web.com) to view—but not reply to—your home e-mail. For more flexibility, you may want to open a free, Web-based e-mail account with **Yahoo! Mail** (mail.yahoo.com) or Microsoft's **Hotmail** (www.hotmail. com). Your home ISP may be able to forward your e-mail to the Web-based account automatically.

WITH YOUR OWN COMPUTER

Major ISPs have **local access numbers** around the world, allowing you to go online by placing a local call. Check your ISP's website or call its toll-free number and ask how you can use your current account away from home, and how much it will cost.

If you're traveling outside the reach of your ISP, the **iPass** network has dial-up numbers in most of the world's countries. You'll have to sign up with an iPass provider, who will tell you how to set up your computer for your destination(s). For a list of iPass providers, go to www.ipass.com and click on "Individuals." One solid provider is **i2roam** (www.i2roam. com; © **866/811-6209** or 920/235-0475).

Wherever you go, bring a **connection kit,** a spare phone cord, and a spare Ethernet network cable.

USING A CELLPHONE

The three letters that define much of the world's **wireless capabilities** are GSM (Global System for Mobiles), a big, seamless network that makes for easy cross-border cellphone use throughout Europe and dozens of other countries worldwide. In the U.S., T-Mobile, AT&T Wireless, and Cingular use this quasi-universal system. In Canada, Microcell and some Rogers customers use GSM. All Europeans and most Australians use GSM.

If your cellphone is on a GSM system, and you have a world-capable phone such as many (but not all) Sony Ericsson, Motorola, or Samsung models, you can make and receive calls across civilized areas on much of the globe. Just call your wireless operator and ask to activate "international roaming" on your account. Per-minute charges can be high—usually $1 to $2.50 in Mexico.

World-phone owners can bring down their per-minute charges with a bit of trickery. Call your cellular operator and say you'll be going abroad for several months and want to "unlock" your phone to use it with a local provider. Usually, the company will oblige. Then, in your destination country, pick up a cheap, prepaid phone chip at a mobile phone store and slip it into your phone. (Show your phone to the salesperson; not all phones work on all networks.) You'll get a local phone number in your destination country—and much, much lower calling rates.

Otherwise, **renting** a phone is a good idea. (Even world-phone owners will have to rent new phones if they're

Online Traveler's Toolbox

- **Visa ATM Locator** (www.visa.com) and **MasterCard ATM Locator** (www.mastercard.com). Find locations of PLUS (Visa) and Cirrus (MasterCard) ATMs worldwide.
- **Foreign Languages for Travelers** (www.travlang.com). Learn basic terms in more than 70 languages and click on any underlined phrase to hear what it sounds like.
- **Intellicast** (www.intellicast.com) and **Weather.com** (www.weather.com). Weather forecasts for all 50 states and cities around the world.
- **Universal Currency Converter** (www.xe.net/currency). See what your dollar or pound is worth in more than 100 other countries.
- **Travel Warnings** (http://travel.state.gov/travel_warnings.html, www.fco.gov.uk/travel, www.voyage.gc.ca, www.dfat.gov.au/consular/advice). These sites report on places where health concerns or unrest might threaten American, British, Canadian, and Australian travelers. Generally, U.S. warnings are the most paranoid, Australian warnings the most relaxed.

traveling to non-GSM regions, such as certain parts of Mexico.) While you can rent a phone from any number of overseas sites, including kiosks at airports and at car-rental agencies, we suggest renting the phone before you leave home. That way you can give loved ones your new number, make sure the phone works, and take the phone wherever you go.

Phone rental isn't cheap. You'll usually pay $40 to $50 per week, plus airtime fees of at least $1 a minute. The bottom line: Shop around.

Two good wireless rental companies are **InTouch USA** (© **800/872-7626;** www.intouchglobal.com) and **Road-Post** (www.roadpost.com; © **888/290-1606** or 905/272-5665). Give

them your itinerary, and they'll tell you what wireless products you need. InTouch will also advise you on whether your existing phone will work overseas; simply call © **703/222-7161** between 9am and 4pm ET, or go to http://intouchglobal.com/travel.htm. This is a free service.

For trips of more than a few weeks in one country, **buying a phone** becomes economically attractive. Many nations have cheap, no-questions-asked prepaid phone systems. Stop by a local cellphone shop and get the cheapest package; you'll probably pay less than $100 for a phone and a starter calling card.

11 Getting There

BY PLANE

The airline situation in Mexico is rapidly improving, with many new regional carriers offering scheduled service to areas previously not served. In addition to regularly scheduled

service, charter service direct from U.S. cities to resorts is making Mexico more accessible. For information about saving money on airfares using the Internet, see "Planning Your Trip Online," earlier in this chapter.

THE MAJOR INTERNATIONAL AIRLINES   The main airlines operating direct or nonstop flights from the United States to Cancún, Cozumel, and Mérida include **Aero-California** (© 800/237-6225), **Aero-mexico** (© 800/237-6639; www.aero mexico.com), **Air France** (© 800/ 237-2747; www.airfrance.com), **American Airlines** (© 800/433-7300; www.aa.com), **Continental** (© 800/ 525-0280; www.continental.com), **Mexicana** (© 800/531-7921; www. mexicana.com), **Northwest/KLM** (© 800/225-2525; www.nwa.com), **United** (© 800/241-6522; www. united.com), and **US Airways** (© 800/ 428-4322; www.usairways.com).

The main departure points in North America for international airlines are Atlanta, Chicago, Dallas/Fort Worth, Denver, Houston, Los Angeles, Miami, New Orleans, New York, Orlando, Philadelphia, Raleigh/ Durham, San Antonio, San Francisco, Seattle, Toronto, Tucson, and Washington, D.C.

GETTING THROUGH THE AIRPORT

With the federalization of airport security, procedures at U.S. airports are more stable and consistent than ever. Generally, you'll be fine if you arrive at the airport **1 hour** before a domestic flight and **2 hours** before an international flight; if you show up late, tell an airline employee and she'll probably whisk you to the front of the line.

Bring a **current, government-issued photo ID** such as a driver's license or passport, and if you have an e-ticket, print out the **official confirmation page;** you'll need to show your confirmation at the security checkpoint, and your ID at the ticket counter or the gate.

Security lines are getting shorter, but some doozies remain. If you have trouble standing for long periods, tell an airline employee; the airline will provide a wheelchair. Speed up security by **not wearing metal objects** such as big belt buckles or clanky earrings. If you have metallic body parts, a note from your doctor can prevent a long chat with the security screeners. Keep in mind that only **ticketed passengers** are allowed past security, except for folks escorting travelers with disabilities or children.

Federalization has stabilized **what you can carry on** and **what you can't.** The general rule is that sharp things are out, nail clippers are okay, and food and beverages must pass through the X-ray machine—but security screeners can't make you drink from your coffee cup. Bring food in your carry-on rather than checking it, because explosive-detection machines used on checked luggage have been known to mistake food for bombs. Travelers in the U.S. are allowed one carry-on bag, plus a "personal item" such as a purse, briefcase, or laptop bag. Carry-on hoarders can stuff all sorts of things into a laptop bag; as long as it has a laptop in it, it's still considered a personal item. The Transportation Security Administration (TSA) has issued a list of restricted items; check its website (www.tsa.gov/ public/index.jsp) for details.

In 2003, the TSA phased out **gate check-in** at all U.S. airports. Passengers with E-tickets and without checked bags can still beat the ticket-counter lines by using **electronic kiosks** or even **online check-in.** Ask your airline which alternatives are available, and if you're using a kiosk, bring the credit card you used to book the ticket. If you're checking bags, you will still be able to use most airlines' kiosks; again, call your airline for up-to-date information. **Curbside check-in** is also a good way to avoid lines, although a few airlines still ban curbside check-in entirely; call before you go.

FLYING FOR LESS: TIPS FOR GETTING THE BEST AIRFARE

Passengers sharing the same airplane cabin rarely pay the same fare. Travelers who need to purchase tickets at the last minute, change their itinerary at a moment's notice, or fly one-way often get stuck paying the premium rate. Here are some ways to keep your airfare costs down.

- Passengers who can book their tickets **far in advance,** who can **stay over Saturday night,** or who **fly midweek** or **at less-trafficked hours** will pay a fraction of the full fare. If your schedule is flexible, say so.
- You can also save on airfares by keeping an eye out in local newspapers for **promotional specials** or **fare wars,** when airlines lower prices on their most popular routes.
- Search **the Internet** for cheap fares (see "Planning Your Trip Online," earlier in this chapter).
- **Consolidators,** also known as bucket shops, are great sources for international tickets, although they usually can't beat the Internet on fares within North America. Start by looking in Sunday newspaper travel sections; U.S. travelers should focus on the *New York Times,* the *Los Angeles Times,* and the *Miami Herald.* For less-developed destinations, small travel agents who cater to immigrant communities in large cities often have the best deals. *Beware:* Bucket shop tickets are usually nonrefundable or rigged with stiff cancellation penalties, often as high as 50% to 75% of the ticket price, and some put you on charter airlines with questionable safety records. Several reliable consolidators are worldwide and available on the Net. **STA Travel** (© **800/781-4040;** www.statravel. com) is now the world's leader in student travel, thanks to its purchase of Council Travel. It also offers good fares for travelers of all ages. **FlyCheap** (© **800/FLY-CHEAP;** www.1800flycheap.com) is owned by package-holiday megalith MyTravel and has especially good access to fares for sunny destinations. **Air Tickets Direct** (© **800/778-3447;** www. airticketsdirect.com) is based in Montreal and leverages the currently weak Canadian dollar for low fares; it'll also book trips to places that U.S. travel agents won't touch, such as Cuba.
- For many more tips about air travel, including a rundown of the major frequent-flier credit cards, pick up a copy of *Frommer's Fly Safe, Fly Smart* (Wiley Publishing, Inc.).

Travel in the Age of Bankruptcy

At press time, two major U.S. airlines were struggling in bankruptcy court and most of the rest weren't doing very well either. To protect yourself, **buy your tickets with a credit card;** the Fair Credit Billing Act guarantees that you can get your money back from the credit card company if a travel supplier goes under (and if you request the refund within 60 days of the bankruptcy). **Travel insurance** can also help, but make sure it covers "carrier default" for your specific travel provider. And be aware that if a U.S. airline goes bust mid-trip, a 2001 federal law requires other carriers to take you to your destination (albeit on a space-available basis) for a fee of no more than $25, provided you rebook within 60 days of the cancellation.

> **Tips Cancelled Plans**
>
> If your flight is cancelled, don't book a new fare at the ticket counter. Find the nearest phone and call the airline directly to reschedule. You'll be relaxing while other passengers are still standing in line.

BY CAR

Driving is not the cheapest way to get to Mexico, but it is the best way to see the country. Even so, you may think twice about taking your own car south of the border once you've pondered the bureaucracy involved. One option is to rent a car once you arrive and tour around a specific region. Rental cars in Mexico are generally new, clean, and well maintained. Although they're pricier than in the United States, discounts are often available for rentals of a week or longer, especially when you make arrangements in advance from the United States. (See "Getting Around: Car Rentals," later in this chapter, for more details.)

For more information on bringing your car into Mexico, call your nearest Mexican consulate or the Mexican Government Tourist Office (see "Visitor Information," earlier in this chapter). Although travel insurance companies are generally helpful, they may not have the most accurate information. To check on road conditions or to get help with any travel emergency while in Mexico, call *C* **01-800/ 903-9200,** or 55/5250-0151 in Mexico City. English-speaking operators staff both numbers.

In addition, check with the **U.S. State Department** (see "Visitor Information," earlier in this chapter) for warnings about dangerous driving areas.

BY SHIP

Numerous cruise lines serve the Mexican Caribbean. Possible trips might cruise from Miami to the Caribbean (which often includes stops in Cancún, Playa del Carmen, and Cozumel). Several cruise-tour specialists offer substantial discounts on unsold cabins if you're willing to take off at the last minute. One such company is **The Cruise Line,** 150 NW 168 St., North Miami Beach, FL 33169 (*C* **800/ 777-0707** or 305/521-2200).

BY BUS

Greyhound-Trailways (or its affiliates) offers service from around the United States to the Mexican border, where passengers disembark, cross the border, and buy a ticket for travel into the interior of Mexico. Many border crossings have scheduled buses from the U.S. bus station to the Mexican bus station.

---

12 Packages for the Independent Traveler

Say the words "package tour," and many people automatically feel as though they're being forced to choose: your money or your lifestyle. This isn't necessarily the case. Most Mexico packages let you have your independence without sacrificing a healthy bank-account balance. Package tours are *not* the same thing as escorted tours. They are simply a way of buying airfare, accommodations, and other pieces of your trip (usually airport transfers, and sometimes meals and activities) in one bundle.

For popular destinations such as the Yucatán's beach resorts, they're often the smart way to go, because they can save you a ton of money. In many cases, a package that includes airfare, hotel, and transportation to and from the airport will cost you less than the hotel alone had you booked it yourself. That's because tour operators buy packages in bulk, then resell them to the public.

You can buy a package at any time of the year, but the best deals usually coincide with the Yucatán's low season—May to early December—when room rates and airfares plunge. But packages vary widely. Some offer a better class of hotels than others. Some offer the same hotels for lower prices. Some offer flights on scheduled airlines, while others book charters. In some packages, your choices of accommodations and travel days may be limited. Each destination usually has some packagers that are better than the rest because they buy in even bigger bulk. Not only can that translate into better prices, it can mean more choices as well. A packager that just dabbles in Mexico may have only a half dozen hotels to choose from, but a packager that focuses energy on south-of-the-border vacations may have dozens of hotels to choose from, with good selections in all price ranges.

WARNINGS

- **Read the fine print.** Make sure you know *exactly* what's included in the price you're being quoted and what's not.
- **Don't compare Mayas and Aztecs.** When evaluating different packagers, compare the deals they offer on similar properties. Most packagers can offer bigger savings on some hotels than others.
- **Know what you're getting yourself into—and if you can get yourself out of it.** Before you commit to a package, make sure you know how much flexibility you have. Often, packagers will offer trip cancellation insurance (for around $25–$30), which will

return your payment if you need to change your plans.
- **Use your best judgment.** Stay away from fly-by-nights and shady packagers. Go with a reputable firm with a proven track record. This is where your travel agent can come in handy.

WHERE TO BROWSE

- For one-stop shopping, go to **www. vacationpackager.com**, an extensive search engine that links you up with more than 30 packagers offering Mexican beach vacations—and even lets you custom design your package.
- Check out **www.2travel.com** and find a page with links to a number of the big-name Mexico packagers, including several of those listed here.
- Another excellent company offering last-minute bargains for both air-only or air-hotel packages is **Vacation Hot Line** (© **800/325-2485;** www.vacationhotline.net).
- Several big **online travel agencies**—Expedia, Travelocity, Orbitz, Site59, and Lastminute. com—also do a brisk business in packages.

RECOMMENDED PACKAGERS

- **Aeromexico Vacations** (© **800/ 245-8585;** www.aeromexico.com) offers year-round packages to Cancún and Cozumel. Aeromexico has a large selection of resorts in these destinations (39 in Cancún, 11 in Cozumel) in a variety of price ranges. The best deals are from Houston, Dallas, San Diego, Los Angeles, Miami, and New York, in that order.
- **American Airlines Vacations** (© **800/321-2121;** http://aav1.aa vacations.com) has year-round deals for Cancún and Cozumel. You don't have to fly with American if you can get a better deal on

another airline; land-only packages include hotel, hotel tax, and airport transfers. American's hubs to Mexico are Dallas/Fort Worth, Chicago, and Miami. The website offers unpublished discounts that are not available through the operators.

- **America West Vacations** (© 800/356-6611; www.americawestvacations.com) has deals to Cancún and Cozumel, mostly from its Phoenix gateway.
- **Apple Vacations** (© 800/365-2775; www.applevacations.com) offers inclusive packages to all the beach resorts, and has the largest choice of hotels: 48 in Cancún and 17 in Cozumel, plus several in the Riviera Maya. Scheduled carriers for the air portion include American, United, Mexicana, Delta, US Airways, AeroCalifornia, and Aeromexico. Apple perks include baggage handling and the services of a company representative at major hotels.
- **Classic Custom Vacations** (© 800/635-1333; www.classiccustom vacations.com) specializes in package vacations to Mexico's finest luxury resorts. It combines discounted first-class and economy airfare (on American, Continental, Mexicana, Alaska, America West, and Delta) with stays at the most exclusive hotels in Cancún, the Riviera Maya, Mérida, and Cozumel. Many packages include meals, private airport transfers, and upgrades.
- **Continental Vacations** (© 800/634-5555 and 888/989-9255; www.continental.com) has year-round packages to Cancún and Cozumel; the best deals are from its hub cities of Houston, Newark, and Cleveland. You have to fly Continental.

- **Delta Vacations** (© 800/872-7786; www.deltavacations.com) has year-round packages to Cancún. Atlanta is the hub, so expect the best prices from there.
- **Funjet Vacations** (book through any travel agent; www.funjet.com for general information) is one of the largest vacation packagers in the United States. Funjet has packages to Cancún, Cozumel, and the Riviera Maya. You can choose a charter or fly on American, Continental, Delta, Aeromexico, US Airways, Alaska Air, or United.
- **GOGO Worldwide Vacations** (book through a travel agent or call © 888/636-3942; www.gogo wwv.com) has trips to the major beach destinations, including Cancún.
- **Mexicana Vacations,** or MexSea-Sun Vacations (© 800/531-9321; www.mexicana.com) offers getaways to all resorts serviced by Mexicana's daily direct flights from Los Angeles to Cancún.
- **Online Vacation Mall** (© 800/839-9851; www.onlinevacation mall.com) allows you to search for and book packages offered by a number of tour operators and airlines to Cancún, Cozumel, and the Riviera Maya.
- **Pleasant Mexico Holidays** (© 800/448-3333; www.pleasant holidays.com) is one of the largest vacation packagers in the United States, with a total of 84 hotels in the most popular destinations, including Cancún and Cozumel.

REGIONAL PACKAGERS

From the East Coast: Liberty Travel (© 888/271-1584; www.liberty travel.com), one of the biggest packagers in the Northeast, often runs a full-page ad in the Sunday papers, with frequent Cancún specials.

(Tips) Sleeping in Style

Mexico lends itself beautifully to the concept of small, private hotels in idyllic settings. These may vary in style from grandiose to a return to the basics of palm-thatched bungalows. **Mexico Boutique Hotels** (www.Mexico BoutiqueHotels.com) specializes in smaller places to stay with a high level of personal attention and service. Most options have fewer than 50 rooms, and the accommodations can consist of entire villas, *casitas,* or bungalows, or a combination of these. The Yucatán is especially noted for the luxury haciendas found throughout the peninsula.

From the West: Suntrips (© 800/ 357-2400, or 888/888-5028 for departures within 14 days; www.sun trips.com) is one of the largest West Coast packagers for Mexico, with departures from San Francisco and Denver on regular charters to Cancún and Cozumel. This company also has a large selection of hotels.

From the Southwest: Town and Country (book through a travel agent) packages regular deals to Cancún and Cozumel with America West from the airline's Phoenix and Las Vegas gateways.

Resort Packages: The biggest hotel chains and resorts also sell packages. To take advantage of these offers, contact your travel agent or call the hotels directly.

QUESTIONS TO ASK BEFORE YOU BOOK

- What are the **accommodation choices** available and are there price differences? Most countries rate their hotels, so ask about the rating of the hotel in question. Or get this information from the government tourist office or its website.
- What **type of room** will you be staying in? Don't take whatever is thrown your way. Request a non-smoking room, a quiet room, a room with a view, or whatever you fancy.
- Look for **hidden expenses.** Ask whether airport departure fees and taxes are included in the total cost.

13 The Active Traveler

Golf courses are plentiful in Mexico, concentrated in the resort areas. Cancún and Playa del Carmen boast excellent options. Visitors can also enjoy **tennis, water-skiing, surfing, bicycling,** and **horseback riding. Scuba diving** is excellent off the Yucatán's Caribbean coast; Cozumel is considered one of the top five dive spots in the world.

PARKS Most of the national parks and nature reserves are understaffed or unstaffed. Reliable Mexican companies (such as **AMTAVE** members; see below) and many U.S.-based companies offer adventure trips.

OUTDOORS ORGANIZATIONS & TOUR OPERATORS AMTAVE (Asociación Mexicana de Turismo de Aventura y Ecoturismo, A.C.) is an active association of eco- and adventure tour operators. It publishes an annual catalog of participating firms and their offerings, all of which must meet certain criteria for security, quality, and training of the guides, as well as for sustainability of natural and cultural environments. For more information, contact AMTAVE (© 800/509-7678; www.amtave.com).

> **Tips Save Money on Diving Packages**
>
> In Cozumel, you may save money by purchasing a diving package that includes accommodations and a fixed number of dives. Many divers, however, save even more money by choosing a hotel that's cheaper than what the package offers, then booking dives directly with a diving concession. This method may be especially practical in the fall, when stormy seas often preclude diving. In this instance, you wouldn't end up paying for unused dives. For more on diving off Cozumel Island, see chapter 4.

The **Archaeological Conservancy,** 5301 Central Ave. NE, Suite 402, Albuquerque, NM 87108 (© **505/266-1540;** www.americanarchaeology.com/tour.html), presents one trip to Mexico per year led by an expert, usually an archaeologist. The trips change from year to year and space is limited; make reservations early.

ATC Tours and Travel, Calle 16 de Septiembre 16, 29200 San Cristóbal de las Casas, Chi. (© **967/678-2550** or 967/678-2557; fax 967/678-3145; www.atctours.com.mx), a Mexico-based tour operator with an excellent reputation, offers specialist-led trips primarily in southern Mexico. In addition to trips to the ruins of Palenque and Yaxchilán (extending into Belize and Guatemala by river, plane, and bus, if desired), ATC offers horseback tours to Chamula or Zinacantán, and day trips to the ruins of Toniná around San Cristóbal de las Casas; birding in the rain forests of Chiapas and Guatemala (including in the El Triunfo Reserve of Chiapas, where you can see the rare quetzal bird and orchids); hikes to the shops and homes of native textile artists of the Chiapas highlands; and walks from the Lagos de Montebello in the Montes Azules Biosphere Reserve, with camping and canoeing. The company can also prepare custom itineraries.

Culinary Adventures, 6023 Reid Dr. NW, Gig Harbor, WA 98335 (© **253/851-7676;** fax 253/851-9532), specializes in a short but select list of cooking tours in Mexico. They feature well-known cooks and travel to regions known for excellent cuisine. The owner, Marilyn Tausend, is the co-author of *Mexico the Beautiful Cookbook* and *Cocinas de la Familia* (Family Kitchens). Most trips take place in central Mexico, but ask about itineraries in the Yucatán.

Mexico Travel Link Ltd. 300-3665 Kingsway, Vancouver, BC V5R 5W2 Canada (© **604/454-9044;** fax 604z454-9088; www.mexicotravel.net), offers cultural, sports, and adventure tours to the Maya Route, and other destinations off the beaten path.

Trek America, P.O. Box 189, Rockaway, NJ 07866 (© **800/221-0596** or 973/983-1144; fax 973/983-8551; www.trekamerica.com), organizes lengthy, active trips that combine trekking, hiking, van transportation, and camping in the Yucatán and Chiapas.

14 Tips on Accommodations

MEXICO'S HOTEL RATING SYSTEM

The hotel rating system in Mexico is called "Stars and Diamonds." Hotels may qualify to earn one to five stars, or five diamonds. Many hotels that have excellent standards are not certified, but all rated hotels adhere to strict standards. The guidelines relate to service, facilities, and hygiene more than to prices.

Five-diamond hotels meet the highest requirements for rating: The beds are comfortable, bathrooms are in excellent working order, all facilities are renovated regularly, infrastructure is top-tier, and services and hygiene meet the highest international standards. Prices are higher than those of other hotels, too.

Five-star hotels usually offer similar quality, but with lower levels of service and detail in the rooms. For example, a five-star hotel may have less luxurious linens, or perhaps room service during limited hours rather than 24 hours. Prices are similar to those at most international resorts.

Four-star hotels are less expensive and more basic, but they still guarantee cleanliness and basic services such as hot water and purified drinking water. Three-, two-, and one-star hotels are at least working to adhere to certain standards: Bathrooms are cleaned and linens are washed daily, and you can expect a minimum standard of service. Two- and one-star hotels generally provide bottled water rather than purified water.

Within this system, telephones, TVs, air-conditioning, and other amenities are not standard. In Mexico, a hotel in a remote beach area, with little or no electricity, may be a five-star property because of the uniqueness of the place and the excellence of the service. Likewise, a hotel in a colonial town might offer cable TV, telephone, and even fax service, yet receive just three stars.

The nonprofit organization Calidad Mexicana Certificada, A.C., known as **Calmecac (www.calmecac.com.mx)**, is responsible for hotel ratings. For additional details about the rating system, visit Calmecac's website or www.starsanddiamonds.com.mx.

HOTEL CHAINS

In addition to the major international chains, you'll run across a number of less-familiar brands as you plan your trip to Mexico. They include:

- **Fiesta Americana** and **Fiesta Inn** (www.posadas.com). Part of the Mexican-owned Grupo Posadas company, these hotels set the country's midrange standard for facilities and services. They generally offer comfortable, spacious rooms and traditional Mexican hospitality. Fiesta Americana hotels offer excellent beach-resort packages. Fiesta Inn hotels are usually more business oriented. Grupo Posadas also owns the more luxurious Caesar Park hotels and the eco-oriented Explorean hotels.

- **Hoteles Camino Real** (www.caminoreal.com). The premier Mexican hotel chain, Camino Real maintains a high standard of service at its properties, all of which carry five stars (see "Mexico's Hotel Rating System," above). Its beach hotels are traditionally located on the best beaches in the area. This chain also focuses on the business market. The hotels are famous for their vivid and contrasting colors.

- **Hoteles Krystal** (www.krystal.com.mx). Grupo Chartwell recently acquired this family-owned chain. The hotels are noted for their family-friendly facilities and five-star standards. The beach properties' signature feature is a pool, framed by columns, overlooking the sea.

- **Plaza Las Glorias** (www.sidek.com.mx/hotel/ing/glorias.asp). Sidek Situr group, the company responsible for building the first mega-developments in Mexico's resort areas, built these hotels. The chain usually represents a more affordable option than its competitors but maintains international hospitality standards.

HOUSE RENTALS & SWAPS

House and villa rentals and swaps are becoming more common in Mexico, but no single recognized agency or business provides this service. In the chapters that follow, we have provided information on independent services that we have found to be reputable.

SAVING ON YOUR HOTEL ROOM

The **rack rate** is the maximum rate that a hotel charges for a room. Hardly anybody pays this price, however. To lower the cost of your room:

- **Ask about special rates or other discounts.** Always ask whether a room less expensive than the first one quoted is available, or whether any special rates apply to you. You may qualify for corporate, student, military, senior, or other discounts. Mention membership in AAA, AARP, frequent-flier programs, or trade unions, which may entitle you to special deals as well. Find out the hotel policy on children— do kids stay free in the room or is there a special rate?
- **Dial direct.** When booking a room in a chain hotel, you'll often get a better deal by calling the individual hotel's reservation desk than by calling the chain's main number.
- **Book online.** Many hotels offer Internet-only discounts, or supply rooms to Priceline, Hotwire, or Expedia at rates much lower than the ones you can get through the hotel itself.
- Consider the pros and cons of **all-inclusive** resorts and hotels. The term "all-inclusive" means different things at different hotels. Many all-inclusive hotels will include three meals daily, sports equipment, spa entry, and other amenities; others may include all or most drinks. In general, you'll save money going the "all-inclusive" way—as long as

you use the facilities provided. The down side is that your choices are limited and you're stuck eating and playing in one place for the duration of your vacation.

- Carefully consider your hotel's meal plan. If you enjoy eating out and sampling the local cuisine, it makes sense to choose a **Continental Plan (CP),** which includes breakfast only, or a **European Plan (EP),** which doesn't include any meals and allows you maximum flexibility. If you're more interested in saving money, opt for a **Modified American Plan (MAP),** which includes breakfast and one meal, or the **American Plan (AP),** which includes three meals. If you must choose a MAP, see if you can get a free lunch at your hotel if you decide to do dinner out.
- **Book an efficiency.** A room with a kitchenette allows you to shop for groceries and cook your own meals. This is a big money saver, especially for families on long stays.

LANDING THE BEST ROOM

Somebody has to get the best room in the house. It might as well be you. You can start by joining the hotel's frequent-guest program, which may make you eligible for upgrades. Always ask about a corner room. They're often larger and quieter, with more windows and light, and they may cost the same as standard rooms. When you make your reservation, ask if the hotel is renovating; if it is, request a room away from the construction. If you're a light sleeper, request a quiet room away from vending machines, elevators, restaurants, bars, and discos. Ask for one of the rooms that have been most recently renovated or redecorated.

If you aren't happy with your room when you arrive, say so. If another room is available, most lodgings will be willing to accommodate you.

In resort areas, particularly in warm climates, ask the following questions before you book a room:

- What's the view like? Cost-conscious travelers may be willing to pay less for a back room facing the parking lot, especially if they don't plan to spend much time in their room.
- Does the room have air-conditioning or ceiling fans? Do the windows open? If they do, and the nighttime entertainment takes place alfresco, you may want to find out when show time is over.
- What's included in the price? Your room may be moderately priced, but if you're charged for beach chairs, towels, sports equipment, and other amenities, you could end up spending more than you bargained for.
- How far is the room from the beach and other amenities? If it's far, is there transportation to and from the beach?

15 Getting Around

An important note: If your travel schedule depends on a vital connection—say, a plane trip or a ferry or bus connection—use the telephone numbers in this book or other resources to find out if the connection you are depending on is still available. Although we've done our best to provide accurate information, transportation schedules can and do change.

BY PLANE

To fly from point to point within Mexico, you'll rely on Mexican airlines. Mexico has two large private national carriers: **Mexicana** (✆ **800/366-5400,** toll-free in Mexico), and **Aeromexico** (✆ **800/021-4000,** toll-free in Mexico), in addition to several up-and-coming regional carriers. Mexicana and Aeromexico offer extensive connections to the United States as well as within Mexico.

Several new regional carriers are operated by or can be booked through Mexicana or Aeromexico. Regional carriers are **AeroCaribe** (see Mexicana), **Aerolitoral** (see Aeromexico), and **Aero Mar** (see Mexicana).

The regional carriers are expensive, but they go to hard-to-reach places. In each applicable section of this book, we've mentioned regional carriers with all pertinent telephone numbers.

Because major airlines can book some regional carriers, read your ticket carefully to see if your connecting flight is on one of these smaller carriers—it may use a different airport or a different counter.

Tips Avoiding Gas Pains

It has never happened to me, but I've heard reports of tourists being shortchanged at gas stations in the Yucatán. When buying gas, I always get out of the car and talk to the attendant, casually making sure that he clears the meter on the pump before filling my tank. When I pay, I keep it simple, preferably using one large bill, either a 200- or 500-peso note. The attendants carry large amounts of cash and are good sources for getting change. When you hand him the money, say out loud the denomination of the bill (*doscientos pesos* or *quinientos pesos*) so that he can't later say that you gave him a smaller denomination. After the transaction, it's customary to tip the attendant a few pesos.

AIRPORT TAXES   Mexico charges an airport tax on all departures. Passengers leaving the country on international flights pay $18—in dollars or the peso equivalent. It has become a common practice to include this departure tax in your ticket price, but double-check to make sure so you're not caught by surprise at the airport. Taxes on each domestic departure within Mexico are around $13, unless you're on a connecting flight and have already paid at the start of the flight, in which case you shouldn't be charged again.

RECONFIRMING   FLIGHTS

Although Mexican airlines say it's not necessary to reconfirm a flight, it's still a good idea. To avoid getting bumped on popular, possibly overbooked flights, check in for an international flight 1½ hours in advance of travel.

BY CAR

Most Mexican roads are not up to U.S. standards of smoothness, hardness, width of curve, grade of hill, or safety markings, with the exception of the roads in and around Cancún. Driving at night is dangerous. The roads are rarely lit; trucks, carts, pedestrians, and bicycles usually have no lights; and you can hit potholes, animals, rocks, dead ends, or uncrossable bridges without warning.

The spirited style of Mexican driving sometimes requires super vision and reflexes. Be prepared for new customs, as when a truck driver flips on his left turn signal when there's not a crossroad for miles. He's probably telling you the road's clear ahead for you to pass. Another custom that's very important to respect is turning left. Never turn left by stopping in the middle of a highway with your left signal on. Instead, pull onto the right shoulder, wait for traffic to clear, then proceed across the road.

You do not need an international driver's license in Mexico—the one issued to you in your home country will suffice.

GASOLINE   There's one government-owned brand of gas and one gasoline station name throughout the country—**Pemex** (Petroleras Mexicanas). There are two types of gas in Mexico: *magna,* 87-octane unleaded gas, and premium 93 octane. In Mexico, fuel and oil are sold by the liter, which is slightly more than a quart (40 liters equal about 10½ gal.). Many franchise Pemex stations have bathroom facilities and convenience stores—a great improvement over the old ones. *Important note:* No credit cards are accepted for gas purchases.

TOLL ROADS   Mexico charges some of the highest tolls in the world for its network of new toll roads; as a result, they are rarely used. Generally speaking, though, using the toll roads will cut your travel time. Older toll-free roads are generally in good condition, but travel times tend to be longer.

BREAKDOWNS   If your car breaks down on the road, help might already be on the way. Radio-equipped green repair trucks operated by uniformed English-speaking officers patrol major highways during daylight hours to aid motorists in trouble. These **"Green Angels"** perform minor repairs and adjustments free, but you pay for parts and materials.

Your best guide to repair shops is the Yellow Pages. For repairs, look under "Automóviles y Camiones: Talleres de Reparación y Servicio"; auto-parts stores are under "Refacciones y Accesorios para Automóviles." To find a mechanic on the road, look for a sign that says TALLER MECANICO.

Places called *vulcanizadora* or *llantera* repair flat tires, and it is common to find them open 24 hours a day on the most traveled highways. Even if the place looks empty, chances are you will find someone who can help you fix a flat.

> **Tips** **Spanish for Bus Travelers**
>
> Little English is spoken at bus stations, so come prepared with your desti-
> nation written down. Then double-check the departure signs.

MINOR ACCIDENTS When possible, many Mexicans drive away from
minor accidents, or try to make an
immediate settlement, to avoid involv-
ing the police. If the police arrive while
the involved persons are still at the
scene, everyone may be locked in jail
until blame is assessed. In any case, you
have to settle up immediately, which
may take days. Foreigners who don't
speak fluent Spanish are at a distinct
disadvantage when trying to explain
their version of the event. Three steps
may help the foreigner who doesn't wish
to do as the Mexicans do: If you were in
your own car, notify your Mexican
insurance company, whose job it is to
intervene on your behalf. If you were in
a rental car, notify the rental company
immediately and ask how to contact the
nearest adjuster. (You did buy insurance
with the rental, right?) Finally, if all else
fails, ask to contact the nearest Green
Angel, who may be able to explain to
officials that you are covered by insurance. See also "Insurance," below.

CAR RENTALS You'll get the best
price if you reserve a car at least a week
in advance in the United States. U.S.
car-rental firms include **Advantage**
(© 800/777-5500 in the U.S. and
Canada), **Avis** (© 800/331-1212 in the
U.S., 800/TRY-AVIS in Canada), **Budget** (© 800/527-0700 in the U.S. and
Canada), **Hertz** (© 800/654-3131 in
the U.S. and Canada), **National**
(© 800/CAR-RENT in the U.S. and
Canada), and **Thrifty** (© 800/
367-2277 in the U.S. and Canada;
www.thrifty.com), which often offers
discounts for rentals in Mexico. For
European travelers, **Kemwel Holiday
Auto** (© 800/678-0678) and **Auto
Europe** (© 800/223-5555) can arrange
Mexican rentals, sometimes through

other agencies. These and some local
firms have offices in Mexico City and
most other large Mexican cities. You'll
find rental desks at airports, all major
hotels, and many travel agencies.

Cars are easy to rent if you are 25 or
over, and have a major credit card,
valid driver's license, and passport
with you. Without a credit card, you
must leave a cash deposit, usually a big
one. One-way rentals are usually simple to arrange but more costly.

Car-rental costs are high in Mexico,
because cars are more expensive. The
condition of rental cars has improved
greatly over the years, and clean new
cars are the norm. The basic cost of the
1-day rental of a Volkswagen Beetle at
press time, with unlimited mileage (but
before 17% tax and $15 daily insur-
ance), was $44 in Cancún and $35 in
Mérida. Renting by the week gives you
a lower daily rate. Avis was offering a
basic 7-day rate for a VW Beetle
(before tax or insurance) of $220 in
Cancún, and $160 in Mérida. Prices
may be considerably higher if you rent
around a major holiday. Also double-
check charges for insurance—some
companies will increase the insurance
rate after several days. Always ask for
detailed information about all charges
you will be responsible for.

Car-rental companies usually write
credit-card charges in U.S. dollars.

Deductibles Be careful—these vary
greatly in Mexico; some are as high as
$2,500, which comes out of your
pocket immediately in case of damage.
On a VW Beetle, Hertz's deductible is
$1,000 and Avis's is $500.

Insurance Insurance is offered in two
parts: **Collision** and **damage** insurance
cover your car and others if the
accident is your fault, and **personal**

Bus Hijackings

The U.S. State Department notes that bandits target long-distance buses traveling at night, but there have been daylight robberies as well. Buses are more common targets than individual cars—they offer thieves more bucks for the bang.

---

accident insurance covers you and anyone in your car. Read the fine print on the back of your rental agreement and note that insurance may be invalid if you have an accident while driving on an unpaved road.

Damage Always inspect your car carefully and note every damaged or missing item, no matter how minute, on your rental agreement, or you may be charged.

BY TAXI

Taxis are the preferred way to get around in almost all the resort areas of Mexico. Short trips within towns are generally preset by zone, and prices are quite reasonable compared with U.S. rates. For longer trips or excursions to nearby cities, taxis can generally be hired for around $10 to $15 per hour, or for a negotiated daily rate. One-way trips—between, say, Cancún and Playa del Carmen—can be arranged. A negotiated one-way price is usually much less than the cost of a rental car for a day, and a taxi travels much faster than a bus. For anyone who is uncomfortable driving in Mexico, this is a convenient, comfortable alternative. A bonus is that you have a Spanish-speaking person with you in case you run into trouble. Many taxi drivers speak at least some English. Your hotel can assist you with the arrangements.

BY BUS

Bus service in the Yucatán is beginning to catch up to the high standards elsewhere in Mexico. Buses are frequent and readily accessible, and can get you to almost anywhere you want to go. They're often the only way to get from large cities to other nearby cities and small villages. Don't hesitate to ask questions if you're confused about anything.

Dozens of Mexican companies operate large, air-conditioned, Greyhound-type buses between most cities. Classes are second *(segunda)*, first *(primera)*, and deluxe *(ejecutiva)*, which goes by a variety of names. Deluxe buses often have fewer seats than regular buses, show video movies, are air-conditioned, and make few stops. Many run express from point to point. They are well worth the few dollars more. In rural areas, buses are often of the school-bus variety, with lots of local color.

Whenever possible, it's best to buy your reserved-seat ticket, often using a computerized system, a day in advance on long-distance routes and especially before holidays. Schedules are fairly dependable, so be at the terminal on time. Current information may be obtained from local bus stations. See Appendix B for a list of helpful bus terms in Spanish.

16 Recommended Books

HISTORY By the time Cortez arrived in Mexico, the indigenous people were already masters of literature, recording their poems and histories by painting in fanfold books *(códices)* made of deerskin and bark paper or by carving on stone. To record history, gifted students were taught the art of bookmaking, drawing, painting, reading, and writing—abilities the general public didn't possess. A contemporary book that tells the story of the natives' "painted books" is *The Mexican Codices and Their Extraordinary History* (Ediciones Lara, 1985), by María Sten.

The ancient Maya produced two important epic works, the *Book of Popol Vuh* and the *Chilam Balam*. Dennis Tedlock produced the most authoritative translation of the *Popol Vuh* (Simon & Schuster, 1985). Anthropologist Michael D. Coe said, "The *Popol Vuh* is generally considered to be the greatest single work of Native American literature." Unfortunately, other than the *Popol Vuh* and the *Chilam Balam*, there are only four surviving códices (or portions of them) because, after the Conquest, the Spaniards deliberately destroyed native books. However, several Catholic priests, among them Bernardo de Sahugun and Diego de Landa (who was one of the book destroyers), encouraged the Indians to record their customs and history. These records are among the best documentation of life before the Conquest.

During the Conquest, Cortez wrote his now-famous five letters to King Charles V, the first printed Conquest literature, but the most important record is that of Bernal Díaz de Castillo. Enraged by an inaccurate account of the Conquest written by a flattering friend of Cortez, 40 years after the conquest, Bernal Díaz de Castillo, himself a conquistador, wrote his lively and very readable version of the event, *True History of the Conquest of Mexico;* it's regarded as the most accurate.

In an attempt to defend himself for burning 27 Maya hieroglyphic rolls in 1562, Diego de Landa collected contemporary Maya customs, beliefs, and history in his *Relación de las Cosas de Yucatán,* known today as *Yucatán Before and After the Conquest* (Dover Press, 1978). It was first published in 1566 and remains the most significant record of its kind.

For an overview of pre-Hispanic cultures, pick up a copy of Michael D. Coe's *Mexico: From the Olmecs to the Aztecs* (Thames and Hudson, 1994) or Nigel Davies's *Ancient Kingdoms of Mexico* (Viking Press, 1991).

CULTURE For the Maya, there are any number of books, of which Michael Coe's *The Maya* (Thames and Hudson, 1999) is probably the best general account. For a survey of Mexican history all the way up to modern times, pick up a copy of *The Course of Mexican History* by Michael C. Meyer, et al. (Oxford University Press, 1998)—it's rather lengthy, but well written and organized.

Passionate Pilgrim (Paragon House, 1993), by Antoinette May, is the fascinating biography of Alma Reed, an American journalist and amateur archaeologist whose life spanned the 1920s to 1960s. Her journalistic assignments included conducting early archaeological digs at Chichén Itzá, Uxmal, and Palenque; breaking the story to the *New York Times* of archaeologist Edward Thompson's role in removing to the Peabody Museum at Harvard the contents of the sacred *cenote* at Chichén Itzá; and serving as a columnist for the *Mexico City News.* She also had a love affair with Felipe Carrillo Puerto, the governor of Yucatán, who commissioned the famous Mexican song "La Peregrina" in her honor. She later championed the career of Mexican muralist José Clemente Orozco at her art gallery in New York.

Anyone going to San Cristóbal de las Casas should read *Living Maya* (Harry N. Abrams, 1987), by Walter F. Morris, with excellent photographs by Jeffrey J. Foxx. The book is all about the Maya living today in the state of Chiapas. Peter Canby's *Heart of the Sky: Travels Among the Maya* (Kodansha International, 1994) takes readers on a rare and rugged journey as he seeks to understand the real issues facing the Maya of Mexico and Guatemala today.

One of the questions in many people's minds is this: What's going on with the Zapatistas? Oppenheimer's book gives a good background to the question. You might want to follow it up with the recent collection of writings by Subcomandante Marcos, *Our Word is Our Weapon* (Seven Stories Press, 2000). Another source would be *Basta! Land and the Zapatista Rebellion* (LPC, 1999) by George Collier, et al. Finally, for those already familiar with Mexico and its culture, Guillermo Bonfil's *Mexico Profundo: Reclaiming a Civilization* (Univ. of Texas Press, 1996), is a rare bottom-up view of Mexico today, which is anthropological in tone and temper.

ART, ARCHAEOLOGY & ARCHITECTURE

Travelers heading for the Yucatán should consider reading amateur archaeologist John L. Stephens's wonderfully entertaining accounts of travel in that region in the 19th century. His book, *Incidents of Travel in Central America, Chiapas, and Yucatán,* and his account of his second trip, *Incidents of Travel in Yucatán,* have been reprinted by Dover Publications. The series also includes Friar Diego de Landa's *Yucatán Before and After the Conquest.*

The Maya (Thames and Hudson, 1993), by Michael D. Coe, is extremely helpful in grasping the different Maya periods. *A Forest of Kings: The Untold Story of the Ancient Maya* (William Morrow, 1990), by Linda Schele and David Freidel, uses the written history of Maya hieroglyphs to tell the incredible dynastic history of selected Maya sites. You'll never view the sky the same way after reading *Maya Cosmos: Three Thousand Years on the Shaman's Path* (William Morrow, 1993), by David Freidel, Linda Schele, and Joy Parker. This scholarly work filled with personal insights takes you along a very readable path into the amazing sky-centered world of the Maya. *The Blood of Kings: Dynasty and Ritual in Maya Art* (George Braziller, Inc., 1986), by Linda Schele and Mary Ellen Miller, is a pioneer work that unlocks the bloody history of the Maya.

In *Breaking the Maya Code* (Thames & Hudson, 1992), readers follow Michael D. Coe on the fascinating 100-year journey of reading the mysterious written texts left by the Maya in partially remaining books, pottery, murals, and carved in stone. Another must-read, and a real page-turner, it's a modern-day mystery complete with a cast of real-life characters. *Maya History,* by Tatiana Proskouriakoff (University of Texas Press, 1993), is the last work of one of the most revered Maya scholars. Linda Schele, a contemporary Maya scholar, calls Proskouriakoff "the person who was to our field as Darwin was to biology." Her contributions included numerous drawings of now-ruined Maya temples and glyphs, of which there are more than 300 in this book.

Try a used bookstore for *Digging in Mexico* (Doubleday, Doran, 1931), by Ann Axtell Morris. The book is as interesting for its photographs of Chichén Itzá before and during the excavations as it is for the author's lively and revealing anecdotes. Morris was the wife of Earl Morris, director of excavations at Chichén Itzá during the Carnegie Institution's work there in the 1920s.

In *Maya Missions* (Espadana Press, 1988), authors Richard and Rosalind Perry reveal the mysteries of the Yucatán Peninsula's many centuries-old colonial-era missions with inviting detail. *An Archaeological Guide to Mexico's Yucatán Peninsula* (University of Oklahoma, 1993), by Joyce Kelly, is a companion to *Maya Missions* that covers the other side of the peninsula's architecture; it is the most comprehensive guide to Maya ruins. Carrying these two books with you will enrich your visit many times over.

Mexico: Splendors of Thirty Centuries (Metropolitan Museum of Art, 1990), the catalog of the 1991 traveling exhibition, is a wonderful resource on Mexico's art from 1500 B.C. through the 1950s. Another superb catalog, *Images of Mexico: The Contribution of*

Mexico to 20th Century Art (Dallas Museum of Art, 1987), is a fabulously illustrated and detailed account of Mexican art gathered from collections around the world. *Art and Time in Mexico: From the Conquest to the Revolution* (Harper & Row, 1985), by Elizabeth Wilder Weismann, illustrated with 351 photographs, covers Mexican religious, public, and private architecture with excellent photos and text. *Casa Mexicana* (Stewart, Tabori & Chang, 1989), by Tim Street-Porter, takes readers through the interiors of some of Mexico's finest homes-turned-museums, public buildings, and private homes. *Mexican Interiors* (Architectural Book Publishing Co., 1962), by Verna Cook Shipway and Warren Shipway, uses black-and-white photographs to highlight architectural details from homes all over Mexico.

NATURE *A Naturalist's Mexico* (Texas A&M University Press, 1992), by Roland H. Wauer, is a fabulous guide to birding in Mexico. *A Hiker's Guide to Mexico's Natural History* (Mountaineers, 1995), by Jim Conrad, covers Mexican flora and fauna and tells how to find both the easy-to-reach and the out-of-the-way spots he describes. *Peterson Field Guides: Mexican Birds* (Houghton Mifflin, 1973), by Roger Tory Peterson and Edward L. Chalif, is an excellent guide to the country's birds. *A Guide to Mexican Mammals and Reptiles* (Minutiae Mexicana), by Normal Pelham Wright and Dr. Bernardo Villa Ramírez, is a small but useful guide to some of the country's wildlife.

 FAST FACTS: Mexico

Abbreviations Dept. (apartments); Apdo. (post office box); Av. (*avenida;* avenue); c/ (*calle;* street); Calz. (*calzada;* boulevard). "C" on faucets stands for *caliente* (hot), "F" for *fría* (cold). PB (*planta baja*) means ground floor; in most buildings the next floor up is the first floor (1).

Business Hours In general, businesses in larger cities are open between 9am and 7pm; in smaller towns many close between 2 and 4pm. Most close on Sunday. In resort areas it is common to find stores open on Sunday, and for shops to stay open late, often until 8pm or even 10pm. Bank hours are Monday to Friday from 9 or 9:30am to anywhere between 3 and 7pm. Increasingly, banks open on Saturday for at least a half day.

Cameras/Film Film costs about the same as in the United States. Tourists wishing to use a video or still camera at any archaeological site in Mexico or at many museums operated by the Instituto de Antropología e Historia (INAH) must pay $4 per camera at each site visited. (Listings for specific sites and museums note this fee.) Also, use of a tripod at any archaeological site requires a permit from INAH. It's courteous to ask permission before photographing anyone. It is never considered polite to take photos inside a church in Mexico. In some areas, such as around San Cristóbal de las Casas, there are other restrictions on photographing people and villages.

Car Rentals See "Getting Around," earlier in this chapter.

Climate See "When to Go," earlier in this chapter.

Currency See "Money," earlier in this chapter.

Doctors/Dentists Every embassy and consulate can recommend local doctors and dentists with good training and modern equipment; some of the doctors and dentists speak English. See the list of embassies and consulates under "Embassies & Consulates," below. Hotels with a large foreign clientele can often recommend English-speaking doctors.

Driving Rules See "Getting Around: By Car," earlier in this chapter.

Drug Laws It may sound obvious, but don't use or possess illegal drugs in Mexico. Mexican officials have no tolerance for drug users, and jail is their solution, with very little hope of getting out until the sentence (usually a long one) is completed or heavy fines or bribes are paid. Remember, in Mexico the legal system assumes you are guilty until proven innocent. **Note:** It isn't uncommon to be befriended by a fellow user, only to be turned in by that "friend," who collects a bounty. Bring prescription drugs in their original containers. If possible, pack a copy of the original prescription with the generic name of the drug.

U.S. Customs officials are on the lookout for diet drugs that are sold in Mexico but illegal in the U.S. Possession could land you in a U.S. jail. If you buy antibiotics over the counter (which you can do in Mexico) and still have some left, U.S. Customs probably won't hassle you.

Drugstores *Farmacias* (pharmacies) will sell you just about anything, with or without a prescription. Most pharmacies are open Monday to Saturday from 8am to 8pm. The major resort areas generally have one or two 24-hour pharmacies. Pharmacies take turns staying open during off hours, so if you are in a smaller town and need to buy medicine during off hours, ask for the *farmacia de turno*.

Electricity The electrical system in Mexico is 110 volts AC (60 cycles), as in the United States and Canada. In reality, however, it may cycle more slowly and overheat your appliances. To compensate, select a medium or low speed on hair dryers. Many older hotels still have electrical outlets for flat two-prong plugs; you'll need an adapter for any plug with an enlarged end on one prong or with three prongs. Many better hotels have three-hole outlets (*trifásicos* in Spanish). Those that don't may have loan adapters, but to be sure, it's always better to carry your own.

Embassies & Consulates They provide valuable lists of doctors and lawyers, as well as regulations concerning marriages in Mexico. Contrary to popular belief, your embassy cannot get you out of jail, provide postal or banking services, or fly you home when you run out of money. Consular officers can provide advice on most matters and problems, however. Most countries have an embassy in Mexico City, and many have consular offices or representatives in the provinces.

The Embassy of the **United States** in Mexico City is at Paseo de la Reforma 305, next to the Hotel María Isabel Sheraton at the corner of Río Danubio (© **55/5209-9100** or 55/5511-9980); hours are Monday to Friday from 8:30am to 5:30pm. Visit www.usembassy-mexico.gov for addresses of the U.S. consulates inside Mexico. There are consular agencies in Cancún (© **998/883-0272**), Cozumel (© **987/872-4574**), and Mérida (© **999/925-5011**).

The Embassy of **Australia** in Mexico City is at Rubén Darío 55, Col. Polanco (© **55/5531-5225**; fax 55/5531-9552). It's open Monday to Thursday from 8:30am to 2pm and 3 to 5pm, and Friday from 8:30am to 2pm.

The Embassy of **Canada** in Mexico City is at Schiller 529, Col. Polanco (📞 **55/5724-7900**); it's open Monday through Friday from 9am to 1pm and 2 to 5pm. At other times, the name of a duty officer is posted on the door. Visit **www.canada.org.mx** for addresses of consular agencies in Mexico. There is a Canadian consulate in Cancún (📞 **998/883-3360**).

The Embassy of **New Zealand** in Mexico City is at José Luis Lagrange 103, 10th Floor, Col. Los Morales Polanco (📞 **55/5283-9460**; kiwimexico @compuserve.com.mx). It's open Monday to Thursday from 8:30am to 2pm and 3 to 5:30pm, and Friday from 8:30am to 2pm.

The Embassy of the **United Kingdom** in Mexico City is at Río Lerma 71, Col. Cuauhtémoc (📞 **55/5207-2089**; www.embajadabritanica.com.mx). It's open Monday to Friday from 8:30am to 3:30pm.

The Embassy of **Ireland** in Mexico City is at Cerrada Blvd. Avila Camacho 76, 3rd floor, Col. Lomas de Chapultepec (📞 **55/5520-5803**). It's open Monday to Friday from 9am to 5pm.

The **South African** Embassy in Mexico City is at Andres Bello 10, 9th floor, Col. Polanco (📞 **55/5282-9260**). It's open Monday to Friday from 8am to 3:30pm.

Emergencies For police emergency numbers, turn to "Fast Facts" in the chapters that follow. The 24-hour **Tourist Help Line** in Mexico City is 📞 **800/903-9200** or 55/5250-0151. A tourist legal assistance office (Procuraduría del Turista) is in Mexico City (📞 **55/5625-8153** or 55/5625-8154). Though the phones are frequently busy, they operate 24 hours, and there is always an English-speaking person available.

Holidays See "Yucatán Calendar of Festivals & Special Events," earlier in this chapter.

Information See "Visitor Information," earlier in this chapter.

Internet Access In large cities and resort areas, a growing number of top hotels offer business centers with Internet access. You'll also find cyber-cafes in destinations that are popular with expats and business travelers. Even in remote spots, Internet access is common. Note that many ISPs automatically cut off your Internet connection after a specified period of time (say, 10 min.), because telephone lines are at a premium. Some Telmex offices also have free Internet kiosks in their reception areas.

Language Spanish is the official language in Mexico. English is spoken and understood to some degree in most tourist areas. Furthermore, you will find that Mexicans are very accommodating with foreigners who try to speak Spanish, even in broken sentences. For basic vocabulary, refer to Appendix B.

Legal Aid International Legal Defense Counsel, 111 S. 15th St., 24th Floor, Packard Building, Philadelphia, PA 19102 (📞 **215/977-9982**), is a law firm specializing in legal difficulties of Americans abroad. See also "Embassies & Consulates" and "Emergencies," above.

Liquor Laws The legal drinking age in Mexico is 18; however, asking for ID or denying purchase is extremely rare. Grocery stores sell everything from beer and wine to national and imported liquors. You can buy liquor 24 hours a day, but during major elections, dry laws often are enacted for as much as 72 hours in advance of the election—and they apply to tourists as well as local residents. Mexico does not have laws that apply to transporting liquor in cars, but authorities are beginning to target drunk drivers more aggressively. It's a good idea to drive defensively.

It is not legal to drink in the street; however, many tourists do so. Use your judgment—if you are getting drunk, you shouldn't drink in the street, because you are more likely to get stopped by the police. As is the custom in Mexico, it is not so much what you do, but how you do it.

Lost & Found To replace a **lost passport,** contact your embassy or nearest consular agent. You must establish a record of your citizenship and fill out a form requesting another FMT (tourist permit) if it, too, was lost. If your documents are stolen, get a police report from local authorities; having one *might* lessen the hassle of exiting the country without all your identification. Without the FMT, you can't leave the country, and without an affidavit affirming your passport request and citizenship, you may have problems at U.S. Customs when you get home. It's important to clear everything up *before* trying to leave. Mexican Customs may, however, accept the police report of the loss of the FMT and allow you to leave.

If you lose your **wallet,** before panicking, retrace your steps—you'll be surprised at how honest people are, and it is likely that you'll find someone trying to find you to return your wallet.

If your wallet is stolen, the police probably won't be able to recover it. Be sure to notify all of your credit card companies right away, and file a report at the nearest police precinct. Your credit card company or insurer may require a police report number or record of the loss. Most credit card companies have an emergency toll-free number to call if your card is lost or stolen; these numbers are not toll-free within Mexico (see "Telephone/Fax," below, for instructions on calling U.S. toll-free numbers). The company may be able to wire you a cash advance off your credit card immediately, and, in many places, can deliver an emergency credit card in a day or 2. The issuing bank's toll-free number is usually on the back of the credit card—which doesn't help you much if the card was stolen. From within Mexico, dial ℂ **001-880/555-1212** (a toll call) to gain access to the toll-free directory. Citicorp Visa's U.S. emergency number is ℂ **800/336-8472.** American Express cardholders and traveler's check holders should call ℂ **800/221-7282.** MasterCard holders should call ℂ **800/307-7309.**

If you carry traveler's checks, keep a record of their serial numbers, separately from the checks, so you're ensured a refund in just such an emergency.

Mail Postage for a postcard or letter is 1 peso (10¢); it may arrive anywhere from 1 to 6 weeks later. A registered letter costs $1.90. Sending a package can be quite expensive—the Mexican postal service charges $8 per kilo (2.2 lb.)—and unreliable; it takes 2 to 6 weeks, if it arrives at all. Packages are frequently lost within the Mexican postal system, although the situation has improved in recent years. The recommended way to send a package or important mail is through FedEx, DHL, UPS, or another reputable international mail service.

Newspapers & Magazines Mexico currently has no national English-language newspaper. Newspaper kiosks in larger Mexican cities carry a selection of English-language magazines.

Pets Taking a pet into Mexico is easy, but requires a little planning. Animals coming from the United States and Canada need to be checked for health within 30 days before arrival in Mexico. Most veterinarians in major cities have the appropriate paperwork—an official health certificate, to be presented to Mexican Customs officials, that ensures the pet's vaccinations are up-to-date. When you and your pet return from Mexico, U.S. Customs officials will require the same type of paperwork. If your stay extends beyond the 30-day time frame of your U.S.-issued certificate, you'll need an updated Certificate of Health issued by a veterinarian in Mexico that states the condition of your pet and the status of its vaccinations. To check last-minute changes in requirements, consult the Mexican Government Tourist Office nearest you (see "Visitor Information," earlier in this chapter).

Police Cancún has a fleet of English-speaking tourist police on hand to help travelers. In other parts of the Yucatán peninsula, you will generally find police officers to be very protective of international visitors.

Restrooms See "Toilets," later in this section.

Safety See "Health & Safety," earlier in this chapter.

Smoking Smoking is permitted and generally accepted in most public places, including restaurants, bars, and hotel lobbies. Nonsmoking areas and hotel rooms for nonsmokers are becoming more common in higher-end establishments, but they tend to be the exception rather than the rule.

Taxes The 15% IVA (value-added) tax applies on goods and services in most of Mexico, and it's supposed to be included in the posted price. This tax is 10% in Cancún and Cozumel. There is a 5% tax on food and drinks consumed in restaurants that sell alcoholic beverages with an alcohol content of more than 10%, and this tax applies whether you drink alcohol or not. Tequila is subject to a new 25% luxury tax. Mexico imposes an exit tax of around $18 on every foreigner leaving the country (see "Airport Taxes" under "Getting Around: By Plane," earlier in this chapter).

Telephone/Fax Mexico's telephone system is slowly but surely catching up with modern times. All telephone numbers have 10 digits. Every city and town that has telephone access has a two-digit (Mexico City, Monterrey, and Guadalajara) or three-digit (everywhere else) area code. In Mexico City, Monterrey, and Guadalajara, local numbers have eight digits; elsewhere, local numbers have seven digits. To place a local call, you do not need to dial the area code. Many fax numbers are also regular telephone numbers; ask whoever answers for the fax tone (*"me da tono de fax, por favor"*). Cellular phones are very popular for small businesses in resort areas and smaller communities. To call a cellular number inside the same area code, dial 044 and then the number. To dial the cellular phone from anywhere else in Mexico, first dial 01, and then the three-digit area code and the seven-digit number. To dial it from the U.S., dial 011-52, plus the three-digit area code and the seven-digit number.

The **country code** for Mexico is **52**.

To call Mexico: If you're calling Mexico from the United States:

1. Dial the international access code: 011
2. Dial the country code: 52
3. Dial the two- or three-digit area code, then the seven- or eight-digit

number. For example, if you wanted to call the U.S. consulate in Acapulco, the whole number would be 011-52-744-469-0556. If you wanted to dial the U.S. embassy in Mexico City, the whole number would be 011-52-55-5209-9100.

To make international calls: To make international calls from Mexico, first dial 00, then the country code (U.S. or Canada 1, U.K. 44, Ireland 353, Australia 61, New Zealand 64). Next, dial the area code and number. For example, to call the British Embassy in Washington, you would dial 00-1-202-588-7800.

For directory assistance: Dial ⓒ **040** if you're looking for a number inside Mexico. *Note:* Listings usually appear under the owner's name, not the name of the business, and your chances to find an English-speaking operator are slim to none.

For operator assistance: If you need operator assistance in making a call, dial 090 to make an international call, and 020 to call a number in Mexico.

Toll-free numbers: Numbers beginning with 800 within Mexico are toll-free, but calling a U.S. toll-free number from Mexico costs the same as an overseas call. To call an 800 number in the U.S., dial 001-880 and the last seven digits of the toll-free number. To call an 888 number in the U.S., dial 001-881 and the last seven digits of the toll-free number. For a number with an 887 prefix, dial 882; for 866, dial 883.

Time Zone Central Time prevails throughout most of Mexico, and for all of the areas covered in this book. Mexico currently observes **daylight saving time.**

Tipping Most service employees in Mexico count on tips for the majority of their income, and this is especially true for bellboys and waiters. Bellboys should receive the equivalent of 50¢ to $1 per bag; waiters generally receive 10% to 20%, depending on the level of service. It is not customary to tip taxi drivers, unless they are hired by the hour or provide touring or other special services.

Toilets Public toilets are not common in Mexico, but an increasing number are available, especially at fast-food restaurants and Pemex gas stations. These facilities and restaurant and club restrooms commonly have attendants, who expect a small tip (about 50¢).

Useful Phone Numbers **Tourist Help Line,** available 24 hours (ⓒ 800/903-9200, toll-free inside Mexico). **Mexico Hot Line** (ⓒ 800/44-MEXICO). **U.S. Department of State Travel Advisory,** staffed 24 hours (ⓒ 202/647-5225). **U.S. Passport Agency** (ⓒ 202/647-0518). **U.S. Centers for Disease Control International Traveler's Hot Line** (ⓒ 404/332-4559).

Water Most hotels have decanters or bottles of purified water in the rooms, and the better hotels have either purified water from regular taps or special taps marked *agua purificada*. Some hotels charge for in-room bottled water. Virtually any hotel, restaurant, or bar will bring you purified water if you specifically request it, but will usually charge you for it. Drugstores and grocery stores sell bottled purified water. Some popular brands are Santa María, Ciel, and Bonafont. Evian and other imported brands are also widely available.

Cancún

3

Mexico's calling card to the world, Cancún perfectly showcases both the country's breathtaking natural beauty and the depth of its 1,000-year history. Simply stated, Cancún is the reason most people travel to Mexico. The sheer number of travelers underscores Cancún's magnetic appeal, with almost three million people visiting this enticing beach resort annually—most of them on their first trip to the country. The reasons for this are both numerous and obvious.

Cancún offers an unrivaled combination of high-quality accommodations, dreamy beaches, easy air access, and a wide diversity of shopping, dining, nightlife, and nearby activities—most of them exceptional values. There is also the lure of ancient cultures evident in all directions and a number of ecologically oriented theme parks.

No doubt about it—Cancún embodies Caribbean splendor, with translucent turquoise waters and powdery white-sand beaches, coupled with coastal areas of great natural beauty. But Cancún is also a modern megaresort. Even a traveler feeling apprehensive about visiting foreign soil will feel completely at ease here. English is spoken, dollars are accepted, roads are well paved, and lawns are manicured. Malls are the mode for shopping and dining, and you could swear that some hotels are larger than a small town. Travelers feel comfortable in Cancún. You do not need to spend a day getting your bearings, because you immediately see familiar names for dining, shopping, nightclubbing, and sleeping.

You may have heard that in 1974 a team of Mexican government computer analysts picked Cancún for tourism development for its ideal mix of elements to attract travelers—and they were right on. It's actually an island, a 14-mile long sliver of land connected to the mainland by two bridges and separated from it by the expansive Nichupté lagoon. (*Cancún* means "golden snake" in Mayan.)

In addition to attractions of its own, Cancún is a convenient distance from the more traditional resorts of Isla Mujeres and from the coastal zone now known as the Riviera Maya—extending down from Cancún, through Playa del Carmen, to the Maya ruins at Tulum, Cozumel, Chichén Itzá, and Cobá. All are within day-trip distance.

You will run out of vacation days before you run out of things to do in Cancún. Snorkeling, jet-skiing, jungle tours, and visits to ancient Maya ruins and modern ecological theme parks are among the most popular diversions. There are a dozen malls with brand-name and duty-free shops (with European goods at prices better than in the U.S.), and more than 350 restaurants and nightclubs. The 24,000-plus hotel rooms in the area offer something for every taste and every budget.

Cancún's luxury hotels have pools so spectacular that you may find it tempting to remain poolside, but don't. Set aside some time to simply gaze into the ocean and wriggle your toes in the fine, brilliantly white sand. It is, after all, what put Cancún on the map.

1 Orientation

GETTING THERE

BY PLANE   If this is not your first trip to Cancún, you'll notice that the airport's facilities and services continue to expand. **Aeromexico** (© **800/237-6639** in the U.S., 01-800/021-4000 toll-free in Mexico, or 998/884-7005 in Cancún; www.aeromexico.com) offers direct service from Atlanta, Houston, Miami, and New York, plus connecting service via Mexico City from Dallas, Los Angeles, and San Diego. **Mexicana** (© **800/531-7921** from the U.S., 01-800/502-2000 toll-free in Mexico, 998/883-4881, 998/881-9090, or 998/887-1245 in Cancún; www.mexicana.com.mx) flies from Chicago, Denver, Los Angeles, Oakland, San Antonio, San Francisco, and San Jose via Mexico City, with nonstop service from Miami and New York. In addition to these carriers, many **charter** companies—such as Apple Vacations, Funjet, and Friendly Holidays—travel to Cancún; these package tours make up as much as 60% of arrivals by U.S. visitors (see "Packages for the Independent Traveler," in chapter 2).

Regional carrier **AeroCaribe,** a Mexicana affiliate (© **998/884-2000**) flies from Cozumel, Havana, Mexico City, Mérida, Chetumal, and other points within Mexico. You'll want to confirm departure times for flights to the U.S.; here are the Cancún airport numbers of major international carriers: **American** (© **998/883-4461;** www.aa.com), **Continental** (© **998/886-0006;** www.continental.com), and **Northwest** (© **998/886-0044** or 998/886-0046; www.nwa.com).

Most major car-rental firms have outlets at the airport, so if you're renting a car, consider picking it up and dropping it off at the airport to save on airport-transportation costs. Another way to save money is to arrange for the rental before you leave home. If you wait until you arrive, the daily cost will be around $45 to $65 for a Chevrolet Chevy or Athos. Major agencies include **Avis** (© 800/331-1212 in the U.S., or 998/886-0222; www.avis.com); **Budget** (© 800/527-0700 in the U.S., or 998/886-0417; fax 998/884-5011); **Dollar** (© 800/800-4000 or 998/886-0775; www.dollar.com); **Hertz** (© 800/654-3131 in the U.S. and Canada, or 998/887-6634; www.hertz.com); and **National** (© 800/328-4567 in the U.S., or 998/886-0152; www.nationalcar.com). The Zona Hotelera (Hotel Zone) is 10km (6½ miles), or about a 20-minute drive, from the airport along wide, well-paved roads.

Rates for a private taxi from the airport are around $25 to downtown Cancún, or $35 to $45 to the Hotel Zone, depending on your destination. Special vans *(colectivos)* run from the airport into town. Buy tickets, which cost about $8, from the booth to the far right as you exit the airport terminal. There's minibus transportation ($9.50) from the airport to the Puerto Juárez passenger ferry to Isla Mujeres, or you can hire a private taxi for about $40. There is no *colectivo* service returning to the airport from Ciudad Cancún or the Hotel Zone, so you'll have to take a taxi, but the rate will be much less than for the trip from the airport. (Only federally chartered taxis may take fares *from* the airport, but any taxi may bring passengers *to* the airport.) Ask at your hotel what the fare should be, but expect to pay about half what you paid from the airport to your hotel.

BY CAR   From Mérida or Campeche, take Highway 180 east to Cancún. This is mostly a winding, two-lane road that branches off into the express toll road 180D between Izamal and Nuevo Xcan. Nuevo Xcan is approximately 42km (26 miles) from Cancún. Mérida is about 83km (52 miles) away—a 3½-hour drive.

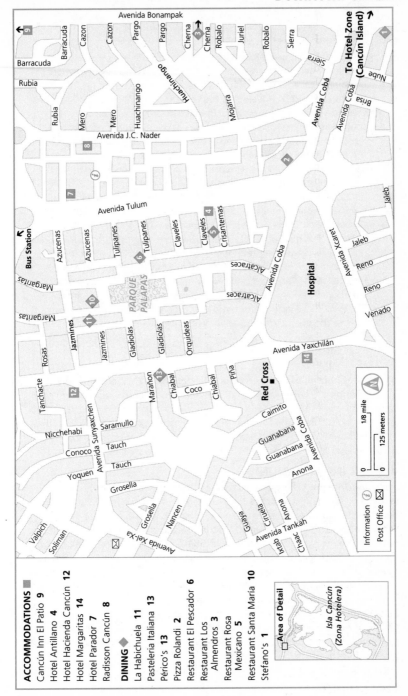

ACCOMMODATIONS ■
Cancún Inn El Patio **9**
Hotel Antillano **4**
Hotel Hacienda Cancún **12**
Hotel Margaritas **14**
Hotel Parador **7**
Radisson Cancún **8**

DINING ◆
La Habichuela **11**
Pasteleria Italiana **13**
Périco's **13**
Pizza Rolandi **2**
Restaurant El Pescador **6**
Restaurant Los Almendros **3**
Restaurant Rosa Mexicano **5**
Restaurant Santa María **10**
Stefano's **1**

Information ⓘ Post Office ⊠

Area of Detail
Isla Cancún
(Zona Hotelera)

> **Tips** **The Best Websites for Cancún**
>
> - **All About Cancún: www.cancunmx.com** This site is a good place to start planning. There's a database of answers to the most common questions, called "The Online Experts." It's slow, but it has input from lots of recent travelers to the region.
> - **Cancún Convention & Visitors Bureau: http://gocancun.com** The official site of the Cancún Convention & Visitors Bureau lists excellent information on events and attractions. Its hotel guide is one of the most complete available, and it offers online booking.
> - **Cancún Online: www.cancun.com** This comprehensive guide has lots of information about things to do and see in Cancún, with most details provided by paying advertisers. You can even reserve a tee time or conduct wedding planning online.
> - **Cancún Travel Guide: www.go2cancun.com** This group specializing in online information about Mexico has put together an excellent resource for Cancún rentals, hotels, and attractions. Note that it lists only paying advertisers, but you'll find most of the major players.
> - **Mexico Web Cancún Chat: www.mexicoweb.com/chats/cancun** This is one of the more active chats online specifically about Cancún. The users share inside information on everything from the cheapest beer to the quality of food at various all-inclusive resorts.

BY BUS Cancún's **ADO bus terminal** (© **998/884-4352** or 998/884-4804) is in downtown Ciudad Cancún at the intersection of avenidas Tulum and Uxmal. All out-of-town buses arrive here. Buses run to Playa del Carmen, Tulum, Chichén Itzá, other nearby beach and archaeological zones, and other points within Mexico. For package deals to popular destinations, see "Day Trips: Archaeological Sites & Eco-Theme Parks," later in this chapter.

VISITOR INFORMATION

The **State Tourism Office,** Avenida Tulum 26 (© **998/881-9000**), is centrally located downtown next to Banco Inverlat, immediately left of the Ayuntamiento Benito Juárez building, between avenidas Cobá and Uxmal. It's open daily from 9am to 8pm. The Convention & Visitors Bureau tourist information office, Avenida Cobá at Avenida Tulum (© **998/884-6531** or 998/884-3438), next to Pizza Rolandi, is open Monday through Friday from 9am to 8pm. Each office lists hotels and their rates, and ferry schedules. For information prior to your arrival in Cancún, call © **800/GO-CANCUN** from the U.S., or visit the Convention Bureau's website, **www.gocancun.com**.

Pick up copies of the free monthly *Cancún Tips* booklet and a seasonal tabloid of the same name. Both are useful and have fine maps. The publications are owned by the same people who own the Captain's Cove restaurants, a couple of sightseeing boats, and time-share hotels, so the information, though good, is not completely unbiased.

CITY LAYOUT

There are really two Cancúns: **Isla Cancún (Cancún Island)** and **Ciudad Cancún (Cancún City).** The latter, on the mainland, has restaurants, shops, and less-expensive hotels, as well as pharmacies, dentists, automotive shops, banks, travel and airline agencies, and car-rental firms—all within an area about 9 blocks square. The city's main thoroughfare is **Avenida Tulum.** Heading south, Avenida Tulum becomes the highway to the airport and to Tulum and Chetumal; heading north, it intersects the highway to Mérida and the road to Puerto Juárez and the Isla Mujeres ferries.

The famed **Zona Hotelera** (the **Hotel Zone,** also called the **Zona Turística,** or **Tourist Zone**) stretches out along Isla Cancún, which is a sandy strip 22km (14 miles) long, shaped like a "7." It connects to the mainland by the Playa Linda Bridge at the north end and the Punta Nizuc Bridge at the southern end. Between the two areas lies Laguna Nichupté. Avenida Cobá from Cancún City becomes Paseo Kukulkán, the island's main traffic artery. Cancún's international airport is just inland from the south end of the island.

FINDING AN ADDRESS   Cancún's street-numbering system is a holdover from its early days. Addresses are still given by the number of the building lot and by the *manzana* (block) or *supermanzana* (group of blocks). The city is relatively compact, and the downtown commercial section is easy to cover on foot.

On the island, addresses are given by kilometer number on Paseo Kukulkán or by reference to some well-known location. In Cancún, streets are named after famous Maya cities. Chichén Itzá, Tulum, and Uxmal are the names of the boulevards in Cancún, as well as nearby archaeological sites.

GETTING AROUND

BY TAXI   Taxi prices in Cancún are clearly set by zone, although keeping track of what's in which zone can take some doing. The minimum fare within the Hotel Zone is $5 per ride, making it one of the most expensive taxi areas in Mexico. In addition, taxis operating in the Hotel Zone feel perfectly justified in having a discriminatory pricing structure: Local residents pay about half of what tourists pay, and prices for guests at higher-priced hotels are about double those for budget hotel guests—these are all established by the taxi union. Rates should be posted outside your hotel; if you have a question, all drivers are required to have an official rate card in their taxis, though it's generally in Spanish.

Within the downtown area, the cost is about $2 per cab ride (not per person); within any other zone, it's $6. Traveling between two zones will also cost $6, and if you cross two zones, that'll cost $8.50. Settle on a price in advance, or check at your hotel. Trips to the airport from most zones cost $15. Taxis can also be rented for $20 per hour for travel around the city and Hotel Zone, but this rate can generally be negotiated down to $12 to $15. If you want to hire a taxi to take you to Chichén Itzá or along the Riviera Maya, expect to pay about $35 per hour—many taxi drivers feel that they are also providing guide services.

BY BUS   Bus travel within Cancún continues to improve and is increasingly popular. In town, almost everything is within walking distance. Ruta 1 and Ruta 2 (HOTELES) city buses travel frequently from the mainland to the beaches along Avenida Tulum (the main street) and all the way to Punta Nizuc at the far end of the Hotel Zone on Isla Cancún. Ruta 8 buses go to Puerto Juárez/Punta Sam for ferries to Isla Mujeres. They stop on the east side of Avenida Tulum. All these city buses operate between 6am and 10pm daily. Beware of private buses along the same route; they charge far more than the public ones. Public buses have the fare painted on the front; at press time, the fare was 5 pesos (50¢).

BY MOPED   Mopeds are a convenient but dangerous way to cruise around through the very congested traffic. Rentals start at $30 for a day, and a credit card voucher is required as security. You should receive a crash helmet (it's the law) and instructions on how to lock the wheels when you park. Read the fine print on the back of the rental agreement regarding liability for repairs or replacement in case of accident, theft, or vandalism.

 FAST FACTS: **Cancún**

American Express The local office is at Avenida Tulum 208 and Agua (© **998/881-4000** or 998/881-4040; www.americanexpress.com), 1 block past the Plaza México. It's open Monday through Friday from 9am to 6pm, Saturday from 9am to 2pm.

Area Code The telephone area code is **998**.

Climate It's hot but not overwhelmingly humid. The rainy season is May through October. August through October is hurricane season, which brings erratic weather. November through February is generally sunny but can also be cloudy, windy, somewhat rainy, and even cool.

Consulates The **U.S. Consular Agent** is in the Plaza Caracol 2, Paseo Kukulkán, Km 8.5, third level, 320–323 (© **998/883-0272**). The office is open Monday through Friday from 9am to 1pm. The **Canadian Consulate** is in the Plaza México 312 (© **998/883-3360**). The office is open Monday through Friday from 9am to 5pm. The **United Kingdom** has a consular office in Cancún (© **998/881-0100**, ext. 6598; fax 998/848-8229; information@britishconsulatecancun.com). Irish, Australian, and New Zealand citizens should contact their embassies in Mexico City.

Crime Car break-ins are just about the only crime here. They happen frequently, especially around the shopping centers in the Hotel Zone. VW Beetles and Golfs are frequent targets.

Currency Exchange Most banks are downtown along Avenida Tulum and are usually open Monday through Friday from 9:30am to 5pm. Many have automated teller machines for after-hours cash withdrawals. In the Hotel Zone, you'll find banks in the Plaza Kukulcan and next to the convention center. There are also many *casas de cambio* (exchange houses). Downtown merchants are eager to change cash dollars, but island stores don't offer very good exchange rates. Avoid changing money at the airport as you arrive, especially at the first exchange booth you see—its rates are less favorable than those of any in town or others farther inside the airport concourse.

Drugstores Next to the Hotel Caribe Internacional, **Farmacia Canto,** Avenida Yaxchilán 36, at Sunyaxchen (© **998/884-9330**), is open 24 hours. It even delivers to hotels (cash only).

Emergencies To report an emergency, dial © **060,** which is supposed to be similar to 911 emergency service in the United States. For first aid, the **Cruz Roja,** or Red Cross (© **998/884-1616;** fax 998/884-7466), is open 24 hours on Avenida Yaxchilán between avenidas Xcaret and Labná, next to the Telmex building. **Total Assist,** Claveles 5, SM 22, at Avenida Tulum (© **998/884-1058** or 998/884-1092; htotal@prodigy.net.mx), is a small (9-room) emergency hospital with English-speaking doctors. It's open 24 hours and accepts

American Express, MasterCard, and Visa. Desk staff may have limited command of English. Air Ambulance service is available by calling © **800/ 305-9400** (toll-free within Mexico). *Urgencias* means "Emergencies."

Internet Access **C@ncunet,** in a kiosk on the second floor of Plaza Kukulcan, Paseo Kukulkán, Km 13 (© **998/885-0055**), offers Internet access at $4 for 15 minutes, or $7 per hour. It's open daily from 10am to 10pm. Downtown, **Sybcom,** in the Plaza Alconde, Local 2, at Avenida Náder, in front of Clinica AMAT (© **998/884-6807**), offers Internet access for $1.50 for 15 minutes, $2.50 for 30 minutes, or $4 per hour. It is open Monday through Saturday from 9am to 11pm.

Luggage Storage/Lockers Hotels will generally tag and store luggage while you travel elsewhere.

Newspapers/Magazines For English-language newspapers and books, go to **Fama,** Avenida Tulum between Tulipanes and Claveles (© **998/ 884-6586**). It's open daily from 8am to 10pm and accepts American Express, MasterCard, and Visa. Most hotel gift shops and newsstands carry English-language magazines and English-language Mexican newspapers.

Police Cancún has a fleet of English-speaking tourist police to help travelers. To reach the **police** (Seguridad Pública), dial © **998/884-1913** or 998/ 884-2342. The *Procuraduría Federal del Consumidor* (consumer protection agency), Avenida Cobá 9–11 (© **998/884-2634** or 998/884-2701), is opposite the Social Security Hospital and upstairs from the Fenix drugstore. It's open Monday through Saturday from 9am to 3pm.

Post Office The main *correo* is at the intersection of avenidas Sunyaxchen and Xel-Ha (© **998/884-1418**). It's open Monday through Friday from 8am to 5pm, Saturday from 9am to noon.

Safety There is very little crime in Cancún. People are generally safe late at night in tourist areas; just use ordinary common sense. As at any other beach resort, don't take money or valuables to the beach. See "Crime," above.

Swimming on the Caribbean side presents a danger because of the undertow. See the information on beaches in "Beaches, Watersports & Boat Tours," later in this chapter, for information about flag warnings

Seasons Technically, high season is from December 15 to Easter; low season is from May to December 15, when prices drop 10% to 30%. Some hotels are starting to charge high-season rates during June and July, when Mexican, European, and school-holiday visitors often travel, although rates may still be lower than in winter months.

Special Events The annual **Cancún Jazz Festival** ★★, featuring internationally known musicians, is held each year over the U.S. Memorial Day weekend, in late May. The **Cancún Marathon** takes place each December and attracts world-class athletes as well as numerous amateur competitors. Additional information is available through the Convention & Visitors Bureau.

Telephones The area code for Cancún is **998** (until 1999, it was 98). All local numbers have seven digits and begin with 8.

2 Where to Stay

Island hotels line the beach like dominoes, almost all of them offering clean, modern facilities. Extravagance is the byword in the newer hotels. Some hotels, while exclusive, affect a more relaxed attitude. The water on the upper end of the island facing Bahía de Mujeres is placid, while beaches lining the long side of the island facing the Caribbean are subject to choppier water and crashing waves on windy days. (For more information on swimming safety, see "Beaches, Watersports & Boat Tours," later in this chapter.) Be aware that the farther south you go on the island, the longer it takes (20–30 min. in traffic) to get back to the "action spots," which are primarily between the Plaza Flamingo and Punta Cancún on the island and along Avenida Tulum on the mainland.

Almost all major hotel chains are represented on Cancún Island, so this list can be viewed as a representative summary, with a select number of notable places. The reality is that Cancún is so popular as a package destination from the U.S. that prices and special deals are often the deciding factor for those traveling here (see "Packages for the Independent Traveler," in chapter 2). Ciudad Cancún offers independently owned, smaller, less expensive lodging; prices are lower here during the off-season (May to early Dec). For condo, home, and villa rentals, check with **Cancún Hideaways** (www.cancun-hideaways.com), a company specializing in luxury properties, downtown apartments, and condos—many at prices much lower than comparable hotel stays. Owner Maggie Rodriguez, a former resident of Cancún, has made this niche market her specialty.

The hotel listings in this chapter begin on Cancún Island and finish in Cancún City, where bargain lodgings are available. Parking is free at all island hotels.

CANCUN ISLAND
VERY EXPENSIVE

Fiesta Americana Grand Coral Beach ★ This is an ideal choice for any type of traveler looking to be at the heart of all that Cancún has to offer. The spectacular hotel, which opened in 1991, has one of the best locations in Cancún, with 303m (1,000 ft.) of prime beachfront and proximity to the main shopping and entertainment centers. The key word here is *big*—everything at the Fiesta Americana seems oversize, from the lobby to the suites. Service is gracious, if cool: The hotel aims for a sophisticated ambience. It's embellished with elegant dark-green granite and an abundance of marble. The large guest rooms are also decorated with marble, and all have balconies facing the ocean. The hotel's great Punta Cancún location (opposite the convention center) has the advantage of facing the beach to the north, meaning that the surf is calm and perfect for swimming.

Paseo Kukulkán, Km 9.5, 77500 Cancún, Q. Roo. ⓒ **800/343-7821** in the U.S., or 998/881-3200. Fax 998/881-3263. www.fiestamericana.com. 602 units. High season $380–$555 double, $529–$650 Club Floor double, $875 Caribbean Suite; low season $277–$424 double, $381–$504 Club Floor double, $695 Caribbean Suite. AE, MC, V. **Amenities:** 2 restaurants; poolside snack bar; 5 bars; 660-ft.-long free-form swimming pool with swim-up bars; 3 indoor tennis courts with stadium seating; gymnasium with weights, sauna, and massage; watersports rentals on the beach; concierge; travel agency; car rental; business center; salon; room service; babysitting; laundry; 2 concierge floors with complimentary cocktails; 2 junior suites for travelers with disabilities are available. *In room:* A/C, TV, minibar, hair dryer, iron, safe.

Hilton Cancún Beach & Golf Resort ★ *Kids* Grand, expansive, and fully equipped, this is a true resort in every sense of the word and is especially perfect for anyone whose motto is "the bigger the better." The Hilton Cancún, formerly the vintage 1994 Caesar Park Resort, joined the Hilton chain in 1999. It sits on

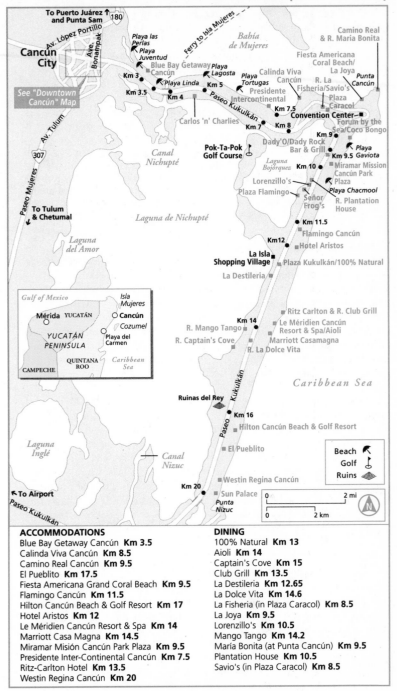

Isla Cancún (Zona Hotelera)

To Puerto Juárez and Punta Sam
180
Av. López Portillo

Cancún City
Av. Bonampak

See "Downtown Cancún" Map

Playa las Perlas
Playa Juventud
Blue Bay Getaway Cancún
Km 3
Km 3.5
Km 4
Playa Linda
Km 5

Ferry to Isla Mujeres

Bahía de Mujeres

Camino Real & R. Maria Bonita
Fiesta Americana Coral Beach/ La Joya
Punta Cancún
Playa Lagosta
Playa Tortugas
Calinda Viva Cancún
R. La Fisheria/Savio's
Presidente Intercontinental
Plaza Caracol
Km 7.5
Convention Center
Forum by the Sea/Coco Bongo
Km 9
Playa Gaviota
Km 9.5
Dady'O/Dady Rock Bar & Grill
Paseo Kukulkán
Km 7
Km 8
Carlos 'n' Charlies

Av. Tulum
307

Canal Nichupté

Pok-Ta-Pok Golf Course
Laguna Bojórquez
Km 10
Miramar Mission Cancún Park
Plaza
Playa Chacmool
Lorenzillo's
Plaza Flamingo
Señor Frog's
R. Plantation House

Paseo Mujeres

To Tulum & Chetumal

Laguna de Nichupté

Km 11.5
Flamingo Cancún
Km12
Hotel Aristos
La Isla Shopping Village
Plaza Kukulkán/100% Natural
La Destileria

Laguna del Amor

Gulf of Mexico
Isla Mujeres
Mérida YUCATÁN
Cancún
Cozumel
YUCATÁN PENINSULA
Playa del Carmen
QUINTANA ROO
Caribbean Sea
CAMPECHE

Ritz Carlton & R. Club Grill
Km 14
Le Méridien Cancún Resort & Spa/Aioli
R. Mango Tango
R. Captain's Cove
Marriott Casamagna
R. La Dolce Vita

Caribbean Sea

Paseo Kukulkán

Laguna Inglé

Ruinas del Rey
Km 16
Hilton Cancún Beach & Golf Resort
El Pueblito

Canal Nizuc

Beach
Golf
Ruins

To Airport
Paseo Kukulkán
Km 20
Westin Regina Cancún
Sun Palace
Punta Nizuc

0   2 mi
0   2 km
N

ACCOMMODATIONS
Blue Bay Getaway Cancún **Km 3.5**
Calinda Viva Cancún **Km 8.5**
Camino Real Cancún **Km 9.5**
El Pueblito **Km 17.5**
Fiesta Americana Grand Coral Beach **Km 9.5**
Flamingo Cancún **Km 11.5**
Hilton Cancún Beach & Golf Resort **Km 17**
Hotel Aristos **Km 12**
Le Méridien Cancún Resort & Spa **Km 14**
Marriott Casa Magna **Km 14.5**
Miramar Misión Cancún Park Plaza **Km 9.5**
Presidente Inter-Continental Cancún **Km 7.5**
Ritz-Carlton Hotel **Km 13.5**
Westin Regina Cancún **Km 20**

DINING
100% Natural **Km 13**
Aioli **Km 14**
Captain's Cove **Km 15**
Club Grill **Km 13.5**
La Destileria **Km 12.65**
La Dolce Vita **Km 14.6**
La Fisheria (in Plaza Caracol) **Km 8.5**
La Joya **Km 9.5**
Lorenzillo's **Km 10.5**
Mango Tango **Km 14.2**
María Bonita (at Punta Cancún) **Km 9.5**
Plantation House **Km 10.5**
Savio's (in Plaza Caracol) **Km 8.5**

250 acres of prime beachfront property, a location that gives every room a sea view (some have both sea and lagoon views), with an 18-hole par-72 golf course across the street. Like the sprawling resort, rooms are grandly spacious and immaculately decorated in minimalist style. Area rugs and pale furnishings soften marble floors and bathrooms throughout. It's a very "kid-friendly" hotel, with one of the island's best children's activity programs, special children's pool, and babysitting available. The hotel is especially appealing to golfers because it's one of only two in Cancún with an on-site course (the other is the Meliá). Greens fees for guests are $77 for 9 holes, $99 for 18 holes, and include the use of a cart.

Paseo Kukulkán, Km 17, Retorno Lacandones, 77500 Cancún, Q. Roo. ✆ 800/228-3000 in the U.S., or 998/881-8000. Fax 998/881-8080. www.hiltoncancun.com. 426 units. High season $350–$415 standard double, $440–$585 Beach Club double, $555–$779 suite; low season $258–$300 standard double, $350–$550 Beach Club double, $395–$500 suite. AE, DC, MC, V. **Amenities:** 2 restaurants; 7 interconnected pools with swim-up bar; golf course across the street, golf clinic; 2 lighted tennis courts; large, fully equipped gym with daily aerobics and Kids Club; 2 whirlpools; sauna; watersports center; concierge; tour desk; car rental; salon; room service; massage; babysitting; laundry. *In room:* A/C, TV, minibar, coffeemaker, hair dryer, iron, safe, robes, house shoes.

Le Méridien Cancún Resort & Spa ★★★   Of all the luxury properties in Cancún, Le Méridien is the most inviting, with a refined yet welcoming sense of personal service. From the intimate lobby and reception area to the best concierge service in Cancún, guests feel immediately pampered. The relatively small establishment is more elegant boutique hotel than immense resort—a welcome relief. The decor throughout the rooms and common areas is classy and comforting, not overdone. Rooms are generous in size, and most have small balconies overlooking the pool, with a view to the ocean. Each has a very large marble bathroom with a separate tub and glassed-in shower. The hotel attracts many Europeans as well as younger, sophisticated travelers, and is ideal for a second honeymoon or romantic break.

A highlight of—or even a reason for—staying here is the **Spa del Mar,** one of Mexico's finest and most complete European spa facilities, with more than 1,394 sq. m (15,000 sq. ft.) of services dedicated to your body and soul. A complete fitness center with extensive cardio and weight machines is on the upper level. The spa consists of a health snack bar, a full-service salon, and 14 treatment rooms, as well as men's and women's steam rooms, saunas, whirlpools, cold plunge pool, inhalation rooms, tranquillity rooms, lockers, and changing areas.

Retorno del Rey Km 14, Zona Hotelera, 77500, Cancún, Q. Roo. ✆ 800/543-4300 in the U.S., or 998/881-2200. Fax 998/881-2201. www.lemeridien.com/mexico/cancun/hotel_mx1658.shtml or www.lemeridien-hotels.com. 213 units. High season $365 standard, $1,050 suite; low season $247 standard, $495 suite. Ask about special

---

⌒Tips   Important Note on Hotel Prices

Cancún's hotels, in all price categories, generally set their rates in dollars, so they are immune to swings in the peso. Travel agents and wholesalers always have air/hotel packages available, and Sunday papers often advertise inventory-clearing packages at prices much lower than the rates listed here. Cancún also has numerous all-inclusive properties, which allow you to take a fixed-cost vacation. Note that the price quoted when you call a hotel's reservation number from the United States may not include Cancún's 12% tax. Prices can vary considerably throughout the year, so it pays to consult a travel agent or shop around.

spa packages. AE, DC, MC, V. Small pets accepted with prior reservation. **Amenities:** 2 restaurants (including Aioli; see "Where to Dine," later in this chapter); lobby bar; 3 cascading swimming pools; 2 lighted championship tennis courts; whirlpool; watersports equipment and massage *palapa* on the beach; supervised children's program with clubhouse, play equipment, wading pool; concierge; tour desk; car rental; business center with Internet access; small shopping arcade; 24-hr. room service; babysitting; laundry; concierge floor. *In room:* A/C, TV, dataport, minibar, hair dryer, iron, safe.

Ritz-Carlton Hotel ★★★   For those who want to feel indulged, this is the place to stay. On 7½ acres, the nine-story Ritz-Carlton sets the standard for elegance in Cancún. The hotel fronts a 360m (1,200-ft.) white-sand beach, and all rooms overlook the ocean, pool, and tropical gardens. The style—in both public areas and guest rooms—is sumptuous and formal, with thick carpets, elaborate chandeliers, and fresh flowers throughout. In all rooms, marble bathrooms have telephones, separate tubs and showers, and lighted makeup mirrors. The hotel has won countless accolades for service.

Retorno del Rey 36, off Paseo Kukulkán, Km 13.5, 77500 Cancún, Q. Roo. 📞 **800/241-3333** in the U.S. and Canada, or 998/881-0808. Fax 998/881-0815. www.ritzcarlton.com. 365 units. High season $425–$475 double, $537–$850 Club floor, $499–$559 suite; low season $235–$302 double, $335–$503 Club floor, $335–$447 suite. Ask about golf, spa, and weekend packages. AE, MC, V. **Amenities:** 5 restaurants (including the Club Grill, 1 of the best restaurants in the city; see "Where to Dine," later in this chapter); Lobby Lounge (see "Cancún After Dark," later in this chapter); 2 connecting swimming pools (heated in winter); deluxe beach cabañas for 2; 3 lighted tennis courts; fully equipped gym and spa with Universal weight training, cardiovascular equipment, personal trainers; steam, sauna, facial, and massage services; Ritz Kids program with supervised activities; concierge; travel agency; business center; shopping arcade; salon; 24-hr. room service; babysitting; laundry; dry cleaning; Club floors. *In room:* A/C, TV, dataport, minibar, hair dryer, iron, safe, robes.

Sun Palace ★   If you're looking for an all-inclusive resort on a great stretch of Caribbean beach, this member of the popular Palace Resorts chain is a prime pick—and the most elegant of the Palace properties in Cancún. The fantastic beach is one of the widest on the island. Located toward the southern end of the island, next to the Westin Regina, this all-suite resort is farther away from the action of the hotel zone—which may be what you want, considering all of the goodies that go with staying here. One of the best perks is that the activities program includes excursions to Tulum, Chichén Itzá, or Isla Mujeres. Suites feature modern Mexican decor, and all have marble floors and a combination bath with whirlpool tub. All units have oceanview balconies or terraces. In addition to the beachside pool, there's an indoor pool, plus a large Jacuzzi with a waterfall. A nicely equipped health club and tennis court complement the ample activities program. Sun Palace also has weekly theme parties. When you stay at any of the Palace resorts, you have the option of playing at any of the other members of the chain—there are two others in Cancún and three others farther south along the Riviera Maya.

Paseo Kukulkán, Km 20, 77500 Cancún, Q. Roo. 📞 **800/346-8225** or 998/85-0533. Fax 998/885-1593. www.palaceresorts.com. 237 suites. High season $310-$398 double. Low-season discounts available. Rates are all-inclusive. AE, DC, MC, V. **Amenities:** 3 restaurants; 2 pools (1 indoor); tennis court; health club; Jacuzzi; 24-hr. room service. *In room:* A/C, TV, hair dryer, iron, safe, robes.

EXPENSIVE

Camino Real Cancún ★★ *Kids*   On 4 acres at the tip of Punta Cancún, the Camino Real is among the island's most appealing places to stay. The architecture is trademark Camino Real style—contemporary and sleek, with bright colors and strategic angles. Rooms in the newer 18-story Camino Real Club have extra services and amenities; rates here include full breakfast. The lower-priced rooms have lagoon views. While the setting is sophisticated, the hotel is also very welcoming to children; it is a favored name in Mexico, where vacations are synonymous with family.

Paseo Kukulkán, 77500 Punta Cancún (Apdo. Postal 14), Cancún, Q. Roo. © **800/722-6466** in the U.S., or 998/848-7000. Fax 998/848-7001. www.caminoreal.com/cancun. 389 units. High season $275 standard double, $264–$465 Camino Real Club double, $1,600 suite; low season $195 standard double, $230 Camino Real Club double, $1,320 suite. AE, DC, MC, V. **Amenities:** 3 restaurants; nightclub; pool; private saltwater lagoon with sea turtles and tropical fish; 3 lighted tennis courts; fitness center with steam bath; watersports center; travel agency; car rental; salon; 24-hr. room service; massage; babysitting (with advance notice); beach volleyball; sailing pier. *In room:* A/C, TV, minibar, hair dryer, iron, safe.

Hyatt Cancun Caribe ⚘

Although this is one of Cancún's older hotels, it remains a favored choice for travelers wanting a more sophisticated place to stay, at a reasonable price. Although the beach here is a bit rocky, there's a precious lagoon-style pool above the beach, with an adjoining pool-bar. Rooms are in a seven-story curved building that backs the pool, or in a collection of villas adjacent to the main building. The rooms, though small, are very comfortable, decorated in muted colors with light wood furnishings. The combination marble tubs have Mexican tile accents, and small furnished balconies overlook the pool and beach (lower floors have terraces). The villa section has quieter rooms that offer more privacy, larger bathrooms, and a large ground-floor terrace.

Paseo Kukulkán, Km 10.5, 77500 Cancún, Q. Roo. © **800/228-9000** in the U.S., or 998/848-7800. Fax 998/848-1514. www.hyatt.com. 226 units. High season $279–$479 double. AE, MC, V. **Amenities:** 3 restaurants; pool; 3 lighted tennis courts; car rental; travel agency; massage; jogging trail. *In room:* A/C, TV, minibar, hair dryer, iron, safe.

Marriott Casa Magna ⚘⚘ (Kids)

This is quintessential Marriott—those who are familiar with the chain's standards will feel at home here and appreciate the hotel's attention to detailed service. Entering through a half circle of Roman columns, you pass through a domed foyer to a wide, lavishly marbled 44-foot-high lobby filled with plants and shallow pools. Guest rooms hold contemporary furnishings, tiled floors, and ceiling fans; most have balconies. The hotel caters to family travelers with specially priced packages (up to 2 children stay free with parents) and the Club Amigos supervised children's program. In 2001, Marriott opened the 450-room luxury **JW Marriott Cancún,** Paseo Kukulkán, Km 14.5, 77500 Cancún, Q. Roo (© **998/848-9600;** www.marriott.com), on the beach next to the Casa Magna.

Paseo Kukulkán, Km 14.5, 77500 Cancún, Q. Roo. © **800/228-9290** in the U.S., or 998/881-2000. Fax 998/881-2071. www.marriott.com. 452 units. High season $260–$285 double, $415 suite; low season $156–$180 double, $345 suite. Ask about packages. AE, MC, V. **Amenities:** 5 restaurants; lobby bar with live music; swimming pool; 2 lighted tennis courts; health club with saunas, whirlpool, aerobics, and juice bar; salon with massage and facials; concierge; travel agency; car rental; room service; babysitting; laundry. *In room:* A/C, TV, dataport, minibar, coffeemaker, hair dryer, iron, safe.

Melía Cancun Beach & Spa Resort ⚘

The large, ultramodern Melía is most popular with weddings, conventions, and other group events, but it's also a great option for individual travelers looking for a lively place to stay. It's a landmark known for the spectacular nine-story atrium garden in the lobby, shaped like a pyramid, with cascading waterfalls and a bevy of palms. The guest rooms are small but adequate, with marble floors, bright decor, and balconies. About half of the units offer ocean or lagoon views; the others overlook the garden atrium. The Melía is one of two hotels in town with an on-site golf course; the other is the Hilton.

Paseo Kukulkán, Km 16.5, 77500 Cancún, Q. Roo. © **800/336-3542** in the U.S., or 998/885-1114. Fax 998/885-1963. www.solmelia.com. 400 units. $190–$330 double. AE, DC, MC, V. **Amenities:** 5 restaurants; 3 bars; 2 pools; 18-hole executive golf course; 3 tennis courts; 2 lighted paddle tennis courts; 558-sq.-m (6,000-sq.-ft.) spa and fitness center; 24-hr. room service. *In room:* A/C, TV, hair dryer, safe.

Presidente InterContinental Cancún ⟨⟨   On the island's best beach, facing the placid Bahía de Mujeres, the Presidente's location is reason enough to stay here, and it's just a 2-minute walk to Cancún's public Pok-Ta-Pok Golf Club (Club de Golf Cancún). For its ambience, I consider it an ideal choice for a romantic getaway or for couples who enjoy indulging in the sports of golf, tennis, or even shopping. Cool and spacious, the Presidente sports a postmodern design with lavish marble and wicker accents and a strong use of color. Guests have a choice of two double beds or one king. All rooms have tastefully simple unfinished pine furniture. Sixteen units on the first floor have patios with outdoor whirlpool tubs. The expansive pool has a pyramid-shaped waterfall. Coming from Cancún City, you'll reach the Presidente on the left side of the street before you get to Punta Cancún.

Paseo Kukulkán, Km 7.5, 77500 Cancún, Q. Roo. ⓒ **800/327-0200** in the U.S., or 998/848-8700. Fax 998/883-2602. www.interconti.com. 299 units. High season $280–$336 double; low season $230–$280 double. Rates include breakfast, coffee with wakeup call, 2 massages on the beach, unlimited golf at Pok-Ta-Pok, 2 bottles of water delivered daily. AE, MC, V. Ask about special packages. **Amenities:** 3 restaurants; 2 swimming pools; marina; lighted tennis courts; fitness center; whirlpool; watersports equipment rental; travel agency; car rental; shopping arcade; 24-hr. room service; babysitting; laundry; nonsmoking floors; Club floors; 2 rooms for travelers with disabilities are available. In room: A/C, TV, dataport, minibar, hair dryer, safe.

Westin Regina Cancún ⟨⟨⟨⟨   The strikingly austere architecture of the Westin Regina, impressive with its elegant use of stone and marble, is the stamp of leading Latin American architect Ricardo Legorreta. The hotel consists of two sections, the main building and the more exclusive six-story hot-pink tower. Standard rooms are unusually large and beautifully furnished with cool, contemporary furniture. Those on the sixth floor have balconies, and first-floor rooms have terraces. Rooms in the tower all have ocean or lagoon views, furniture with Olinalá lacquer accents, Berber area rugs, oak tables and chairs, and terraces with lounge chairs. It's important to note that this hotel is a 15- to 20-minute ride from the lively strip that lies between the Plaza Flamingo and Punta Cancún, so it's a good choice for those who want a little more seclusion than Cancún typically offers. However, it is easy to join the action—buses stop in front, and taxis are readily available.

Paseo Kukulkán, Km 20, 77500 Cancún, Q. Roo. ⓒ **800/228-3000** in the U.S., 800/215-7000 in Mexico, or 998/848-7400. Fax 998/885-0296. www.westin.com. 293 units. High season $350–$450 double; low season $147–$415 double. AE, DC, MC, V. **Amenities:** 2 restaurants; 2 bars; 5 swimming pools; 2 lighted tennis courts; gym with Stairmaster, bicycle, weights, aerobics, sauna, steam, massage; 3 whirlpools; concierge; travel agency; car rental; pharmacy/gift shop; salon; room service; babysitting; laundry. In room: A/C, TV, dataport, minibar, coffeemaker, hair dryer, iron, safe.

MODERATE

Blue Bay Getaway Cancún ⟨⟨⟨⟨   The adults-only Blue Bay Getaway Cancún is a spirited yet relaxing all-inclusive resort favored by young adults. Surrounded by acres of tropical gardens, it's ideally located at the northern end of the Hotel Zone, close to the major shopping plazas, restaurants, and nightlife. It has a terrific beach with calm waters for swimming. The comfortable, modern rooms are in two sections. The central building features 72 rooms decorated in rustic wood, the main lobby, administrative offices, restaurants, and Tequila Sunrise bar. The remaining nine buildings feature colorful Mexican decor; rooms have lagoon, garden, and ocean views. Safes are available for an extra charge. During the evenings, guests may enjoy a variety of theme-night dinners, nightly shows, and live entertainment in an outdoor theater.

Paseo Kukulkán, Km 3.5, 77500 Cancún, Q. Roo. ℂ **998/848-7900**. Fax 998/848-7994. www.bluebayresorts. com. 216 units. High season $320 double; low season $230 double. Rates include food, beverages, and activities. AE, MC, V. **Amenities:** 4 restaurants; 4 bars; 2 swimming pools; marina; tennis court; exercise room with daily aerobics classes; 4 whirlpools; watersports equipment; game room with pool and Ping-Pong tables; snorkeling and scuba lessons; bicycles; wheelchair-accessible rooms available. *In room:* A/C, TV, dataport, hair dryer.

Calinda Viva Cancún   From the street, this hotel looks like a blockhouse; on the ocean side you'll find a small but pretty patio garden and Cancún's best beach for safe swimming. The location is ideal, close to all the shops and restaurants near Punta Cancún and the Convention Center. Rooms overlook the lagoon or the ocean. They are large and undistinguished in decor, but comfortable, with marble floors and either two double beds or a king-size bed. Several studios have kitchenettes.

Paseo Kukulkán, Km 8.5, 77500 Cancún, Q. Roo. ℂ **800/221-2222** in the U.S., or 998/883-0800. Fax 998/883-2087. 216 units. High season $198–$275 double; low season $147–$215 double. AE, MC, V. **Amenities:** Restaurant; 2 snack bars; 3 bars; 2 swimming pools (1 for adults, 1 for children); marina; 2 lighted tennis courts; watersports equipment rental; nonsmoking areas; wheelchair access. *In room:* A/C, TV.

El Pueblito ★ *Kids*   This hotel offers perhaps the top all-inclusive value in Cancún. Dwarfed by its ostentatious neighbors, the El Pueblito lobby resembles a traditional Mexican hacienda, with several three-story buildings (no elevators) terraced in a V-shape down a gentle hillside toward the sea. A meandering swimming pool with waterfalls runs between the two series of buildings. Rooms are very large, with modern rattan furnishings, travertine marble floors, and large bathrooms. Each has either a balcony or a terrace. In addition to a constant flow of buffet-style meals and snacks, there's also the choice of a nightly theme party, complete with entertainment. Mini-golf and a water slide, plus a full program of kids' activities, make this an ideal place for families with children. The hotel is located toward the southern end of the island past the Hilton Resort.

Paseo Kukulkán, Km 17.5, 77500 Cancún, Q. Roo. ℂ **998/881-8800** or 998/881-8814. Fax 998/885-2066. www.pueblitohotels.com. 349 units. High season $270 double; low season $198 double. Rates are all-inclusive. Ask about specials. AE, MC, V. **Amenities:** 3 restaurants; 2 bars; lobby cafe; large pool; tennis courts; babysitting ($10 per hr.); aerobics; volleyball, nonmotorized watersports; cooking classes. *In room:* A/C, TV.

Flamingo Cancún ★   The Flamingo seems to have been inspired by the dramatic, slope-sided architecture of the Camino Real, but it's considerably smaller and less expensive. The comfortable, modern guest rooms—all with balconies—border a courtyard facing the interior swimming pools and *palapa* pool bar. A second pool with a sun deck overlooks the ocean. The Flamingo is in the heart of the island hotel district, opposite the Flamingo Shopping Center and close to other hotels, shopping centers, and restaurants. It's a friendly, accommodating choice for families.

Paseo Kukulkán, Km 11.5, 77500 Cancún, Q. Roo. ℂ **998/883-1544**. Fax 998/883-1029. www.flamingocancun. com. 221 units. All-Inclusive: High season $200 double; low season $180 double. Room only: High season $165 double; low season $145 double. AE, MC, V. **Amenities:** 2 restaurants; 2 pools; small gym; watersports equipment rentals; tour desk; car rental; babysitting; laundry; dry cleaning. *In room:* A/C, TV, minibar.

Miramar Misión Cancún Park Plaza   Each of the ingeniously designed rooms here has a partial view of both the lagoon and the ocean. Public spaces throughout the hotel have lots of dark wood accents, but the most notable feature is the large, rectangular swimming pool that extends through the hotel and down to the beach, with built-in, submerged sun chairs. There's also an oversize whirlpool (the largest in Cancún), a sun deck, and a snack bar on the seventh-floor roof. Rooms are on the small side but are bright and comfortable, with small balconies and bamboo furniture; bathrooms have polished limestone vanities. A popular nightclub, **Batacha,** has live music for dancing from 9pm to 4am Tuesday through Sunday.

Paseo Kukulkán, Km 9.5, 77500 Zona Hotelera Cancún, Q. Roo. © **800/215-1333** in the U.S., or 998/883-1755. Fax 998/883-1136. www.hotelesmision.com. 266 units. High season $290 double; low season $190 double. AE, MC, V. **Amenities:** 3 restaurants; 2 bars; rooftop snack bar; swimming pool; whirlpool. *In room:* A/C, TV, minibar, hair dryer, safe.

INEXPENSIVE

Hotel Aristos   This was one of the island's first hotels, and it continues to welcome repeat guests, especially European and senior travelers. The recently remodeled rooms have upgraded wood furnishings and decor. Though small, they are very clean and cool, with red tile floors and small balconies. All rooms face either the Caribbean or the *paseo* and lagoon; the best views face the Caribbean side (without noise from the *paseo*). A central pool overlooks the ocean and a wide stretch of beach one level below the lobby. Beware of spring break, when the hotel rocks with loud music poolside all day. The hotel wisely books the spring-breakers into their own section, facing the *paseo,* and reserves the beach-facing rooms for other guests.

Paseo Kukulkán, Km 12, 77500 Cancún, Q. Roo. © **998/883-0011.** Fax 998/883-0078. aristcun@ prodigy.net.mx. 245 units. High season $135 double, $175 double with 3 meals and drinks; low season $105 double, $140 double with 3 meals and drinks. AE, MC, V. **Amenities:** Restaurant; 3 bars; swimming pool; 2 lighted tennis courts; marina with watersports equipment; travel agency; room service; babysitting; laundry. *In room:* A/C, TV.

CANCUN CITY
MODERATE

Radisson Hacienda Cancún ★★ *Value*   This is the nicest hotel in downtown Cancún, and one of the best values in the area. The Radisson offers all the expected comforts of a chain, yet in an atmosphere of Mexican hospitality. Resembling a hacienda, rooms are set off from a large rotunda-style lobby, lush gardens, and a pleasant pool area. All have Talavera tile inlays and brightly colored fabric accents; views of the garden, the pool, or the street; and a small sitting area and balcony. Bathrooms have a combination tub and shower. Guests have access to the facilities of the Avalon Bay Beach Club, with complimentary shuttle service. The hotel is behind the State Government building, within walking distance of downtown Cancún dining and shopping.

Av. Nader 1, SM2, Centro, 77500 Cancún, Q. Roo. © **998/887-4455.** Fax 998/884-7954. 248 units. High season $125 standard, $145 junior suite; low season $94 standard, $115 junior suite. Ask about special all-inclusive rates. AE, MC, V. **Amenities:** 2 restaurants; lively lobby bar; pool with adjoining bar and separate wading area for children; tennis courts; small gym with sauna; travel agency; car rental; salon. *In room:* A/C, TV, coffeemaker, hair dryer, iron, safe.

INEXPENSIVE

Cancún Inn El Patio ★ *Finds*   Many guests at this small hotel stay for up to a month, drawn by its combination of excellent value and warm hospitality. The European-style guesthouse caters to travelers looking for more of the area's culture. You won't find bars, pools, or loud parties; you will find excellent service and impeccable accommodations. Rooms face the plant-filled interior courtyard, dotted with groupings of wrought-iron chairs and tables. Each room has slightly different appointments and amenities, but all have white tile floors and rustic wood furnishings. Some rooms have kitchenettes, and there's a common kitchen area with purified water and a cooler for stocking your own supplies. There is a public phone in the entranceway, and the staff can arrange for a cellular phone in your room on request. A game and TV room has a large-screen cable TV, a library stocked with books on Mexican culture, backgammon, cards, and board games.

Av. Bonampak 51 and Cereza, SM2A, Centro, 77500 Cancún, Q. Roo. © 998/884-3500. Fax 998/884-3540. www.cancun-suites.com. 12 units. $56 double. Spanish-lesson packages available. Ask about discounts for longer stays. AE, MC, V. **Amenities:** Small restaurant (breakfast and dinner). *In room:* A/C, safe.

Hotel Antillano   A quiet and very clean choice, the Antillano is close to the Ciudad Cancún bus terminal. Rooms overlook Avenida Tulum, the side streets, or the interior lawn and pool. Pool-view rooms are most desirable because they are quietest. The recently remodeled rooms feature coordinated furnishings, one or two double beds, a sink area separate from the bathroom, and red-tile floors. Guests have the use of the hotel's beach club on the island.

Av. Claveles 1 (corner of Av. Tulum, opposite Restaurant Rosa Mexicano), 77500 Cancún, Q. Roo. © 998/884-1532. Fax 998/884-1878. www.hotelantillano.com. 48 units. High season $72 double; low season $60 double. AE, MC, V. Street parking. **Amenities:** Small bar; travel agency; babysitting. *In room:* A/C, TV.

Hotel Hacienda Cancún *Value*   This extremely pleasing little hotel is a great value. The facade has been remodeled to look like a hacienda. The guest rooms are very comfortable; all have rustic Mexican furnishings and two double beds, but no views. There's a nice small pool and cafe under a shaded *palapa* in the back.

Sunyaxchen 39–40, 77500 Cancún, Q. Roo. © 998/884-3672. Fax 998/884-1208. hhda@cancun.com.mx. 35 units. High season $45 double; low season $38 double. MC, V. Street parking. From Avenida Yaxchilán, turn west on Sunyaxchen; it's on the right next to the Hotel Caribe International, opposite 100% Natural. **Amenities:** Restaurant; pool. *In room:* A/C, TV, safe.

Hotel Margaritas ★ *Value*   Located in downtown Cancún, this four-story hotel (with elevator) is comfortable and unpretentious, offering one of the best values in Cancún. The pleasantly decorated rooms, with white tile floors and small balconies, are exceptionally clean and bright. Lounge chairs surround the attractive pool, which has a wading section for children. The hotel offers complimentary safes at the front desk.

Av. Yaxchilán 41, SM22, Centro, 77500 Cancún, Q. Roo. © 998/884-9333 or 01-800/711-1531. Fax 998/884-1324. 100 units. High season $95 double; low season $78 double. AE, MC, V. **Amenities:** Restaurant; pool; travel agency; room service; babysitting; medical service; money exchange. *In room:* A/C, TV.

Hotel Parador   The conveniently located three-story Parador is one of the most popular downtown hotels. Recently remodeled guest rooms are arranged around two long, narrow garden courtyards leading back to a pool (with a separate children's pool) and grassy sunning area. Each modern room has two double beds and a shower. Guests can help themselves to bottled drinking water in the hall. The hotel is next to Pop's restaurant, almost at the corner of Uxmal.

Av. Tulum 26, 77500 Cancún, Q. Roo. © 998/884-1043 or 998/884-1310. Fax 998/884-9712. 66 units. High season $73 double. Low season $50 double. Ask about promotional rates. MC, V. Limited street parking. **Amenities:** Restaurant and bar; pool. *In room:* A/C, TV.

3 Where to Dine

U.S.–based franchise chains, which really need no introduction, dominate the Cancún restaurant scene. These include Hard Rock Cafe, Planet Hollywood, Rainforest Cafe, Tony Roma's, TGI Friday's, Ruth's Chris Steak House, and the gamut of fast-food burger places. The establishments listed here are locally owned, one-of-a-kind restaurants or exceptional selections at area hotels. Many schedule live music. Unless otherwise indicated, parking is free.

One unique way to combine dinner with sightseeing is aboard the **Lobster Dinner Cruise** (© 998/849-4621). Cruising around the tranquil, turquoise waters of the lagoon, passengers feast on lobster dinners accompanied by wine. Cost is $69 per person. There are two daily departures from the Royal Mayan Marina. A sunset cruise leaves at 4pm during the winter and 5pm during the summer; a moonlight cruise leaves at 7pm winter, 8pm summer.

CANCUN ISLAND
VERY EXPENSIVE

Aioli ★★★ FRENCH   For the quality and originality of the cuisine, coupled with excellent service, this is my top pick for the best fine-dining value in Cancún. The Provençal—but definitely not provincial—Aioli offers exquisite French and Mediterranean gourmet specialties in a warm and cozy country French setting. Though it serves perhaps the best breakfast buffet in Cancún (for $16), most diners from outside the hotel come here in the evening, when low lighting and superb service make it a top choice for a romantic dinner. Starters include traditional patés and a delightful escargot served in the shell with white wine and herbed butter sauce. A specialty is duck breast in honey and lavender sauce. Equally scrumptious is rack of lamb, prepared in Moroccan style and served with couscous. Pan-seared grouper is topped with a paste of black olives, crushed potato, and tomato, and bouillabaisse contains an exceptional array of seafood. Desserts are decadent; the signature "Fifth Element" is a sinfully delicious temptation rich with chocolate.

In Le Méridien Cancún Resort & Spa, Retorno del Rey Km 14. © 998/881-2260. www.lemeridien.com/mexico/cancun/restaurants_mx1658.shtml. Reservations required. Main courses $22–$36. AE, DC, MC, V. Daily 6:30am–11pm.

Club Grill ★★★ INTERNATIONAL   This is the place for that special night out. Cancún's most elegant and stylish restaurant is also among its most delicious. Even rival restaurateurs give it an envious thumbs up. The gracious service starts as you enter the anteroom, with its comfortable seating and selection of fine tequilas and Cuban cigars. It continues in a candlelit dining room with shimmering silver and crystal. Elegant plates of peppered scallops, truffles, and potatoes in tequila sauce; grilled lamb; or mixed grill arrive at a leisurely pace. The restaurant has smoking and nonsmoking sections. A band plays romantic music for dancing from 8pm on.

In the Ritz-Carlton Hotel, Paseo Kukulkán, Km 13.5. © 998/885-0808. Reservations required. No sandals or tennis shoes; men must wear long pants. Main courses $30–$40. AE, DC, MC, V. Tues–Sun 7–11pm.

The Plantation House ★ *Overrated* CARIBBEAN/FRENCH   This casually elegant, pale-yellow-and-blue clapboard restaurant overlooking Nichupté lagoon takes you back to the time when the Caribbean first experienced European tastes and culinary talents. The decor combines island-style colonial charm with elegant touches. The service is excellent, but the food is only mediocre, especially considering the price. For starters, try the signature poached shrimp with lemon juice and olive oil, or creamy crabmeat soup. Move on to the main event, which may consist of classic veal Wellington in puff pastry with duck paté, fish filet crusted in spices and herbs and topped with vanilla sauce, or lobster *medaillons* in mango sauce. Flambéed desserts are a specialty, and the Plantation House has one of the most extensive wine lists in town. It's generally quite crowded, which makes it a bit loud for a romantic evening.

Paseo Kukulkán, Km 10.5. ℂ **998/883-1433** or 998/883-2120. Reservations recommended. Main courses $13–$35. AE, MC, V. Daily 5pm–12:30am.

EXPENSIVE

Blue Bayou ⚹ CAJUN   You may not associate Cancún with Cajun dining, but this restaurant receives plenty of raves—not to mention repeat diners. It flies in crawfish daily from Louisiana. The signature Maya blackened seafood platter is a favorite, combining Caribbean with Cajun. Blue Bayou serves certified Angus beef; the Green Goddess rib-eye is excellent. The two-level setting is remarkable—the lower level has a lush hanging garden with a waterfall. Adding to the ambience is nightly live jazz, as well as a special "dine and dance" Thursday through Saturday.

In the Hyatt Cancun Caribe Hotel, Paseo Kukulkán, Km 10.5. ℂ **998/848-7800.** Main courses: $15-$33. AE, MC, V. Daily 6–11pm.

Captain's Cove ⚹ INTERNATIONAL/SEAFOOD   Though it sits almost at the end of Paseo Kukulkán, far from everything, the Captain's Cove continues to pack in customers with its consistent value. Diners sit on several levels, facing big open windows overlooking the lagoon and Royal Yacht Club Marina. For breakfast there's an all-you-can-eat buffet. Main courses of USDA Angus steak and seafood are the norm at lunch and dinner, and there's a children's menu. For dessert there are flaming coffees, crepes, and Key lime pie. The restaurant is on the lagoon side, opposite the Omni Hotel.

Paseo Kukulkán, Km 15. ℂ **998/885-0016.** Main courses $16–$30; breakfast buffet $12. AE, MC, V. Daily 7am–11pm.

La Dolce Vita ⚹⚹ ITALIAN/SEAFOOD   Casually elegant La Dolce Vita is Cancún's favorite Italian restaurant. Appetizers include paté of quail liver and carpaccio in vinaigrette, and mushrooms Provençal. The chef specializes in homemade pastas combined with fresh seafood. You can order green tagliolini with lobster *medaillons,* linguine with clams or seafood, or rigatoni Mexican-style (with *chorizo,* mushrooms, and chives) as a main course, or as an appetizer for half price. Other main courses include veal with morels, fresh salmon with cream sauce, and fresh fish in a variety of sauces. Recently added choices include vegetarian lasagna and grilled whole lobster. You have a choice of dining in air-conditioned comfort or on an open-air terrace with a view of the lagoon. Live jazz plays from 7 to 11:30pm Monday through Saturday.

Paseo Kukulkán, Km 14.6, on the lagoon, opposite the Marriott Casa Magna. ℂ **998/885-0150** or 998/885-0161. Fax 998/885-0590. www.cancun.com/dining/dolce. Reservations required for dinner. Main courses $12–$33. AE, MC, V. Daily noon–midnight.

La Fishería ⚹ *Kids* SEAFOOD   If you're at the mall shopping, this is your best bet. Patrons find a lot to choose from at this restaurant overlooking Paseo Kukulkán and the lagoon. The expansive menu includes shark fingers with jalapeño dip, grouper filet stuffed with seafood in lobster sauce, Acapulco-style *ceviche* (in tomato sauce), New England clam chowder, steamed mussels, grilled red snapper with pasta—you get the idea. The menu changes daily, but there's always *tikin xik,* that great Yucatecan grilled fish marinated in *achiote* sauce. For those not inclined toward seafood, a pizza from the wood-burning oven, or perhaps a grilled chicken or beef dish, might do. La Fishería has a nonsmoking section.

Plaza Caracol shopping center, Paseo Kukulkán, Km 8.5, 2nd floor. ℂ **998/883-1395.** Main courses $7–$30. AE, MC, V. Daily 11am–midnight.

La Joya ★ MEXICAN/INTERNATIONAL   La Joya (the Jewel) is truly a gem of a dining experience, with a menu of gourmet Mexican cuisine is a suitably upscale atmosphere. For starters, try lobster quesadillas, with mellow panela cheese. Baked pumpkin flower soup and a rich, lobster-infused version of the Mexican classic *pozole* are equally tempting first courses. Main dishes range from red snapper Cozumel (grilled and topped with a rainbow of coco-infused sauces), to beef medallions on a bed of sautéed cactus petals in creamy chipotle sauce. Entertaining touches include a cigar show, guided tequila tastings, and live music nightly, ranging from mariachis to classical piano.

In the Fiesta Americana Grand Coral Beach hotel, Paseo Kukulkán, Km 9.5. ℂ 998/881-3200. Main courses $25–$40. AE, MC, V. Daily 6:30pm–midnight.

Lorenzillo's ★★★ *Kids* SEAFOOD   This festive, friendly restaurant is a personal favorite—I never miss a lobster stop here when I'm in Cancún. Live lobster is the overwhelming favorite, and part of the appeal is selecting your dinner out of the giant lobster tank. Lorenzillo's sits on the lagoon under a giant *palapa* roof. A dock leads down to the main dining area, and when that's packed (which is often), a wharf-side bar handles the overflow. In addition to lobster—which comes grilled, steamed, or stuffed—good bets are shrimp stuffed with cheese and wrapped in bacon, the Admiral's filet coated in toasted almonds and light mustard sauce, and seafood-stuffed squid. Desserts include the tempting "Martinique": Belgian chocolate with hazelnuts, almonds, and pecans, served with vanilla ice cream. The sunset pier offers a lighter menu of cold seafood, sandwiches, and salads. Children are very welcome.

Paseo Kukulkán, Km 10.5. ℂ 998/883-1254. www.lorenzillos.com.mx. Reservations recommended. Main courses $8–$50. AE, MC, V. Daily noon–midnight. Valet parking available.

Mango Tango ★★ INTERNATIONAL   The beauty of dining here is that you can stay and enjoy a hot nightspot. Mango Tango has made a name for itself with sizzling floor shows and live reggae music (see "Cancún After Dark," later in this chapter), but its kitchen deserves attention as well. Try the peel-your-own shrimp, Argentine-style grilled meat with *chimichurri* sauce, and other grilled specialties. Mango Tango salad is shrimp, chicken, avocado, red onion, tomato, and mushrooms served on mango slices. Entrees include rice with seafood and fried bananas. Creole gumbo comes with lobster, shrimp, and squid, and coconut-and-mango cake is a suitable finish to the meal.

Paseo Kukulkán, Km 14.2, opposite the Ritz-Carlton Hotel. ℂ 998/885-0303. Reservations recommended. Main courses $12–$57; dinner show $40. AE, MC, V. Daily 2pm–2am.

María Bonita ★ *Kids* REGIONAL/MEXICAN/NOUVELLE MEXICAN   In a stylish setting overlooking the water, María Bonita captures the essence of the country through its music and food. Prices are higher and the flavors more institutionalized than at traditional Mexican restaurants in Ciudad Cancún, but this is a good choice for the Hotel Zone. There are three sections: La Cantina Jalisco, with an open kitchen and tequila bar; the Salón Michoacán, which features that state's cuisine; and the Patio Oaxaca. The menu encompasses the best of Mexico's other cuisines, with a few international dishes. Prix-fixe dinners include appetizer, main course, and dessert. Trios, marimba and jarocho music, and mariachis serenade you while you dine. A nice starter is Mitla salad, with slices of the renowned Oaxaca cheese dribbled with olive oil and coriander dressing. Wonderful stuffed chile La Doña—a mildly hot poblano pepper filled with lobster and *huitlacoche,* in a cream sauce—comes as an appetizer or a main course.

In the Hotel Camino Real, Punta Cancún (enter from the street). ℂ **998/848-7000**, ext. 8060 or 8061. Reservations recommended. Prix-fixe dinner $30–$45; main courses $17–$31. AE, DC, MC, V. Daily 6:30–11:45pm.

Savio's ⭐ ITALIAN   Centrally located at the heart of the Hotel Zone, Savio's is a great place to stop for a quick meal or coffee. Its bar is always crowded with patrons sipping everything from cappuccino to imported beer. Repeat diners look forward to large fresh salads and rich, subtly herb-flavored Italian dishes. Ravioli stuffed with ricotta and spinach comes in delicious tomato sauce. Stylish, with black-and-white decor and tile floors, it has two levels and faces Paseo Kukulkán through two stories of awning-shaded windows.

Plaza Caracol shopping center, Paseo Kukulkán, Km 8.5. ℂ/fax **998/883-2085**. Main courses $10–$30. AE, MC, V. Daily 10am–midnight.

MODERATE

La Destilería MEXICAN   If you want to experience tequila in its native habitat, you won't want to miss this place—even though it's across the country from the region that produces the beverage. La Destilería is more than a tequila-inspired restaurant; it's a mini-museum honoring the "spirit" of Mexico. It serves over 150 brands of tequila, including some treasures that never find their way across the country's northern border, so be adventurous! The margaritas are among the best on the island. When you decide to have some food with your tequila, the menu is refined Mexican, with everything from quesadillas with squash blossom flowers, to shrimp in a delicate tequila-lime sauce.

Paseo Kukulkán, Km 12.65, across from Plaza Kukulcan. ℂ **998/885-1086** or 998/885-1087. Main courses $8–30. AE, MC, V. Daily 1pm–midnight.

100% Natural VEGETARIAN/MEXICAN   If you want a healthy reprieve from an overindulgent night—or just like your meals as fresh and natural as possible—this is your oasis. No matter what your dining preference, you owe it to yourself to try a Mexican tradition, the fresh-fruit *liquado*. The blended drink combines fresh fruit, ice, and either water or milk. More creative combinations may mix in yogurt, granola, or other goodies. And 100% Natural serves more than just meal-quality drinks—there's a bountiful selection of basic Mexican fare and terrific sandwiches served on whole-grain bread, both with options for vegetarians. Breakfast is a delight as well as a good value. The space abounds with plants and cheery colors. There are a few locations in town; the branch in Plaza Terramar (ℂ 998/883-3636) is open 24 hours.

Plaza Kukulcan, Paseo Kukulkán, Km 13. ℂ **998/885-2904**. Main courses $2.80–$13. MC, V. Daily 8am–11pm.

CANCUN CITY
EXPENSIVE

La Habichuela ⭐ GOURMET SEAFOOD/CARIBBEAN/MEXICAN   In a garden setting with soft music playing in the background, this restaurant is ideal for a romantic evening. For an all-out culinary adventure, try *habichuela* (string bean) soup; shrimp in any number of sauces, including Jamaican tamarind, tequila, or ginger-and-mushroom; and Maya coffee with *xtabentun* (a strong, sweet, anise-based liqueur). Grilled seafood and steaks are excellent, but this is a good place to try a Mexican specialty such as *enchiladas suizas* or *tampiqueña*-style beef (thinly sliced, marinated, and grilled). For something totally divine, try *Cocobichuela*, which is lobster and shrimp in curry sauce served in a coconut shell and topped with fruit.

Margaritas 25. ℂ **998/884-3158**. habichuela@infosel.net.mx. Reservations recommended in high season. Main courses $12–$35. AE, MC, V. Daily noon–midnight.

Périco's ★/★★ MEXICAN/SEAFOOD/STEAKS   Périco's has colorful murals that almost dance off the walls, a bar area with saddles for barstools, colorful leather tables and chairs, and accommodating waiters; it's always booming and festive. The extensive menu offers well-prepared steak, seafood, and traditional Mexican dishes for reasonable rates (except for lobster). This is a place not only to eat and drink, but also to let loose and join in the fun, so don't be surprised if everybody drops their forks and dons huge sombreros to shimmy and snake in a conga dance around the dining room. It's fun whether or not you join in, but it's definitely not the place for a romantic evening alone. There's marimba music from 7:30 to 9:30pm, and mariachis from 9:30pm to midnight.

Yaxchilán 61. ℂ **998/884-3152.** Reservations recommended. Main courses $11–$25. AE, MC, V. Daily 1pm–1am.

MODERATE

Restaurant El Pescador ★ SEAFOOD   Locals all seem to agree: This is the best spot for fresh seafood in Cancún. There's often a line for the well-prepared fresh seafood served on a street-side patio and in an upstairs space overlooking Tulipanes. Feast on shrimp cocktail, conch, octopus, *camarones à la criolla* (Creole-style shrimp), charcoal-broiled lobster, and stone crabs. *Zarzuela* is a combination seafood plate cooked in white wine and garlic. There's a Mexican specialty menu as well. Another branch, **La Mesa del Pescador,** is in the Plaza Kukulcan on Cancún Island and keeps the same hours, but it's more expensive.

Tulipanes 28, off Av. Tulum. ℂ **998/884-2673.** Fax 998/884-3639. Main courses $10–$55; Mexican plates $7–$12. AE, MC, V. Daily 11am–11pm.

Restaurant Rosa Mexicano MEXICAN HAUTE CUISINE   This beautiful little place has candlelit tables and a plant-filled patio in back, and is almost always packed. Colorful paper banners and piñatas hang from the ceiling, efficient waiters wear bow ties and cummerbunds that match the Mexican flag, and a trio plays romantic Mexican music nightly. The menu features "refined" Mexican specialties. Try *pollo almendro* (chicken covered in cream sauce and sprinkled with ground almonds), or pork baked in a banana leaf with a sauce of oranges, lime, ancho chile, and garlic. Steak *tampiqueño* is a huge platter that comes with guacamole salad, quesadillas, beans, salad, and rice.

Claveles 4. ℂ **998/884-6313.** Fax 998/884-2371. Reservations recommended for parties of 6 or more. Main courses $8–$15; lobster $30. AE, MC, V. Daily 5–11pm.

INEXPENSIVE

Pizza Rolandi (Kids) ITALIAN   This is an institution in Cancún, and the Rolandi name is synonymous with dining in both Cancún and neighboring Isla Mujeres. Pizza Rolandi and its branch in Isla (see chapter 4) have become standards for dependably good casual fare. At this shaded outdoor patio restaurant, you can choose from almost two dozen wood-oven pizzas and a full selection of spaghetti, calzones, Italian-style chicken and beef, and desserts. There's a full bar as well.

Cobá 12. ℂ **998/884-4047.** Fax 998/884-3994. www.rolandi.com. Pasta $7–$12; pizza and main courses $7–$17. AE, MC, V. Daily 12:30pm–midnight.

Restaurant Los Almendros ★ YUCATECAN   To steep yourself in Yucatecan cuisine and music, head directly to this large, colorful restaurant opposite the bullring. Readers have written to say they ate here almost exclusively because the food and service are good; the illustrated menu, with color pictures of dishes, makes ordering easy. Regional specialties include lime soup, *poc chuc* (marinated, barbecue-style pork), chicken or pork *pibil* (sweet and spicy shredded meat), and such appetizers as *panuchos* (soft fried tortillas with refried beans and shredded turkey or pork *pibil*). The *combinado* Yucateco is a sampler of four typical main courses: chicken, *poc chuc,* sausage, and *escabeche* (onions marinated in vinegar and sour-orange sauce).

Av. Bonampak and Sayil. ℰ **998/887-1332.** Main courses $6–$10. AE, MC, V. Daily 11am–10pm.

Restaurant Santa María MEXICAN   The open-air Santa María is a clean, gaily decked-out place to sample authentic Mexican food. It's cool and breezy, with a patio dining area that's open on two sides and furnished with leather tables and chairs covered in multicolored cloths. A bowl of *frijoles de olla* (beans cooked in a clay pot) and an order of beefsteak tacos will fill you up for a low price. You may want to try tortilla soup or enchiladas, or go for one of the specialty grilled U.S.–cut steaks, fajitas, ribs, or grilled seafood, all of which arrive with a baked potato. The restaurant also serves traditional Yucatecan dishes.

Azucenas at Parque Palapas. ℰ **998/884-3158.** Fax 998/884-0940. Main courses $3.50–$9; tacos 75¢–$5. AE, MC, V. Daily 5pm–1am.

Stefano's ITALIAN/PIZZA/PASTA   Stefano's began primarily as a local restaurant, serving Italian food with a few Mexican accents, and now it's equally popular with tourists. On the menu you'll find ravioli stuffed with *huitlacoche;* rigatoni in tequila sauce; and seafood with chile peppers. Pizza options include the Stefano special, with fresh tomato, cheese, and pesto, and three-cheese-and-shrimp. Stefano's offers vegetarian pizza, calzones stuffed with spinach, mozzarella, and tomato sauce, and other options for non-meat-eaters. For dessert, ricotta strudel is something out of the ordinary. There are lots of coffees and mixed drinks, plus a wine list.

Bonampak 177. ℰ **998/887-9964.** Main courses $6–$9; pizza $5.75–$9.75. AE, MC, V. Daily noon–1am.

COFFEE & PASTRIES

Pastelería Italiana ℰ COFFEE/PASTRIES/ICE CREAM   More a casual neighborhood coffeehouse than a tourist destination, this shady little spot has been doing business since 1977. A white awning covers the small outdoor, plant-filled table area. Inside are refrigerated cases of tarts and scrumptious-looking cakes, ready to be carried away whole or by the piece. The coffeehouse is in the same block as Périco's.

Av. Yaxchilán 67-D (between Maraño and Chiabal), SM 25, near Sunyaxchen. ℰ **998/884-0796.** Pastries $1.75–$2.25; ice cream $2; coffee $1–$2. AE. Mon–Sat 9am–11pm; Sun 1–9pm.

4 Beaches, Watersports & Boat Tours

THE BEACHES   Big hotels dominate the best stretches of beach. All of Mexico's beaches are public property, so you can use the beach of any hotel by walking through the lobby or directly onto the sand. Be especially careful on beaches fronting the open Caribbean, where the undertow can be quite strong. By contrast, the waters of Mujeres Bay (Bahía de Mujeres), at the north end of the island, are usually calm and ideal for swimming. Get to know Cancún's water-safety pennant system, and be sure to check the flag at any beach or hotel before entering the water. Here's how it goes:

- **White**   Excellent
- **Green**   Normal conditions (safe)
- **Yellow**   Changeable, uncertain (use caution)
- **Black** or **red**   Unsafe; use the swimming pool instead!

In the Caribbean, storms can arrive and conditions can change from safe to unsafe in a matter of minutes, so be alert: If you see dark clouds heading your way, make for the shore and wait until the storm passes.

Playa Tortuga (Turtle Beach), Playa Langosta (Lobster Beach), Playa Linda (Pretty Beach), and **Playa Las Perlas (Beach of the Pearls)** are some of the public beaches. At most beaches, you can rent a sailboard and take lessons, ride a parasail, or partake in a variety of watersports. There's a small but beautiful portion of public beach on **Playa Caracol,** by the Xcaret Terminal. It faces the calm waters of Bahía de Mujeres and, for that reason, is preferable to those facing the Caribbean.

WATERSPORTS   Many beachside hotels offer watersports concessions that rent rubber rafts, kayaks, and snorkeling equipment. On the calm Nichupté lagoon are outlets for renting **sailboats, jet skis, windsurfers,** and **water skis.** Prices vary and are often negotiable, so check around.

For windsurfing, go to the Playa Tortuga public beach, where there's a **Windsurfing School** (no phone) with equipment for rent.

DEEP-SEA FISHING   You can arrange a day of **deep-sea fishing** at one of the numerous piers or travel agencies for around $220 to $360 for 4 hours, $420 for 6 hours, and $520 for 8 hours for up to four people. Marinas will sometimes assist in putting together a group. Charters include a captain, a first mate, bait, gear, and beverages. Rates are lower if you depart from Isla Mujeres or from Cozumel—and frankly, the fishing is better closer to those departure points.

SCUBA & SNORKELING   Known for its shallow reefs, dazzling color, and diversity of life, Cancún is one of the best places in the world for beginning **scuba diving.** Punta Nizuc is the northern tip of the **Great Mesoamerican Reef (Gran Arrecife Maya),** the largest reef in the Western Hemisphere and one of the largest in the world. In addition to the sea life along this reef system, several sunken boats add a variety of dive options. Inland, a series of caverns and *cenotes* (wellsprings) are fascinating venues for the more experienced diver. Drift diving is the norm here, with popular dives going to the reefs at **El Garrafón** and the **Cave of the Sleeping Sharks**—although be aware that the famed "sleeping sharks" have departed, driven off by too many people watching them snooze.

A variety of hotels offer resort courses that teach the basics of diving—enough to make shallow dives and slowly ease your way into this underwater world of unimaginable beauty. Scuba trips run around $64 for two-tank dives at nearby reefs, and $100 and up for locations farther out. **Scuba Cancún,** Paseo Kukulkán, Km 5 (© **998/849-7508** or 998/849-4736; www.scubacancun.com.mx), on the lagoon side, offers a 4-hour resort course for $64. Phone reservations are available from 7:30 to 10:30pm using the fax line, 998/884-2336. Full certification takes 4 to 5 days and costs around $350. Scuba Cancún is open daily from 9am to 6pm, and accepts major credit cards. The largest operator is **Aquaworld,** across from the Meliá Cancún at Paseo Kukulkán, Km 15.2 (© **998/885-2288** or 998/848-8300; www.aquaworld.com.mx). It offers resort courses and diving from a man-made anchored dive platform, Paradise Island. Aquaworld has the **Sub See Explorer,** a submarine-style boat with picture windows that hang beneath the surface. The boat doesn't submerge—it's an updated version of a glass-bottom boat—but it does provide nondivers with a look at life beneath the sea. This outfit is open 24 hours a day and accepts all major credit cards.

Scuba Cancún also offers diving trips, in good weather only, to 20 nearby reefs, including Cuevones (9m/30 ft.) and the open ocean (9–18m/30–60 ft.).

The average dive is around 11m (35 ft.). One-tank dives cost $55, and two-tank dives cost $65. Discounts apply if you bring your own equipment. Dives usually start around 9am and return by 2:15pm. Snorkeling trips cost $35 and leave every afternoon after 2pm for shallow reefs about a 20-minute boat ride away.

Besides **snorkeling** at **El Garrafón Natural Park** (see "Boating Excursions," below), travel agencies offer an all-day excursion to the natural wildlife habitat of **Isla Contoy,** which usually includes time for snorkeling. The island, 90 minutes past Isla Mujeres, is a major nesting area for birds and a treat for nature lovers. Only two boats hold permits for excursions, which depart at 9am and return by 5pm. The price ($70) includes drinks and snorkeling equipment.

The Great Mesoamerican Reef also offers exceptional snorkeling opportunities. In Puerto Morelos, 37km (23 miles) south of Cancún, this reef hugs the coastline for 9 miles. The reef is so close to the shore (about 455m/500 yd.) that it forms a natural barrier for the village and keeps the waters calm on the inside of the reef. The water here is shallow, from 1.5 to 9m (5–30 ft.), resulting in ideal conditions for snorkeling. Stringent environmental regulations implemented by the local community have kept the reef here unspoiled. Only a select few companies are allowed to offer snorkel trips, and they must adhere to guidelines that will ensure the reef's preservation. **Cancún Mermaid** (© **998/843-6517** or 998/886-4117; www.cancunmermaid.com) is considered the best—it's a family-run ecotour company that has operated in the area since the 1970s. It's known for highly personalized service. The tour typically takes snorkelers to two sections of the reef, spending about an hour in each area. When conditions allow, the boat drops off snorkelers and then follows them along with the current—an activity known as "drift snorkeling," which enables snorkelers to see as much of the reef as possible. The trip costs $45 for adults, $35 for children, and includes boat, snorkeling gear, life jackets, a light lunch, bottled water, sodas, and beer, plus round-trip transportation to and from Puerto Morelos from Cancún hotels. Departures are Monday through Saturday at 9am or noon, a minimum of four snorkelers is required for a trip, and reservations are required.

JET SKI TOURS   Several companies offer the popular **Jungle Cruise,** which takes you by jet ski or WaveRunner (you drive your own watercraft) through Cancún's lagoon and mangrove estuaries out into the Caribbean Sea and a shallow reef. The excursion runs about 2½ hours and costs $40 to $55, including snorkeling and beverages. Some of the motorized miniboats seat one person behind the other—meaning that the person in back gets a great view of the driver's head; others seat you side by side.

The operators and names of boats offering excursions change often. To find out what's available, check with a local travel agent or hotel tour desk. The popular **Aquaworld,** Paseo Kukulkán, Km 15.2 (© **998/885-2288**), calls its trip the Jungle Tour and charges $55 for the 2½-hour excursion, which includes 45 minutes of snorkeling time. It even gives you a free snorkel, but has the less-desirable one-behind-the-other seating configuration. Departures are at 9am, noon, and 2:30pm daily.

BOATING EXCURSIONS

ISLA MUJERES   The island of **Isla Mujeres,** just 13km (8 miles) offshore, is one of the most pleasant day trips from Cancún. At one end is **El Garrafón Natural Park,** which is excellent for snorkeling. At the other end is a captivating village with small shops, restaurants, and hotels, and **Playa Norte,** the island's best beach. If you're looking for relaxation and can spare the time, it's worth several days. For complete information about the island, see chapter 4.

There are four ways to get there: **public ferry** from Puerto Juárez, which takes between 15 and 45 minutes; **shuttle boat** from Playa Linda or Playa Tortuga—an hour-long ride, with irregular service; **Watertaxi** (more expensive, but faster), next to the Xcaret Terminal; and daylong **pleasure-boat trips,** most of which leave from the Playa Linda pier.

The inexpensive Puerto Juárez **public ferries** 🌟 are just a few kilometers from downtown Cancún. From Cancún City, take the Ruta 8 bus on Avenida Tulum to Puerto Juárez. The *Caribbean Express* (20 min.) costs $4.50 per person. Departures are every half hour, starting between 6 and 7am and ending between 9 and 11pm. The *Caribbean Savage* (45–60 min.) is a bargain at about $2. It departs every 2 hours, or less frequently depending on demand. Upon arrival, the ferry docks in downtown Isla Mujeres near all the shops, restaurants, hotels, and Norte beach. You'll need a taxi to get to El Garrafón park, at the other end of the island. You can stay as long as you like on the island (even overnight) and return by ferry, but be sure to double-check the time of the last returning ferry.

Pleasure-boat cruises to Isla Mujeres are a favorite pastime. Modern motor yachts, catamarans, trimarans, and even old-time sloops—more than 25 boats a day—take swimmers, sun lovers, snorkelers, and shoppers out on the translucent waters. Some tours include a snorkeling stop at El Garrafón, lunch on the beach, and a short time for shopping in downtown Isla Mujeres. Most leave at 9:30 or 10am, last about 5 or 6 hours, and include continental breakfast, lunch, and rental of snorkel gear. Others, particularly sunset and night cruises, go to beaches away from town for pseudo-pirate shows and include a lobster dinner or Mexican buffet. If you want to actually see Isla Mujeres, go on a morning cruise, or travel on your own using the public ferry from Puerto Juárez. Prices for the day cruises run around $55 per person.

In the El Garrafón park area is **El Garrafón Natural Park** 🌟🌟, which is under the same management as Xcaret (© **998/883-3143;** see "Eco-Theme Parks & Reserves," later in this chapter). The basic entrance fee of $22 includes access to the reef and a museum, as well as use of kayaks, inner tubes, life vests, the pool, hammocks, and public facilities and showers. Snorkel gear and lockers can be rented for an extra charge. There are also nature trails as well as several restaurants on-site. An all-inclusive option is available for $46, which includes dining on whatever you choose at any of the restaurants, plus unlimited domestic drinks and use of snorkel gear, locker, and towel. El Garrafón also has full dive facilities and gear rentals, plus an expansive gift shop.

Other excursions go to the **reefs** in glass-bottom boats, so you can have a near-scuba-diving experience and see many colorful fish. However, the reefs are some distance from the shore and are impossible to reach on windy days with choppy seas. They've also suffered from overvisitation, and their condition is far from pristine. The glass-bottomed **Nautibus** (© **998/883-3732** or 998/883-2119) has been around for years. Trips begin at 9:30 and 11am, and 12:30 and 2pm from the El Embarcadero Pier. The journey to the Chitale coral reef to see colorful fish takes about 1 hour and 20 minutes, with about 50 minutes of transit time back and forth. Tickets cost $35 for adults, $16 for children 6 to 12. Nautibus's **Atlantis Submarine** takes you close to the aquatic action. Departures vary, depending on weather conditions. Prices range from $44 to $65, depending on the length of the trip. Reservations are recommended for both. Other boat excursions visit

Isla Contoy, a **national bird sanctuary** that's well worth the time. If you are planning to spend time in Isla Mujeres, the Contoy trip is easier and more pleasurable to take from there.

5 Outdoor Activities & Attractions

OUTDOOR ACTIVITIES

DOLPHIN SWIMS   On Isla Mujeres, you have the opportunity to swim with dolphins at **Dolphin Discovery** ⭐ (© **998/849-4757;** fax 998/849-4758; www.dolphindiscovery.com). Each session lasts 1 hour, with an educational introduction followed by 30 minutes of swim time. The price is $119 (MC, V), with transportation to Isla Mujeres an additional $15. Advance reservations are required. Assigned swimming times are 9am, 11am, 1pm, or 3pm, and you must arrive 1 hour before your scheduled swim time. In Cancún, the **Parque Nizuc** (© **998/881-3030**) marine park offers guests a chance to swim with dolphins and view them in their dolphin aquarium, Atlántida. The price of the dolphin swim ($132) includes admission to the park. It's a fun place for a family to spend the day, with its numerous pools, waterslides, and rides. Visitors can also snorkel with manta rays, tropical fish, and tame sharks. It's at the southern end of Cancún, between the airport and the Hotel Zone. Admission is $33 for adults, $25 for children 3 to 11 (AE, MC, V). Open daily from 10am to 5:30pm.

La Isla Shopping Center, Bulevar Kukulkán, Km 12.5, has an **Interactive Aquarium** (© **998/883-0413,** 998/883-0436, or 998/883-5077), with dolphin swims and the chance to feed a shark. Prices for interactive encounters and swims start at $110.

GOLF & TENNIS   The 18-hole **Pok-Ta-Pok Club,** or Club de Golf Cancún (© **998/883-0871;** poktapok@sybcom.com), a Robert Trent Jones, Sr., design, is on the northern leg of the island. Greens fees run $120 per 18 holes, with clubs renting for $26 and shoes for $15. Hiring a caddy costs $22. The club is open daily, accepts American Express, MasterCard, and Visa, and has tennis courts.

The **Hilton Cancún Golf & Beach Resort** (© **998/881-8016;** fax 998/881-8084) has a championship 18-hole, par-72 course designed around the Ruinas Del Rey. Greens fees for the public are $88 for 9 holes, $121 for 18 holes; Hilton Cancún guests pay $77 and $99, respectively, which includes a golf cart. Golf clubs and shoes are available for rent. The club is open daily from 6am to 6pm.

The **Meliá Cancún** (© **998/881-1100**) has an 18-hole executive course; the fee is $35. The club is open daily from 8am to 4pm and accepts American Express, MasterCard, and Visa.

Tips **An All-Terrain Tour**

Cancún Mermaid (© **998/843-6517** or 998/886-4117; www.cancun mermaid.com), in Cancún, offers all-terrain-vehicle (ATV) jungle tours for $49 per person. The ATV tours travel through the jungles of Cancún and emerge on the beaches of the Riviera Maya. The 2½-hour tour includes equipment, instruction, the services of a tour guide, and bottled water; it departs daily at 8am and 1:30pm. The company picks you up at your hotel. Another ATV option is Rancho Loma Bonita; see "Horseback Riding," below.

HORSEBACK RIDING **Rancho Loma Bonita** (© **998/887-5465** or 998/887-5423), about 30 minutes south of town, is Cancún's most popular option for horseback riding. Five-hour packages include 2 hours of riding through the mangrove swamp to the beach, where you have time to swim and relax. The tour costs $72 for adults, $65 for children 6 to 12. The ranch also offers a four-wheel ATV ride on the same route as the horseback tour. It costs $72 per person if you want to ride on your own, $55 if you double up. Prices for both tours include transportation to the ranch, riding, soft drinks, and lunch, plus a guide and insurance. Visa is accepted, but cash is preferred.

IN-LINE SKATING You can rent in-line skates outside Plaza Las Glorias Hotel and in front of Playa Caracol, where the valet parking is located. The jogging track that runs parallel to Paseo Kukulkán along the Hotel Zone is well maintained and safe.

ATTRACTIONS

A MUSEUM To the right side of the entrance to the Cancún Convention Center is the **Museo Arqueológico de Cancún** (© **998/883-0305**), a small but interesting museum with relics from archaeological sites around the state. Admission is $3.50; free on Sunday and holidays. It's open Tuesday through Sunday from 9am to 7pm.

BULLFIGHTS Cancún has a small bullring, **Plaza de Toros** (© **998/884-8372**; bull@prodigy.net.mx), near the northern (town) end of Paseo Kukulkán opposite the Restaurant Los Almendros. Bullfights take place every Wednesday at 3:30pm during the winter tourist season. A sport introduced to Mexico by the Spanish viceroys, bullfighting is now as much a part of Mexican culture as tequila. The bullfights usually include four bulls, and the spectacle begins with a folkloric dance exhibition, followed by a performance by the *charros* (Mexico's sombrero-wearing cowboys). You're not likely to see Mexico's best bullfights in Cancún—the real stars are in Mexico City. Keep in mind that if you go to a bullfight, *you're going to see a bullfight*, so stay away if you're an animal lover or you can't bear the sight of blood. Travel agencies in Cancún sell tickets, which cost $35 for adults, free for children; seating is by general admission. American Express, MasterCard, and Visa are accepted.

SIGHTSEEING Get the best possible view of Cancún atop the new **La Torre Cancún,** Paseo Kukulkán, Km 4 (© **998/849-4848** or 998/889-7777), a rotating tower at the El Embarcadero park and entertainment complex. One ride costs $9; a day and night pass goes for $14. Open daily from 9am to 11pm.

Panoramic **helicopter tours** allow you to see a complete overview of this island paradise and the surrounding areas. Both day and evening flights are available. Tours to the ruins and flights south along the Riviera Maya are also an option. **Heli Data** (© **998/883-3104**) offers customized tours with hourly rates depending upon the length of flight and time of day. Hotel pickup is provided. **HeliTours** (© **998/849-4222** or 998/849-4230) offers a 15-minute ride over the Cancún Hotel Zone for $79.

6 Shopping

Despite the surrounding natural splendor, shopping has become a favorite activity. Cancún is known throughout Mexico for its diverse shops and festive malls catering to a large number of international tourists. Visitors from the United

States may find apparel more expensive in Cancún, but the selection is much broader than at other Mexican resorts. Numerous duty-free shops offer excellent value on European goods. The largest is **UltraFemme,** Avenida Tulum, Super-manzana 25 (© **998/884-1402** or 998/885-0804), specializing in imported cosmetics, perfumes, and fine jewelry and watches. The downtown Cancún location offers slightly lower prices than branches in Plaza Caracol, Plaza Kukul-can, Plaza Mayafair, Flamingo Plaza, and the international airport.

Handicrafts and other *artesanía* works are more limited and more expensive in Cancún than in other regions of Mexico because they are not produced here. They are available, though; several **open-air crafts markets** are on Avenida Tulum in Cancún City and near the convention center in the Hotel Zone. One of the biggest is **Coral Negro,** Paseo Kukulkán, Km 9.5 (© **998/883-0758;** fax 998/883-0758), open daily from 7am to 11pm. A small restaurant inside, Xtabentun, serves Yucatecan food and pizza slices, and metamorphoses into a disco from 9 to 11pm.

Cancún's main venues are the **malls**—not quite as grand as their U.S. coun-terparts, but close. All are air-conditioned, sleek, and sophisticated. Most are on Paseo Kukulkán between Km 7 and Km 12. They offer everything from fine crystal and silver to designer clothing and decorative objects, along with numer-ous restaurants and clubs. Stores are generally open daily from 10am to 10pm, with clubs and restaurants remaining open much later.

The **Plaza Kukulcan** (© **998/885-2200;** www.kukulcanplaza.com) offers the largest selection—more than 300—of shops, restaurants, and entertainment. There's a branch of Banco Serfin; OK Maguey Cantina Grill; a theater with U.S. movies; an Internet access kiosk; Tikal, which sells Guatemalan textile clothing; several crafts stores; a liquor store; several bathing-suit specialty stores; record and tape outlets; a leather goods store (including shoes and sandals); and a store specializing in silver from Taxco. The Fashion Gallery features designer clothing. In the food court are a number of U.S. franchise restaurants, including Ruth's Chris Steak House, plus one featuring specialty coffee. For entertainment, there's a bowling alley, Q-Zar laser game pavilion, and video game arcade. There's also a large indoor parking garage. The mall is open daily from 10am to 10pm, until 11pm during high season. Assistance for those with disabilities is available upon request, and wheelchairs, strollers, and lockers are available at the information desk.

Planet Hollywood anchors the **Plaza Flamingo** (© **998/883-2945**), which has branches of Bancrecer, Subway, and La Casa del Habano (Cuban cigars).

The long-standing **Plaza Caracol** (© **998/883-1038**) holds Cartier jewelry, Guess, Waterford Crystal, Señor Frog clothing, Samsonite luggage, Gucci, and La Fisheria restaurant.

Maya Fair Plaza/Centro Comercial Maya Fair, frequently called "Mayfair" (© **998/883-2801**), is the oldest mall. The lively center holds open-air restau-rants and bars, and several stores sell silver, leather, and crafts.

The entertainment-oriented **Forum by the Sea,** Paseo Kukulkán, Km 9 (© **998/883-4425**), has shops including Tommy Hilfiger, Levi's, Diesel, Swatch, and Harley Davidson. Most people come here for the food and fun, choosing from Hard Rock Cafe, Coco Bongo, Rainforest Cafe, Sushi-ito, and Santa Fe Beer Factory, plus an extensive food court. It's open daily from 10am to midnight (bars remain open later).

La Isla Shopping Village, Paseo Kukulkán, Km 12.5 (© **998/883-5025;** www.cancunmalls.com), is an open-air festival mall that looks like a small village.

Walkways lined with shops and restaurants cross little canals. It also has a "river-walk" alongside the Nichupté lagoon, and an interactive aquarium and dolphin swim facility. Shops include Zara clothing, Benetton, Guess, Swatch, H. Stern, UltraFemme, and the Warner Bros. Studio Store. Dining choices include Johnny Rockets, the Food Court (actually an Anderson's restaurant), and the beautiful Mexican restaurant La Casa de las Margaritas. There's also a first-run movie theater, a video arcade, and several nightclubs, including Max-O's and Alebrijes. It's across from the Sheraton, on the lagoon side of the street.

7 Cancún After Dark

One of Cancún's main draws is its active nightlife. The hottest centers of action are the **Centro Comercial Maya Fair, Forum by the Sea,** and **La Isla Shopping Village.** Hotels also compete, with happy-hour entertainment and special drink prices to entice visitors and guests from other resorts. (Lobby-bar-hopping at sunset is one great way to plan next year's vacation.)

THE CLUB & MUSIC SCENE

Clubbing in Cancún, still called "discoing," is a favorite part of the vacation experience and can go on each night until the sun rises over that incredibly blue sea. Several big hotels have nightclubs (usually discos) or schedule live music in their lobby bars. At discos, expect to stand in long lines on weekends, pay a cover charge of $15 to $25 per person, and pay $5.50 to $8.50 for a drink. Some of the higher-priced discos include an open bar or live entertainment. The places listed in this section are air-conditioned and accept credit cards (AE, MC, V).

A great idea to get you started is the **Bar Crawl Tour** ★★ offered by American Express Travel Agency (© 998/881-4050; fax 998/884-6942). For $49, it takes you by bus from bar to club—generally four to five top choices—where you'll bypass any lines and spend about an hour. The price includes entry to the clubs, one welcome drink at each, and transportation by air-conditioned bus, allowing you to get a great sampling of the best of Cancún's nightlife.

Numerous restaurants, such as **Carlos 'n' Charlie's, Planet Hollywood, Hard Rock Cafe, Señor Frog's, TGI Friday's,** and **Iguana Wana,** double as nighttime party spots, offering wild-ish fun at a fraction of the price of more costly discos.

Bulldog Café, in the Hotel Krystal, Paseo Kukulkán, Km 7.5 (© 998/848-9800), is a former hotspot's attempt to lure back the crowds (it used to be the opulent disco Christine). To the impressive space, signature laser-light shows, infused oxygen, and large video screens, the club added updated music and a funkier ambience. The music ranges from hip-hop to Latino rock, with a heavy emphasis on infectious dance tunes. Bulldog is open nightly from 10pm until the party winds down. The cover charge is $12 per person, or $25 for an open bar all night (national drinks).

Carlos 'n' Charlie's, Paseo Kukulkán, Km 4.5 (© 998/849-4052), is a reliable place to find both good food and packed-frat-house entertainment in the evening. There's a dance floor; live music starts nightly around 8:30pm. A cover charge kicks in if you're not planning to eat. It's open daily from 11am to 2am.

With recorded music, **Carlos O'Brian's,** Tulum 107, SM 22 (© 998/884-1659), is only slightly tamer than other Carlos Anderson restaurants and nightspots in town (Señor Frog and Carlos 'n' Charlie's). It's open daily from 9am to midnight.

Maintaining its reputation as the hottest spot in town is **Coco Bongo** in Forum by the Sea, Paseo Kukulkán, Km 9.5 (© **998/883-5061;** www.cocobongo. com.mx). Its main appeal is that it has no formal dance floor, so you can dance anywhere—and that includes on the tables, on the bar, or even on the stage with the live band! This place can—and regularly does—pack in up to 3,000 people. You have to experience it to believe it. Despite its capacity, lines are long on weekends and in high season. The music alternates between Caribbean, salsa, techno, and classics from the 1970s and '80s. It draws a mixed crowd, but the young and hip dominate. Choose between a $15 cover or $25 with an open bar.

Dady'O, Paseo Kukulkán, Km 9.5 (© **998/883-3333**), is a highly favored rave with frequent long lines. It opens nightly at 9:30pm and generally charges a cover of $15.

Dady Rock Bar and Grill, Paseo Kukulkán, Km 9.5 (© **998/883-1626**), the offspring of Dady'O, opens early (7pm) and goes as long as any other nightspot, offering a new twist on entertainment with a combination of live bands and DJ-orchestrated music, along with an open bar, full meals, a buffet, and dancing.

Hard Rock Cafe, in Plaza Lagunas Mall and Forum by the Sea (© **998/ 881-8120** or 998/883-2024; www.hardrock.com), schedules a live band at 10:30pm Thursday through Tuesday night. At other times you get lively recorded music to munch by—the menu combines the most popular foods from American and Mexican cultures. It's open daily from 11am to 2am.

La Boom, Paseo Kukulkán, Km 3.5 (© **998/883-1152;** fax 998/883-1458, www.laboom.com.mx), has two sections: one side is a video bar, the other a bi-level disco with cranking music. Each night there's a special deal: no cover, free bar, ladies' night, bikini night, and others. Popular with early-20-somethings, it's open nightly from 10pm to 6am. A sound-and-light show begins at 11:30pm in the disco. The cover varies depending on the night—most nights, women enter free, and men pay $15 to $30, which includes an open bar.

The most refined and upscale of Cancún's nightly gathering spots is the **Lobby Lounge** at the **Ritz-Carlton Hotel** ★ (© **998/885-0808**), with live dance music and a list of more than 120 premium tequilas for tasting or sipping.

Planet Hollywood, Flamingo Shopping Center, Paseo Kukulkán, Km 11 (© **998/885-3003;** www.planethollywood.com), is the still-popular brainchild of Sylvester Stallone, Bruce Willis, and Arnold Schwarzenegger. One of the last remaining branches of the chain, it's both a restaurant and a nighttime music and dance spot with mega-decibel live music. It's open daily from 11am to 2am.

THE PERFORMING ARTS

Performances of the **Ballet Folklórico de Cancún** (© **998/849-7777**) are held at the Teatro de Cancún, at the El Embarcadero Pier. The show, **Voces y Danzas de México (Voices and Dances of Mexico)** takes place Monday through Friday at 7pm. The cost is $29 per person, and includes an open bar of national drinks. American Express, MasterCard, and Visa accepted.

Another show, **Tradición del Caribe (Caribbean Traditions)** also takes place at the Teatro de Cancún (© **998/849-7777**), Monday through Friday at 9pm. Over 80 performers showcase the dance and music of the Mexican Caribbean, Trinidad and Tobago, Costa Rica, Cuba, and Puerto Rico. At the conclusion of the show, guests are welcome to dance to the tempting tropical rhythms. The cost of $29 per person includes an open bar of national drinks.

Several hotels host **Mexican fiesta nights,** including a buffet dinner and a folkloric dance show; admission, including dinner, ranges from $35 to $50. In the Costa Blanca shopping center, **El Mexicano** restaurant (© **998/884-4207**) offers a tropical dinner show every night and has live music for dancing. The entertainment is a folkloric show that starts at 8:30pm. Cover charge is $5.

You can also get in the party mood at **Mango Tango** ☆, Paseo Kukulkán, Km 14.2 (© **998/885-0303**), a lagoon-side restaurant and dinner-show establishment opposite the Ritz-Carlton Hotel. Diners can choose from two levels, one nearer the music and the other overlooking it all. Music is loud and varied but mainly features reggae or salsa. A 45-minute floor shows start nightly at 8:30pm. A variety of packages are available—starting at $40 per person—depending on whether you want dinner and the show, open bar and the show, or the show alone. For dancing, which starts at 9:30, there's a $10 cover charge. See "Where to Dine," earlier in this chapter, for a restaurant review.

Tourists mingle with locals at the downtown **Parque de las Palapas** (the main park) for *Noches Caribeñas,* which involves free live tropical music for anyone who wants to listen and dance. Performances begin at 7:30pm on Sunday, and sometimes there are performances on Friday and Saturday.

8 Day Trips: Archaeological Sites & Eco-Theme Parks

One of the best ways to spend a vacation day is exploring the nearby archaeological ruins or an ecological theme park near Cancún. Within easy driving distance are historical and natural treasures unlike any you've likely encountered before. Cancún can be a perfect base for day or overnight trips, or the starting point for a longer expedition.

Organized day trips are popular and easy to book through any travel agent in town, or you can plan a journey on your own and travel by bus or rental car. The Maya ruins to the south at **Tulum** or **Cobá** should be your first goal, and then perhaps the *caleta* (cove) of **Xel-Ha** or the ecological theme park **Xcaret.** If you're going south, consider staying a night or 2 on the island of **Cozumel** or at one of the budget resorts on the **Tulum coast** or **Punta Allen,** south of the Tulum ruins. **Isla Mujeres** is an easy day trip off mainland Cancún.

> **More Info**
> For more information on the destinations covered in this section, see chapters 4, 5, and 6.

Greenline (© **998/883-4545**) buses offer packages *(paquetes)* to popular nearby destinations. The package to **Chichén Itzá** ($68) departs at 8:30am and includes the round-trip air-conditioned bus ride, a video of a current movie that plays during the 3-hour trip, entry to the ruins, 2 hours at the ruins, and lunch. The tour returns to Cancún by 7:30pm. Although I don't recommend it, by driving fast or catching the right buses you can go inland to Chichén Itzá, explore the ruins, and return in a day. It's much better to spend at least 2 days seeing Chichén Itzá, Mérida, and Uxmal.

ARCHAEOLOGICAL SITES

TULUM   A popular excursion combines a visit to the ruins at Tulum with the ecological water park Xel-Ha (discussed below). **Ancient Tulum** ☆☆☆ is a stunning site, and my personal favorite of all the ruins. (For another take on Tulum, see "Tulum: A Friendly Difference of Opinion" on p. 151.)

A wall surrounds the site on three sides, which explains the name (*tulum* means fence, trench, or wall). Its ancient name is believed to have been *Záma,* a derivative of the Maya word for "morning" or "dawn," and sunrise at Tulum is certainly dramatic. The wall is believed to have been constructed after the original buildings, to protect the interior religious altars from a growing number of invaders. It is considered to have been principally a place of worship, but members of the upper classes later took up residence here. Between the two most dramatic structures—the Castle and the Temple of the Wind—lies Tulum Cove. A small inlet with a beach of fine, white sand, it was a point of departure for Maya trading vessels in ancient times. Today it's a playground for tourists, and you can enjoy a refreshing swim. Admission to the site without a tour is $2, parking costs $1, and use of a video camera requires a $4 permit.

RUINAS DEL REY   Cancún has its own **Maya ruins** (© **998/884-8073**)— a small site that's less impressive than the ruins at Tulum, Cobá, or Chichén Itzá. Fishermen built the small ceremonial center and settlement very early in the history of Maya culture. It was then abandoned, to be resettled again near the end of the post-Classic period, not long before the arrival of the conquistadors. The platforms of numerous small temples are visible amid the banana plants, papayas, and wildflowers. The Hilton Cancún hotel golf course surrounds the ruins, which have a separate entrance for sightseers. You'll find the ruins about 21km (13 miles) from town, at the southern reach of the Zona Hotelera, almost to Punta Nizuc. Look for the Hilton hotel on the left (east) and the ruins on the right (west). Admission is $4.50; free on Sunday and holidays. It's open daily from 8am to 5pm.

A new theme restaurant, **El Rey Mundo Maya,** Paseo Kukulkán, Km 18.5 (© **998/883-2080;** www.elreycancun.com), adjacent to the ruins, offers a more comprehensive "taste" of what life was once like on Cancún Island. The restaurant is styled like an ancient Mayan village, complete with an astronomical observatory and market. The Royal Dining Room serves a three-course dinner of traditional cooking, accompanied by a folkloric show, and nocturnal tour of the ruins. Dinner starts at 7pm Monday through Saturday, and the cost is $62 per person, including drinks, the show, and the tour. It's a unique alternative to other nighttime attractions.

ECO-THEME PARKS & RESERVES

The popularity of Xcaret and Xel-Ha has inspired entrepreneurs to ride the wave of interest in ecological and adventure theme parks. Be aware that "theme park" is the more pertinent part of the phrase. The newer parks of Aktun Chen and Tres Ríos are—so far—less commercial and more focused on nature than their predecessors. Included here are several true reserves, which have less in the way of facilities but offer an authentic encounter with the natural beauty of the region.

AKTUN CHEN ☆   This park, consisting of a spectacular 5,000-year-old grotto and an abundance of wildlife, is the first above-the-ground cave system in the Yucatán to be open to the public. The name means "cave with an underground river inside," and the main cave (of 3) is more than 600 yards long, with a magnificent vault. Discreet illumination and easy walking paths make visiting the caves comfortable, without appearing to alter them much from their natural state. The caves contain thousands of stalactites, stalagmites, and sculpted rock formations, along with a 40-foot-deep *cenote* with clear blue water. Aktun Chen was once underwater, and fossilized shells and fish embedded in the limestone are visible as you walk along the paths. Knowledgeable guides provide explanations of what you see and offer mini–history lessons in the Maya's association with these caves. Tours have no set times—guides are available to take you when you arrive—and the maximum group size is 20. Surrounding the caves, nature trails wind throughout the 988-acre park, where spottings of deer, spider monkeys, iguanas, and wild turkeys are common. A small informal restaurant and gift shop are also on-site.

It's easy to travel by yourself to Aktun Chen (© **998/892-0662** or 998/850-4190; www.aktunchen.com); from Cancún, go south along Highway 307, the road to Tulum. Just past the turnoff for Akumal, a sign on the right side of the highway indicates the turnoff to Aktun-Chen, and from there it's a 3km (2-mile) drive west along a smooth but unpaved road. Travel time from Cancún is about an hour. The park is open daily from 9am to 5pm; the last tour departs at 4pm. The entry fee of $19 for adults, $10 for children includes the services of a guide.

EL EDEN RESERVA ECOLOGICA   Established in 1990, this is a privately owned 500,000-acre reserve dedicated to research for biological conservation in Mexico. It takes around 2 hours to reach the center of this reserve deep in the jungle, yet it's only 48km (30 miles) northwest of Cancún. It's intended as an overnight (or more) excursion for people who want to know more about the biological diversity of the peninsula.

Within the reserve, or near it, are marine grasslands, mangrove swamps, rainforests, savannas, wetlands, and sand dunes, as well as evidence of archaeological sites and at least 205 species of birds, plus orchids, bromeliads, and cacti. Among the local animals are the spider monkey, jaguar, cougar, deer, and ocelot. The "eco-scientific" tours include naturalist-led birding, animal tracking, stargazing, spotlight surveys for nocturnal wildlife, and exploration of *cenotes* and Maya ruins. Comfortable, basic accommodations are provided. Tours include transportation from Cancún, 1 or 2 nights of accommodation at La Savanna Research Station, meals, nightly cocktails, guided nature walks, and tours. The tours cost $235 to $380, depending on the length of stay, plus $95 per extra night. American Express is accepted. Contact **Ecocolors,** Camarón 32 SM 27 (© **998/884-3667;** fax 998/884-9580; www.ecotravelmexico.com), which specializes in ecologically oriented tours around the Cancún area.

SIAN KA'AN BIOSPHERE RESERVE 🐾   About 128km (80 miles) south of Cancún, this 1.3-million-acre area was set aside in 1986 to preserve a region of tropical forests, savannas, mangroves, canals, lagoons, bays, *cenotes,* and coral reefs, all of which are home to hundreds of birds and land and marine animals. The Friends of Sian Ka'an, a nonprofit group based in Cancún, offers biologist-escorted day trips, weather permitting, from the **Cabañas Ana y José** (www. anayjose.com), just south of the Tulum ruins. They cost $68 per person in a company vehicle, or $58 per person if you drive yourself. The price includes chips and soft drinks, round-trip van transportation to the reserve, a guided boat and birding trip through one of the reserve's lagoons, and use of binoculars. Tours can accommodate up to 18 people. Trips start from the Cabañas Monday through Saturday at 9am and return there around 3pm. For reservations, contact **Amigos de Sian Ka'an,** Crepúsculo 18, and Amanecer, Supermanzana 44, Manzana 13 Residencial Alborada, Cancún (© **998/848-2136,** 998/848-1618, or 998/848-1593; fax 998/848-1618; sian@cancun.com.mx). Office hours are from 9am to 5pm.

TRES RIOS 🐾   This eco-adventure park 25 minutes south of Cancún is actually a nature reserve on more than 150 acres of land. Tres Ríos (© **998/887-8077** in Cancún; www.tres-rios.com) offers guests a beautiful natural area for kayaking, canoeing, snorkeling, horseback riding, or biking along jungle trails. It's definitely less commercial than the other eco-theme parks and is essentially just a great natural area for participating in these activities. The entrance fee—$22 for adults, $19 for children—includes canoe trips; the use of bikes, kayaks, and snorkeling equipment; and the use of hammocks and beach chairs once you tire yourself out. Extra charges apply for scuba diving, horseback riding, and other extended, guided tours through the reserve and its estuary. You can also opt for an all-inclusive package that covers admission, diving, horseback riding, and all food and beverages. It costs $75 per adult, $62 for children under 12, and reservations are required. Tres Ríos also has bathroom facilities, showers, and a convenience store. Most Cancún travel agencies sell a half-day Kayak Express tour to Tres Ríos. Priced at $48, it includes admission and activities, plus round-trip transportation, lunch, and two nonalcoholic drinks. The park is open daily from 9am to 5pm.

XCARET: A DEVELOPED NATURE PARK   Eighty kilometers (50 miles) south of Cancún and 10km (6½ miles) south of Playa del Carmen is the turnoff to Xcaret (pronounced "ish-cah-*ret*"), an ecological and archaeological theme park that is one of the area's most popular tourist attractions. It's the closest thing to Disneyland that you'll find in Mexico, with myriad attractions in one location, most of them participatory. Signs throughout Cancún advertise Xcaret, which has its own bus terminal to take tourists there at regular intervals. Plan to spend a full day.

Xcaret may celebrate Mother Nature, but its builders rearranged quite a bit of her handiwork in completing it. If you're looking for a place to escape the commercialism of Cancún, this may not be it; it's relatively expensive and may be very crowded, diminishing the advertised "natural" experience. Children love it, however, and the jungle setting and palm-lined beaches are beautiful. Once past the entrance booths (built to resemble small Maya temples), you'll find pathways that meander around bathing coves, the snorkeling lagoon, and the remains of a group of real Maya temples. You'll have access to swimming beaches; limestone tunnels to snorkel through; marked palm-lined pathways; a wild-bird breeding aviary; a *charro* exhibition; horseback riding; scuba diving; a botanical garden and nursery; a sea turtle nursery that releases the turtles after their first year; a pavilion showcasing regional butterflies; a tropical aquarium where visitors can touch underwater creatures such as manta rays, starfish, and octopi; and a "Dolphinarium," where visitors (on a 1st-come, 1st-served basis) can swim with the dolphins for an extra charge of $90.

Another attraction at Xcaret is a replica of the ancient Maya game pok-ta-pok, where six "warriors" bounce around a 9-pound ball with their hips. The Seawalker is a watersport designed for nonswimmers. By donning a special suit and helmet with a connected air pump, you can walk on the ocean floor or examine a coral reef in a small bay.

There is also a visitor center with lockers, first aid, and gifts. Visitors aren't allowed to bring in food or drinks, so you're limited to the rather expensive on-site restaurants. No personal radios are allowed, and you must remove all suntan lotion if you swim in the lagoon (to avoid poisoning the habitat).

Xcaret is open Monday through Saturday from 8:30am to 8pm, Sunday from 8:30am to 5:30pm. The admission price of $49 per person entitles you to all the facilities—boats, life jackets, and snorkeling equipment for the underwater tunnel and lagoon, and lounge chairs and other facilities. Other attractions, such as snorkeling ($32), horseback riding ($49), scuba diving ($55 for certified divers; $75 for a resort course), and the dolphin swim ($80), cost extra. There may be more visitors than equipment (such as beach chairs), so bring a beach towel and your own snorkeling gear. Travel agencies in Cancún offer day trips to Xcaret that include transportation, admission, and a guide. They depart at 8am, return at 6pm, and cost $75 for adults and $55 for children. The "Xcaret Day and Night" package includes round-trip transportation from Cancún, a *charreada* festival, lighted pathways to Maya ruins, dinner, and a folkloric show. It's $89 for adults, $40 for children ages 5 to 11, free for children under 5. Buses leave the terminal at 9 and 10am daily, with the "Day and Night" tour returning at 9:30pm. You can also buy tickets to the park at the **Xcaret Terminal** (© **998/883-3143**), next to the Fiesta Americana Grand Coral Beach hotel on Cancún Island.

XEL-HA   The eco-park at Xel-Ha (© **998/884-9422;** www.xelha.com.mx), 13km (8 miles) south of Akumal, attracts throngs of snorkelers and divers with its warm waters and brilliant fish. The beautiful, calm cove is a perfect place to bring kids for their first snorkeling experience.

Xel-Ha (shell-*hah*) also offers dolphin swims and has food and beverage service, changing rooms, showers, and other facilities. For a complete description, see chapter 5.

Just south of the Xel-Ha turnoff on the west side of the highway, don't miss the ruins of **ancient Xel-Ha** ★. You'll likely be the only one there as you walk over limestone rocks and through the tangle of trees, vines, and palms. There is a huge, deep, dark *cenote* to one side, a temple palace with tumbled-down columns, a jaguar group, and a conserved temple group. A covered *palapa* on one pyramid guards a partially preserved mural. Admission is $3.50.

Xel-Ha is close to **Tulum** (discussed earlier in this chapter) and makes a good place for a dip when you've finished climbing those Maya ruins. You can even make the 8-mile hop north from Tulum to Xel-Ha by public bus. When you get off at the junction for Tulum, ask the restaurant owner when the next buses come by; otherwise, you may have to wait as long as 2 hours on the highway.

4

Isla Mujeres & Cozumel

Mexico's two main Caribbean islands are good places to get away from the hustle and bustle of Cancún and the Riviera Maya. Neither Isla Mujeres nor Cozumel is particularly large, and they have that island feel—small roads that don't go very far, lots of mopeds, few buses and trucks, and a sense of being set apart from the rest of the world. Yet they're just a short ferry ride from the mainland. Both offer a variety of lodging choices, ample outdoor activities, and a laid-back atmosphere that makes a delightful contrast with the mainland experience.

EXPLORING MEXICO'S CARIBBEAN ISLANDS

ISLA MUJERES A day trip to Isla Mujeres on a party boat is one of the most popular excursions from Cancún. This fish-shaped island is just 13km (8 miles) northeast of Cancún, a quick boat ride away, allowing ample time to get a taste of the peaceful pace of life. To fully explore the village and its shops and cafes, relax at the broad, tranquil Playa Norte, or snorkel or dive El Garrafón Reef (an underwater park), you'll need more time. Overnight accommodations range from rustic to offbeat chic.

Passenger ferries go to Isla Mujeres from Puerto Juárez, and car ferries leave from Punta Sam, both near Cancún. More expensive passenger ferries, with less frequent departures, leave from the Playa Linda pier on Cancún Island.

COZUMEL Cozumel is larger than Isla Mujeres and farther from the mainland (19km/12 miles off the coast from Playa del Carmen). It has its own international airport. Life here turns around two major activities: scuba diving and being a port of call for cruise ships. It is far and away the most popular destination along this coast for both. Despite the cruise ship traffic and all the stores that it has spawned, life on the island moves at a relaxed and comfortable pace. There is just one town, San Miguel de Cozumel. North and south of town are resorts; the rest of the shore is deserted and predominantly rocky, with a scattering of small sandy coves that you can have practically all to yourself.

1 Isla Mujeres ★★★

16km (10 miles) N of Cancún

Isla Mujeres (Island of Women) is a casual, laid-back refuge from the conspicuously commercialized action of Cancún, visible across a narrow channel. Just 8km (5 miles) long and 4km (2½ miles) wide, it's known as the best value in the Caribbean, assuming that you favor an easy-going vacation pace and prefer simplicity to pretense.

This is an island of white-sand beaches and turquoise waters, complemented by a town filled with Caribbean-colored clapboard houses and rustic, open-air restaurants. Hotels are clean and comfortable, but if you're looking for lots of

Tips **The Best Websites for Isla Mujeres & Cozumel**

- **Cozumel.net: www.cozumel.net**   This site is a cut above the typical dining/lodging/activities sites. Click on "About Cozumel" to find schedules for ferries and island-hop flights, and to check the latest news. There's also a comprehensive listing of B&Bs and vacation home rentals, plus great info on diving, maps, and a chat room.
- **Cozumel Travel Planner: go2cozumel.com**   This is a well-done guide to area businesses and attractions, by an online Mexico specialist.
- **Travel Notes: travelnotes.cc**   This site boasts more than 1,000 pages of information on and photos of Cozumel island—with an emphasis on diving, deep sea fishing, and other water-bound activities.
- **Cozumel Hotel Association: www.islacozumel.com.mx**   Operated by the tourism-promotion arm of the hotel association, this site gives more than just listings of the member hotels. There's info on packages and specials, plus brief descriptions of most of the island's attractions, restaurants, and recreational activities.
- **Viva Cozumel: viva-cozumel.com**   With weather forecasts, links to dive shops, and listings of restaurants and hotels, this site can come in handy—just don't expect objectivity; the businesses pay for space to advertise. They do offer some Internet-only deals that can make a visit worthwhile, though.

action or opulence, you'll be happier in Cancún. A few recent additions provide more luxurious lodging, but they still maintain a decidedly casual atmosphere.

Francisco Hernández de Córdoba, seeing figurines of partially clad females along the shore, gave the island its name when he landed in 1517. These are now believed to have been offerings to the Maya goddess of fertility and the moon, Ixchel. Their presence indicates that the island was probably sacred to the Maya.

At midday, suntanned visitors hang out in open-air cafes and stroll streets lined with frantic souvenir vendors. Calling attention to their bargain-priced wares, they give a carnival atmosphere to the hours when tour-boat traffic is at its peak. Befitting the size of the island, most of the traffic consists of golf carts, *motos* (mopeds), and bicycles. Once the tour boats leave, however, Isla Mujeres reverts to its more typical, tranquil way of life.

Days in "Isla"—as the locals call it—can alternate between adventurous activity and absolute repose. Trips to the Isla Contoy bird sanctuary are popular, as are the excellent diving, fishing, and snorkeling—in 1998, the island's coral coast became part of Mexico's Marine National Park. The island and several of its traditional hotels attract regular gatherings of yoga practitioners. In the evening, most people find the slow, casual pace one of the island's biggest draws. The cool night breeze is a perfect accompaniment to casual open-air dining and drinking in small street-side restaurants. Many people pack it in as early as 9 or 10pm, when most of the businesses close. Those in search of a party, however, will find kindred souls at the bars on Playa Norte that stay open late.

ESSENTIALS
GETTING THERE & DEPARTING   Puerto Juárez (© **998/877-0618**), just north of Cancún, is the dock for passenger ferries to Isla Mujeres, the least

expensive way to travel to Isla. The *Caribbean Savage* makes the 45-minute trip every 2 hours and costs just $2. The newer, air-conditioned *Caribbean Express* leaves every half-hour, makes the trip in 20 minutes, has storage space for luggage, and costs about $3.50. These boats operate daily, starting between 6 and 7am and ending between 9 and 11pm. They leave early if they're full. Pay at the ticket office—or, if the ferry is about to leave, aboard.

Note: Upon arrival by taxi or bus in Puerto Juárez, be wary of pirate "guides" who tell you either that the ferry is canceled or that it's several hours until the next ferry. They'll offer the services of a private *lancha* (small boat) for about $40—and it's nothing but a scam. Small boats are available and, on a co-op basis, charge $15 to $25 one-way, based on the number of passengers. They take about 50 minutes and are not recommended on days with rough seas. Check with the clearly visible ticket office—the only accurate source—for information.

Taxi fares are posted by the street where the taxis park, so be sure to check the rate before agreeing to a taxi for the ride back to Cancún. Rates generally run $12 to $15, depending upon your destination. Moped and bicycle rentals are also readily available as you depart the ferry. This small complex also has public bathrooms, luggage storage, a snack bar, and souvenir shops.

Isla Mujeres is so small that a vehicle isn't necessary, but if you're taking one, you'll use the **Punta Sam** port a little beyond Puerto Juárez. The ferry (40 min.) runs five or six times daily between 8am and 8pm, year-round except in bad weather. Times are generally as follows: Cancún to Isla 8am, 11am, 2:45pm, 5:30pm, and 8:15pm; Isla to Cancún 6:30am, 9:30am, 12:45pm, 4:15pm, and 7:15pm. Always check with the tourist office in Cancún to verify this schedule. Cars should arrive an hour before the ferry departure to register for a place in line and pay the posted fee, which varies depending on the weight and type of vehicle. The sole gas pump in Isla is at the intersection of Avenida Rueda Medina and Calle Abasolo, just northwest of the ferry docks.

There are also ferries to Isla Mujeres from the **Playa Linda,** known as the Embarcadero pier in Cancún, but they're less frequent and more expensive than those from Puerto Juárez. A **Water Taxi** (*©* 998/886-4270 or 998/886-4847; asterix1@prodigy.net.mx) to Isla Mujeres operates from **Playa Caracol,** between the Fiesta Americana Coral Beach Hotel and the Xcaret terminal on the island, with prices about the same as those from Playa Linda and about four times the cost of the public ferries from Puerto Juárez. Scheduled departures are at 9am, 11am, and 1pm, with returns from Isla Mujeres at noon and 5pm. Adult round-trip fares are $15; kids 3 to 12 pay $7.50; free for children under 3.

To get to Puerto Juárez or Punta Sam from **Cancún,** take any Ruta 8 city bus from Avenida Tulum. If you're coming from **Mérida,** you can fly to Cancún and proceed to Puerto Juárez or take a bus directly to Puerto Juárez. From **Cozumel,** you can fly to Cancún (there are daily flights) or take a ferry to Playa del Carmen (see "Cozumel," later in this chapter), then travel to Puerto Juárez.

Arriving   Ferries arrive at the ferry docks (*©* 998/877-0065) in the center of town. The main road that passes in front is Avenida Rueda Medina. Most hotels are close by. Tricycle taxis are the least expensive and most fun way to get to your hotel; you and your luggage pile in the open carriage compartment, and the driver pedals through the streets. Regular taxis are always lined up in a parking lot to the right of the pier, with their rates posted. If someone on the ferry offers to arrange a taxi for you, politely decline, unless you'd like some help with your luggage down the short pier—it just means an extra, unnecessary tip for your helper.

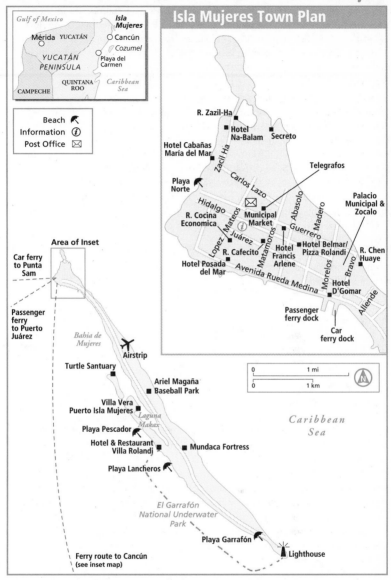

Isla Mujeres Town Plan

VISITOR INFORMATION   The **City Tourist Office** (☎/fax **998/877-0767**) is on Avenida Rueda Medina, on your left as you reach the end of the pier. It's open Monday through Friday from 8am to 8pm, Saturday from 8am to 2pm. Also look for *Islander,* a free publication with local information, advertisements, and event listings.

ISLAND LAYOUT   Isla Mujeres is about 8km (5 miles) long and 4km (2½ miles) wide, with the town at the northern tip. "Downtown" is a compact 4 blocks by 6 blocks, so it's very easy to get around. The **ferry docks** are at the center of town, within walking distance of most hotels, restaurants, and shops. The street running along the waterfront is **Avenida Rueda Medina,** commonly called the *malecón* (boardwalk). The **Mercado Municipal** (market) is by the post office on **Calle Guerrero,** an inland street at the north edge of town, which, like most streets in the town, is unmarked.

GETTING AROUND   A popular form of transportation on Isla Mujeres is the electric **golf cart,** available for rent at many hotels for $12 per hour or $40 per day. **El Sol Golf Cart Rental,** Avenida Francisco I. Madero 5 (© 998/877-0068), will deliver, or you can pick one up. The golf carts don't go more than 20 mph, but they're fun. Anyway, you aren't on Isla Mujeres to hurry. Many people enjoy touring the island by *moto* (motorized bike or scooter). Fully automatic versions are available for around $25 per day or $7 per hour. They come with seats for one person, but some are large enough for two. There's only one main road with a couple of offshoots, so you won't get lost. Be aware that the rental price does not include insurance, and any injury to yourself or the vehicle will come out of your pocket. **Bicycles** are also available for rent at some hotels for $3 per hour or $7 per day, including a basket and a lock.

If you prefer to use a taxi, rates are about $2.50 for trips within the downtown area, or $4.50 for a trip to the southern end of Isla. You can also hire them for about $10 per hour.

FAST FACTS: Isla Mujeres

Area Code The telephone area code is **998**.

Consumer Protection The local branch of **Profeco** consumer protection agency has a local phone number, © **998/877-0106**.

Currency Exchange Isla Mujeres has numerous *casas de cambios,* or money exchanges, that you can easily spot along the main streets. Most of the hotels listed here change money for their guests, although often at less favorable rates than the commercial enterprises. There is only one bank in Isla, Banco Bital, across from the ferry docks. It's open Monday through Friday from 9am to 5pm.

Hospital The **Hospital de la Armada** is on Avenida Rueda Medina at Ojon P. Blanco (© **998/877-0001**). It's half a mile south of the town center. It will only treat you in an emergency.

Internet Access **Compulsla,** Abasolo 11, between Medina and Juárez streets (© **998/877-0898**), offers Internet access for $4 per hour Monday through Friday from 8am to 10pm, Saturday from 9am to 4pm.

Pharmacy **Isla Mujeres Farmacia** (© **998/877-0178**) has the best selection of prescription and over-the-counter medicines. It's on Calle Benito Juárez, between Morelos and Bravo, across from Van Cleef & Arpels.

Post Office/Telegraph Office The *correo* is at Calle Guerrero 12 (© **998/877-0085**), at the corner of López Mateos, near the market. It's open Monday through Friday from 9am to 4pm.

Taxis To call for a taxi, dial © **998/877-0066**.

Telephone Ladatel phones accepting coins and prepaid phone cards are at the plaza and throughout town.

Tourist Seasons Isla Mujeres's tourist season (when hotel rates are higher) is a bit different from that of other places in Mexico. High season runs December through May, a month longer than in Cancún. Some hotels raise their rates in August, and some raise their rates beginning in mid-November. Low season is from June to mid-November.

BEACHES & OUTDOOR ACTIVITIES

THE BEACHES   The most popular beach in town used to be called Playa Cocoteros ("Cocos," for short). Then, in 1988, Hurricane Gilbert destroyed the coconut palms on the beach. Gradually, the name has changed to **Playa Norte** ★. The long stretch of beach extends around the northern tip of the island, to your left as you get off the boat. This is a truly splendid beach—a wide stretch of fine white sand and calm, translucent, turquoise-blue water. Topless sunbathing is permitted. The beach is easily reached on foot from the ferry and from all downtown hotels. Watersports equipment, beach umbrellas, and lounge chairs are available for rent. Those in front of restaurants usually cost nothing if you use the restaurant as your headquarters for drinks and food.

El Garrafón Natural Park ★★ (see "Snorkeling," below) is best known as a snorkeling area, but there is a nice stretch of beach on either side of the park. **Playa Lancheros** is on the Caribbean side of Laguna Makax. Local buses go to Lancheros, then turn inland and return downtown. The beach at Playa Lancheros is nice, but the few restaurants there are expensive.

SWIMMING   Wide Playa Norte is the best swimming beach, with Playa Lancheros second. There are no lifeguards on duty on Isla Mujeres, which does not use the system of water-safety flags employed in Cancún and Cozumel.

SNORKELING   By far the most popular place to snorkel is **El Garrafón Natural Park** ★★. It is at the southern end of the island, where you'll see numerous schools of colorful fish. The well-equipped park has two restaurant-bars, beach chairs, a swimming pool, kayaks, changing rooms, rental lockers, showers, a gift shop, and snack bars. The park is under the same management as Xcaret, south of Cancún. Admission is $22 for adults, $15 for children (AE, MC, V). You can also choose a package ($46) that includes food, beverages, locker rental, and snorkeling gear rental. Day-trip packages from Cancún (✆ **998/884-9422** in Cancún, or 984/875-6000 [Xel-Ha, which also provides information on El Garrafón]) are also available. Prices start at $22 and include round-trip transportation from the pier on Km 4 outside Cancún. The park is open daily from 8am to 6pm.

Also good for snorkeling is the **Manchones Reef,** off the southeastern coast. The reef is just offshore and accessible by boat.

Another excellent location is around the lighthouse *(el faro)* in the **Bahía de Mujeres** at the southern tip of the island, where the water is about 2m (6 ft.) deep. Boatmen will take you for around $25 per person if you have your own snorkeling equipment or $30 if you use theirs.

DIVING   Most of the dive shops on the island offer the same trips for the same prices: one-tank dives cost $55, two-tank dives $70. **Bahía Dive Shop,** Rueda Medina 166, across from the car-ferry dock (✆ **998/877-0340**), is a full-service shop that offers resort and certification classes as well as dive equipment for sale or rent. The shop is open daily from 9am to 7pm, and accepts MasterCard and Visa. Another respected dive shop is **Coral Scuba Center,** at Matamoros 13A and Rueda Medina (© **998/877-0061** or 998/877-0763). It's open daily from 8am to 12:30pm and 3 to 10pm, and accepts American Express, MasterCard, and Visa. It offers discounted prices for those who bring their own gear.

The best season for diving is from June to August, when the water is calm and warm. **Cuevas de los Tiburones (Caves of the Sleeping Sharks)** ✪, Isla's most famous dive site, costs $70 to $80 for a two-tank dive at a depth of 21 to 24 meters (70–80 ft.), advisable only for experienced divers. The sleeping sharks have mostly been driven off, and a storm collapsed the arch featured in a Jacques Cousteau film showing them, but the caves survive. Other dive sites include a **wreck** 15km (9 miles) offshore; **Banderas** reef, between Isla Mujeres and Cancún, where there's always a strong current; **Tabos** reef on the eastern shore; and **Manchones** reef, 1km (½ mile) off the southeastern tip of the island, where the water is 4.5 to 11m (15–35 ft.) deep. **The Cross of the Bay** is close to Manchones reef. A bronze cross, weighing 1 ton and standing 12m (39 ft.) high, was placed in the water between Manchones and Isla in 1994, as a memorial to those who have lost their lives at sea.

In May 1999, a shrimp boat suffering engine failure ran aground on a portion of a large coral reef just north of Isla. A section of the reef suffered significant damage, and officials have placed buoys in the area to steer as much traffic as possible away from the damaged area.

FISHING   To arrange a day of fishing, ask at the **Sociedad Cooperativa Turística** (the boatmen's cooperative), on Avenida Rueda Medina (no phone), next to Mexico Divers and Las Brisas restaurant, or the travel agency mentioned in "A Visit to Isla Contoy," below. Four to six others can share the cost, which includes lunch and drinks. Year-round you'll find bonito, mackerel, kingfish, and amberjack. Sailfish and sharks (hammerhead, bull, nurse, lemon, and tiger) are in good supply in April and May. In winter, larger grouper and jewfish are prevalent. Four hours of fishing close to shore costs around $110; 8 hours farther out goes for $250. The cooperative is open Monday through Saturday from 8am to 1pm and 5 to 8pm, and Sunday from 7:30 to 10am and 6 to 8pm.

YOGA   Increasingly, Isla is becoming known as a great place to combine a relaxing beach vacation with yoga practice and instruction. The trend began at **Hotel Na Balam** (© **998/877-0279;** www.nabalam.com), which offers yoga classes under its large poolside *palapa,* complete with yoga mats and props. The classes, which begin at 9am Monday through Friday, are free to guests, $10 per class to visitors. Na Balam is also the site of frequent yoga instruction vacations featuring respected teachers and a more extensive practice schedule.

The **Casa de la Cultura,** on Avenida Guerrero, between Abasolo and Madero streets (© **998/877-0639**), holds yoga classes frequently. Call to check and confirm the available classes. The center is open Monday through Saturday from 9am to 1pm and 4 to 8pm. It also offers dance classes, drawing classes, and a book exchange that's the closest thing to a library on Isla.

MORE ATTRACTIONS

DOLPHIN DISCOVERY   You can swim with live dolphins (© **998/877-0207,** or 998/849-4757 in Cancún; fax 998/849-4751; www.dolphindiscovery.com) in an enclosure at Treasure Island, on the side of Isla Mujeres that faces Cancún. Groups of six people swim with two dolphins and one trainer. Swimmers view an educational video and spend time in the water with the trainer and the dolphins before enjoying 30 minutes of free swimming time with them. Reservations are recommended, and you must arrive an hour before your assigned swimming time, at 9am, 11am, 1pm, or 3pm. The cost is $119 per person, plus $15 if you need round-trip transportation from Cancún.

A TURTLE SANCTUARY ★★ This reserve, dedicated to preserving Caribbean sea turtles and to educating the public about them, makes a worthwhile outing.

As recently as 20 years ago, fishermen converged on the island nightly from May to September, waiting for the monster-size turtles to lumber ashore to deposit their Ping-Pong-ball-shaped eggs. Totally vulnerable once they begin laying their eggs, and exhausted when they have finished, the turtles were easily captured and slaughtered for their highly prized meat, shell, and eggs. Then a concerned fisherman, Gonzalez Cahle Maldonado, began convincing others to spare at least the eggs, which he protected. It was a start. Following his lead, the fishing secretariat founded the **Centro de Investigaciones** 11 years ago; both the government and private donations fund it. Since then, at least 28,000 turtles have been released, and every year local schoolchildren participate in the event, bringing the notion of protecting the turtles to a new generation of islanders.

Six species of sea turtles nest on Isla Mujeres. An adult green turtle, the most abundant species, measures 1 to 1.5m (4–5 ft.) in length and can weigh as much as 450 pounds. At the center, visitors walk through the indoor and outdoor turtle pool areas, where the creatures paddle around. The turtles are separated by age, from newly hatched up to 1 year. Besides protecting the turtles that nest on Isla Mujeres of their own accord, the program also captures turtles at sea, brings them to enclosed compounds to mate, and later frees them to nest on Isla Mujeres after they have been tagged. People who come here usually end up staying at least an hour, especially if they opt for the guided tour, which I recommend. The sanctuary is on a piece of land separated from the island by Bahía de Mujeres and Laguna Makax; you'll need a taxi to get there. Admission is $2.30; the shelter is open daily from 9am to 5pm. For more information, call ⓒ 998/877-0595.

A MAYA RUIN ★★ Just beyond the lighthouse, at the southern end of the island, are the strikingly beautiful remains of a small Maya temple, believed to have been built to pay homage to the moon and fertility goddess, Ixchel. The location, on a lofty bluff overlooking the sea, is worth seeing and makes a great place for photos. It is believed that Maya women traveled here on annual pilgrimages to seek Ixchel's blessings of fertility. If you're at El Garrafón park and want to walk, it's not too far. Turn right from El Garrafón. When you see the lighthouse, turn toward it down the rocky path.

A PIRATE'S FORTRESS The Fortress of Mundaca is about 4km (2½ miles) in the same direction as El Garrafón, about half a mile to the left. A slave trader who claimed to have been the pirate Mundaca Marecheaga built the fortress. In the early 19th century, he arrived at Isla Mujeres and set up a blissful paradise, while making money selling slaves to Cuba and Belize. According to island lore, he decided to settle down and build this hacienda after being captivated by the charms of an island girl. However, she reputedly spurned his affections and married another islander, leaving him heartbroken and alone on Isla Mujeres. Admission is $2; the fortress is open daily from 10am to 6pm.

A VISIT TO ISLA CONTOY ★ If possible, plan to visit this pristine uninhabited island, 30km (19 miles) by boat from Isla Mujeres, that became a national wildlife reserve in 1981. Lush vegetation covers the oddly shaped island, which is 6km (3¾ miles) long and harbors 70 species of birds as well as a host of marine and animal life. Bird species that nest on the island include pelicans, brown boobies, frigates, egrets, terns, and cormorants. Flocks of flamingos arrive in April. June, July, and August are good months to spot turtles burying their eggs in the sand at night. Most excursions troll for fish (which will be your lunch), anchor en route for a snorkeling expedition, skirt the island at a leisurely pace for close viewing of the birds without disturbing the habitat, and then pull ashore. While the captain prepares lunch, visitors can swim, sun, follow the nature trails, and visit the fine nature museum, which has bathroom facilities. The trip from Isla Mujeres takes about 45 minutes each way and can be longer if the waves are choppy. Because of the tight-knit boatmen's cooperative, prices for this excursion are the same everywhere: $40. You can buy a ticket at the **Sociedad Cooperativa Turística** on Avenida Rueda Medina, next to Mexico Divers and Las Brisas restaurant (no phone), or at one of several travel agencies, such as **La Isleña,** on Morelos between Medina and Juárez (© **998/877-0578**). La Isleña is open daily from 7:30am to 9:30pm and is a good source for tourist information. Isla Contoy trips leave at 8:30am and return around 4pm. The price (cash only) is $37 for adults, $18 for children. It usually includes snorkeling equipment, but double-check before heading out.

Three types of boats go to Isla Contoy. Small boats have one motor and seat eight or nine. Medium-sized boats have two motors and hold 10. Large boats have a toilet and hold 16. Most boats have a sun cover. The first two types are being phased out in favor of larger, better boats. Boat captains should respect the cooperative's regulations regarding capacity and should have enough life jackets to go around.

SHOPPING

Shopping is a casual activity here. There are only a few shops of any sophistication. Shop owners will bombard you, especially on Avenida Hidalgo, selling Saltillo rugs, onyx, silver, Guatemalan clothing, blown glassware, masks, folk art, beach paraphernalia, and T-shirts in abundance. Prices are lower than in Cancún or Cozumel, but with such overeager sellers, bargaining is necessary.

The one treasure you're likely to take back is a piece of fine jewelry—Isla is known for its excellent, duty-free prices on gemstones and handcrafted work made to order. Diamonds, emeralds, sapphires, and rubies can be purchased as loose stones and then mounted while you're off exploring. The superbly crafted gold, silver, and gems are available at very competitive prices in the workshops near the central plaza. The stones are also available in the rough. **Van Cleef & Arpels** (© **998/877-0331**) has a store at the corner of Morelos and Juárez streets, with a broad selection of jewelry at competitive prices. Easily the largest store in Isla, it's open daily from 9am to 9pm and accepts all major credit cards.

WHERE TO STAY

You'll find plenty of hotels in all price ranges on Isla Mujeres. Rates peak during high season, which is the most expensive and most crowded time to go. Elizabeth Wenger of **Four Seasons Travel** in Montello, Wisconsin (© **800/552-4550**), specializes in Mexico travel and books a lot of hotels in Isla Mujeres. Her service is invaluable in the high season. Those interested in private home rentals or longer-term stays can contact **Mundaca Travel and Real Estate** in Isla Mujeres (© **998/877-0025;** fax 998/877-0076; www.mundacatravel.com).

In the last few years, Isla has gained several smaller but decidedly upscale places to stay. Anyone wanting the proximity and ease of arrival that Cancún offers but not its excesses should seriously consider these new options.

VERY EXPENSIVE

Hotel Villa Rolandi Gourmet & Beach Club ★★★   Isla's newest hotel is adding to the island's options for guests who enjoy its tranquillity—but also like being pampered. Despite a price increase, Villa Rolandi remains a great value for a luxury stay, with Mediterranean-style rooms that offer every conceivable amenity, as well as its own small, private beach in a sheltered cove. Each of the oversize suites has an ocean view and a large terrace or balcony with a full-size private whirlpool. TVs offer satellite music and movies, and rooms all have a sophisticated in-room sound system. A recessed seating area extends out to the balcony or terrace. Bathrooms are large and tastefully decorated in deep-hued Tikal marble. The stained-glassed shower has dual showerheads, stereo speakers, and jet options, and converts into a steam room.

Dining is an integral part of a stay at Villa Rolandi. Its owner is a Swiss-born restaurateur who made a name for himself with his restaurants on Isla Mujeres and in Cancún (see "Where to Dine," below). This intimate hideaway with personalized service is ideal for honeymooners, who receive a complimentary bottle of domestic champagne upon arrival, when notified in advance.

Fracc. Lagunamar SM 7 Mza. 75 L 15 and 16, 77400 Isla Mujeres, Q. Roo. © **998/877-0700**. Fax 998/877-0100. www.rolandi.com. 20 units. High season $450 double; low season $290 double. Rates include round-trip transportation from Playa Linda in Cancún aboard a private catamaran yacht; continental breakfast; and a la carte lunch or dinner in the on-site restaurant. AE, MC, V. Children under 14 not accepted. **Amenities:** Restaurant (see "Where to Dine," below); breakfast delivery; Infinity pool with waterfall; small fitness room with basic equipment and open-air massage area; concierge; tour desk; 24-hr. room service. *In room:* TV/VCR, dataport, minibar, hair dryer, iron, safe.

Villa Vera Puerto Isla Mujeres ★   The concept here—an exclusive glide-up yachting and sailing resort—is unique not only to Isla Mujeres, but also to most of Mexico. Facing an undeveloped portion of the glass-smooth, mangrove-edged Makax Lagoon, Puerto Isla Mujeres is a collection of modern suites and villas with sloping white-stucco walls and red-tile roofs spread across spacious palm-filled grounds. Beautifully designed with Scandinavian and Mediterranean elements, guest quarters feature tile, wood-beam ceilings, natural teakwood, and marble accents. Suites have a large, comfortable living area with minibar on a lower level, with the bedroom above, loft-style. Villas have two bedrooms upstairs with a full bathroom, and a small bathroom downstairs with a shower. Each villa also holds a small kitchen area. A whirlpool is on the upper patio off the master bedroom. Nightly turndown service leaves the next day's weather forecast on the pillow beside the requisite chocolate. The beach club, with refreshments, is a water-taxi ride across the lagoon on a beautiful stretch of beach. A staff biologist can answer questions about birds and water life on Isla Mujeres.

Puerto de Abrigo Laguna Macax, 77400 Isla Mujeres, Q. Roo. Reservations: Km 4.5 Paseo Kukulkán, 77500 Cancún, Q. Roo. © **800/960-ISLA** in the U.S., or 998/877-0413. 24 units. High season $290–$350 suite, $550 villa; low season $280 suite, $350 villa. Rates include boat transportation from office in Playa Linda, continental breakfast. AE, MC, V. **Amenities:** 2 restaurants (1 indoor, 1 poolside); breakfast delivery; free-form swimming pool with swim-up bar; on-site spa with complete massage services; mopeds, golf carts, bikes, and watersports equipment for rent; laundry; nearby beach club; full-service marina with 60 slips for 30- to 60-ft. vessels, fueling station, charter yachts and sailboats, and sailing school; video and CD library. *In room:* TV/VCR, minibar, safe, stereo with CD.

EXPENSIVE

Hotel Na Balam ★★ *Finds*   Na Balam is known as a haven for yoga students and those interested in an introspective vacation. This popular, two-story hotel near the end of Playa Norte has comfortable rooms on a quiet, ideally located portion of the beach. Rooms are in three sections; some face the beach, and others are across the street in a garden setting with a swimming pool. All rooms have a terrace or balcony, with hammocks. Each spacious suite contains a king bed or two double beds, a seating area, and folk-art decorations. Though other rooms are newer, the older section is well kept, with a bottom-floor patio facing the peaceful, palm-filled, sandy inner yard and Playa Norte. Yoga classes (free for guests; $10 per class for nonguests) start at 9am Monday through Friday. The restaurant, **Zazil Ha,** is one of the island's most popular (see "Where to Dine," below). A beachside bar serves a selection of natural juices and is one of the most popular spots for sunset watching.

Zazil Ha 118, 77400 Isla Mujeres, Q. Roo. ℂ **998/877-0279.** Fax 998/877-0446. www.nabalam.com. 31 units. High season $217–$302 suite; low season $155–$225 suite. Ask about weekly and monthly rates. AE, MC, V. **Amenities:** Restaurant (Mexican/Caribbean); 2 bars; swimming pool; diving and snorkeling trips available; mopeds, golf carts, and bikes for rent; salon services; in-room massage; babysitting; laundry; library; Internet access; rec room with TV, VCR, and Ping-Pong tables; yoga classes. *In room:* Fan.

Secreto ⭐ *Finds*   This new boutique hotel looks like a Hamptons beach house, but it is one of the best B&B values in the Caribbean. What sets Secreto apart— aside from the stunning setting and outstanding value—is the exemplary service. The sophisticated, romantic property has nine suites that overlook a central pool area to the private beach beyond. Located on the northern end of the island, Secreto is within walking distance of town, yet feels removed enough to make for an idyllic, peaceful retreat. The captivating contemporary design features clean, white spaces and sculpted architecture in a Mediterranean style. Tropical gardens surround the pool area, and an outdoor living area offers comfy couches and places to dine. All rooms have private verandas with comfortable seating, ideal for ocean-gazing beyond Halfmoon Beach, and are accented with original artwork. Three suites have king beds, draped in mosquito netting, while the remaining six have two double beds; all rooms are nonsmoking. Transportation from Cancún airport can be arranged on request, for an additional $50 per van (not per person).

Sección Rocas, lote 1, 77400 Isla Mujeres, Q. Roo. ℂ **877/278-8018** in the U.S., or 998/877-1039. Fax 998/ 877-1048. www.hotelsecreto.com. 9 units. High season $150–$200 double; low season $125–$150 double. Extra person $15. 1 child under 5 stays free in parent's room. Rates include continental breakfast. MC, V. **Amenities:** Pool; sun terrace; private cove beach; tours, diving and snorkeling available; dinner delivery from Rolandi's restaurant available. *In room:* A/C, TV, CD player, mini-fridge, safe-deposit box, robes.

MODERATE

Hotel Cabañas María del Mar ⭐   A good choice for simple beach accommodations, the Cabañas María del Mar is on the popular Playa Norte. The older two-story section behind the reception area and beyond the garden offers nicely outfitted rooms facing the beach. All have two single or double beds, refrigerators, and oceanview balconies strung with hammocks. Eleven single-story cabañas closer to the reception area were remodeled in late 1999, in a rustic Mexican style, with new bathroom fixtures and the addition of a mini-fridge. The newer **El Castillo** section is across the street, over and beside Buho's restaurant. It contains all "deluxe" rooms, but some are larger than others; the five rooms on the ground floor have large patios. Upstairs rooms have small balconies. All have ocean views, blue-and-white tile floors, and tile baths, and contain colonial-style furniture. There's a small pool in the garden.

Av. Arq. Carlos Lazo 1 (on Playa Norte, ½ block from the Hotel Na Balam), 77400 Isla Mujeres, Q. Roo. ℂ **800/ 223-5695** in the U.S., or 998/877-0179. Fax 998/877-0213 or 998/877-0156. 73 units. High season $100–$130 double; low season $55–$88 double. MC, V. From the pier, walk left 1 block and turn right on Matamoros. After 4 blocks, turn left on Lazo (the last street); hotel is at end of block. **Amenities:** Standard-size pool; bus for tours and boat for rent; golf-cart and *moto* rentals.

INEXPENSIVE

Hotel Belmar ⭐⭐   Situated in the center of Isla's small-town activity, this hotel sits above Pizza Rolandi (consider the restaurant noise) and is run by the same people. Each of the simple but stylish tile-accented rooms comes with two twin or double beds. Prices are high considering the lack of views, but the rooms are pleasant. This is one of the few island hotels that have televisions (with U.S. channels) in the room. It has one large colonial-decorated suite with a whirlpool and a patio.

Av. Hidalgo 110 (between Madero and Abasolo, 3½ blocks from the passenger-ferry pier), 77400 Isla Mujeres, Q. Roo. © **998/877-0430.** Fax 998/877-0429. www.rolandi.com/about_hotel.htm. 11 units. High season $54–$95 double; low season $25–$90 double. AE, MC, V. **Amenities:** Restaurant/bar (see "Where to Dine," below); room service until 11:30pm; laundry. *In room:* A/C, TV, fan.

Hotel D'Gomar *Value*   This hotel is known for comfort at reasonable prices. You can hardly beat the value for basic accommodations, which are regularly updated. Rooms—each with two double beds—have new mattresses, drapes, and tiled bathrooms with new fixtures. A wall of windows offers great breezes and views. The higher prices are for air-conditioning, which is hardly needed with the breezes and ceiling fans. The only drawback is that there are five stories and no elevator. But it's conveniently located cater-cornered (look right) from the ferry pier, with exceptional rooftop views. The name of the hotel is the most visible sign on the "skyline."

Rueda Medina 150, 77400 Isla Mujeres, Q. Roo. © **998/877-0541.** 16 units. High season $55 double; low season $30 double. No credit cards. *In room:* Fan.

Hotel Francis Arlene ⭐   The Magaña family operates this neat little two-story inn built around a small, shady courtyard. This hotel is very popular with families and seniors, and it welcomes many repeat guests. You'll notice the tidy cream-and-white facade from the street. Some rooms have ocean views, and all are remodeled or updated each year. They are comfortable, with tile floors, tiled bathrooms, and a very homey feel. Each downstairs room has a coffeemaker, refrigerator, and stove; each upstairs room comes with a refrigerator and toaster. Some have either a balcony or a patio. Higher prices are for the 14 rooms with air-conditioning; other units have fans. Rates are substantially better if quoted in pesos and are reflected below. In dollars they are 15% to 20% higher.

Guerrero 7 (5½ blocks inland from the ferry pier, between Abasolo and Matamoros), 77400 Isla Mujeres, Q. Roo. ©/fax **998/877-0310** or 998/877-0861. 26 units. High season $45–$60 double; low season $38–$48 double. No credit cards. **Amenities:** Money exchange; in-room massage; safe. *In room:* No phone.

Hotel Posada del Mar *Kids*   Simply furnished, quiet, and comfortable, this long-established hotel faces the water and a wide beach 3 blocks north of the ferry pier. It has one of the few swimming pools on the island. This is probably the best choice in Isla for families. The ample rooms are in a three-story building or one-story bungalow units. For the spaciousness of the rooms and the location, this is among the best values on the island and is very popular with readers, though I consistently find the staff to be the least gracious on the island. A wide, seldom-used but appealing stretch of Playa Norte is across the street, where watersports equipment is available for rent. A great, casual *palapa*-style bar and a lovely pool are on the back lawn, and the restaurant **Pinguino** (see "Where to Dine," below) is by the sidewalk at the front of the property.

Av. Rueda Medina 15 A, 77400 Isla Mujeres, Q. Roo. © **800/544-3005** in the U.S., or 998/877-0044. Fax 998/877-0266. www.mexhotels.com/pdm.html. 62 units. High season $70–$88 double; low season $33–$44 double. Children under 12 stay free in adult's room. AE, MC, V. From the pier, go left for 4 blocks; hotel is on the right. **Amenities:** Restaurant/bar; pool.

WHERE TO DINE

At the **Municipal Market,** next to the telegraph office and post office on Avenida Guerrero, obliging, hard-working women operate several little food stands. At the **Panadería La Reyna** (no phone), at Madero and Juárez, you can pick up inexpensive sweet bread, muffins, cookies, and yogurt. It's open Monday through Saturday from 7am to 9:30pm.

Cocina económica (literally, "economic kitchen") restaurants usually aim at the local population. These are great places to find good food at rock-bottom prices, and especially so on Isla Mujeres, where you'll find several, most of which feature delicious regional specialties. But be aware that the hygiene is not what you'll find at more established restaurants, so you're dining at your own risk.

EXPENSIVE

Casa Rolandi ⭐ ITALIAN/SEAFOOD   The gourmet Casa Rolandi restaurant and bar has become Isla's favored fine-dining experience. It boasts a view of the Caribbean and the most sophisticated menu in the area. There's a colorful main dining area as well as more casual, open-air terrace seating for drinks or light snacks. The food is the most notable on the island, but the overall experience falls short—the lights are a bit too bright and the music a bit too close to what you'd hear on an elevator. Along with seafood and northern Italian specialties, the famed wood-burning-oven pizzas are a good bet. Careful—the oven-baked bread, which arrives looking like a puffer fish, is so divine that you're likely to fill up on it. This is a great place to enjoy the sunset, and it offers a selection of more than 80 premium tequilas.

On the pier of Villa Rolandi, Lagunamar SM 7. ☎ **998/877-0430.** Main courses $6–$31. AE, MC, V. Daily 11am–11pm.

MODERATE

Las Palapas Chimbo's ⭐ SEAFOOD   If you're looking for a beachside *palapa*-covered restaurant where you can wiggle your toes in the sand while relishing fresh seafood, this is the best of them. It's the locals' favorite on Playa Norte. Try the delicious fried whole fish, which comes with rice, beans, and tortillas. You'll notice a bandstand and dance floor in the middle of the restaurant, and sex-hunk posters all over the ceiling—that is, when you aren't gazing at the beach and the Caribbean. Chimbo's becomes a lively bar and dance club at night, drawing a crowd of drinkers and dancers (see "Isla Mujeres After Dark," below).

Norte Beach. No phone. Sandwiches and fruit $2.50–$4.50; seafood $6–$9. No credit cards. Daily 8am–midnight. From the pier, walk left to the end of the *malecón,* then right onto the Playa Norte; it's about ½ block on the right.

Pinguino MEXICAN/SEAFOOD   The best seats on the waterfront are on the deck of this restaurant and bar, especially in late evening, when islanders and tourists arrive to dance and party. This is the place to feast on sublimely fresh lobster—you'll get a large, beautifully presented lobster tail with a choice of butter, garlic, and secret sauces. The grilled seafood platter is spectacular, and fajitas and barbecued ribs are also popular. Breakfasts include fresh fruit, yogurt, and granola, or sizable platters of eggs, served with homemade wheat bread. Pinguino also has nonsmoking areas.

In front of the Hotel Posada del Mar (3 blocks west of the ferry pier), Av. Rueda Medina 15. ☎ **998/877-0044.** Main courses $4–$7; daily special $7. AE, MC, V. Daily 7am–10pm; bar closes at midnight.

Pizza Rolandi ⭐⭐ ITALIAN/SEAFOOD   You're bound to dine at least once at Rolandi's, which is practically an Isla institution. The plate-size pizzas and calzones feature exotic ingredients—including lobster, black mushrooms, pineapple, and Roquefort cheese—as well as more traditional tomatoes, olives, basil, and salami. A wood-burning oven provides the signature flavor of the pizzas, as well as baked chicken, roast beef, and mixed seafood casserole with lobster. The extensive menu also offers a selection of salads and light appetizers, as well as an ample array of pasta dishes, steaks, fish, and scrumptious desserts. The setting is the open courtyard of the Hotel Belmar, with a porch overlooking the action on Avenida Hidalgo.

Av. Hidalgo 10 (3½ blocks inland from the pier, between Madero and Abasolo). © 998/877-0430. Main courses $3.70–$13. AE, MC, V. Daily 11am–11:30pm.

Zazil Ha ★★ CARIBBEAN/INTERNATIONAL Here you can enjoy some of the island's best food while sitting at tables on the sand among palms and gardens. The food—terrific pasta with garlic, shrimp in tequila sauce, fajitas, seafood pasta, and delicious *mole* enchiladas—enhances the serene environment. Caribbean specialties include cracked conch, coconut sailfish, jerk chicken, and stuffed squid. A selection of fresh juices complements the vegetarian menu, and there's even a special menu for those participating in yoga retreats. Between the set meal times, you can order all sorts of enticing food, such as vegetable and fruit drinks, tacos and sandwiches, *ceviche,* and terrific nachos. It's likely you'll stake this place out for several meals.

At the Hotel Na Balam (at the end of Playa Norte, almost at the end of Calle Zazil Ha). © 998/877-0279. Fax 998/877-0446. Main courses $8.50–$16. AE, MC, V. Daily 7:30–10:30am, 12:30–3:30pm, and 7–10pm.

INEXPENSIVE

Cafecito ★ CREPES/ICE CREAM/COFFEE/FRUIT DRINKS Sabina and Luis Rivera own this cute, Caribbean-blue corner restaurant where you can begin the day with flavorful coffee and a croissant and cream cheese, or end it with a hot-fudge sundae. Terrific crepes come with yogurt, ice cream, fresh fruit, or chocolate sauce, as well as ham and cheese. The two-page ice cream menu satisfies almost any craving, even one for waffles with ice cream and fruit. The three-course fixed-price dinner includes soup, a main course (such as fish or curried shrimp with rice and salad), and dessert.

Calle Matamoros 42, at Juárez (4 blocks from the pier). © 998/877-0438. Crepes $2–$4.50; breakfast $2.50–$4.50; sandwiches $2.80–$2.90. No credit cards. Year-round daily 8am–2pm. High season Fri–Wed 5:30–10:30 or 11:30pm.

Cocina Económica Carmelita MEXICAN/HOME COOKING Few tourists find their way to this tiny restaurant, but locals know they can get a filling, inexpensive, home-cooked meal. Carmelita prepares food in the back kitchen, and her husband serves it at the three cloth-covered tables in the front room of their home. Two or three *comida corridas* are available each day until they run out. They begin with the soup of the day and include a fruit water drink *(agua fresca)*. Common selections include *paella, cochinita pibil,* and fishstuffed chiles. Menu specialties include chicken in *mole* sauce, pork cutlet in a spicy sauce, and breaded shrimp. For fancier tastes, the least expensive lobster in town—served grilled or in a garlic sauce—costs $13 for an ample portion.

Calle Juárez 14 (2 blocks from the pier, between Bravo and Allende). No phone. Main dishes $4–$6; daily lunch special $4. No credit cards. Year-round Mon–Sat 12:30–3pm; Dec–Mar Mon–Sat 4–8pm.

ISLA MUJERES AFTER DARK

Those in a party mood by day's end might want to start out at the beach bar of the **Hotel Na Balam** on Playa Norte, which draws a crowd until around midnight. On Saturday and Sunday there's live music from 4 to 7pm. **Las Palapas**

Chimbo's restaurant on the beach becomes a jammin' dance joint with a live band from 9pm until whenever. Farther along the same stretch of beach, **Buho's,** the restaurant and beach bar of the Cabañas María del Mar, has its moments as a popular, low-key hangout. **Pinguino** at the Hotel Posada del Mar offers a convivial late-night hangout; a band plays nightly during high season from 9pm to midnight. Near Mateos and Hidalgo, **KoKo Nuts** caters to a younger crowd, with alternative music for late-night dancing.

2 Cozumel ★★★

70km (44 miles) S of Cancún; 19km (12 miles) SE of Playa del Carmen

Cozumel was a well-known diving spot before Cancún ever existed, and it has ranked for years among the top five dive destinations in the world. Tall reefs line the southwest coast, creating towering walls that offer divers a fairy-tale landscape to explore. For nondivers, it has the beautiful water of the Caribbean with all the accompanying watersports and seaside activities. The island is 45km (28 miles) long and 18km (11 miles) wide, and lies 19km (12 miles) from the mainland. Most of the terrain is flat, undisturbed scrubland.

The only town on the island is San Miguel, which, despite the growth of the last 20 years, can't be called anything more than a small town. It's not particularly attractive, but the place and its inhabitants are agreeable—on Sunday evenings, everybody congregates around the plaza to be sociable and have a good time. Staying in town can be fun and convenient. You get a choice of a number of restaurants and nightspots. Because Cozumel enjoys such popularity with the cruise ships, the waterfront section of town holds wall-to-wall jewelry stores and souvenir shops. This and the area around the town's main square are as far as most cruise ship passengers venture into town. Elsewhere you find mainly offices, restaurants, small hotels, and dive shops.

Should you come down with a case of island fever, **Playa del Carmen** and the mainland are a convenient 25-to-45-minute ferry ride away, weather permitting. Some travel agencies on the island can set you up with a tour of the major ruins on the mainland, such as **Tulum** or **Chichén Itzá,** or a visit to a nature park such as **Xel-Ha** or **Xcaret** (see "Trips to the Mainland," later in this chapter).

The island has its own ruins, but they cannot compare with the major cities of the mainland. During pre-Hispanic times, Maya women traveled by boat to the island to worship the goddess of fertility, Ixchel. More than 40 sites containing shrines remain around the island, and archaeologists still uncover the small dolls customarily offered in the fertility ceremony.

ESSENTIALS
GETTING THERE & DEPARTING
BY PLANE In recent years, the number of international commercial flights in and out of Cozumel (airport code: CZM) has decreased, while charter flights have increased. You might want to inquire about buying a ticket from a packager. Some packagers work with several of Cozumel's hotels, even the small ones; others will let you buy a ticket without making it part of a package. Flight availability changes between high season and low season. **Continental** (© **800/231-0856** in the U.S., or 987/872-0487 in Cozumel) flies to and from Houston and Newark. **U.S. Airways** (© **800/428-4322** in the U.S., or 987/872-2824 in Cozumel but only on days when the flight is operating, or 998/886-0549 in Cancún) flies to and from Charlotte. **Aerocozumel** (© **987/872-3456,** or 998/884-2002 in Cancún), an

Cozumel

affiliate of Mexicana, has numerous flights to and from Cancún and Mérida. **Mexicana** (*C* **800/531-7921** in the U.S.; 987/872-0157 or 987/872-2945 at the airport) and **Aeromexico** (*C* **800/237-6639** in the U.S., or 01-800/021-4000 in Cozumel) fly from Mexico City. Vans are available from the airport to the town ($4) and the outlying hotels (see "Arriving," below).

BY FERRY   Passenger ferries run to and from Playa del Carmen. **Barcos México** (*C* **987/872-1508** or 987/872-1588) offers departures almost every hour between 5am and midnight. The trip takes 30 to 45 minutes, depending on the boat, and costs $9 one-way. The boats are air-conditioned. In Playa del Carmen, the ferry dock is 1½ blocks from the main square. In Cozumel, the ferries use the town pier (Muelle Fiscal), a block from the main square. Schedules are subject to change, so check at the docks for departure times—especially the time of the last returning ferry, if that's the one you intend to use. Luggage storage at the Cozumel dock costs $2 per day.

There is a car ferry to Cozumel from Puerto Morelos (32km/20 miles north of Playa del Carmen), which takes longer, is more expensive, and should be avoided unless you need to take your vehicle across. Double-check the schedule, which is usually daily at 5:30am, 10:30am, and 4pm, by calling the **terminal** (© 998/871-0008). On Sunday the last trips are sometimes canceled. The crossing takes 2½ hours. The ferry arrives at the International Pier just south of town, near La Ceiba hotel. Cargo takes precedence over private cars. Officials suggest that camper drivers stay overnight in the parking lot to be first in line for tickets. Return trips to Puerto Morelos depart at 8am, 1:30pm, and 7pm daily; double-check the schedule by calling © **987/872-0950.** *Always arrive at least 3 hours before the ferry's departure to purchase a ticket and get in line.* The fare is $55 for a car, $100 for a van.

BY BUS   If you plan to continue your trip on the mainland, there are two offices where you can purchase tickets in advance. Look for signs reading ADO. One is at the ferry pier, next to the counter for ferry tickets (no phone). The other is on Calle 2 Norte between avenidas 5 and 10 (© **987/872-1706**). Hours for both are from 8am to 9:30pm daily.

ORIENTATION

ARRIVING   Cozumel's **airport** is immediately inland from downtown. **Transportes Terrestres** provides hotel transportation in air-conditioned Suburbans. Buy your ticket as you exit the terminal. To hotels downtown, the fare is $4 per person; to hotels along the north shore, $6, and to hotels along the south shore, $7 to $9. Passenger ferries arrive at Muelle Fiscal, the dock by the town's main square. Cruise ships dock at the **Punta Langosta** pier, a few blocks south of the Muelle Fiscal; at the **International Pier,** near La Ceiba hotel; and at the **Puerta Maya** pier.

VISITOR INFORMATION   The **Municipal Tourism Office** (©/fax **987/ 869-0212**) is on the second floor of the Plaza del Sol commercial building facing the central plaza. It is open Monday through Friday from 8:30am to 5pm and Saturday from 9am to 1pm. The office operates information booths at the ferry pier and at Puerta Maya; open Monday through Saturday from 8:30am to 4pm.

CITY LAYOUT   San Miguel's main waterfront street is **Avenida Rafael Melgar.** Running parallel to Avenida Rafael Melgar and the coast are other avenidas numbered in multiples of five—5, 10, 15—which increase as you go inland. **Avenida Juárez** runs perpendicular, starting at the ferry dock, passing by the main square, and heading inland. Avenida Juárez divides the town into northern and southern halves. The streets *(calles)* that run parallel Juárez to the north have even numbers. The ones to the south have odd numbers, with the exception of Calle Rosado Salas, which runs between calles 1 and 3.

Tips Be Streetwise

North-south streets—the avenidas—have the right of way, and traffic doesn't slow down or stop.

ISLAND LAYOUT   One road runs along the western coast of the island, which faces the Yucatán mainland. It has different names. North of town it's **Santa Pilar** or **San Juan;** in the city it is **Avenida Rafael Melgar;** south of town it's **Costera Sur.** Hotels stretch along this road north and south of town. The road runs to the southern tip of the island (Punta Sur), passing **Chankanaab National Park. Avenida Juárez** (and its extension, the **Carretera Transversal**) runs east from the town across the island. It passes the airport and the turnoff to the ruins of San Gervasio before reaching the undeveloped ocean side of the island. It then turns south and follows the coast to the southern tip of the island, where it meets the Costera Sur.

GETTING AROUND   You can walk to most destinations in town. Getting to outlying hotels and beaches requires a taxi or rental car.

Car rentals are roughly the same price as on the mainland, depending on demand. **Avis** (© 987/872-0099) and **Executive** (© 987/872-1308) have counters in the airport. Other major rental companies have offices in town. Rentals are easy to arrange through your hotel or at any of the many local rental offices.

Moped rentals are available all over the village and cost $15 to $30 for 24 hours, depending upon the season. If you rent a moped, be careful. Riding a moped made a lot more sense when Cozumel had less traffic; now it involves a certain amount of risk as taxi drivers and other motorists have become more numerous and pushier. Moped accidents easily rank as the greatest cause of injury in Cozumel. Before renting one, inspect it carefully to see that all the gizmos—horn, light, starter, seat, mirror—are in good shape. I've been offered mopeds with unbalanced wheels, which made them unsteady at higher speeds, but the renter quickly exchanged them for another upon my request. You are required to stay on paved roads. It's illegal to ride a moped without a helmet outside of town (subject to a $25 fine).

Cozumel has lots of **taxis** and a strong drivers' union. Fares have been standardized—there's no bargaining. Here are a few sample fares for two people (there is an additional charge for extra passengers to most destinations): island tour, $60; town to southern hotel zone, $5 to $18; town to northern hotels, $5 to $6; town to Chankanaab, $9 (for up to 4 people); in and around town, $3 to $4.

 FAST FACTS: **Cozumel**

Area Code The telephone area code is **987.**

Climate From October to December there can be strong winds all over the Yucatán, as well as some rain. May through September is the rainy season.

Diving Bring proof of your diver's certification and your log. Underwater currents can be strong, and many of the reef drops are quite steep, so dive operators want to make sure divers are experienced.

Internet Access Several cybercafes are in and about the main square. If you go just a bit off Avenida Rafael Melgar and the main square, prices drop. **Modutel,** Av. Juárez 15 (at Av. 10) offers good rates. Hours are Monday through Saturday from 10am to 8pm.

Money Exchange The island has several banks and *casas de cambio,* as well as ATMs. Most places accept dollars, but you usually get a better deal paying in pesos.

Post Office The *correo* is on Avenida Rafael Melgar at Calle 7 Sur (© **987/ 872-0106**), at the southern edge of town. It's open Monday through Friday from 9am to 6pm, Saturday from 9am to noon.

Recompression Chamber There are four recompression chambers *(cámaras de recompresión)*. **Buceo Médico Mexicano,** staffed 24 hours, is at Calle 5 Sur 21-B, between Avenida Rafael Melgar and Avenida 5 Sur (© **987/872-2387** or 987/872-1430). The **Hyperbaric Center of Cozumel** (© **987/872-3070**) is at Calle 4 Norte, between avenidas 5 and 10.

Seasons High season is August and from Christmas to Easter.

EXPLORING THE ISLAND

For **diving** and **snorkeling,** there are plenty of dive shops to choose from, including those recommended below. For **island tours, ruins tours** on and off the island, **glass-bottom boat tours, fiesta nights, fishing,** and other activities, go to a travel agency. I recommend **InterMar Cozumel Viajes,** Calle 2 Norte 101-B, between avenidas 5 and 10 (© **987/872-1535** or 987/872-2022; fax 987/872-0895; cozumel@travel2mexico.com). Office hours are Monday through Saturday from 8am to 8pm, Sunday from 9am to 5pm.

WATERSPORTS

SCUBA DIVING Cozumel is the number one dive destination in the Western Hemisphere. Don't forget your dive card and dive log. Dive shops will rent you scuba gear, but won't take you out on a boat until you show some documentation. If you have a medical condition, bring a letter signed by a doctor stating that you've been cleared to dive. A two-tank morning dive costs around $55; some shops offer an additional afternoon one-tank dive for $9 for those who took the morning dives. A lot of divers save some money by buying a dive package with a hotel. These usually include two dives a day.

Diving in Cozumel is drift diving, which can be a little disconcerting for novices. The current that sweeps along Cozumel's reefs, pulling nutrients into them and making them as large as they are, also dictates how you dive here. The problem is that it pulls at different speeds at different depths and in different places. When it's pulling strong, it can quickly scatter a dive group. The role of the dive master becomes more important, especially with choosing the dive location. Cozumel has a lot of dive locations. To mention but a few: the famous **Palancar Reef,** with its caves and canyons, plentiful fish, and a wide variety of sea coral; the monstrous **Santa Rosa Wall,** famous for its depth, sea life, coral, and sponges; the **San Francisco Reef,** which has a shallower drop-off wall and fascinating sea life; and the **Yucab Reef,** with its beautiful coral.

Finding a dive shop in town is even easier than finding a jewelry store. Of Cozumel's more than 50 dive operators, I recommend Bill Horn's **Aqua Safari,** which has a location on Avenida Rafael Melgar at Calle 5 (© **987/872-0101;** fax 987/872-0661; www.aquasafari.com) and a PADI five-star instructor center with full equipment and parts in the Hotel Plaza Las Glorias (© **987/872-3362** or 987/872-2422); and **Dive House,** on the main plaza (© **987/872-1953;** fax 987/872-0368), which offers PADI, NAUI, and SSI instruction.

A popular activity in the Yucatán is *cenote* diving. The peninsula's underground *cenotes* (seh-*noh*-tehs)—sinkholes or wellsprings—lead to a vast system of underground caverns. The gently flowing water is so clear that divers seem to

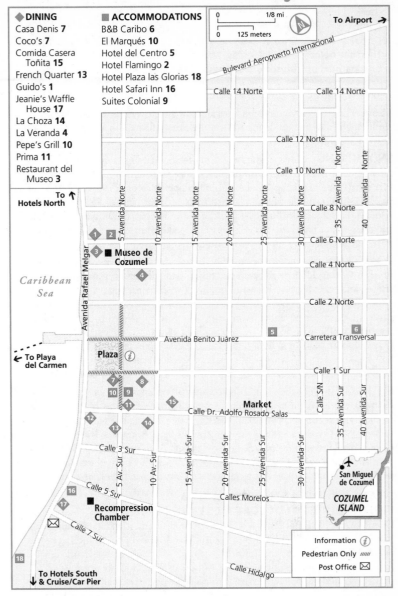

◆ DINING
Casa Denis **7**
Coco's **7**
Comida Casera
  Toñita **15**
French Quarter **13**
Guido's **1**
Jeanie's Waffle
  House **17**
La Choza **14**
La Veranda **4**
Pepe's Grill **10**
Prima **11**
Restaurant del
  Museo **3**

■ ACCOMMODATIONS
B&B Caribo **6**
El Marqués **10**
Hotel del Centro **5**
Hotel Flamingo **2**
Hotel Plaza las Glorias **18**
Hotel Safari Inn **16**
Suites Colonial **9**

0 _____ 1/8 mi
0 ____ 125 meters

To Airport →

Bulevard Aeropuerto Internacional

Calle 14 Norte   Calle 14 Norte

Calle 12 Norte

Calle 10 Norte

To ↑
Hotels North

Calle 8 Norte

Calle 6 Norte

Museo de
Cozumel

Calle 4 Norte

*Caribbean
Sea*

Calle 2 Norte

Avenida Benito Juárez

Carretera Transversal

← To Playa
  del Carmen

Plaza ⓘ

Calle 1 Sur

Market
Calle Dr. Adolfo Rosado Salas

Calle 3 Sur

✈
San Miguel
de Cozumel

Calle 5 Sur

Calles Morelos

**COZUMEL
ISLAND**

Recompression
Chamber

Calle 7 Sur

Information ⓘ
Pedestrian Only ▨
Post Office ✉

To Hotels South
↓ & Cruise/Car Pier

Calle Hidalgo

float on air through caves complete with stalactites and stalagmites. If you want to try this but didn't plan a trip to the mainland, contact **Yucatech Expeditions,** Av. 15 no.144, between Calle 1 and Rosado Salas (ℂ/fax **987/872-5659;** yucatech @cozumel.czm.com.mx), which offers a trip five times a week. Cenotes are 30 to 45 minutes from Playa del Carmen, and a dive in each cenote lasts around 45 minutes. Dives are within the daylight zone, about 39m (130 ft.) into the caverns, and no more than 18m (60 ft.) deep. Company owner Germán Yañez

---

Moments Mardi Gras

Carnaval (Mardi Gras) is Cozumel's most colorful fiesta. It begins the Thursday before Ash Wednesday, with daytime street dancing and night-time parades on Thursday, Saturday, and Monday (the best).

Mendoza inspects diving credentials carefully, and divers must meet his list of requirements before cave diving is permitted. For information and prices, call or drop by the office.

SNORKELING   Anyone who can swim can snorkel. One shop that specializes in snorkeling trips is the **Kuzamil Snorkeling Center,** 50 Av. bis 565 Int. 1, between 5 Sur and Hidalgo, Colonia Adolfo López Mateos (© **987/872-4637** or 987/872-0539). A full-day snorkel trip costs $65 per person, $50 for children under 8. It includes the boat, the guide, a buffet lunch, and snorkel equipment, and it visits four reefs. You can call directly or make arrangements through a local travel agency. Half-day trips are $40 adults, $30 children.

BOAT TRIPS   Travel agencies and hotels can arrange boat trips, a popular pastime on Cozumel. There are evening cruises, cocktail cruises, glass-bottom boat cruises, and other options. It's worth inquiring whether the trip will be filled with cruise-ship passengers, because trips that cater to the cruise-ship crowds can be packed. One rather novel trip is a ride in a submarine, offered by **Atlantis Submarines** (© **987/872-5671**). The sub can hold 48 people. It operates almost 3km (2 miles) south of town in front of the Casa del Mar hotel and costs $76 per adult, $39 for kids 3 to 12 years old. This is a superior experience to the **Sub See Explorer** offered by **Aqua World,** which is really a glorified glass-bottom boat.

FISHING   Travel agents can also arrange fishing trips. The best months for fishing are from April to September, when the catch includes blue and white marlin, sailfish, tarpon, swordfish, dorado, wahoo, tuna, and red snapper. One agency that specializes in deep sea and fly fishing is **Aquarius Travel Fishing,** Calle 3 Sur 2 between Avenida Rafael Melgar and Avenida 5 (© **987/872-1092;** gabdiaz@yahoo.com). Or contact the owners of Cocos Cozumel restaurant (see later in this chapter), who can recommend an experienced guide and boat.

CHANKANAAB NATIONAL PARK & PUNTA SUR ECOLOGICAL RESERVE

Chankanaab National Park *★★* is the pride of many islanders. Chankanaab means "little sea," which refers to a beautiful land-locked pool connected to the sea through an underground tunnel—a sort of miniature ocean. Snorkeling in this natural aquarium is not permitted, but the park has a lovely ocean beach for sunbathing and snorkeling. Arrive early to stake out a chair and *palapa* before the cruise-ship crowd arrives. Likewise, the snorkeling is best before noon. There are bathrooms, lockers, a gift shop, several snack huts, a restaurant, and a *palapa* for renting snorkeling gear.

You can also swim with dolphins. **Dolphin Discovery** (© 998/849-4757 in Cancún; www.dolphindiscovery.com) has several programs for experiencing these sea creatures. You'll need to make reservations well in advance. The surest way is by e-mail (salesinternet@dolphindiscovery.com.mx) or through the website. The dolphin swim and other programs are very popular, so your best bet is to plan ahead. Still, if you're already in Cozumel, you can try by calling © **987/872-9702.**

The dolphin swim costs $119 and features close interaction with the beautiful swimmers. There's also a swim and snorkel program for $89 that gets you in the water with them but offers less interaction. Dolphin Discovery also offers a program only in Cozumel where you can swim with sea lions ($59); make reservations for this. There is also a sea lion show, which doesn't require reservations. It costs $5 per adult, $3.50 per kid. Tickets are available through any travel agency in town. The show also includes some scarlet macaws, which, like the sea lions, were rescued from illegal captivity.

Surrounding the land-locked pool is a botanical garden with shady paths and 351 species of tropical and subtropical plants from 22 countries, as well as 451 species from Cozumel. Several Maya structures have been re-created within the gardens to give visitors an idea of Maya life in a jungle setting. There's a small natural history museum as well. Admission to the park costs $10; it's open daily from 8am to 5pm. The park is south of town, just past the Fiesta Americana Hotel. Taxis run constantly between the park, the hotels, and town ($9 from town for up to 4 people).

Punta Sur Ecological Reserve (admission $10) is a large area that encompasses the southern tip of the island, including the Columbia Lagoon. The only practical way of going there is to rent a car or scooter; there is no taxi stand, and, usually, few people. This is an ecological reserve, not a park, so don't expect much infrastructure. The reserve has an information center, several observation towers, and a snack bar. In addition, there are four boat rides per day around the Colombia Lagoon, where guides point out things of interest about the habitat (bring bug spray). Punta Sur has some interesting snorkeling (bring your own gear), and lovely beaches kept as natural as possible. Regular hours are from 9am to 5pm. A special program (© **987/872-2940** for info) allows visitors to observe turtle nests in season, and you can participate as a volunteer in the evenings during the nesting season.

THE BEACHES

Along both the west and east sides of the island you'll see signs advertising beach clubs. A "beach club" in Cozumel usually means a *palapa* hut that's open to the public and serves soft drinks, beer, and fried fish. Some are more elaborate. **Nachi Cocom,** south of Chankanaab, even has a swimming pool, a good restaurant, and watersports equipment rental. A little farther south you'll come to **Playa San Francisco** ★★ and, south of it, **Playa Palancar** ★★. Food (usually overpriced) and equipment rentals are available.

Other beach clubs include **Paradise Cafe,** on the southern tip of the island across from Punta Sur nature park, and **Playa Bonita, Chen Río,** and **Punta Morena,** on the eastern side. They are scattered along the coast and do a big business on Sunday, when the locals head for the beaches; otherwise they aren't crowded. Most of the east coast is unsafe for swimming because of the surf. Small beaches occupy the spaces between rocky promontories, and you can have one all to yourself.

If you're not trying to get away from the crowds, there is an all-inclusive beach park, **Playasol** (© **987/872-9030;** www.playasol.com.mx). It sells different packages for people wanting a day at the beach for $50 to $70, depending on the package. The park offers guests the use of a pool, restaurant, bar, and a number of watersports. The owner of Playasol operates the ferries from Playa. It promotes the park on the mainland offering direct transportation there. The park also gets cruise-ship passengers, so it can be crowded.

TOURS OF THE ISLAND

To be frank, the best part of Cozumel isn't on land; it's in the water. Still, you might want to try a tour to do something different. Travel agencies can book you on a group tour of the island for around $40; the price depends on whether it includes lunch and a stop for snorkeling and swimming at Chankanaab Park. (If all you're interested in is Chankanaab, go by yourself and save money.) A taxi driver charges $60 for a 4-hour tour of the island, which most people would consider only mildly amusing, depending on the driver's personality. Also available are horseback tours of the island's interior jungle, a jungle Jeep tour, and a jungle ATV tour. The tours aren't spectacular: Most of the terrain is flat, and the interior is more scrublike than the term "jungle" would indicate. If you're interested in riding horseback, your best bet is to talk to the people at Cocos Cozumel restaurant (see the listing later in this chapter, making sure to note the limited hours). The owners are English speakers and are friends with the rancher who offers the tours. They can tell you about it and set you up if you're interested.

OTHER ATTRACTIONS

MAYA RUINS   One of the most popular island excursions is to **San Gervasio** (100 B.C.–A.D. 1600). Follow the paved transversal road. You'll see the well-marked turnoff about halfway between town and the eastern coast. Stop at the entrance gate and pay the $1 road-use fee. About 3km (2 miles) farther, pay the $5 fee to enter; still and video camera permits cost $5 each. A small tourist center at the entrance sells cold drinks and snacks.

When it comes to Cozumel's Maya remains, getting there is most of the fun—do it for the mystique and for the trip, not for the size or scale of the ruins. The buildings, though preserved, are crudely made and would not be much of a tourist attraction if they were not the island's principal ruins. More significant than beautiful, this site was once an important ceremonial center where the Maya gathered, coming even from the mainland. The important deity was Ixchel, the goddess of weaving, women, childbirth, pilgrims, the moon, and medicine. Although you won't see any representations of Ixchel at San Gervasio today, Bruce Hunter, in his *Guide to Ancient Maya Ruins,* writes that priests hid behind a large pottery statue of her and became the voice of the goddess, speaking to pilgrims and answering their petitions. Ixchel was the wife of Itzamná, the sun god.

Guides charge $10 for a tour for one to six people. A better option is to find a copy of the green booklet *San Gervasio,* sold at local checkout counters and bookstores, and tour the site on your own. Seeing it takes 30 minutes. Taxi drivers offer a tour to the ruins for about $25; the driver will wait for you outside the ruins.

A HISTORY MUSEUM   The **Museo de la Isla de Cozumel** ✈, Avenida Rafael Melgar between calles 4 and 6 Norte (© **987/872-1475**), is more than just a nice place to spend a rainy hour. On the first floor an excellent exhibit illustrates endangered species, the origin of the island, and its present-day topography and plant and animal life, including an explanation of coral formation. The second-floor galleries feature the history of the town, artifacts from the island's pre-Hispanic sites, and colonial-era cannons, swords, and ship paraphernalia. It's open daily from 9am to 5pm. Admission is $3. A good rooftop restaurant serves breakfast and lunch.

GOLF   Cozumel has a new 18-hole course designed by Jack Nicklaus. It's at the **Cozumel Country Club** (© **987/872-9570**), just north of San Miguel. Greens fees are $144, including tax. Tee times can be made 3 days in advance. A few hotels have special memberships with discounts for guests and advance tee times; Playa Azul Golf and Beach Club guests pay no greens fees, just the cart cost.

TRIPS TO THE MAINLAND

PLAYA DEL CARMEN & XCARET   Going on your own to the nearby sea-side village of **Playa del Carmen** and the **Xcaret** nature park is as easy as a quick ferry ride from Cozumel (for ferry information, see "Getting There & Depart-ing," earlier in this chapter). For information on Playa, see chapter 5; Xcaret is covered in chapter 3. Cozumel travel agencies offer an Xcaret tour that includes the ferry ride, transportation to the park, and the admission fee. The price is $90 for adults, $48 for kids. Available Monday through Saturday.

CHICHEN ITZA, TULUM & COBA   Travel agencies can arrange day trips to the fascinating ruins of **Chichén Itzá** ✦✦✦ by air or bus. The ruins of **Tulum** ✦, overlooking the Caribbean, and **Cobá** ✦, in a dense jungle setting, are closer and cost less to visit. These cities are quite a contrast to Chichén Itzá. Cobá is a grandiose, mostly unrestored city beside a lake in a remote jungle setting, while Tulum is smaller, more compact, and right on the beach. It's more intact than Cobá. A trip to both Cobá and Tulum begins at 8am and returns around 6pm. A shorter, more relaxing excursion goes to Tulum and the nearby nature park of Xel-Ha.

SHOPPING

If you like shopping for silver jewelry, you can spend a great deal of time examin-ing the wares of all the jewelers along Avenida Rafael Melgar. Some duty-free stores sell items such as perfumes and designer wares. If you're interested in Mexican folk art, there are three stores on Avenida Rafael Melgar that have merchandise better than what most stores offer: **Los Cinco Soles** (© **987/872-2040**), **Indigo** (© **987/ 872-1076**), and **Viva México** (© **987/872-5466**). There are also some import/export stores in the new Punta Langosta Shopping Center in the southern part of town in front of the Punta Langosta Pier. Prices for serapes, T-shirts, and the like are lower on the side streets off Avenida Melgar. Also off Melgar is a branch of **ARIPO,** the state-run Oaxacan handicrafts store (© **987/869-2145**). It's at the corner of Av. 5 and Calle 5 and displays some lovely merchandise. Across the street is a small gallery called **Casa Chaak** (no phone), which is the joint effort of eight island artists.

WHERE TO STAY

I've grouped Cozumel's hotels by location—**north** of town, **in town,** and **south** of town—and I describe them in that order. The prices I've quoted include the 12% tax. High season is from December to Easter, with a mini high season in August, when Mexican families vacation. Expect rates from Christmas to New Year's to be still higher than the regular high-season rates quoted here. Low sea-son is the rest of the year, though a few hotels raise their rates in August. All offer free parking.

All the large hotels and many smaller ones offer dive packages. All the large waterfront hotels have dive shops and a pier. And it's quite okay to stay at one hotel and dive with another operator—any dive boat can pull up to any hotel pier to pick up customers. Most dive shops don't pick up from the hotels north of town, so it's best to dive with the in-house operator at these places.

As an alternative to a hotel, you can try **Cozumel Vacation Villas and Con-dos,** Av. Rafael Melgar 685 (between calles 3 and 5 Sur), 77600 Cozumel, Q. Roo (© **800/224-5551** in the U.S., or 987/872-0729; www.cvvmexico.com), which offers accommodations by the week.

NORTH OF TOWN

Carretera Santa Pilar, or San Juan, is the name of Avenida Rafael Melgar's northern extension. All the hotels lie close to each other on the beach side of the road a short distance from town and the airport.

Expensive

Playa Azul Golf and Beach Hotel ★★★ This quiet hotel is perhaps the most relaxing of the island's beachfront properties. Its small, sandy beach, with shade *palapas*, is one of the best on this side of the island. Service is attentive and personal. Almost all the rooms have balconies and ocean views. The units in the original section are all suites—very large, with oversize bathrooms with showers. The new wing has mostly standard rooms that are comfortable and large, decorated with light tropical colors and rattan furniture. The corner rooms are master suites and have large balconies with Jacuzzis overlooking the sea. If you prefer lots of space over having a Jacuzzi, opt for a suite in the original building. Rooms contain a king bed or two double beds; suites offer two convertible single sofas in the separate living room. This is an especially good hotel for golfers, who play free (except for cart costs). The hotel also offers deep-sea- and fly-fishing trips. For a family or group, the hotel rents a garden house with lovely rooms.

Carretera San Juan Km 4, 77600 Cozumel, Q. Roo. © **987/872-0199** or 987/872-0043. Fax 987/872-0110. www.playa-azul.com. 50 units. High season $210–$230 double, $235–$335 suite; low season $125–$145 double, $180–$290 suite. Discounts and packages sometimes available. AE, MC, V. **Amenities:** Restaurant; 2 bars; medium-sized pool; unlimited golf privileges at Cozumel Country Club; watersports equipment/rentals; game room; tour info; room service until 11pm; in-room massage; babysitting; overnight laundry. *In room:* A/C, TV, fridge, coffeemaker, hair dryer on request, safe.

Moderate

Condumel Condobeach Apartments If you want some distance from the crowds, consider lodging here. It's not a full-service hotel, but in some ways it's more convenient. The one-bedroom apartments are designed and furnished in practical fashion—large and airy, with glass sliding doors that face the sea and allow for good cross-ventilation (especially in the upper units). They also have ceiling fans, air-conditioning, and two twin beds or one king. Each apartment has a separate living room and a full kitchen with a partially stocked fridge, so you don't have to run to the store on the first day. There's a small, well-tended beach area (with shade *palapas* and a grill for guests' use) that leads to a low, rocky fall-off into the sea.

Carretera Hotelera Norte s/n, 77600 Cozumel, Q. Roo. © **987/872-0892.** Fax 987/872-0661. www.aquasafari. com. 10 units. High season $135 double; low season $110 double. No credit cards. *In room:* A/C, kitchen, no phone.

Sol Cabañas del Caribe This hotel offers good rates for oceanfront lodging. It's quaint and a little worn. There's a small beach on one side and a nice snorkeling area by the rocky section in front of the restaurant (which is at the water's edge). You have a choice of two types of rooms for the same price. Medium-sized standard rooms in the two-story main section face the water and are comfortable but a little dark. These units have one double and one twin bed, a small sitting area, and a porch or a balcony. I prefer them to the one-story cabañas, which are smaller, with one double bed, but have patios near the pool. Bathrooms are small. Service is friendly. The owners also run the Paradisus, an all-inclusive hotel a little way up the coast.

Carretera Santa Pilar Km 4.5 (Apdo. Postal 9), 77600 Cozumel, Q. Roo. © **800/33MELIA** in the U.S. and Canada, or 987/872-0017. Fax 987/872-1599. paradisu@cozumel.com.mx. 48 units. High season $147–$164

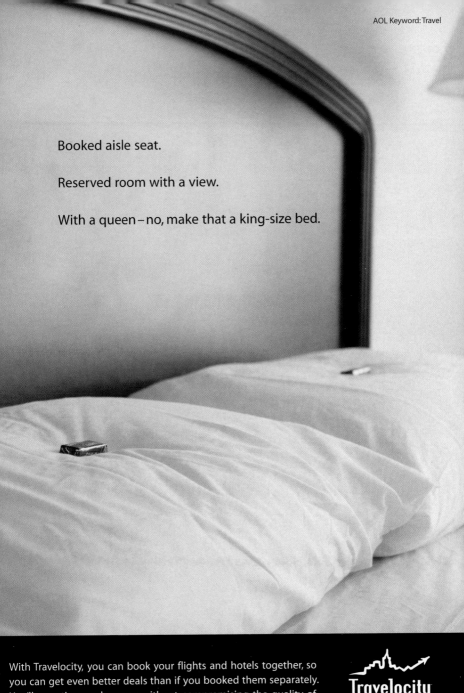

Booked aisle seat.

Reserved room with a view.

With a queen – no, make that a king-size bed.

With Travelocity, you can book your flights and hotels together, so you can get even better deals than if you booked them separately. You'll save time and money without compromising the quality of your trip. Choose your airline seat, search for alternate airports, pick your hotel room type, even choose the neighborhood you'd like to stay in

Travelocity®

Visit www.travelocity.com or call 1-888-TRAVELOCITY

double; low season $110 double. Honeymoon packages available. AE, MC, V. Free secured parking. **Amenities:** Restaurant; bar; small pool; wading pool; membership in local golf club; watersports equipment; tour desk; car rental; room service until 10:30pm; babysitting; overnight laundry. *In room:* A/C, no phone.

IN TOWN

Staying in town is not like staying in Playa del Carmen, where you can walk to the beach. The oceanfront in town is too busy for swimming, and there's no beach, only the *malecón*. Consequently, there's no real premium for staying close to the water. You'll have to drive or take a cab to the beach; it's pretty easy. The hotels in town are the most economical on the island (except for Hotel Plaza Las Glorias, which is an oceanfront hotel away from the harbor). The staff at almost all of them speaks English.

Very Expensive

Hotel Plaza Las Glorias ★★   This all-suite five-story hotel combines the top-notch amenities of the expensive hotels farther out with the convenience of being 5 blocks from town. For people who must have a beach, this is not the right hotel. Don't dismiss it out of hand, though; it has a smart terraced sunning area above the water, and easy access to the sea (a small dock with swimming-pool ladders). The split-level rooms are large and have separate sitting areas. The furniture and beds are comfortable, and the bathrooms are large, with stone countertops and tub/shower combinations. Bed choices include two doubles, two twins, or one king. All rooms face out over the water and have a balcony or a terrace. The dive shop comes highly recommended.

Av. Rafael Melgar Km 1.5, 77600 Cozumel, Q. Roo. © **800/342-AMIGO** in the U.S. and Canada, or 987/872-2588. Fax 987/872-1937. www.sidek.com.mx. 174 units. High season $280 double; low season $130 double. Promotional rates sometimes available. AE, MC, V. **Amenities:** Restaurant; 2 bars (1 swim-up); large pool; whirlpool; dive shop; watersports equipment rental; tour desk; car and moped rental; room service until 11pm; babysitting; same-day laundry. *In room:* A/C, TV, fridge, hair dryer, safe.

Moderate

Hotel del Centro   Five long blocks from the waterfront, this stylish two-story hotel is a bargain for those wanting a pool. The rooms are small to medium in size but modern and attractive. They come with two double beds or one king (costing $10 less). Bathrooms are medium-sized. The rooms surround a garden courtyard with an oval pool framed by comfortable lounge chairs.

Av. Juárez 501, 77600 Cozumel, Q. Roo. © **987/872-5471.** Fax 987/872-0299. hcentro@cozumel.com.mx. 14 units. High season $65–$75 double; low season $50–$60 double. Special discounts available. No credit cards. **Amenities:** Medium-sized pool. *In room:* A/C, TV.

Hotel Flamingo ★   A small hotel just off Avenida Rafael Melgar, the Flamingo offers three stories of attractive, comfortable rooms around a small, plant-filled inner courtyard. Highlights include an inviting rooftop terrace and a comfortable bar and coffee bar that serves breakfast. Second- and third-story rooms, which have air-conditioning and TV, cost more. Rooms are large, with two double beds, white-tile floors, medium-sized bathrooms, and ceiling fans. A penthouse suite comes with a full kitchen and sleeps up to six. The English-speaking staff is helpful and friendly.

Calle 6 Norte 81, 77600 Cozumel, Q. Roo. © **800/806-1601** in the U.S., or ©/fax 987/872-1264. www.hotel flamingo.com. 22 units. $39–$77 double. Discounts sometimes available. AE, MC, V. From the plaza, walk 3 blocks north on Av. Rafael Melgar and turn right on Calle 6; hotel is on the left. **Amenities:** Cafe; bar; scuba rental; tour info; car rental; overnight laundry. *In room:* A/C, no phone.

Suites Colonial   Around the corner from the main square, on a pedestrian-only street, you'll find this pleasant four-story hotel. Standard rooms, called "studios," are large, with large bathrooms and attractive red-tile floors, but they could be better lit. These units have one double and one twin bed and are trimmed in yellow pine, which seems oddly out of place here. The suites hold two double beds, a kitchenette, and a sitting and dining area. There's free coffee and sweet bread in the morning. When calling, specify the Colonial.

Av. 5 Sur 9 (Apdo. Postal 286), 77600 Cozumel, Q. Roo. © 877/228-6747 or 987/872-9080. Fax 987/872-9073. www.suitescolonial.com. 28 units. High season $57–$65 studio, $68–$75 suite; low season $50 studio, $58–$63 suite. Rates include continental breakfast. Extra person $14–$16. AE, MC, V. From the plaza, walk ½ block south on Av. 5 Sur; the hotel is on the left. *In room:* A/C, TV, fridge.

Inexpensive

B&B Caribo ★ *Value* Cindy Cooper, the American owner of this smartly painted blue-and-white B&B, goes out of her way to make guests feel at home. The rates are a good deal and include air-conditioning, breakfast, and several little extras. Six neatly decorated rooms come with cool tile floors, white furniture, and big bottles of purified drinking water; these units share a guest kitchen. The six apartments (3 have 1-month minimums) have small kitchens. Rooms have a double bed and a twin bed. There are a number of common rooms and a rooftop terrace. Breakfasts are full, and the cooking is good.

Av. Juárez 799, 77600 Cozumel, Q. Roo. © 987/872-3195. www.visit-caribo.com. 12 units. High season $50 double, $60 apartment; low season $35 double, $40 apartment. Rates include full breakfast. Long-term discounts available. Ask about yoga vacations. AE, MC, V. From the plaza, walk 6½ blocks inland on Juárez; Caribo is on the left. **Amenities:** Massage. *In room:* A/C.

Hotel Safari Inn This budget hotel offers a convenient location for divers: directly above the Aqua Safari Dive Shop and across the street from the shop's pier, which means that you don't have to lug your gear very far. The large rooms have little in the way of furniture aside from beds. They have small bathrooms with good hot showers. Some rooms could use better lighting, and in some the air-conditioning is noisy. The hotel becomes a real bargain when four or five people are willing to share a room (some units hold a king and 2 or 3 twin beds).

Av. Rafael Melgar, between calles 5 and 7 Sur (Apdo. Postal 41), 77600. Cozumel, Q. Roo. © 987/872-0101. Fax 987/872-0661. dive@aquasafari.com. 12 units. $45 double. MC, V. From the pier, turn right (south) and walk 4½ blocks on Melgar. *In room:* A/C, no phone.

SOUTH OF TOWN

The hotels in this area tend to be more spread out and farther from town than hotels to the north. Some are on the inland side of the road; some are on the beach side, which means a difference in price. Those farthest from town are all-inclusive properties. The beaches along this part of the coast tend to be slightly better than those to the north, but all the hotels have swimming pools and piers from which you can snorkel, and all of them accommodate divers. Head south on Avenida Rafael Melgar, which becomes the coastal road **Costera Sur** (also called **Carretera a Chankanaab**).

Very Expensive

Presidente InterContinental Cozumel ★★★ This is Cozumel's finest hotel in terms of location, on-site amenities, and service. Palatial in scale and modern in style, the Presidente spreads out across a long stretch of coast with only distant hotels for neighbors. Rooms come in four categories distributed throughout four buildings (2–5 stories tall). The "superior" or "garden-view" rooms are large and comfortable. Most are in the five-story building. The deluxe rooms are in a long two-story building facing the water. They described as "oceanfront" (2nd floor) and "beachfront" rooms (ground floor, with direct access to the beach). These two are pretty much the same except that one comes with a patio, the other with a balcony. They are oversize and have large, well-lit bathrooms. Guests in beachfront rooms can request in-room dining on the patio with a serenading trio. Most rooms come with a choice of one king-size or two double beds and are furnished in understated modern style. The 17 suites and reef rooms are extremely large and well furnished. A long stretch of sandy beach area dotted with *palapas* and palm trees fronts the entire hotel.

Costera Sur Km 6.5, 77600 Cozumel, Q. Roo. ⓒ **800/327-0200** in the U.S., or 987/872-9500. Fax 987/872-9528. www.cozumel.intercontinental.com. 253 units. High season $224–$280 garden-view, $352–$392 oceanfront/beachfront, reef rooms and suites from $730; low season $197–$224 garden-view, $258–$308 oceanfront/beachfront, reef rooms and suites from $615. Discounts and packages available. AE, DC, MC, V. **Amenities:** 2 restaurants (international, Mexican); snack bar; 2 bars; large pool; wading pool; access to golf club; 2 lighted tennis courts; fully equipped gym; whirlpool; dive shop; watersports equipment rental; children's activities center; concierge; tour desk; car rental; business center; shopping arcade; 24-hr. room service; in-room massage; babysitting; same-day laundry; dry cleaning; nonsmoking rooms. *In room:* A/C, TV w/pay movies, dataport, minibar, hair dryer.

Expensive

El Cid La Ceiba ★★   On the beach side of the road, La Ceiba is a fun place to stay. It has snorkeling and shore diving to a submerged airplane (the hotel provides unlimited tanks) in front of the hotel. Lots of divers come here: it is the Mares Hub system center for Cozumel and was voted one of the world's top 15 dive resorts in *Rodale's Scuba Diving* magazine. All rooms have ocean views, balconies, and two doubles or one king bed. Bathrooms are roomy and well lit, with granite countertops and strong water pressure. Superior rooms are larger than standard and have more furniture. Some suites are available for limited periods and only to guests who make direct reservations, not to groups. The emphasis here is on watersports, particularly scuba diving, but nondivers can enjoy the large pool area, tennis court, and seaside restaurant.

Costera Sur Km 4.5 (Apdo. Postal 284), 77600 Cozumel, Q. Roo. ⓒ **800/435-3240** in the U.S., or 987/872-0844. Fax 987/872-0065. www.elcid.com. 98 units. $105–$165 standard; $126–$188 superior. Ask for the Frommer's discount. AE, MC, V. **Amenities:** 2 restaurants; 2 bars; 2 large pools; access to golf club; lighted tennis court; small exercise room with sauna; whirlpool; dive shop; watersports equipment rental; tour desk; car rental; room service until 10:30pm; in-room massage; babysitting; laundry. *In room:* A/C, TV, fridge, coffeemaker.

WHERE TO DINE

The island offers a number of good restaurants. Taxi drivers will often steer you toward restaurants that pay them commissions, so don't heed their advice.

    Zermatt (ⓒ **987/872-1384**), a terrific little bakery, is on Avenida 5 at Calle 4 Norte.

VERY EXPENSIVE

Cabaña del Pescador (Lobster House) ★★★ LOBSTER   The thought I often have when I eat a prepared lobster dish is that the cook could have simply boiled the lobster to better effect. The owner of this restaurant seems to agree. The only item on the menu is lobster boiled with a hint of spices and served with melted butter, accompanied by sides of rice, vegetables, and bread. The weight of the lobster you select determines the price, with side dishes included. Candles and soft lights illuminate the inviting dining rooms set amid gardens, fountains, and a small duck pond—*muy romántico*. The owner, Fernando, welcomes you warmly and will even send you next door to his brother's excellent Mexican seafood restaurant, El Guacamayo, if you must have something other than lobster.

Km 4 Carretera Santa Pilar (across from Playa Azul Hotel). No phone. Lobster (by weight) $19–$30. No credit cards. Daily 6–10:30pm.

Pepe's Grill ★★ STEAKS/SEAFOOD The chefs at Pepe's seem fascinated with fire; what they don't grill in the kitchen, they flambé at your table. The most popular grilled items are the good-quality beef (prime rib or filet mignon) and the lobster. For something out of the ordinary, try shrimp Bahamas, flambéed with a little banana and pineapple in a curry sauce. Pepe's is a second-story restaurant with one large air-conditioned dining room under a massive beamed ceiling. The lighting is soft, and a guitar trio plays background music. Large windows look out over the harbor. The children's menu offers breaded shrimp and broiled chicken. For dessert there are more incendiary specialties: bananas Foster, crêpes Suzettes, and café Maya (coffee, vanilla ice cream, and 3 liqueurs).

Av. Rafael Melgar (at Salas). © 987/872-0213. Reservations recommended. Main courses $18–$35; children's menu $7. AE, MC, V. Daily 5–11:30pm.

EXPENSIVE

French Quarter ★★ LOUISIANA/SOUTHERN In a pleasant upstairs open-air setting, French Quarter serves Southern and Creole classics. I found the jambalaya and étouffée delicious. You also have the choice of dining indoors or having a cocktail in the downstairs bar. The menu lists blackened fish (very good) and fresh lump crabmeat. Filet mignon with red-onion marmalade is a specialty of the house.

Av. 5 Sur 18. © 987/872-6321. Reservations recommended during Carnaval. Main courses $10–$27. AE, MC, V. Daily 5–10:30pm.

La Veranda ★★★ SEAFOOD/INTERNATIONAL This is the perfect place to go if you're getting tired of fried fish or fish with achiote sauce, or if you just want something different. The highly inventive menu emphasizes tropical ingredients and fuses West Indian with European cooking. Every dish I tried here was delicious and artfully presented. The spiced mussel soup had a delicious broth scented with white wine. Veranda mango fish included a mango sauce that was both light and satisfying. And Palancar coconut shrimp consisted of shrimp boiled in a coconut sauce with little bits of raw (not sweet) coconut. The indoor and outdoor dining areas are airy and quite pleasant. You can hear soft jazz and the whirring of ceiling fans in the background. The tables are well separated and attractively set.

Calle 4 Norte (between avs. 5 and 10). © 987/872-4132. Reservations recommended during high season. Main courses $14–$20. MC, V. Daily 4:30pm–midnight.

Prima ★★★ NORTHERN ITALIAN Everything at this ever-popular hangout is fresh—pastas, vegetables, and seafood. Owner Albert Domínguez grows most of the vegetables in his local hydroponic garden. The menu changes daily and concentrates on seafood. It might include shrimp scampi, fettuccine with pesto, and lobster and crab ravioli with cream sauce. The fettuccine Alfredo is wonderful, the salads crisp, and the steaks USDA choice. Pizzas are cooked in a wood-burning oven. Desserts include Key lime pie and tiramisu. Dining is upstairs on the breezy terrace.

Calle Rosado Salas 109A (corner of Av. 5) © 987/872-4242. Reservations recommended during high season. Pizzas and pastas $6–$10; seafood $10–$20; steaks $15–$20. AE, MC, V. Daily 5–11pm.

MODERATE

El Moro ★ REGIONAL Crowds flock to El Moro for its good food, service, and prices—but not its decor, which is orange, orange, orange, and Formica. And it's 12 blocks inland, away from everything; a taxi, costing around $2.25, is a must. But all misgivings will disappear as soon as you taste the food (and especially if you sip one of the giant, wallop-packing margaritas). Portions are generous. *Pollo Ticuleño,* a specialty from the town of Ticul, is a rib-sticking, delicious, layered plate of smooth tomato sauce, mashed potatoes, crispy baked corn tortilla, and batter-fried chicken breast, all topped with shredded cheese and green peas. Besides the regional food, other specialties include enchiladas and seafood prepared many ways, plus grilled steaks and sandwiches.

75 BIS Norte 124 (between calles 2 and 4 Norte). ⓒ **987/872-3029.** Reservations not accepted. Main courses $6–$15. MC, V. Fri–Wed 1–11pm.

Guido's ⭐ MEDITERRANEAN   The inviting interior, with sling chairs and rustic wood tables, makes this a restful place in daytime and a romantic spot at night. The specialty is oven-baked pizzas. Also keep an eye out for the daily specials, which may include an appetizer of sea bass carpaccio, a couple of meat dishes, and usually a fish dish. The other thing that people love here is *pan de ajo*—a house creation of bread made with olive oil, garlic, and rosemary. There's a good, well-priced wine list.

Av. Rafael Melgar, between calles 6 and 8 Norte. ⓒ **987/872-0946.** Main courses $8–$13; daily specials $10–$14. AE. Mon–Sat 11am–11pm.

La Choza ⭐ YUCATECAN/MEXICAN   Local residents consider this one of the best Mexican restaurants in town. Platters of poblano chiles stuffed with shrimp, *fajitas,* and *pollo en relleno negro* (chicken in a sauce of scorched chiles) are among the specialties. The table sauces and guacamole are great, and the daily specials can be good, too. This is an open-air restaurant with well-spaced tables under a tall thatched roof.

Rosado Salas 198 (at Av. 10 Sur). ⓒ **987/872-0958.** Reservations accepted for groups of 6 or more. Breakfast $4; main courses $9–$15. AE, MC, V. Daily 7am–11pm.

INEXPENSIVE

Casa Denis REGIONAL/MEXICAN   This yellow wooden house, one of the few remaining residences built in the old island style, is a great home-style Mexican restaurant. Small tables are scattered outside on the pedestrian-only street. More tables are in back, on the shady patio. You can make a light meal of empanadas filled with potatoes, cheese, or fish. Better yet, try one of the Yucatecan specialties, such as *pollo pibil, panuchos,* or *tacos de cochinita pibil.*

Calle 1 Sur 267 (just off the main plaza). ⓒ **987/872-0067.** Breakfast $3–$5; main courses $7–$10. No credit cards. Mon–Sat 7am–11pm; Sun 5–11pm.

Cocos Cozumel MEXICAN/AMERICAN   Cocos offers the largest breakfast menu on the island, including all the American and Mexican classics, from *huevos divorciados* to ham and eggs. Indulge in stateside favorites like hash browns, corn flakes and bananas, gigantic blueberry muffins, cinnamon rolls, and bagels, or go for something with tropical ingredients, like a blended fruit drink. The service and the food are excellent. The American and Mexican owners, Terri and Daniel Ocejo, are good folk and can set you up with a horseback ride or a fishing or snorkeling trip.

Av. 5 Sur 180 (1 block south of the main plaza). ⓒ **987/872-0241.** Breakfast $3–$6. No credit cards. Tues–Sun 6am–noon. Closed Sept–Oct.

Comida Casera Toñita HOME-STYLE YUCATECAN   The owners have made the living room of their home into a comfortable dining room, complete with filled bookshelves and classical music playing in the background. Whole fried fish, fish filet, and fried chicken are on the regular menu. Daily specials give you a chance to taste authentic regional food, including *pollo a la naranja* (chicken in bitter-orange sauce), chicken *mole* (in a vinegar-based sauce), *pollo en escabeche* (chicken stewed in a lightly pickled sauce), and pork chops with achiote seasoning.

Calle Rosado Salas 265 (between avs. 10 and 15). (© 987/872-0401. Breakfast $1.75–$3; main courses $4–$7; daily specials $3; fruit drinks $2. No credit cards. Mon–Sat 8am–6pm.

Restaurant del Museo BREAKFAST/MEXICAN   The most pleasant place in San Miguel to have breakfast or lunch (weather permitting) is at this rooftop cafe above the island's museum. It offers a serene view of the water, removed from the traffic noise below and sheltered from the sun above. The tables and chairs are comfortable and the food reliable. Choices are limited to the mainstays of American and Mexican breakfasts, and lunch dishes such as enchiladas and guacamole.

Av. Rafael Melgar (corner of Calle 6 Norte). (© 987/872-0838. Reservations not accepted. Breakfast $4–$5; lunch main courses $5–$9. No credit cards. Daily 7am–2pm.

COZUMEL AFTER DARK

Cozumel attracts divers and other active visitors who play hard all day and wind down at night. The nightlife scene is often low-key and peaks in the early evening. The exception is the cruise-ship crowd. Most of the music and dance venues are in two areas: one is just north of the main plaza on Rafael Melgar, and includes the **Hard Rock Cafe** (© 987/872-5271); the other is in the Punta Langosta shopping center, in front of the pier of the same name, not far from Hotel Plaza Las Glorias. Here you'll find **Carlos 'n' Charlie's** (© 987/869-1646) and **Señor Frog's** (© 987/869-1651). On Sunday evenings the place to be is the main square, which usually has a free concert and lots of people strolling about and visiting with friends. People sit in outdoor cafes enjoying the cool night breezes until the restaurants close.

The town of San Miguel has three movie theaters. Your best option is **Cinépolis,** the modern multicinema in the Chedraui Plaza Shopping Center, across Avenida Melgar from the Plaza Las Glorias Hotel. It mainly shows Hollywood movies. Most of these are in English with Spanish subtitles *(película subtitulada),* but before buying your tickets, make sure the movie hasn't been dubbed *(doblada).*

The Riviera Maya

5

Perhaps it's worth reiterating that the Riviera Maya has "endless stretches of pristine beaches of soft white sand gently caressed by the turquoise-blue waters of the Caribbean," yadda, yadda, yadda . . . but my bet is that you've already heard it all. You've seen the brochures, the articles in the Sunday travel sections, and the ads. (And if you haven't, then where have you been?) Even so, I don't think I have it in me to join the chorus of travel writers singing the region's praises. And I suspect that your reason for buying this book was different anyway. So let's get down to it.

Mexico has 384km (240 miles) of Caribbean coast, stretching from Cancún south all the way to Chetumal, at the border with Belize. The northern half of the coast has been dubbed the "Riviera Maya"; the southern half, the "Costa Maya."

A large reef system, the second largest in the world, protects most of the shore. Where there are gaps in the reef—Playa del Carmen, Xpu-Ha, and Tulum—you find good beaches. The action of the surf washes away silt and seagrass and erodes rocks, leaving a sandy bottom. Where the reef is prominent, you get good snorkeling and diving with lots of fish and other sea creatures. Here mangrove often occupies the shoreline; the beaches are usually sandy up to the water's edge, but shallow, with a silty or rocky floor.

Inland, you'll find jungle, caverns, the famous *cenotes* (wells), and the even more famous ruins of the Maya. Activities abound.

So do lodging options. On this coast you can stay in a wide variety of communities or distance yourself from all of them. There's just about every choice you can think of: rustic cabins, secluded spa resorts, boutique hotels, B&B's, all-inclusive megaresorts, whatever you want. The problem is that with so many options, you need to make some decisions. I hope that what follows will help.

EXPLORING MEXICO'S CARIBBEAN COAST

A single road, Highway 307, runs down the coast from Cancún to Chetumal. The section between Cancún and Playa del Carmen (51km/32 miles) is a four-lane divided highway with speed limits up to 110kmph (68 mph). There are a couple of traffic lights and several reduced-speed zones around the major turnoffs. From Playa to Tulum (131km/82 miles from Cancún), the road becomes a smooth two-lane highway with wide shoulders. Speed limits are the same, but more places require you to reduce your speed. It takes around 1½ hours to drive from the Cancún airport to Tulum.

From Tulum, the highway turns inland to skirt the edges of Sian Ka'an. The roadway is narrower, without shoulders, and in some areas the forest crowds in on both sides. The speed limit is mostly 90kmph (56 mph), but you'll need to slow down in several places, and you must watch for speed bumps *(topes)* where the road passes through villages and towns. To drive from Tulum to Chetumal takes a little more than 3 hours.

Tips **The Best Websites for Playa del Carmen &**
the Caribbean Coast

- **Cancún South: www.cancunsouth.com**   Billed as a guide for independent travelers, this site has itineraries and detailed driving instructions, plus tips on lodgings and attractions in the areas south of Cancún.
- **Ecotravels in Mexico: www2.planeta.com/mader/ecotravel/mexico/mexico.html**   This site covers the whole country and has a nice section on the Yucatán (about halfway down the page).
- **Kuartos.com: www.kuartos.com**   Here's a well-designed and easy-to-use site for finding hotels and making reservations throughout Cancún and the Riviera Maya. Each hotel listing has a photo and detailed description (plus lowest rates) and allows you to check availability and make reservations. It also features super specials for selected properties.
- _Playa_ **Magazine Online: www.playadelcarmen.com**   This online version of the popular guide offers plenty of tips, news, and tourist information for those bound for Playa del Carmen.
- **The Net Traveler: www.thenettraveler.com**   This site specializes in information about the Yucatán, Quintana Roo (home state of Cancún), and Chiapas, as well as other areas in the old Maya empire. Its information on archaeological sites, as well as on diving in the region's caves and _cenotes,_ is especially good.

PLAYA DEL CARMEN   Playa, as it is called, is the most happening place on the coast—lots of beach (especially when the wind and currents are flowing in the right direction), hotels for every budget, a good choice of restaurants, and an active nightlife, most of which is on or around Avenida 5, Playa's very popular promenade. In the last few years the town has grown quickly, and local residents and the tourism board are working hard to keep it from becoming a smaller version of Cancún. They are encouraging builders to use the same kind of tropical, slightly quirky architectural style that the town has become known for.

PUERTO MORELOS   This town 30 minutes south of Cancún remains a sleepy little village affectionately known by the locals as "Muerto Morelos." It has a few small hotels and rental houses, and in the vicinity are a few secluded spa resorts. The coast is sandy and well protected by an offshore reef, which means good snorkeling and diving nearby, but the lack of surf means lots of seagrass and shallow water. If you're looking for good swimming, you should head farther down the coast. If you're looking for a quiet seaside retreat, this might work for you.

AKUMAL   The community at Akumal and Half Moon Bay is relatively old for this shore, which means that it's already built up and doesn't have the boomtown feel of Playa and Tulum. Akumal has a strong ecological orientation. The locals are a mix of Americans and Mexicans, who enjoy the unhurried lifestyle of the tropics, making this a good place to relax and work on your hammock technique. There are a few hotels; most of the lodging is rental houses. Consequently, the town is a favorite with families who enjoy the calmness of the place and can save money by buying groceries and cooking for themselves.

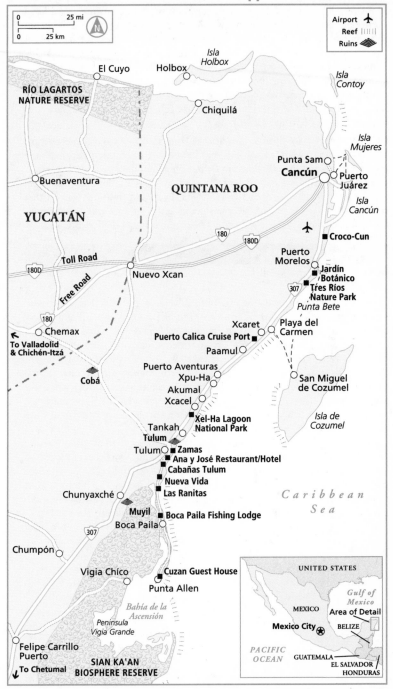

0   25 mi
0   25 km

N

Airport ✈
Reef ||||||
Ruins

Isla Holbox

El Cuyo   Holbox

Isla Contoy

RÍO LAGARTOS NATURE RESERVE

Chiquilá

Isla Mujeres

Punta Sam
Cancún
Puerto Juárez

Buenaventura   **QUINTANA ROO**

Isla Cancún

YUCATÁN

■ Croco-Cun

180

180D

Puerto Morelos

■ **Jardín Botánico**

307

■ **Tres Ríos Nature Park**

Toll Road

180D

Punta Bete

Free Road

Nuevo Xcan

180

Chemax

Xcaret   Playa del Carmen

← To Valladolid & Chichén-Itzá

Puerto Calica Cruise Port ■

Paamul

Puerto Aventuras
Xpu-Ha

Cobá

Akumal
Xcacel

San Miguel de Cozumel

■ **Xel-Ha Lagoon National Park**

Tankah

Isla de Cozumel

Tulum
Tulum ■ ■ **Zamas**
■ **Ana y José Restaurant/Hotel**
■ **Cabañas Tulum**
■ **Nueva Vida**
■ **Las Ranitas**

C a r i b b e a n S e a

Chunyaxché

Muyil ■
Boca Paila

■ **Boca Paila Fishing Lodge**

307

Chumpón

Vigia Chíco   ■ **Cuzan Guest House**
Punta Allen

Bahía de la Ascensión

Península Vigia Grande

Felipe Carrillo Puerto

↙ To Chetumal

SIAN KA'AN BIOSPHERE RESERVE

UNITED STATES

Gulf of Mexico

MEXICO

Area of Detail

Mexico City ✪

BELIZE

PACIFIC OCEAN

GUATEMALA

EL SALVADOR
HONDURAS

TULUM   The town of Tulum (near the ruins of the same name) has a hotel district of about 30 *palapa* hotels, which stretch down the coast of the Punta Allen peninsula. A few years ago it was mainly a destination for backpacker types, but with some of the most beautiful beaches on this coast and many improvements in hotel amenities, it now attracts people with bigger budgets. Construction is booming, both in the town and along the coast. Here you can enjoy the beach in relative solitude and quiet (unless your hotel is busy building additional rooms). The flip side of this is that Tulum doesn't have the variety of restaurants that Playa and Cancún do.

COSTA MAYA   South of Tulum lies the large Sian Ka'an Biosphere Preserve and, beyond that, what is known as the Costa Maya, a term that designates the rest of the coast all the way down to Belize. This coast does not have beaches as good as those of the Riviera Maya. Most of the coast is along the Majahual Peninsula, which is very attractive for scuba divers and fly fishermen. Farther south is Lake Bacalar, a large, clear freshwater lake fed by *cenotes* (wells or sinkholes). Inland from here are the many fascinating ruins of the Río Bec area.

1 Playa del Carmen ★★★

32km (20 miles) S of Puerto Morelos, 70km (44 miles) S of Cancún, 10km (6½ miles) N of Xcaret, 13km (8 miles) N of Puerto Calica

Though it no longer has the feel of a village, Playa still provides that rare combination of simplicity (it's a small town that can be traversed on foot) and variety (in the many one-of-a-kind hotels, restaurants, and stores). The town has a casual, comfortable feel. The local architecture has adopted elements of native building—rustic clapboard walls, thatched roofs, lots of tropical foliage, roughhewn wood, and a ramshackle, unplanned look to many structures that reflects the town's taste for third-world chic. Slicker architecture has appeared, with chain restaurants and stores, which detract from Playa's individuality. But it remains a cosmopolitan counterculture getaway, and that's what makes it so different from the rest of the coast.

Playa is perfect for enjoying the simple (and perhaps the best) pleasures of a seaside vacation—taking in the sun and the sea air while working your toes into the sand; cooling down with a swim in clear water; and strolling aimlessly down the beach while listening to the wash of waves and feeling the light touch of tropical breezes on your skin. A strong European influence has made topless sunbathing (nominally against the law in Mexico) a nonchalantly accepted practice anywhere there's a beach. The beach grows and shrinks, from broad and sandy to narrower with occasional rocks, depending on the currents and wind. When this happens, head to the beaches in north Playa.

From Playa it's easy to shoot out to Cozumel on the ferry, to drive south to the nature parks and the ruins at Tulum and Cobá, or to drive north to Cancún. Directly south of town is the Playacar development, which has a golf course, 13 large all-inclusive resorts, and a residential section. Farther south, at Calica, is the cruise-ship pier.

ESSENTIALS

GETTING THERE & DEPARTING   By Air   You can fly into Cancún and take a bus directly from the airport (see "By Bus," below), or fly into Cozumel and take the passenger ferry.

■ ACCOMMODATIONS
Albatros Royale **8**
Deseo Hotel & Lounge **5**
El Faro Hotel & Beach Club **7**
Hotel Jungla Caribe **11**
Hotel La Tortuga **1**
Hotel Lunata **12**
Treetops **9**
Villa Catarina Rooms
  & Cabañas **2**

◆ DINING
Ambasciata D'Italia **4**
Casa Mediterranea **13**
Estas Son Las Mañanitas **14**
La Casa del Agua **15**
La Parrilla **10**
Media Luna **3**
Tarraya Restaurant & Bar **16**
Yaxché **6**

BY CAR Highway 307, which connects Cancún with Tulum, is the only highway that passes through Playa. As you approach Playa from Cancún, the highway divides. Stay left; you'll be able to make a left turn at either of two traffic lights. The first is Avenida Constituyentes, which works well for destinations in northern Playa. The second is Avenida Juárez, the artery connecting the highway to the town's main square and ferry pier. If you don't get over to the left when the highway divides, you must continue past Playa until you get to a turnaround, then double back, this time staying to your right.

BY THE PLAYA DEL CARMEN–COZUMEL PASSENGER FERRY Air-conditioned passenger ferries run to and from Cozumel. **Barcos México (© 987/872-1508** or 987/872-1588) offers departures almost every hour between 5am and midnight. The trip takes 30 to 45 minutes, depending on the boat, and costs $9 one-way. In Playa, the ferry dock is 1½ blocks from the main square. In Cozumel, ferries use the town pier (Muelle Fiscal), a block from the main square. Schedules are subject to change, so check at the docks for departure times—especially the time of the last returning ferry, if you intend to use it.

For information about the car ferry that connects Cozumel and Puerto Morelos, 32km (20 miles) north of Playa, see "Getting There & Departing" in the Cozumel section of chapter 4.

BY TAXI Taxi fares from the Cancún airport are high—about $70 one-way.

> ### ⟨*Tips* Pickpocket Alert
>
> I have spoken with travelers who've had their pockets picked while trying to claim their luggage after the ferry ride to or from Cozumel. Crowds form around the baggage claim area, creating excellent working conditions for pickpockets. By waiting only a couple of minutes for the crowd to dissipate, you can avoid this risk.

BY BUS   Autobuses Riviera offers service from the Cancún airport about 12 times a day. Cost is $7 one-way. You'll see a ticket counter in the corridor leading out of the airport. Buses to Playa from the Cancún bus station are plentiful.

ORIENTATION

ARRIVING   The **ferry** dock in Playa del Carmen is 1½ blocks from the main square and within walking distance of hotels. Playa has two **bus** stations. Buses coming from Cancún and places along the coast, such as Tulum, arrive at the Riviera bus station, at the corner of Juárez and Avenida 5, by the town square. Buses coming from destinations in the interior of the peninsula arrive at the new ADO station, on Avenida 20 between 12th and 14th streets. The Puerto Calica **cruise ship** pier is 13km (8 miles) south of Playa del Carmen; taxis meet each ship.

CITY LAYOUT   Locals know and use street names, but few street signs exist. The main street, **Avenida Juárez,** leads to the *zócalo* (town square) from Highway 307. As it does so, it crosses several numbered avenues that run parallel to the beach, all of which are multiples of 5. Avenida 5 is closest to the beach; it's closed to traffic from the *zócalo* to Calle 6 (and some blocks beyond, in the evening). On this avenue are many hotels, restaurants, and shops. Almost all of the town is north and west of the *zócalo.* Immediately south are the ferry pier and the Continental Plaza Playacar Hotel. This is the southern edge of town. Beyond it are the airstrip and the golf course development called Playacar, with lots of private residences and a dozen resort hotels.

 FAST FACTS: **Playa del Carmen**

Area Code   The telephone area code is **984.**

Doctor   Dr. E. Medina Peniche (© **984/873-0134**) speaks English and can be reached around the clock.

Internet Access   There are plenty of Internet cafes with fast connections. Sometimes it seems as if there is one on every block.

Money Exchange   Playa has several banks with ATMs. Many currency-exchange houses are close to the pier or along Avenida 5 at Calle 8. There is a bank and teller machine at the corner of Avenida 10 and Calle 12.

Parking   Because of Playa's pedestrian-only blocks and increasing population and popularity, parking close to hotels has become more difficult. The most accessible parking lot is the Estacionamiento Mexico, at Avenida Juárez and Avenida 10. It's open daily 24 hours and charges $1.25 per hour, $8 per day. There's also a 24-hour lot a block from the pier, where you can leave your car while you visit Cozumel.

Pharmacy The **Farmacia del Carmen,** Avenida Juárez between avenidas 5 and 10 (© 984/873-2330), states on its sign that it's open 24 hours, but sometimes it closes at midnight. If it's not open, there are a few others on that same avenue.

Post Office The *correo,* on Avenida Juárez 3 blocks from the plaza, is on the right past the Hotel Playa del Carmen and the launderette.

Seasons The main high season is from mid-December to Easter. There is a mini high season in August. Low season is all other months.

EXPLORING PLAYA DEL CARMEN

The main activity in Playa is hanging out on the beach and enjoying the Avenida 5 nightlife. But, as is the case just about anywhere on this coast, you can always line up a snorkel or scuba trip. A number of shops, including **Tank-Ha Dive Center** (© **984/873-0302;** fax 984/873-1355; www.tankha.com), arrange reef and cavern diving. The owner, Alberto Leonard, came to Playa by way of Madrid and offers reef and *cenote* diving excursions. He and his staff speak English. Snorkeling trips cost around $30 and include soft drinks and equipment. Two-tank dive trips are $55; resort courses with SSI and PADI instructors cost $75.

If golf is your bag, an 18-hole championship **golf course** (© **984/873-0624**), designed by Robert Von Hagge, is adjacent to the Continental Plaza Playacar. Greens fees are $120 (including tax and cart), caddies cost $20, and club rental costs $20. The club also has two **tennis** courts.

Day-trip possibilities include **Xcaret, Xel-Ha,** and **Tulum.** (See the Tulum section later in this chapter and "Eco-Theme Parks & Reserves," in chapter 3.) The magnificent ruins of Chichén Itzá are 2½ hours away. Several agencies offer tours to these and other places; most run large tour buses from the all-inclusive resorts in Playacar. They usually add stops (sometimes welcome, sometimes annoying) at places where you can buy food, drinks, or souvenirs. For smaller tours, contact **Alltournative** (© **984/873-2036;** www.alltournative.com), or book one of its tours through one of the local travel agencies. In addition to trips to the ruins, Alltournative offers adventure and ecological tours to places such as Sian Ka'an.

Cozumel, a 30-minute ferry ride, can be a day trip, but I don't believe it appears to best advantage in a short visit. You'll pretty much see exactly what the cruise-ship passengers see—lots of duty-free, souvenir, and jewelry shops. To enjoy Cozumel, you have to spend at least a couple of nights there. See chapter 4.

WHERE TO STAY

Playa has a lot of small hotels with affordable prices that can be more fun than one of the resorts outside of town. Don't hesitate to book a place that's not on the beach. Town life here is much of the fun, and staying on the beach in Playa has its disadvantages—in particular, the noise of a couple of beachside bars. Beaches are public property in Mexico, and you can lay out your towel anywhere you like without anyone bothering you. If you want a quiet room on the beach, consider the **Shangri-La Caribe,** listed below. It's on the outskirts of town, far from the bars but within walking distance or a short taxi ride of downtown.

High season is from mid-December to Easter. Late July and August is high season for some hotels and low season for others. In low season you can come to Playa and look for walk-in offers. The rates listed below include the 12%

hotel tax. I don't include the rates for Christmas and New Year's, which are higher than the standard high-season rates.

VERY EXPENSIVE

El Faro Hotel and Beach Club ★★   Rooms encircle a lawn graced by palm trees and gardens fronting 75m (82 yd.) of sandy beachfront. A stunning pool (heated in winter) has islands of palms inside and is bordered by cushioned lounges and a *palapa* bar. The rooms, most of which are in a long three-story building running perpendicular to the beach, are attractive, with clay-tile and marble floors, ceiling fans, and rattan furniture. The bathrooms are large and smart looking, with lots of marble countertop. Bed choices include one king, one queen, or two double beds. Most rooms have a balcony or terrace. Rates for deluxe rooms vary according to location—"oceanfront," "oceanview," or "gardenview"—and the time of year. Oceanfront rooms are right on the beach and are larger than the others, but occasionally the music from the beach bars can drift in. Five smaller "standard" rooms in the back of the property come without air-conditioning and are cheaper. A working lighthouse fronts the beach.

Calle 10 Norte, 77710 Playa del Carmen, Q. Roo. ⓒ 888/243-7413 from the U.S., or 984/873-0970. Fax 984/873-0968. www.hotelelfaro.com. 28 units. High season $190–$240 deluxe with A/C, $110–$150 without A/C; low season $150–$185 deluxe with A/C, $97–$134 without A/C. Rates include full breakfast. Look for Internet specials. AE, MC, V. Limited free guarded parking. **Amenities:** Restaurant; bar; pool; watersports equipment; tour info; ground transfer; limited room service; massage; babysitting. *In room:* Hair dryers in room or available on request.

Shangri-La Caribe ★★★   This hotel—a grouping of cabanas on one of the best beaches in Playa—is hard to beat for sheer fun and leisure. And it's far enough from the center of town to be quiet yet convenient. The older, south side of the hotel (the "Caribe" section) consists of one- and two-story cabanas. The north ("Playa") side is a few larger buildings, generally holding several rooms. A preference for one or the other section is a matter of taste; the units in both are similar in amenities, privacy, and price. The real difference in price depends on the proximity to the water—beachfront, oceanview, or garden view. Garden view is the best bargain, being only a few steps farther from the water. Many garden-view rooms (mostly in a 3rd section called "Pueblo") have air-conditioning, which adds only $6 to the price. All rooms have a patio or porch complete with hammock. Most come with two double beds, but a few have a king bed. Windows are screened, and ceiling fans circulate the breeze. Book well in advance during high season.

Calle 38 (Apdo. Postal 253), 77710 Playa del Carmen, Q. Roo. ⓒ 800/538-6802 in the U.S. or Canada, or 984/873-0611. Fax 984/873-0500. www.shangri-la.com.mx. 107 units. High season $180 garden view, $200–$250 oceanview or beachfront; low season $140 garden view, $160–$200 oceanview or beachfront. Rates include breakfast and dinner. AE, MC, V. Free guarded parking. From Hwy. 307 from Cancún, U-turn at the light for Av. Constituyentes, making sure to get into the far right lane. Backtrack to the Volkswagen dealership, turn right, and head for the beach. This will be Calle 38. **Amenities:** 2 restaurants; poolside grill; 3 bars; 2 large pools; whirlpool; watersports equipment; game room; tour desk; car rental; ground transfer; dive shop; in-room massage; babysitting; overnight laundry. *In room:* Hair dryer, no phone.

EXPENSIVE

Deseo Hotel + Lounge ★★★   In a town where being hip is a *raison d'être*, there is no hotel hipper than this one. Its creators, the owners of Habita in Mexico City, seem to want to redefine the idea of hotel. In the interest of accentuating the social aspect of travel, the lounge is central to their concept. It appropriates the functions that in a conventional hotel would be filled by the lobby, the restaurant, the bar, and the pool area. This lounge is an expansive, open-air platform with a pool, a bar, and large daybeds for sunning during the day or for sitting on at night, when the bar is in full swing. It's all very hip. The clientele is predominantly 25- to 45-year-olds, and the tunes tend to be contemporary chill-out music.

The guest rooms are off the lounge; most have sliding doors of wood and frosted glass that make me think of Japan. An Asian-style scarcity of furniture reminds me of Japan, too. The mattresses, however, are thick, luxurious, and inviting. All rooms come with king beds. From the bottom of the bed, a little drawer slides out with a night kit provided by the hotel. It contains three things: incense, earplugs, and condoms.

Av. 5 (at Calle 12), 77710 Playa del Carmen, Q. Roo. (©) **984/879-3620.** Fax 984/879-3621. www.hoteldeseo. com. 15 units. High season $160 loungeview, $180 balcony, $220 suite; low season $140 loungeview, $160 balcony, $190 suite. Rates include continental breakfast. AE, MC, V. No parking. Children not accepted. **Amenities:** Bar; small rooftop pool; Jacuzzi; tour info; ground transfer; room service until 11pm; in-room massage; overnight laundry. *In room:* A/C, minibar, hair dryer on request, safe.

MODERATE

Albatros Playa   The Albatros consists of several two-story buildings on a narrow lot facing the beach and one three-story building in back. All rooms have tile floors and bathrooms with marble countertops and showers. Deluxe units have air-conditioning, microwave, fridge, coffeemaker, and king-size bed. Other rooms have two double beds or a queen bed. Each of the bungalow units has a balcony or terrace with a hammock. Most have two double beds, but seven have queen beds.

Calle 8, between Av. 5 and the beach (Apdo. Postal 31), 77710 Playa del Carmen, Q. Roo. (©) **800/538-6802** in the U.S. and Canada, or 984/873-0001. 39 units. High season $82 double, $92 deluxe; low season $40 double, $65 deluxe. Promotional rates sometimes available. AE, MC, V. **Amenities:** Tour info; overnight laundry.

Hotel Jungla Caribe ✮   Located right in the heart of the Avenida 5 action, "La Jungla" is an imaginative piece of work—a colorful execution of neoclassical *a la tropical.* Its quirkiness is perfectly in keeping with the rest of the town. Owner Rolf Albrecht envisioned space and comfort for guests, so all but the eight standard *(sencilla)* rooms are large, with gray-and-black marble floors, the occasional Roman column, and large bathrooms. Catwalks connect the "tower" section of suites to the main building. These suites are the quietest because they are in back. There's an attractive pool in the courtyard beneath a giant *ramón* tree. The *sencilla* rooms are fun, too. These are medium size with ample bathrooms. They come with one double bed and a balcony overlooking Calle 8. They aren't air-conditioned, and cost $35 to $60 depending on the season.

Av. 5 Norte (at Calle 8), 77710 Playa del Carmen, Q. Roo. (©)/fax **984/873-0650.** www.jungla-caribe.com. 25 units. High season $95 double, $110–$135 suite; 30% low-season discount. AE, MC, V. **Amenities:** Restaurant; 2 bars; tour info; room service until 11pm. *In room:* A/C, TV, no phone.

Hotel Lunata ✮✮   A combination of location, comfort, and attractiveness makes this hotel a great choice for those wanting to stay in central Playa. It's built in hacienda style, with cut stone, wrought iron, and contemporary Mexican colors. The rooms show a lot of polish, with good air-conditioning and nicely finished bathrooms. The majority of rooms are deluxe, which are large and come with a king bed or two doubles and a minibar. Breakfast is served in the garden, and the third-story terrace makes a nice place to hang out. The front rooms facing Avenida 5 are noisier than the back ones.

Av. 5 (between calles 6 and 8), 77710 Playa del Carmen, Q. Roo. (©) **984/873-0884.** Fax 984/873-1240. www. lunata.com. 10 units. High season $85–$100 standard, $95–$115 deluxe and junior suite; low season $65–$80 standard, $75–$100 deluxe and junior suite. Rates include continental breakfast. Promotional rates available. AE, MC, V. Children under 13 not accepted. **Amenities:** Snorkel and bike rentals; tour desk; in-room massage; overnight laundry; nonsmoking rooms. *In room:* A/C, TV, hair dryer on request, safe, no phone.

Hotel Quinto Sol ★ *Value*   This lovely 3-story hotel wraps around an ancient-looking tree laden with orchids. The rooms are large, with attractive tilework, good air-conditioning, and ample bathrooms. The design has an Italian touch, with a lot of curves and rounded corners in the stuccowork. Highlights include a rooftop Jacuzzi, and easy access to the lovely beaches on Playa's north side. "Studios" are comparable to "standards" but come with kitchenettes. Minisuites are larger than either, have a few extra details, and have balconies. This part of Avenida 5 is fairly quiet, so noise isn't usually a problem.

Av. 5 Norte 330 (at Calle 28), 77710 Playa del Carmen, Q. Roo. ⓒ **984/873-3292** or 984/873-3293. Fax 984/873-3294. www.hotelquintosol.com. 20 units. High season $70–$80 standard or studio, $90–$110 suite; low season $55–$65 standard or studio, $75–$95 suite. Rates include continental breakfast. Ask for Frommer's discount. MC. V. Street parking. **Amenities:** Restaurant; bar; free access to Playa Mamita's beach club; Jacuzzi; tour info; room service until 11pm; overnight laundry; nonsmoking rooms. *In room:* A/C, TV, minibar, coffeemaker on request, hair dryer, safe.

La Tortuga   The exterior of this two-story hotel goes native, with *palapa* roofs and lots of raw-wood bracing. The rooms, however, offer comfort and polish. Most have a king bed; some have two queen beds. The bathrooms are large, and the suites contain whirlpool tubs. They have balconies or terraces facing lovely garden courtyards. The hotel is 3 blocks from the beach. Guests get a voucher for the nearby Tukan Beach Club, which offers some food and drink service on one of the nicest stretches of beach in Playa.

Av. 10 no. 732 (between calles 12 and 14), 77710 Playa del Carmen, Q. Roo. ⓒ/fax **984/873-1484** or 984/873-0626. Fax 984/873-0798. www.hotellatortuga.com. 33 units. High season $95 double, $135 suite; low season $75 double, $115 suite. AE, MC, V. Rates include continental breakfast. **Amenities:** Restaurant; bar; 2 pools; bike rental; tour info; limited room service; in-room massage; overnight laundry and dry cleaning. *In room:* A/C, TV, minibar, fridge, hair dryer, safe.

INEXPENSIVE

Treetops ★ *Value*   The rooms at Treetops encircle a patch of preserved jungle (and a small *cenote*) that shades the hotel and lends it the proper tropical feel. Rooms are large and comfortable and have balconies or patios that overlook the "jungle." Some of the upper rooms, especially the honeymoon suite, have the feel of a treehouse. The two other suites are large, with fully loaded kitchenettes— good for groups of four. The location is excellent: half a block from the beach, half a block from Avenida 5. That little bit of distance keeps the rooms quiet. A bar and snack bar is open nights. The American owners are helpful, attentive hosts.

Calle 8 s/n, 77710 Playa del Carmen, Q. Roo. ⓒ/fax **984/873-0351**. www.treetopshotel.com. 18 units. High season $45–$78 double, $90–$110 suite; low season $35–$65 double, $80–$90 suite. Rates include continental breakfast. Dive and honeymoon packages available. MC, V. **Amenities:** Bar; small pool. *In room:* A/C, fridge, no phone.

Villa Catarina Rooms & Cabañas ★ *Value*   A rare combination of style and economy, this hotel is a grouping of two- and three-story structures nestled among palms and fruit trees. The architecture, decor, and furnishings are stylish yet rustic—thatched roofs, stucco walls, rough-hewn wood steps and planking, and hammocks hanging from the rafters. Rooms vary considerably: a few have air conditioning, though most have ceiling fans; floors are wood, tile, brick, or carpet. The attractive *palapa* cabañas are cheapest; each has a brick floor, a loft area that holds a second double bed, and a small bathroom. Garden rooms, the next step up, vary a lot—medium to large in size, with a queen or king bed. *Palapa* tower rooms are large and have king beds and sitting areas. Almost all the rooms have some kind of porch. There's good cross-ventilation through well-screened windows. Coffee is available every morning.

Calle Privada Norte (between calles 12 and 14), 77710 Playa del Carmen, Q. Roo. © **984/873-2098.** Fax 984/873-2097. 14 units. High season $65–$85 double; low season $45–$60 double. Rates include morning coffee. MC, V.

WHERE TO DINE

Playa, with its large population of European and American transplants, offers a wide variety of dining options. I actually prefer the restaurant scene here over Cancún's. But good and varied Mexican food can be hard to find. If you're looking for the people's food, I can recommend a taco place, **El Sarape Grill,** on Avenida Juárez between avenidas 20 and 25. For something farther off the beaten path, try **Pozolería Mi Abuelita** (no phone) on Avenida 30, between calles 20 and 22. It's open in the evenings and serves good *pozole rojo* and *enchiladas verdes.* If pizza is what you want, the consensus favorite is **La Siesta,** where you can order to go (© **984/879-3982**). It's at Avenida 1 Norte 238, between calles 12 and 16. (Av. 1 is in north Playa between Av. 5 and the ocean.)

EXPENSIVE

Ambasciata D'Italia ★ NORTHERN ITALIAN   The predominantly Italian crowd filling the tables here is a telling sign that the food is authentic and delicious. Entrees cover a range of homemade pasta and northern Italian specialties, with seafood prominently featured. There's an admirable selection of wines, and the espresso is exceptional. The ambience is lively and sophisticated. Good choices include fresh-made pastas, *strozzapreti alla marinara* (a pasta dish), Italian and Mexican weekly specials, and pizza.

Av. 5 (at Calle 12). © **984/873-0553.** Main courses $8–$12. AE, MC, V. Daily 7pm–midnight.

La Casa del Agua ★★★ EUROPEAN/MEXICAN   Dining here is a pleasure—the food is great and the surroundings are lovely. Instead of loud music, you hear only the sound of falling water. The Swiss owners, who have lived in Mexico a long time, work at combining what they like best about Old and New Worlds. For starters, among other things, are mushrooms flavored with white wine, garlic, and *epazote* (a Mexican herb). For a mild dish, try chicken in a wonderfully scented sauce of fine herbs accompanied by fettuccine; for something heartier, there's the tortilla soup listed as "Mexican soup." The restaurant offers a number of cool and light dishes that would be appetizing for lunch or an afternoon meal, for example, an avocado stuffed with shrimp and flavored with a subtle horseradish sauce on a bed of alfalfa sprouts and julienne carrots—a good mix of tastes and textures. For dessert, try the chocolate mousse. This is an upstairs restaurant under a large and airy *palapa* roof.

Av. 5 (at Calle 2). © **984/803-0232.** Main courses $9–$22. AE, MC, V. Daily noon–midnight.

La Parrilla ★ MEXICAN/GRILL   One of the most popular restaurants in town, this place has an open-air dining area where the aroma of grilling meats permeates the air. The chicken fajitas fill the plate. Grilled lobster is also on the menu. The cooks do a good job with Mexican standards such as tortilla soup, enchiladas, and quesadillas. Mariachis show up around 8pm; if you want to avoid them and dine in relative tranquillity, get a table on the upper terrace in back.

Av. 5 (at Calle 8). © **984/873-0687.** Reservations recommended in high season. Main courses $8–$20. AE, MC, V. Daily noon–1am.

Yaxché ★★ MAYA/YUCATECAN   The menu here makes use of many native foods and spices to produce a style of cooking different from what you usually get when ordering Yucatecan food. You find such things as a cream of *chaya* (a native leafy vegetable), and xcatic chile stuffed with *cochinita* (pork). I also like the classic fruit salad, done Mexican style with lime juice and dried powdered chile. The menu is varied and includes a lot of seafood dishes; the ones I had were fresh and well prepared.

Calle 8 (between avs. 5 and 10). ℂ **984/873-2502**. Reservations recommended in high season. Main courses $9–$25. AE, MC, V. Daily noon–midnight.

MODERATE

Casa Mediterránea ★★★ ITALIAN   Tucked away on a quiet little patio off Avenida 5, this small, homey restaurant serves excellent food. One of the owners, Maurizio Gabrielli and Giovanna Furian, usually attends the customers and makes recommendations. They came to Mexico to enjoy the simple life, and this inclination shows in the restaurant's welcoming, unhurried atmosphere. The menu is mostly northern Italian, with several dishes from the rest of the country as well as daily specials. Pastas (except penne and spaghetti) are made in-house, and none is precooked. Try fish and shrimp ravioli or penne alla Veneta. There are several wines, mostly Italian, to choose from. The salads are good and are carefully prepared—dig in without hesitation.

Av. 5 (between calles 6 and 8; look for a sign for Hotel Marieta). ℂ **044-984/876-3926**. Reservations recommended in high season. Main courses $8–$15. No credit cards. Daily 1–11pm.

Estas Son Las Mañanitas ★ MEXICAN/ITALIAN   For dependably good food in an advantageous spot for people-watching, I really like this restaurant. It's simple outdoor dining on Avenida 5—comfortable chairs and tables under *palapa* umbrellas. It's not noisy, and the Italian owner is vigilant about maintaining quality and consistency. He offers an excellent *sopa de lima*. After that, try seafood pasta if you're really hungry, or grilled shrimp with herbs. Also available are such Tex-Mex specialties as chili and fajitas. The hot sauces are good.

Av. 5 (between calles 4 and 6). ℂ **984/873-0114**. Main courses $7–$12. AE, MC, V. Daily 7am–11:30pm.

La Vagabunda ITALIAN/MEXICAN   This place is old-style Playa in its simplicity and charm. A large, attractive *palapa* shelters several simple wood and rattan tables well spread out over the gravel-covered ground. The ambience is low key and quiet, and the food is prepared under the watchful eye of the Italian owner. This is one of my favorite places for breakfast, with many options, including delicious blended fruit drinks, waffles, and omelets. The specials are a good value. In the afternoon and evening you can order light fare such as *panini* (sandwiches), pastas, and *ceviche,* or more substantial dishes such as fajitas or seafood.

Av. 5 (between calles 24 and 26). ℂ **984/873-3753**. Breakfast $3–$5; main courses $6–$14. MC, V. High season daily 7am–11:30pm; low season daily 7am–3:30pm.

Media Luna ★★★ FUSION   The owner-chef has come up with an outstanding menu that favors grilled seafood, sautés, and pasta dishes. Everything is fresh and prepared beautifully. On my last visit, I tried the pan-fried fish cakes with mango and honeyed hoisin sauce—very good. I also enjoyed the black-pepper-crusted fish. Be sure to eye the daily specials. For lunch you can get lovely sandwiches and salads, as well as black-bean quesadillas and crepes. The decor is primitive-tropical chic.

Av. 5 (between calles 12 and 14). ℂ **984/873-0526**. Breakfast $4–$6; main courses $7–$15; sandwich with salad $4–$8. No credit cards. Daily 8am–11:30pm.

INEXPENSIVE

Tarraya Restaurant/Bar ★ SEAFOOD/BREAKFAST   THE RESTAURANT THAT WAS BORN WITH THE TOWN, proclaims the sign. This is also the restaurant locals recommend for seafood. It's right on the beach, with the water practically lapping at the foundations. Because the owners are fishermen, the fish is so fresh it's practically still wiggling. The wood hut doesn't look like much, but you can have your fish prepared in several ways. If you haven't tried the Yucatecan specialty *tik-n-xic* fish (with achiote and bitter-orange sauce, cooked in a banan.. leaf), this is a good place to do so. Tarraya is on the beach opposite the basketball court. It serves a set breakfast menu that includes hot cakes, French toast, and eggs any style.

Calle 2 Norte. ☎ 984/873-2040. Main courses $4–$7; whole fish $8 per kg. No credit cards. Daily 7am–9pm.

PLAYA DEL CARMEN AFTER DARK

It seems as if everyone in town is out on Avenida 5 or on the square until 10 or 11pm; there's pleasant strolling, meals and drinks at streetside cafes, shops to browse, and a few bars with live music. The other nightspot is the beach. The beach bar at the **Blue Parrot** (☎ **984/873-0083**) is the most popular hangout in town and a classic example of its genre. Down by the ferry dock is a **Señor Frog's** (☎ **984/873-0930**), which dishes out its patented mix of thumping dance music, Jell-O shots, and frat-house antics. Also on the beach is **Captain Tutiz** (no phone), which is designed like a pirate ship and has a large bar area, dance floor, and live entertainment nightly. Each time I go, the live bands are worse than the ones before.

A new club called **Alux** (no phone) is a one-of-a-kind establishment in a large cave with two dramatically lit chambers and several nooks and sitting areas. It's worth going to, if only for the novelty. The local conservancy group approved all the work, and great care was taken not to contaminate the water, which is part of a large underground river system. Take Avenida Juárez across to the other side of the highway. Alux is a couple of blocks down on your left. The club books a variety of music acts, usually with no cover. I saw a good acoustic band playing an imaginative hybrid of Latin and North American music. The bar is cash only and is open Tuesday to Sunday from 7pm to 2am.

Cine Hollywood, Avenida 10 and Calle 8, in the Plaza Pelícanos shopping center, shows a lot of films in English with Spanish subtitles *(subtitulada)*. Before you buy your ticket, make sure the film is subtitled and not dubbed *(doblada)*.

2 North of Playa del Carmen to the Puerto Morelos Area

EN ROUTE TO PUERTO MORELOS

As you drive north from Playa del Carmen, you'll pass a number of roadside attractions, all-inclusive hotels, small cabaña hotels, secluded resorts, and the nature park of Tres Ríos. The turn-off for Puerto Morelos is only 32km (20 miles) from Playa.

Midway between Playa and Puerto Morelos is **Tres Ríos** (☎ **998/887-8077;** www.tres-rios.com), a nature park along the same lines as Xcaret and Xel-Ha. See the "Eco-Theme Parks & Reserves" section of chapter 3.

Just before you get to the Puerto Morelos turn-off, you'll pass Rancho Loma Bonita, which has all the markings of a tourist trap and offers horseback riding and ATV tours. For horseback riding, I prefer Rancho Punta Venado, south of Playa (see listing later in this chapter). You'll also come across **Jardín Botánico Dr. Alfredo Barrera** (no phone). Opened in 1990 and named after a biologist who studied tropical forests, the botanical garden is open Monday to Saturday from 9am to 5pm. Admission is $6. It will be of most interest to gardeners and plant enthusiasts, but I'm afraid will bore children. They are much more likely to enjoy the interactive zoo at Croco Cun (see "Exploring In & Around Puerto Morelos," later in this chapter).

BEACH CABAÑAS Five kilometers (3 miles) north of Playa are some economical lodgings on a mostly rocky beach. A sign that says PUNTA BETE marks the access road to Xcalacoco. The last time I visited, there was a large warehouse-like structure and a sign advertising a subdivision somewhere that read ARBOLEDAS. The road is rough in places, but in a short time you arrive at the water. Before you do, the road forks off in a few places, and you'll see signs for different cabañas. The word conjures up visions of idyllic native-style dwellings with thatched roofs, but as often as not on the Yucatecan coast, it means simple lodging. This is mostly the case here, with rates running $30 to $50 a night for two people. Of the four groupings of cabañas in Xcalacoco, the one I like best is **Coco's Cabañas** (© 998/ 874-7056; www.travel-center.com), which has electricity and ceiling fans; a good, inexpensive little restaurant; and a small pool. It's operated by a friendly Swiss gentleman named Helmut. His establishment shares a wall with Ikal del Mar, a spa resort (see "Spa Resorts Near Puerto Morelos," later in this chapter). In the future, one or two of the rooms might have air-conditioning.

A few minutes after passing Xcalacoco/Punta Bete, you'll see a large sign on the right side of the road marking the entrance to La Posada del Capitán Lafitte. Take the same road to reach KaiLuum II.

KaiLuum II ⚑⚑ This lodging is for those who want an unfiltered beach experience and time off from civilization. KaiLuum is simplicity. The things that matter here are the beach, the water, the stars, the quiet, and the soft light of candles. Things that don't seem to matter are electricity, noise, and bustle. Thirty large tents spread across an immaculately kept beach. Each stands under a thatched roof and contains chairs, a couple of hammocks, some shelving, and a queen-size bed. A couple of buildings house showers, sinks, and toilets; a tall beach *palapa* serves breakfast, cocktails, and dinner. The food is good. This is the kind of place where you take off your sandals and don't put them on again until it's time to leave.

Carretera Cancún–Tulum Km 62, 77710 Playa del Carmen, Q. Roo. © 800/538-6802 in the U.S. and Canada, or ©/fax 984/801-3502. www.mexicoholiday.com. 30 units. High season $120–$140 double; low season $85–$100 double. Rates include breakfast and dinner. AE, MC, V for reservations only; no credit cards accepted on site. Children under 17 not accepted. **Amenities:** Restaurant; bar.

La Posada del Capitán Lafitte ⚑ Two kilometers (1¼ mile) from the highway, down a dirt road, this lovely seaside retreat sits on a solitary stretch of sandy beach next to KaiLuum II. Here you can enjoy being isolated while still having all the amenities of a relaxing vacation. The beach is the same for both hotels— powdery white sand, but with a rocky bottom below the water. The one- and two-story white stucco bungalows hold one to four rooms each. They are small to medium in size but comfortable, with tile floors, tiled bathrooms, either two double beds or one king-size bed, and an oceanfront porch. Twenty-nine bungalows have air-conditioning; the rest have fans. Coffee can be served as early as 6:30am in the game room.

Carretera Cancún–Tulum Km 62, 77710 Playa del Carmen, Q. Roo. © 800/538-6802 in the U.S. and Canada, or 984/873-0214. Fax 984/873-0212. www.mexicoholiday.com. 62 units. High season $200–$225 double; low season $130–$140 double. Christmas and New Year's rates are higher. Minimum 2–4 nights. Rates include breakfast and dinner. MC, V. Free guarded parking. **Amenities:** Restaurant; poolside grill; bar; medium-size pool; watersports equipment; game/TV room; activities desk; dive shop; car rental; limited room service; laundry. *In room:* Minibar.

PUERTO MORELOS

Puerto Morelos remains a quiet place—perfect for a relaxed vacation of lying on the beach and reading, with perhaps the occasional foray into watersports, especially snorkeling, diving, and kayaking. Offshore is a prominent reef, which has been declared a national park for its protection. Because of the reef, the beaches in Puerto Morelos have a lot of sea grass growing on the bottom. But the water is as clear as anywhere along the coast, and if a little sea grass doesn't bother you, you'll find this a cozy spot. Another attraction of the town is a large English-language new and used bookstore that stocks 20,000 titles. Puerto Morelos is also the terminus for the car ferry to Cozumel.

ESSENTIALS
GETTING THERE   By Car   At Km 31 there's a traffic light at the intersection, and a large sign pointing to Puerto Morelos.

By Bus   Buses from Cancún to Tulum and Playa del Carmen usually stop here, but be sure to ask in Cancún if your bus makes the Puerto Morelos stop.

By Ferry   The Puerto Morelos–Cozumel car ferry (© **998/871-0008**) runs daily. To get to the ferry dock, head south from the main square. You can't miss it. See the "Cozumel" section of chapter 4 for details on the car ferry schedule, but a couple of points bear repeating here: The schedule may change, so double-check it, and always arrive at least 3 hours before the ferry's departure to purchase a ticket and get in line.

In the winter of 2003, a car ferry made weekly trips to and from Tampa, Florida, but they have stopped. (Service between Tampa and Progreso, near Mérida, continued until Apr.) To see whether service has resumed, check with **Yucatan Express** (© **866/208-4235** in the U.S., or 01-800/514-4235 in Mexico; www.yucatanexpress.com).

EXPLORING IN & AROUND PUERTO MORELOS
Puerto Morelos attracts visitors who seek seaside relaxation without crowds and high prices. The town has several hotels, a few restaurants, and an English-language bookstore. For outdoor recreation, there are two dive shops and plenty of recreational boats for fishing or snorkeling. On the main square, you'll find the bookstore, **Alma Libre** (© **998/871-0713**; www.almalibrebooks.com). It has more English-language books than any other in the Yucatán, and not just whodunits, sci-fi, and spy novels. The owners, Rob and Joanne Birce, stock everything from volumes on Mayan culture to English classics to maps of the region. The store is open from October through the first week in June. Hours are Tuesday to Sunday from 10am to 3pm and 6 to 9pm.

On the ocean side of the main square is **Mystic Divers** (©/fax **998/871-0634**; www.mysticdiving.com). It's well recommended, not only for diving but for fishing trips, too. The owner, Victor Reyes, speaks English and takes small groups. He is a PADI and NAUI instructor and gives his customers a lot of personal attention. The shop is open all year. A two-tank dive costs $45. The reef directly offshore is very shallow and is protected by law. Snorkelers are required to wear a life vest to prevent them from damaging the reef. I snorkeled for a bit and wasn't bothered by the vest. Much of the reef is within a foot or two of the water's surface and, at its deepest, is only about 10 feet. There was abundant life, and in a short time I spotted four different eels and sea snakes, lots of fish, and a ray. The dive sites are, of course, farther out.

From Playa, if you continue along Highway 307 towards Cancún, you'll pass **Croco Cun** (© **998/884-4782**), a zoological park that raises crocodiles. It's a lot more than just your average roadside attraction. There's an interactive zoo with crocodiles in all stages of development, as well as animals of nearly all the species that once roamed the Yucatán Peninsula. A visit to the new reptile house is fascinating, though it may make you think twice about venturing into the jungle. The rattlesnakes and boa constrictors are particularly intimidating, and the tarantulas are downright enormous. The guided tour lasts 1½ hours. Children enjoy the guides' enthusiasm and are entranced by the spider monkeys and wild pigs. Wear plenty of bug repellent. The restaurant sells refreshments. Croco Cun is open daily from 8:30am to 5:30pm. As with other attractions of this sort along the coast, entrance fees are high: $15 adult, $9 children 6 to 12, free for children under 6. The park is at Km 31 on Highway 307.

WHERE TO STAY

Amar Inn   Simple, rustic rooms on the beach, in a home-style setting, make this small inn a good place for people wanting a quiet seaside retreat. The cordial hostess, Ana Luisa Aguilar, is the daughter of Luis Aguilar, a Mexican singer and movie star of the 1940s and '50s. Besides running her little B&B, she keeps busy promoting environmental and equitable-development causes. She can line up snorkeling and fishing trips and jungle tours for guests. There are three cabañas in back, opposite the main house, and four upstairs rooms with views of the beach. There is something unselfconsciously Mexican in the decor. The cabañas get less of a cross-breeze than the rooms in the main house but still have plenty of ventilation. They are large and come with kitchenettes. Rooms in the main building are medium to large. Bedding choices include one or two doubles, one king, or five twin beds. A full Mexican breakfast is served in the garden.

Av. Javier Rojo Gómez (at Lázaro Cárdenas), 77580 Puerto Morelos, Q. Roo. © **998/871-0026.** amar_inn@ hotmail.com. 7 units. High season $65 double; low season $45 double. Rates include full breakfast. No credit cards. From the plaza, turn left; it's 1km (½ mile) farther, immediately after the Hotel Ojo de Agua. **Amenities:** Tour and rental info. *In room:* Fridge, fan, no phone.

Casita del Mar ⭐   An attractive hotel on the beach, Casita del Mar offers pleasant rooms and good prices. Rooms come with either two full beds or one king. The standard units are medium size and well furnished. The beds I tried had soft mattresses. Oceanview rooms are larger, with larger bathrooms; three have tubs. There's a pretty terrace overlooking the beach.

Calle Roberto Frías, SMZA 2, MZA 14, Lote 6, 77580 Puerto Morelos, Q. Roo. ©/fax **998/871-0301.** www.hotel casitadelmar.com. 19 units. High season $60 standard double, $70 oceanview double; low season $52 standard double, $60 oceanview double. Rates include full breakfast. MC, V. Street parking. **Amenities:** Restaurant; bar; large pool; dive shop; tour info; massage; limited laundry service. *In room:* A/C, no phone.

Hotel Ojo de Agua ⭐ *Value*   What I like best about this hotel is that it offers great convenience and service for the price. It has a good dive shop and watersports equipment rental. Two three-story buildings stand on the beach at a right angle to each other. The simply furnished rooms have balconies or terraces; most have a view of the ocean. Standard rooms have one double bed. Deluxe rooms are large and have two doubles. Studios have a double and a twin and a small kitchenette but no air-conditioning (the rest of the rooms do have A/C). Some rooms come with TV and phone. A highly respected instructor heads the dive shop. If you've wanted to try windsurfing, this is the place. The American who operates the shop takes his time with customers and doesn't just put them on a board and send them out into the water.

Av. Javier Rojo Gómez. Supermanzana 2, lote 16, 77580 Puerto Morelos, Q. Roo. © **998/871-0027** or 998/871-0507. Fax 998/871-0202. www.ojo-de-agua.com. 36 units. High season $45–$55 double, $60–$75 studio or deluxe; low season $30–$40 double, $40–$55 studio or deluxe. Weekly and monthly rates available. AE, MC, V. **Amenities:** Restaurant; bar; pool; watersports equipment; tour info; scuba shop; room service until 10pm; in-room massage.

WHERE TO DINE

Puerto Morelos has a few restaurants. They are on or around the main square and include the ever-popular **Palapa Pizza, Los Pelicanos** for seafood, **Hola Asia** for Asian food, and **Le Café d'Amancia** for coffee and pastries.

SPA RESORTS NEAR PUERTO MORELOS

In the area around Puerto Morelos, four spa resorts offer different versions of the hedonistic resort experience. Only 20 to 30 minutes from the Cancún airport, they are well situated for a quick weekend escape from the daily grind. You can jet down to Cancún, get whisked away by the hotel car, and be on the beach with a cocktail in hand before you can figure out whether you crossed a time zone. All four resorts pride themselves on their service, amenities, and full range of spa and salon treatments. Being in the Yucatán, they like to add the healing practices of the Maya, especially the use of the steam bath known as a *temascal.* Rates quoted below include taxes but not the 5% to 10% service charge.

Ceiba del Mar   Eight three-story buildings make up this resort, the largest of the four in this section. Each building has a rooftop terrace with Jacuzzi and service area. The carefully tended white sand beach adjoins a seaside pool with Jacuzzi and bar. I like it a tad less than Maroma's and Paraíso de la Bonita's. Rooms are large and have a terrace or balcony. The bathtub area can be opened up to the entire room. Service is attentive and unobtrusive, as exemplified by the delivery of coffee and juice each morning, accomplished without disturbing the guests through the use of a closed pass-through.

Av. Niños Héroes s/n, 77580 Puerto Morelos, Q. Roo. © **877/545-6221** from the U.S. or 998/872-8060. Fax 998/872-8061. www.ceibadelmar.com. 126 units. High season $336–$390 deluxe double, $708 2-bedroom suite; low season $242–$300 deluxe double, $538 2-bedroom suite. Rates include continental breakfast and ground transfer. Spa packages available. AE, MC, V. Free parking. **Amenities:** 2 restaurants; 2 bars; 2 pools; lighted tennis court; complete state-of-the-art gym with sauna, steam room, whirlpool, and Swiss showers; spa offering a wide variety of treatments; 8 rooftop Jacuzzis; dive shop with watersports equipment; bikes for guests' use; concierge; tour info; car rental; salon; 24-hr. room service; babysitting; overnight laundry; non-smoking rooms. *In room:* A/C, TV/VCR, CD player, minibar, hair dryer, safe.

Ikal del Mar   The smallest and most private of the four resorts in this section, Ikal has 30 well-separated bungalows, each with its own piece of jungle, a little pool, and an outdoor shower. The bungalows are large, filled with amenities, and decorated in modern style. The bathrooms have only a shower. Service here is the most personal of the four—the numerous staff members will get you just about anything you need. A bar and restaurant (with excellent food) overlooking an inviting pool make for an attractive common area. If there's a drawback, it's the beach, which is rockier than the beaches at the other three.

Playa Xcalacoco, Carretera Cancún-Tulum, 77710 Q. Roo. © **888/230-7330** in the U.S. and Canada or 984/877-3000. Fax 713/528-3697. www.ikaldelmar.com. 30 units. High season $616 double; low season $532 double. Packages available. AE, MC, V. Free secured parking. Children not accepted. **Amenities:** Restaurant; 2 bars; large pool; spa; 2 Jacuzzis; steam bath; watersports equipment; concierge; tour info; car rental; courtesy shuttle to Playa; salon; 24-hr. room service; in-room massage; overnight laundry. *In room:* A/C, TV/DVD, fridge, hair dryer, safe.

> ### ⌐Tips⌐ In Case of Emergency
>
> The Riviera Maya south of Playa del Carmen is susceptible to power fail-
> ures that can last for hours. Gas pumps and cash machines shut down
> when this happens, and once the power returns, they attract long lines.
> It's a good idea to keep a reserve of gas and cash with you to guard
> against such an inconvenience.

Maroma   This resort has been around the longest, owns a large parcel of land
inland that it protects from development, and has a gorgeous beach and beautifully
manicured grounds. Two- and three-story buildings contain the large guest rooms;
most have king beds and rattan furniture. It is not the retreat into the jungle that
Ikal is. Still, my two most vivid memories of the place are the sound of the sea
breeze softly rustling the lush palm trees, and the sight of a pair of toucans—most
uncommon on this coast. I also have a fond memory of the beach bar. I could do
without the staff dressing in native peasant garb, but they don't seem to mind. As
at Ikal, the smaller size makes for more personal service and a deeper sense of escape.
Carretera 307, Km 51, 77710 Q. Roo. ℂ 866/454-9351 in the U.S. or 998/872-8200. Fax 998/872-8220. www.
orient-express.com. 58 units. $225 gardenview double; $364–$476 premium or deluxe double; from $728 suite.
Rates include ground transfer, full breakfast, 1 snorkeling tour. AE, MC, V. Free valet parking. Children under 16
not accepted. **Amenities:** Restaurant; 3 bars; 3 outdoor spring-fed pools; fitness center; spa; Jacuzzi; steam bath;
watersports equipment rental; game room; concierge; tours; car rental; salon; room service until 11pm; in-room
massage; same-day laundry/dry cleaning. *In room:* A/C, hair dryer.

Paraíso de la Bonita   This recently opened resort has the most elaborate spa
of all. I'm not a regular spa-goer and cannot discuss the relative merits of different treatments, but in my work I've seen plenty of spas, and this one, which
operates under the principles of the French system of thalassotherapy, is like no
other I've visited. This therapy uses seawater, sea salts, and sea algae in its treatments, and to be certified by the authorities, you have to jump through a lot of
hoops. Just viewing the different apparatuses is impressive. InterContinental
manages the hotel part of the resort and handles the hospitality smoothly. The
beach is lovely and open, without the mature palms and vegetation that grace
Maroma and Ikal. The pool area and the common areas of the spa, which are
open to guests, are uncommonly attractive. The rooms occupy some unremarkable three-story buildings on the opposite side of the property from the spa. The
interiors are lovely and far from the standard hotel room. They are, in decor and
furnishings, more impressive than those of Maroma and Ceiba del Mar. I especially like the tribal art pieces from Asia and Africa. The ground-floor rooms
have a plunge pool; upstairs rooms come with a balcony.
Carretera Cancún-Chetumal Km 328, Bahía Petenpich, 77710 Q. Roo. ℂ 800/327-0200 in the U.S. or
998/873-8300. Fax 998/872-8301. www.paraisodelabonitaresort.com. 90 units. $530–$640 suite; $1,400
2-bedroom master suite. Rates include ground transfer. AE, MC, V. Free valet parking. Children under 12 not
accepted. **Amenities:** 2 restaurants; 2 bars; 4 pools; 1 lighted tennis court; spa; 2 Jacuzzis; watersports equipment rental; concierge; tour info; rental cars; salon; 24-hr. room service; in-room massage; same-day laundry
and dry cleaning; nonsmoking rooms. *In room:* A/C, TV/DVD, dataport, minibar, hair dryer, safe.

3 South of Playa del Carmen to Tulum

South of Playa del Carmen you'll find a succession of nature parks, resort communities, and beaches. From north to south, this section covers them in the

following order: Xcaret, Paamul, Puerto Aventuras, Xpu-Ha, Akumal, Xel-Ha, Punta Solimán, and Tankah. The distance from Playa del Carmen to Xel-Ha is 54km (33 miles).

HEADING SOUTH FROM PLAYA DEL CARMEN   The best way to travel this coast is in a rental car; Playa has many rental agencies. The wide, well-paved highway to Tulum makes for a 1-hour drive. Buses to Chetumal depart fairly regularly from Playa. Most stop several times along the highway; however, from the highway it can be a hot walk to the coast and to your final destination. There's also bus service to and from Cobá three times a day. Another option is to hire a car and driver.

Along the road, you'll see several signs advertising roadside attractions. Between Xcaret and Paamul is **Rancho Punta Venado** (© **984/877-9701**), which offers horseback riding. This is a better option than Rancho Loma Bonita, near Puerto Morelos. It's less touristy and noisy (no ATVs), and the owner, a rancher, takes good care of his horses. Beyond Paamul, you'll see signs for this or that *cenote* (well) or cave. There are thousands of *cenotes* in the Yucatán, and each is slightly different. These turn-offs are less visited than the major attractions and can make for a pleasant visit. Two major attractions bear specific mention: **Hidden Worlds,** offering remarkable snorkeling and diving tours of a couple of *cenotes,* and **Aktun Chen** cavern with a small nature park. Both are south of Akumal and described later in this chapter.

XCARET: A DEVELOPED NATURE PARK

Ten kilometers (6½ miles) south of Playa del Carmen and 80km (50 miles) south of Cancún is the turn-off to Xcaret (pronounced "eesh-ca-*ret*"), an **ecological and archaeological theme park** that is the Riviera Maya's most popular tourist attraction. It attracts hordes of visitors from Cancún and the cruise ships. Everywhere you look in Cancún, signs advertise Xcaret or someone hands you a leaflet about it. It even has its own bus terminal to take tourists from Cancún at regular intervals. It's open Monday to Saturday from 8:30am to 8:30pm, Sunday from 8:30am to 5:30pm.

Four kilometers (2½ miles) south of the entrance to Xcaret is the turn-off for **Puerto Calica,** the cruise-ship pier. Passengers disembark here for tours of Playa, Xcaret, the ruins, and other attractions on the coast. Fewer ships arrive on weekends than on weekdays, which makes the weekend a good time for visiting the major attractions on this coast.

PAAMUL: SEASIDE GETAWAY

About 16km (10 miles) beyond Xcaret, 26km (16 miles) from Playa del Carmen, and 96km (60 miles) from Cancún is Paamul, which in Maya means "a destroyed ruin." The exit is clearly marked. At Paamul (also written Pamul), you can enjoy the Caribbean with relative quiet; the water at the out-of-the-way beach is wonderful, but the shoreline is rocky. There are 18 rooms for rent, a restaurant, and many trailer and RV lots with hook-ups.

There's also a dive shop. **Scubamex** (© **984/873-0667;** fax 984/874-1729; www.scubamex.com) is a fully equipped PADI-, NAUI-, and SSI-certified dive shop next to the cabañas. Using two boats, the staff takes guests on dives 8km (5 miles) in either direction. If it's too choppy, the reefs in front of the hotel are also good. The cost for a two-tank dive is $45, plus $25 to rent gear. Snorkeling is also excellent in this protected bay and the one next to it. The shop offers a great 3-hour snorkeling trip ($25).

WHERE TO STAY & DINE

Cabañas Paamul ★ Lodging options here include eight rooms in a couple of long one-story concrete buildings and 10 freestanding wood cabañas, all just a few steps from the water. The rooms are large and clean, with ample bathrooms. Each comes with two double beds, tile floors, rattan furniture, air-conditioning, and a ceiling fan. In front of each is a porch with hammocks. Remodeling has made them much more attractive. The cabañas are also attractive, with a more native feel. They have wooden floors, stucco walls, *palapa* roofs, two double beds with comfortable mattresses, and a private porch. The trailer park isn't what you might expect—some trailers have decks or patios and thatched *palapa* shade covers. Trailer guests have access to 12 showers and separate bathrooms for men and women. Laundry service is available nearby. Turtles nest here from June to September. The large, breezy *palapa* restaurant is a Brazilian-style grill. The restaurant and the rooms are under the new management of Kalu da Silva, a retired Brazilian soccer player, who closed his restaurant in León, Guanajuato, to live on the coast. Restaurant customers are welcome to use the beach.

Km 85 Carretera Cancún–Tulum. ✆ **984/875-1053**. paamulmx@yahoo.com. 18 units; 190 trailer spaces (all with full hookups). July–Aug and Dec–Feb $60–$70 double; Mar–June and Sept–Nov $40–$50 double. Ask about discount for stays longer than 1 week. RV space with hookups $22 per day, $475 per month. No credit cards. **Amenities:** Restaurant; bar.

PUERTO AVENTURAS: A RESORT COMMUNITY

Five kilometers (3 miles) south of Paamul and 104km (65 miles) from Cancún is the glitzy development of Puerto Aventuras, on Chakalal Bay. It's a condo-marina community with a nine-hole golf course. At the center of the development is a collection of restaurants bordering a dolphin pool. They offer a variety of food— Mexican, Italian, steaks, even a popular pub. The major attraction is the dolphins. To swim with them in a highly interactive program, you must make reservations ahead of time by contacting **Dolphin Discovery** (✆ **998/849-4757** in Cancún; www.dolphindiscovery.com). It's best to make reservations well in advance. The surest way is by e-mail to salesinternet@dolphindiscovery.com.mx or through the link on the website. A 1-hour session costs $119.

There is also a museum called **Museo CEDAM** (no phone). CEDAM stands for Center for the Study of Aquatic Sports in Mexico, and the museum houses displays on the history of diving on this coast from pre-Hispanic times to the present. There are also displays of pre-Hispanic pottery and artifacts found in the *cenotes* of Chichén Itzá, shell fossils, and the like. For most people, the museum won't merit a special trip. It's open daily from 10am to 1pm and 2 to 6pm. Donations are requested.

I don't find this town interesting and prefer to stay elsewhere on the coast. It's like a mini Cancún, but lacking Cancún's vibrancy. There are a couple of fancy hotels. The main one is the **Omni Puerto Aventuras** (✆ **800/THE-OMNI** or 984/873-5101). It looks larger than its 30 rooms would indicate and was probably intended to be bigger but didn't get the expected traffic.

XPU-HA: BEAUTIFUL BEACH

Three kilometers (2 miles) beyond Puerto Aventuras is **Xpu-Ha** (eesh-poo-*hah*) ★★★, a wide bay lined by a broad, beautiful sandy beach, perhaps the best beach on the entire coast. All-inclusive resorts sit at each end of the bay (Xpu-Ha Palace and Robinson Club) and in the middle (Hotel Copacabana). The beach is big enough to accommodate the hotel crowds (who usually stay on the beach in front of their lodgings) as well as the people trucked in on weekdays from the cruise ships that dock at Calica. The cruise-ship vans usually pull in to the beach entrance called La Playa, on the far side (south) of the Copacabana, which means that you'll want to take one of the entrances before the hotel.

There are some restaurants and small hotels at Xpu-Ha. The rooms in these hotels are simple: two twin or full beds, private bathroom, cement floor. Most are rented on a first-come, first-served basis. Rates vary from $35 to $50 a night, depending upon how busy they are. The nicest establishment is **Villas del Caribe Xpu-Ha** (© 984/873-2194, cafedelmarxpuha@yahoo.com.mx), run by a personable Mexican named León who speaks English. Rooms are on the beach and have private bathrooms with hot water and 24-hour electricity, but no ceiling fans. León also runs a little beach restaurant next to the hotel. It serves seafood and is a pleasant place to have lunch. If you find a good lodging deal in nearby Akumal or Paamul, you might consider staying there and driving here for the day. That's what a lot of locals do.

If you're considering an all-inclusive resort, one of the hotels here might be what you're looking for. The **Robinson Club** (© 984/871-3000) is the oldest. It has small rooms that tend to be rather plain. The hotel markets 80% of its rooms to Germans, making it an excellent choice if you've taken German lessons and are looking for an opportunity for cultural immersion without actually having to go to Germany. Otherwise, consider the other two.

The **Copacabana** (© 984/875-1800; www.hotelcopacabana.com) consists of several three-story buildings housing large, comfortable rooms with a king or two queen beds. Like most of the large all-inclusives on this coast, it has several restaurants serving Mexican, Italian, and fast food; bars; lovely pools; and several Jacuzzis. It's built ecologically, with lots of conservation techniques and a minimal footprint on the land. It works for families or couples and has a kids' club.

And then there's the **Xpu-Ha Palace** (© 984/875-1010; www.palaceresorts. com), occupying the failed ecopark. It has a couple of lovely natural features, including a large lagoon and extensive mangrove. Unlike the Copacabana, this hotel is very spread out; staying here will involve some walking. It, too, has a strong ecological orientation. It's well geared up for families, providing lots of activities and attractions for youngsters, including a crocodile hatchery. The rooms are in two-story cabañas. The prominent feature is a large Jacuzzi tub open to the room, but the bathrooms are on the small side. The rooms are more interesting than the Copacabana's, but less practical.

To stay at any of these all-inclusives, you do best to go through your travel agent or a packager. Don't try to contact the hotel directly; you don't get the best price that way—strange, but that's how the business works.

AKUMAL: BEAUTIFUL BAYS AND CAVERN DIVING

Continuing south on Highway 307 for 2km (1¼ miles), you'll come to the turn-off for Akumal, a small, modern, ecologically oriented community built on the shores of two beautiful bays. This community has been around long enough that it feels more relaxed than developing places such as Playa and Tulum. It draws a lot of families. You'll see a turtle icon everywhere you go because the name Akumal means "place of the turtles." From the highway, turn off at the sign that reads PLAYA AKUMAL. (Don't be confused by other signs reading VILLAS AKUMAL or AKUMAL AVENTURAS or AKUMAL BEACH RESORT.) Instead of making a left, you'll exit to the right and then turn left, and cross the highway. Less than 1km (½ mile) down the road is a white arch. Just before it are a couple of convenience stores (the one named Super Chomak has an ATM) and a laundry service.

Just after it (to the right) is the Club Akumal Caribe/Hotel Villas Maya. If you follow the road to the left and keep to the left, you'll come to Half Moon Bay, lined with two- and three-story condos, and eventually to Yal-ku Lagoon, which is a snorkeling park. Families can rent most of these condos for a week at a time. Contact **Akumal Vacations** (℗ **800/448-7137;** www.akumalvacations.com), **Caribbean Fantasy** (℗ **800/523-6618;** www.caribbfan.com), or **Loco Gringo** (℗ **984/875-9140;** www.locogringo.com).

You don't have to be a guest to enjoy the beach, swim or snorkel, or eat at one of the restaurants. This is a comfortable place to spend a day on a trip down the coast. There are three dive shops in town and at least 30 dive sites offshore. The **Akumal Dive Shop** (℗ **984/875-9032;** www.akumal.com), one of the oldest and best dive shops on the coast, offers courses in technical diving and cavern diving trips. It and **Akumal Dive Adventures** (℗ **984/875-9157**), at the Vista del Mar hotel on Half Moon Bay, offer resort courses as well as complete certification. The operator of Akumal Dive Adventures is an American who is competent and personable. He took me to one of his favorite dive sites, where we had some close encounters with a couple of nursing sharks, a ray, and a turtle.

Yal-ku Lagoon is a park that is like a miniature and more primitive Xel-Ha. It's open daily from 8am to 5:30pm. Admission is $6 for adults, $3 for children 3 to 14. The lagoon is about 700 meters long and about 200 meters at its widest. You can paddle around comfortably in sheltered water with little current and see fish and a few other creatures. It makes for a relaxing outing, but for sheer variety, I prefer snorkeling along the reefs.

WHERE TO STAY

Rates below are for two people and include taxes. Most hotels and condo rentals charge higher rates for the holidays than those listed here.

Club Akumal Caribe/Hotel Villas Maya Club ★★ (Kids) The hotel rooms and garden bungalows of this hotel sit along Akumal Bay. Both are large and comfortable, with tile floors and good-sized bathrooms. The 40 **Villas Maya Bungalows** are simply and comfortably furnished and have kitchenettes. The 21 rooms in the three-story beachfront **hotel** are more elaborately furnished and come with refrigerators. They have a king bed or two queen beds, tile floors, and Mexican accents. There is a large pool on the grounds. Other rooms belonging to the hotel are condos and the lovely **Villas Flamingo** on Half Moon Bay. The villas have two or three bedrooms and large living, dining, and kitchen areas, as well as a lovely furnished patio just steps from the beach. The four villas share a pool.

Km 104 Carretera Cancún–Tulum (Hwy. 307). ℗ **984/875-9010.** (Reservations: P.O. Box 13326, El Paso, TX 79913. ℗ 800/351-1622 in the U.S., 800/343-1440 in Canada, or 915/584-3552.) www.hotelakumalcaribe. com. 70 units. High season $110 bungalow, $140 hotel room, $165–$425 villa or condo; low season $66 bungalow, $84 hotel room, $80–$233 villa or condo. Reservations with prepayment by check only. AE, MC, V; cash only at restaurants. Low-season packages available. **Amenities:** 2 restaurants; bar; large pool; tour desk; children's activities (seasonal); dive shop; in-room massage; babysitting. *In room:* A/C, fridge, coffeemaker; no phone.

Vista del Mar Hotel and Condos ★ This beachfront property is a great place to stay for several reasons. It offers hotel rooms at good prices, and large, fully equipped condos that you don't have to rent by the week. The lovely, well-tended beach in front of the hotel has chairs and umbrellas. There's an on-site dive shop with an experienced staff, which eliminates the hassle of organizing dive trips. Hotel rooms are small and contain either a queen bed or a double and a twin bed; all have air conditioning. The 12 condos are large and have ceiling fans and good cross-ventilation; some come with air conditioning for $22 above the prices quoted below. They consist of a well-equipped kitchen, a living area, two or three bedrooms, and one or two bathrooms. All have balconies or terraces facing the sea and are furnished with hammocks. Several rooms come with whirlpool tubs.

Half Moon Bay, Akumal. © **877/425-8625.** Fax 505/988-3882 in the U.S. www.akumalinfo.com. 27 units. High season $85 double, $175–$240 condo; low season $51 double, $84–$125 condo. MC, V. **Amenities:** Restaurant; bar; small pool; watersports equipment rental; dive shop. *In room:* A/C, TV, CD player, fridge, coffeemaker, no phone.

WHERE TO DINE

There are about 10 places to eat in Akumal, and a convenient grocery store, **Super Chomak,** by the archway. The **Turtle Bay Café and Bakery** is good for breakfast or a light lunch. A good dining spot for lunch or dinner is **La Buena Vida,** on Half Moon Bay.

XEL-HA: SNORKELING & SWIMMING ⭐⭐

A bit beyond Akumal is the turn-off for **Aktun Chen** ⭐ cavern. Of the several caverns that I've toured in the Yucatán, this is one of the best—lots of geological features, good lighting, several underground pools, and large chambers, all carefully preserved. The tour takes about an hour and requires a good amount of walking. The footing is good. You exit not far from where you enter. There is also a zoo with specimens of the local fauna. Some of the critters are allowed to run about freely. In my opinion, the cost of admission is high—$17 for adults, $9 for children—but this is true of several attractions on this coast. The cavern is open 9am to 5pm daily. The turn-off is to the right, and the cave is 3 to 5km (2–3 miles) from the road.

Thirteen kilometers (8 miles) south of Akumal is a nature park called **Xel-Ha** (© **998/884-9422** in Cancún, 984/873-3588 in Playa, or 984/875-6000 at the park; www.xelha.com.mx). The centerpiece of Xel-Ha (shell-*hah*), a 10-acre ecological park, is a large, beautiful lagoon where you can swim, float, and snorkel in beautifully clear water surrounded by jungle. A small train takes guests upriver to the drop-off point. The water moves calmly toward the sea, and you can float right with it. Snorkeling here offers a higher comfort level than the open sea—there are no waves and currents to pull you about, but there are a lot of fish to view. The park entertains a lot of visitors, mainly families.

Inside the park, you can rent snorkeling equipment and an underwater camera. Platforms allow nonsnorkelers to view the fish. When swimming, be careful to observe the signs directing you where not to swim. (You can see the greatest variety of fish right near the ropes marking the no-swimming areas and near any group of rocks.) Another way to view fish is to use the park's "snuba" gear—a contraption that allows you to breath air through 6m (20-ft.) tubes connected to scuba tanks floating on the surface. It frees you of the cumbersome tank and weights while allowing you to stay down without having to hold your breath. Rental costs $39 for approximately an hour. Like snuba but more elaborate is "sea-trek," a device consisting of an elaborate plastic helmet with air hoses. It allows you to walk around on the bottom breathing normally and perhaps participate in feeding the park's stingrays.

Another attraction is swimming with dolphins. A 1-hour swim costs $90; a 15-minute program costs $35. Make reservations (© **998/887-6840**) at least 24 hours in advance for one of the four daily times.

Xel-Ha is open daily from 8:30am to 5pm. Parking is free. Admission for adults is $25 on weekdays, $19 on weekends; for children age 4 to 11 it's $13 on weekdays, $10 on weekends; children under 4 enter free. Admission includes use of inner tubes, life vest, and shuttle train to the river. Changing rooms and showers are available. An all-inclusive option includes snorkeling equipment rental, locker rental, towels, food, and beverages for $52 for adults and $26 for children (no weekend discounts). The park has five restaurants, two ice cream shops, and a store. It accepts American Express, MasterCard, and Visa, and has an ATM.

Signs clearly mark the turn-off to Xel-Ha. One kilometer (½ mile) of paved road leads to the entrance. Xel-Ha is close to the ruins of Tulum. A popular day tour from Cancún combines the two. If you're traveling on your own, the best time to enjoy Xel-Ha without the crowds is during the weekend from 9am to 2 pm.

About 2km (1 mile) south of Xel-Ha is the **Hidden Worlds Cenotes** ★★★ (© **984/877-8535;** www.hiddenworlds.com.mx), which offers an excellent opportunity to snorkel or dive in a couple of nearby caverns. The caverns are part of a vast network that makes up a single underground river system. The water is crystalline (and a bit cold) and the rock formations impressive. These caverns were filmed for the IMAX production "Journey into Amazing Caves." The people running the show are resourceful. When I was last there, they were putting together a new way to view the caverns using 90 to 120m (300–400 ft.) of submerged half-sections of tubes that will create a long air pocket for viewing the cavern. This is their own invention (which they've dubbed "tube-a-scuba"), and I'm curious to see if it will work. The snorkel tour costs $40 and takes you to different caverns. The main form of transportation is "jungle mobile," with a guide who throws in tidbits of information and lore about the jungle plant life that you see. There is some walking involved, so take shoes or sandals. I've toured several caverns, but floating through one gave me an entirely different perspective.

PUNTA SOLIMAN AND TANKAH BAYS

The next couple of turnoffs to the left lead to Punta Solimán and Tankah bays. On Punta Solimán Bay is a good beach restaurant called **Oscar y Lalo's.** Here you can rent kayaks and snorkel equipment and paddle out to the reefs for some snorkeling. Three kilometers (2 miles) farther is the turn-off for Tankah, where there are a handful of lodgings. The most interesting is **Casa Cenote** (© **998/874-5170;** www.casacenote.com). It has an underground river that surfaces at a *cenote* in the back of the property then goes underground and bubbles up into the sea just a few feet offshore. Casa Cenote has seven rooms, all on the beach. The double rate, including breakfast and dinner at the restaurant, is $168. The owner, an American, provides kayaks and snorkeling gear and can arrange dives, fishing trips, and sailing charters.

A beach road connects the two bays. I found the snorkeling in Tankah better than in Punta Solimán. Snorkeling in the latter was both interesting and frustrating. I've never before experienced so many thermoclines, which are produced by freshwater seeping from the floors of the bay and coming in contact with the warmer saltwater. Light passing through the water is refracted in funny ways. At first I found the effect interesting—it lent an ethereal shininess to everything I was seeing—but then it just got annoying as it cut down sharply on visibility. At one point I was floating through some of the worst of it, trying not to stir up the water, when a giant silvery barracuda came ghostlike through the shimmering water and crossed my field of vision about 6 feet away. As he passed slowly by me I was astonished at how beautiful and luminescent he looked. Still, I will take clear water over shimmering water every time.

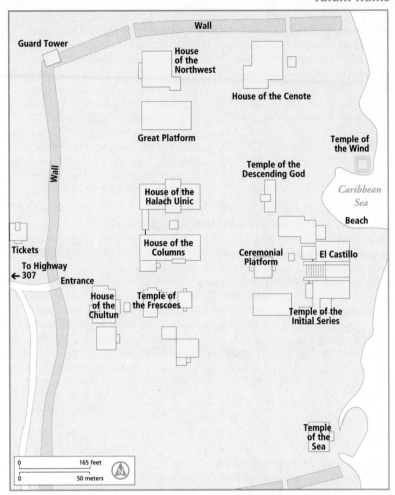

Wall

Guard Tower

House of the Northwest

House of the Cenote

Great Platform

Temple of the Wind

Wall

Temple of the Descending God

Caribbean Sea

House of the Halach Uinic

Beach

Tickets

House of the Columns

Ceremonial Platform

El Castillo

To Highway
← 307

Entrance

House of the Chultun

Temple of the Frescoes

Temple of the Initial Series

Temple of the Sea

0		165 feet
0		50 meters

4 Tulum, Punta Allen & Sian Ka'an

Tulum (130km/81 miles from Cancún) and the Punta Allen Peninsula border the northern edge of the Sian Ka'an biopreserve. The walled Maya city of Tulum is a large post-Classic site overlooking the Caribbean in dramatic fashion. Tour companies and public buses make the trip regularly from Cancún and Playa del Carmen; get there early to avoid the crowds. Tulum also has wonderful, sandy beaches and no large resort hotels. It's a perfect spot for those who like to splash around in the water and lie on the beach away from the resort scene. The town has a dozen restaurants, five pharmacies, three cybercafes, a bank, two cash machines, and several stores.

For those who really want to leave the modern world behind, there's the Punta Allen Peninsula. Getting to the end of the peninsula from Tulum can take 1½ to 3 hours, depending on the condition of the road. It's a place without crowds, frenetic action, or creature comforts; the generator (if there is one) shuts down at 10pm. You'll find great fishing and snorkeling, the natural riches of the Sian Ka'an Biosphere Reserve, and a chance to rest up at what truly feels like the end of the road. A few beach cabañas offer reliable power, telephones, and hot showers.

ORIENTATION   Highway 307 passes the entrance to the ruins (on your left) before running through town. After the entrance to the ruins but before entering the town you'll come to a highway intersection with a traffic light. The light wasn't functioning the last time I was there. To the right is the highway leading to the ruins of Cobá (see "Cobá Ruins," later in this chapter); to the left is the Tulum hotel zone, which begins about 2km (1½ miles) away. The road sign reads BOCA PAILA, which is a place halfway down the **Punta Allen Peninsula.** This road eventually goes all the way to the tip of the peninsula and the town of Punta Allen, a lobstering and fishing village. It is a rough road that is slow going for most of the way. A few miles down the road, you will enter the **Sian Ka'an Biosphere Reserve.**

EXPLORING THE TULUM ARCHAEOLOGICAL SITE

Thirteen kilometers (8 miles) south of Xel-Ha are the ruins of Tulum, a Maya fortress-city overlooking the Caribbean. The ruins are open to visitors daily from 7am to 5pm in the winter, 8am to 6pm in the summer. It's always best to go early, before the crowds start showing up (around 9:30am). The entrance to the ruins is about a 5-minute walk from the archaeological site. There are artisans' stands, a bookstore, a museum, a restaurant, several large bathrooms, and a ticket booth. Admission fee to the ruins is $4. If you want to ride the shuttle from the visitor center to the ruins, it's another $1.50. Parking is $3. A video camera permit costs $4. Licensed guides have a stand next to the path to the ruins and charge $20 for a 45-minute tour in English, French, or Spanish for up to four persons. In some ways, they are like performers and will tailor their presentation to the responses they receive from you. Some will try to draw connections between the Maya and Western theology. But they will point out architectural details that you might otherwise miss.

By A.D. 900, the end of the Classic period, Maya civilization had begun its decline, and the large cities to the south were abandoned. Tulum is one of the small city-states that rose to fill the void. It came to prominence in the 13th century as a seaport, controlling maritime commerce along this section of the coast, and remained inhabited well after the arrival of the Spanish. The primary god here was the diving god, depicted on several buildings as an upside-down figure above doorways. Seen at the Palace at Sayil and Cobá, this curious, almost comical figure is also known as the bee god.

The most imposing building in Tulum is a large stone structure above the cliff called the **Castillo** (castle). Actually a temple as well as a fortress, it was once covered with stucco and painted. In front of the Castillo are several unrestored palace-like buildings partially covered with stucco. On the **beach** below, where the Maya once came ashore, tourists swim and sunbathe, combining a visit to the ruins with a dip in the Caribbean.

The **Temple of the Frescoes,** directly in front of the Castillo, contains interesting 13th-century wall paintings, though entrance is no longer permitted. Distinctly Maya, they represent the rain god Chaac and Ixchel, the goddess of weaving, women, the moon, and medicine. On the cornice of this temple is a relief of the head of the rain god. If you pause a slight distance from the building, you'll see the eyes, nose, mouth, and chin. Notice the remains of the red-painted stucco—at one time all the buildings at Tulum were painted bright red.

Much of what we know of Tulum at the time of the Spanish Conquest comes from the writings of Diego de Landa, third bishop of the Yucatán. He wrote that Tulum was a small city inhabited by about 600 people who lived in platform dwellings along a street and who supervised the trade traffic from Honduras to the Yucatán. Though it was a walled city, most of the inhabitants probably lived outside the walls, leaving the interior for the residences of governors and priests and ceremonial structures. Tulum survived about 70 years after the Conquest, when it was finally abandoned. Because of the great number of visitors this site receives, it is no longer possible to climb all of the ruins. In many cases, visitors are asked to remain behind roped-off areas to view them.

WHERE TO STAY IN & AROUND TULUM

Unless you're just passing through, the place to stay is at one of the more than 30 *palapa* hotels that stretch along the coast from just south of the ruins down to the Punta Allen peninsula. This stretch of coast has great beaches. The seven or eight hotels in town are cheaper than all but the most basic of beach accommodations, but they aren't as much fun. They offer no-frills lodging for $20 to $50 a night. All the beach hotels must generate their own electricity, and this raises the price of lodging. Most of them are simple affairs without a lot of luxuries. Turn east at the highway intersection. Three kilometers (2 miles) ahead, you come to a T junction. North are most of the cheap cabañas. Over the years, I've heard from several sources about cases of theft at a few of these establishments. To the south are most of the *palapa* hotels, including some moderately

---

(Fun Fact   Tulum: A Friendly Difference of Opinion

Two of us cover the entirety of Mexico for Frommer's, and almost without exception we agree on the country's top destinations. However, we have an ongoing dialogue regarding the relative merits and beauty of the ruins at Tulum. Herewith we present our respective cases, and leave it for you to decide with whom you agree.

Lynne says: Ancient Tulum is my favorite of all the ruins, poised as it is on a rocky hill overlooking the transparent, turquoise Caribbean. It's not the largest or most important of the Maya ruins in this area, but it's the only one by the sea, which makes it the most visually impressive. Intriguing carvings and reliefs decorate the well-preserved structures, which date to the 12th to 16th centuries A.D., in the post-Classic period.

David says: Aside from the spectacular setting, Tulum is not as impressive a city as Chichén Itzá, Uxmal, or Ek Balam (discussed in chapter 6). The stonework is cruder than that at these other sites, as if construction of the platforms and temples had been hurried. The city's builders were concerned foremost with security and defense. They chose the most rugged section on this coast and then built stout walls on the other three sides. This must have absorbed a tremendous amount of energy that might otherwise have been used to build the large ceremonial centers and more varied architecture that we see in other sites in the Yucatán.

priced places. The pavement quickly turns into sand, and on both sides of the road you start seeing cabañas. You can try your luck at one of many places.

Very Expensive

Las Ranitas ⭐ This property offers more solitude than Ana y José and more luxury than Nueva Vida. The owners built it with ecological principles and privacy in mind. Footpaths through the native vegetation connect the two-story stucco beach houses and look as if they were meant to blend into the landscape as much as possible. Each house holds two rooms: upstairs ("premier") with a king bed, and downstairs ("conventional") with two double beds. The hotel has four suites, which are quite a bit larger and fancier. The rooms are probably the nicest on this stretch of coast; each has a large tile bathroom, chairs, a writing table, and a private patio or balcony. Solar and wind generators provide electricity. The restaurant closes for supper in the off-season. Some consider the French owners difficult to deal with. Each time I call the hotel, I have to speak to a new manager.

Punta Allen Peninsula, Km 9 Carretera Punta Allen, 77780 Tulum, Q. Roo. ⓒ 984/877-8554. Fax 984/845-0861. www.lasranitas.com. 17 units. $165–$210 double; $242–$275 suite. No credit cards. Rates include continental breakfast during high season, full breakfast during low season. **Amenities:** Restaurant; bar; small pool.

Expensive

Hotel Nueva Vida ⭐ I like this place because it's so different, with few rooms, much space, and an ecological orientation. It has 150m (164 yd.) of beautiful beachfront, but the cabañas are built behind the beach, in the jungle, which has been preserved as much as possible. Most of the rooms are in freestanding thatched cabañas 4m (12 ft.) off the ground. Each is medium size with a private bathroom, a double and a twin bed with mosquito netting, and a ceiling fan (solar cells and wind generators provide energy 24 hr. a day; there are no electrical outlets in the units). The owners are from South America and operate a family-style restaurant. When I was last there, they were building a couple of units in a concrete building, which were going to be larger and have a few more amenities.

Km 8.5 Carretera Punta Allen, 77780 Tulum, Q. Roo. ⓒ 984/877-8512. Fax 984/871-2092. www.tulumnv.com. 7 units. High season $100 double; low season $70 double. Rates include continental breakfast. MC, V. **Amenities:** Restaurant; tour information; limited room service; massage; limited laundry service; nonsmoking rooms.

Restaurant y Cabañas Ana y José ⭐⭐ This comfortable hotel sits on a great beach with a good beach restaurant. The rock-walled cabañas in front (called "oceanfront"), closest to the water, are a little larger than the others and come with two double beds. I also like the attractive second-floor "vista al mar" rooms, which have tall *palapa* roofs. The standard rooms are much like the others but don't face the sea. New construction has crowded them in back, making them much less desirable. The hotel has one suite. There is 24-hour electricity for lights and ceiling fans. Sometimes you can book a package deal that includes hotel and a rental car waiting for you at the Cancún airport. Ana y José is 6.5km (4 miles) south of the Tulum ruins.

Punta Allen Peninsula, Km 7 Carretera Punta Allen (Apdo. Postal 15), 77780 Tulum, Q. Roo. ⓒ 998/887-5470 in Cancún. Fax 998/887-5469. www.anayjose.com. 15 units. High season $110–$150 double; low season $90–$130 double. Rates higher at Christmas and New Year's. Internet specials sometimes available. MC, V. Free parking. **Amenities:** Restaurant; small pool; tour info; car rental.

Moderate

Cabañas Tulum Next to Ana y José's is a row of bungalows facing the same beautiful ocean and beach. This place offers basic accommodations. Rooms are simple yet attractive and large, though poorly lit. The large bathrooms are tiled. All rooms have two double beds (most with new mattresses), screens on the windows, a table, one electric light, and a porch facing the beach. Electricity is available from 7 to 11am and 6 to 11pm. There are billiard and Ping-Pong tables. The cabañas are often full between December 15 and Easter, and in July and August.

Punta Allen Peninsula, Km 7 Carretera Punta Allen (Apdo. Postal 63), 77780 Tulum, Q. Roo. ℭ 984/879-7395. Fax 984/871-2092. www.hotelstulum.com. 32 units. $50–$70 double. No credit cards. **Amenities:** Restaurant; game room.

Zamas ⭐   The owners of these cabañas, a couple from San Francisco, have made their rustic getaway most enjoyable by concentrating on the essentials: comfort, privacy, and good food. The cabañas are simple, attractive, well situated for catching the breeze, and not too close together. Most rooms are in individual structures; the suites and oversized rooms are in modest two-story buildings. For the money, I like the six individual garden *palapas,* which are attractive and comfortable, with either two double beds or a double and a twin. Two small beachfront cabañas with one double bed go for a little less. The most expensive rooms are the upstairs oceanview units, which enjoy a large terrace and lots of sea breezes. I like these especially. They come with a king and a queen bed or a double and a queen bed. The restaurant serves the freshest seafood—I've seen the owner actually flag down passing fishermen to buy their catch. A nice white sand beach stretches between large rocky areas.

Km 5 Carretera Punta Allen, 77780 Tulum, Q. Roo. ℭ 415/387-9806 in the U.S. www.zamas.com. 20 units. High season $80–$115 beachfront double, $90 garden double, $110–$145 oceanview double; low season $60–$90 beachfront double, $50 garden double, $80–$110 oceanview double. No credit cards. **Amenities:** Restaurant.

WHERE TO DINE

There are several restaurants in the town of Tulum. They are reasonably priced and do an okay job. On the main street are **Charlie's** (ℭ 984/871-2136), my favorite for Mexican food, and **Don Cafeto's** (ℭ 984/871-2207). A good Italian-owned Italian restaurant, **Il Giardino di Toni e Simone** (ℭ 984/804-1316; closed Wed), is 1 block off the highway—you'll see a large building supply store called ROCA. It's on the opposite side of the road, 1 block away. Also in town are a couple of roadside places that grill chicken and serve it with rice and beans. Out on the coast, you can eat at **Zamas** or at **Ana y José** (see above).

EXPLORING THE PUNTA ALLEN PENINSULA

If you've been captured by an adventurous spirit and have an excessively sanguine opinion of your rental car, you might want to take a trip down the Punta Allen Peninsula, especially if your interests lie in fly-fishing, birding, or simply exploring new country. The far end of the peninsula is only 48km (30 miles) away, but it can be a very slow trip (up to 3 hr., depending on the condition of the road). Not far from the last cabaña hotel is the entrance to the 1.3-million-acre **Sian Ka'an Biosphere Reserve** (see below). Halfway down the peninsula, at Boca Paila, a bridge crosses to the lower peninsula, where the Boca Paila Fishing Lodge is. On your right is a large lagoon. Another 24km (15 miles) gets you to the village of **Punta Allen,** where you can arrange a birding expedition (available June–Aug, with July being best) or a boat trip (see the entry for Cuzan Guest House in "Where to Stay," below).

WHERE TO STAY

The peninsula offers simple but comfortable lodgings. One or two have electricity for a few hours in the evening, but it goes off around 10pm. Halfway down the peninsula, the **Boca Paila Fishing Lodge** (ℭ 800/245-1950, or 412/935-1577 in the U.S.) specializes in hosting fly-fishers. Its weeklong packages include everything, even the boat and guide. Prices start at $1,500 per person.

The Sian Ka'an Biosphere Reserve

Down the peninsula a few miles south of the Tulum ruins, you'll pass the guardhouse of the Sian Ka'an Biosphere Reserve. The reserve is a tract of 1.3 million acres set aside in 1986 to preserve tropical forests, savannas, mangroves, coastal and marine habitats, and 112km (70 miles) of coastal reefs. The area is home to jaguars, pumas, ocelots, margays, jaguarundis, spider and howler monkeys, tapirs, white-lipped and collared peccaries, manatees, brocket and white-tailed deer, crocodiles, and green, loggerhead, hawksbill, and leatherback sea turtles. It also protects 366 species of birds—you might catch a glimpse of an ocellated turkey, a great curassow, a brilliantly colored parrot, a toucan or trogon, a white ibis, a roseate spoonbill, a jabiru (or wood stork), a flamingo, or one of 15 species of herons, egrets, and bitterns.

The park has three parts: a "core zone" restricted to research; a "buffer zone," to which visitors and families already living there have restricted use; and a "cooperation zone," which is outside the reserve but vital to its preservation. Driving south from Tulum on Highway 307, everything on the left side of the highway is part of the reserve, but there's no access to any of it except at the ruins of Muyil/Chunyaxche. At least 22 archaeological sites have been charted within Sian Ka'an. The best place to check out the reserve is on the Punta Allen Peninsula, part of the "buffer zone." The inns were already in place when the reserve was created. Of these, only the Cuzan Guest House (see below) offers birding trips. But bring your own binoculars and birding books and have at it—the bird life here is rich. Birding is best just after dawn, especially during the April to July nesting season.

Visitors can arrange day trips in Tulum at **Sian Ka'an Tours** (© **984/ 871-2363**; siankaan_tours@hotmail.com), on the east side of the road, 1 block south of the highway intersection. This outfit offers a general-interest day tour and a sunset tour.

Between Boca Paila and Punta Allen are a couple of small, comfortable hotels run by Americans, perfect for getting away from it all. One is **Rancho Sol Caribe** (no phone; www.cancun.com), which has only two or three rooms on a private beach. Punta Allen is a lobstering and fishing village on a palm-studded beach. Isolated and rustic, it's the most laid-back end of the line you'll find for a long time. The small town has a lobster cooperative, a few streets with modest homes, and a lighthouse at the very end of the peninsula.

Cuzan Guest House ⋆ *Finds* This place has a rustic charm perfectly in character with its location at the end of the road, plus the great benefits of hot water, 24-hour solar electricity, comfortable beds, and private bathrooms. You have a choice of Maya-style stucco buildings with thatched roofs, concrete floors, and a combination of twin and king beds with mosquito netting, or raised wooden cabins with thatched roofs and little porches that overlook the water. These have two double beds each. The hotel's restaurant, a large *palapa* with a sand floor, serves three meals a day. Full breakfast and lunch run about $5 each, and dinner costs $12 to $15. The menu sometimes includes lobster in season

(July–Apr). The food is good, and, of course, the seafood is fresh. Payment for meals must be in cash or traveler's checks.

Co-owner Sonja Lilvik, a Californian, offers fly-fishing trips for bone, permit, snook, and tarpon to the nearby saltwater flats and lagoons of Ascension Bay. One-week packages (priced per person, double occupancy) include lodging, three meals a day, a boat, and a guide. She also offers a fascinating 3-hour boat tour of the coastline that includes snorkeling, slipping in and out of mangrove-filled canals for birding, and skirting the edge of an island rookery loaded with frigate birds. November to March is frigate mating season, when the male shows off his big, billowy red breast pouch to impress potential mates. You can also go kayaking along the coast or relax in a hammock on the beach.

Punta Allen. (Reservations: Apdo. Postal 24, 77200 Felipe Carrillo Puerto, Q. Roo. ☎ 983/834-0358. Fax 983/834-0292.) www.flyfishmx.com. 12 units. High season $40–$80 double. Low-season discounts available. All-inclusive fly-fishing packages $1,999 per week. No credit cards. **Amenities:** Restaurant; tours and activities desk.

7 Cobá Ruins

168km (105 miles) SW of Cancún

Older than most of Chichén Itzá and much larger than Tulum, Cobá was the dominant city of the eastern Yucatán before a.d. 1000. The site is large and spread out, with thick forest growing between the temple groups. Rising high above the forest canopy are tall, steep classic Maya pyramids. Of the major sites, this one is the least reconstructed and so disappoints those who expect another Chichén Itzá. Appreciating it requires a greater exercise of the imagination. Bordering the ruins are two lakes, an uncommon feature in the Yucatán, where surface water is rare.

ESSENTIALS
GETTING THERE & DEPARTING   By Car   The road to Cobá begins in Tulum, across Highway 307 from the turn-off to the Punta Allen Peninsula. Turn right when you see signs for Cobá, and continue on that road for 64km (40 miles). Watch out for both *topes* (speed bumps) and potholes. Enter the village, proceed straight until you see the lake, then turn left. The entrance to the ruins is a short distance down the road past some small restaurants. There's a large parking area.

By Bus   Several buses a day leave Tulum and Playa del Carmen for Cobá. Several companies offer bus tours.

EXPLORING THE COBA RUINS
The Maya built many intriguing cities in the Yucatán, but few grander than Cobá ("water stirred by wind"). Much of the 67 sq. km (42 sq. mile) site remains unexcavated. A 96km (60-mile) *sacbé* (a pre-Hispanic raised road or causeway) through the jungle linked Cobá to Yaxuná, once a large, important Maya center 48km (30 miles) south of Chichén Itzá. It's the Maya's longest known *sacbé,* and at least 50 shorter ones lead from here. An important city-state, Cobá flourished from A.D. 632 (the oldest carved date found here) until after the flourishing of Chichén Itzá, around 800. Then Cobá slowly faded in importance and population until it was finally abandoned. Scholars believe Cobá was an important trade link between the Yucatán Caribbean coast and inland cities.

Once at the site, keep your bearings—you can get turned around in the maze of dirt roads in the jungle. And bring bug spray. As spread out as this city is, renting a bike (which you can do at the entrance for a reasonable fee) is a good option. Branching off from every labeled path, you'll notice unofficial narrow paths into the jungle, used by locals as shortcuts through the ruins. These are good for birding, but be careful to remember the way back.

The **Grupo Cobá** boasts an impressive pyramid, the **Temple of the Church (La Iglesia),** which you'll find if you take the path bearing right after the entrance. As you approach, notice the unexcavated mounds on the left. Though the urge to climb the temple is great, the view is better from El Castillo in the Nohoch Mul group farther back.

From here, return to the main path and turn right. You'll pass a sign pointing right to the ruined *juego de pelota* (ball court), but the path is obscure.

Continuing straight ahead on this path for 5 to 10 minutes, you'll come to a fork in the road. To the left and right you'll notice jungle-covered, unexcavated pyramids, and at one point, you'll see a raised portion crossing the pathway—this is the visible remains of the *sacbé* to Yaxuná. Throughout the area, intricately carved stelae stand by pathways or lie forlornly in the jungle underbrush. Although protected by crude thatched roofs, most are weatherworn enough that they're indiscernible.

The left fork leads to the **Nohoch Mul Group,** which contains **El Castillo.** With the exception of Structure 2 in Calakmul, this is the tallest pyramid in the Yucatán (rising even higher than the great El Castillo at Chichén Itzá and the Pyramid of the Magician at Uxmal). So far, visitors are still permitted to climb to the top. From this magnificent lofty perch, you can see unexcavated jungle-covered pyramidal structures poking up through the forest all around.

The right fork (more or less straight on) goes to the **Conjunto Las Pinturas.** Here, the main attraction is the **Pyramid of the Painted Lintel,** a small structure with traces of its original bright colors above the door. You can climb up to get a close look. Though maps of Cobá show ruins around two lakes, there are really only two excavated groups.

Admission is $4, free for children under age 12. Parking is $1. A video camera permit costs $4. The site is open daily from 8am to 5pm, sometimes longer.

WHERE TO STAY & DINE

El Bocadito   El Bocadito, on the right as you enter town (next to the hotel's restaurant of the same name), offers rooms arranged in two rows facing an open patio. They're simple, with tile floors, two double beds, no bedspreads, a ceiling fan, and a washbasin separate from the toilet and cold-water shower cubicle. The open-air restaurant offers good meals at reasonable prices, served by a friendly, efficient staff.

Calle Principal, Cobá, Q. Roo. (Reservations: Apdo. Postal 56, 97780 Valladolid, Yuc.) No phone. 8 units. $18–$25 double. No credit cards. Free unguarded parking.

Villas Arqueológicas Cobá   This lovely lakeside hotel is a 5-minute walk from the ruins. It is laid out like its Club Med counterparts in Chichén Itzá and Uxmal. The beautiful grounds hold a pool and tennis court. The restaurant is top-notch, though expensive, and the rooms are stylish and modern, but small. Beds occupy niches that surround the mattress on three sides and can be somewhat uncomfortable for those taller than about 2m (6 ft.). The hotel also has a library on Mesoamerican archaeology (with books in French, English, and Spanish). Make reservations—this hotel fills with touring groups.

For Your Comfort at Cobá

Visit Cobá in the morning or after the heat of the day has passed. Mosquito repellent, drinking water, and comfortable shoes are imperative.

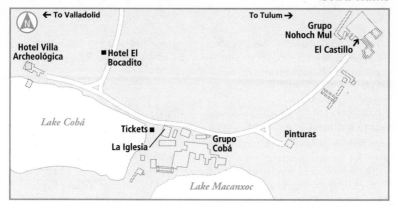

Cobá, Q. Roo. ℂ **800/258-2633** in the U.S., or 55/5203-3086 in Mexico City. 41 units. $90 double. Rates include continental breakfast. ¹⁄₂-board (breakfast plus lunch or dinner) $29 per person; full board (3 meals) $58 per person. AE, MC, V. Free guarded parking. Drive through town and turn right at lake; hotel is straight ahead on the right. **Amenities:** Restaurant; bar; medium-size pool.

EN ROUTE TO THE LOWER CARIBBEAN COAST: FELIPE CARRILLO PUERTO

Mexico's lower Caribbean coast is often called the Costa Maya. This area attracts fishermen, divers, and travelers looking to get away from the crowds. For divers it's especially interesting for the highly regarded Chinchorro reefs, which lie 20 miles offshore (see below). You'll find sandy beaches good for sunbathing—but not for swimming, because the shore usually has a muddy bottom below the water. For swimming, the beaches around Tulum and Playa del Carmen are better. But if you want to snorkel or dive among pristine reefs, kayak in calm turquoise water, or perhaps do some fly-fishing away from the crowds, this area is a good option. And there's fine swimming in Lake Bacalar.

You also might enjoy the astounding Maya ruins in the Río Bec area, west of Bacalar. I prefer them over Tulum or Cobá. Here, too, you'll find a richer ecosystem than the northern part of the peninsula. The forest canopy is higher, and the wildlife is more abundant. If you're interested in exploring this territory, see "The Río Bec Ruin Route," later in this chapter.

Continue south on Highway 307 from Tulum. The road narrows, the speed limit drops, and you begin to see *topes* (speed bumps). Down the road some 24km (15 miles), a sign points to the small but interesting ruins of **Muyil.** Take bug spray. The principal ruins are a small group of buildings and a plaza dominated by the Castillo, a pyramid of medium height but unusual construction. From here, a canal dug by the Maya enters what is now the Sian Ka'an preserve and empties into a lake, with other canals going from there to the saltwater estuary of Boca Paila. The local community offers a boat ride ($35) through these canals and lakes. The 3¹⁄₂-hour tour includes snorkeling the canal and letting the current carry you along. Soft drinks are also included. A few travel agencies in Playa and Tulum offer this tour among their Sian Ka'an trips. The agencies charge more but provide transportation, better interpretation, and lunches.

Felipe Carrillo Puerto (pop. 60,000) is the first large town you pass on the road to Ciudad Chetumal. It has two gas stations, a market, a bus terminal, and

> **Tips Last Gas**
>
> Felipe Carrillo Puerto is the only place to buy **gasoline** between Tulum and Chetumal. If you're desperate, there is a guy who sells gas in Bacalar; just ask when you get there.

a few modest hotels and restaurants. Next to the gas station in the center of town is a bank with an ATM. Highway 184 goes from here into the interior of the peninsula, leading eventually to Mérida, which makes Carrillo Puerto a turning point for those making the "short circuit" of the Yucatán Peninsula.

The town is of interest for having been a rebel stronghold during the War of the Castes and the center of the intriguing millenarian cult of the "Talking Cross." The town is still home to a strong community of believers in the cult who practice their own brand of religion and are respected by the whole town. Every month a synod of sorts is held here for the church leaders in 12 neighboring towns.

8 Majahual, Xcalak & the Chinchorro Reef

South of Felipe Carrillo Puerto, the speed bumps begin in earnest. In 45 minutes you reach the turn-off for Majahual and Xcalak, which is at the town of Limones. This year there has been work on the road between Limones and Majahual and Limones and Bacalar. It might be completed by the time you read this. (And it might not.) The roadwork is being done to facilitate bus tours from the new cruise-ship pier in **Majahual** (mah-hah-*wahl*) to some of the Maya ruins close by, especially Chacchoben. Many passengers elect to enjoy some beach time in Majahual instead. Even before the cruise-ship pier came to Majahual, I saw little that was attractive about the town. The best option is to keep your distance and stay farther down the peninsula in the area of Xcalak. You'll come to the turn-off for Xcalak before you get to Majahual. Xcalak has better lodging than Majahual, a decent dive shop, and more interesting coastal features. It used to take about 1½ hours to get there from Highway 307, but it will be quicker when the new road is finished. On the route, you'll see a sign for the turn-off for the **Maya-Ha Dive Resort** (see below).

Xcalak (eesh-kah-*lahk*) is a depopulated, weather-beaten fishing village with a few comfortable places to stay and a couple of restaurants. It once had a population as large as 1,200 before the 1958 hurricane washed most of the town away; now it has only 300 permanent residents. It's charming in a run-down way, and you'll certainly feel miles away from the crush of the crowds. From here you work your way back up the coast to get to one of the several small inns just beyond the town.

ORIENTATION

ARRIVING   By Car   Driving south from Felipe Carrillo Puerto, you'll come to the turn-off (left) onto Highway 10, 2.5km (1½ miles) after Limones; then it's a 48km (30 mile) drive to the coastal settlement of **Majahual.** Before Majahual, there's a military guard station. Tell the guard your destination and turn right to continue to **Xcalak** on the paved highway for 56km (35 miles) more.

DIVING THE CHINCHORRO REEF

The **Chinchorro Reef Underwater National Park** is 38km (24 miles) long and 13km (8 mile) wide. The oval reef is as shallow as 1m (3 ft.) on its interior and as deep as 910m (3,000 ft.) on its exterior. It lies 32km (20 miles) offshore. Locals

The Yucatán's Lower Caribbean Coast

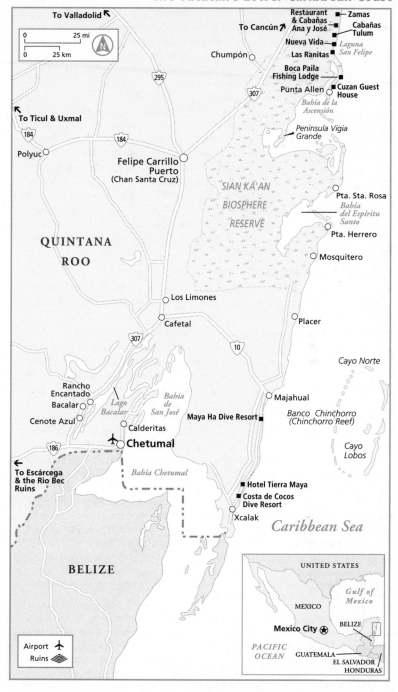

To Valladolid

0   25 mi
0   25 km

Restaurant
& Cabañas
Ana y José
To Cancún

Zamas

Cabañas
Tulum

Nueva Vida
Chumpón
Las Ranitas

Laguna
San Felipe

Boca Paila
Fishing Lodge

Punta Allen

Cuzan Guest
House

To Ticul & Uxmal

Bahía de la
Ascensión

184

184

Polyuc

295

307

Peninsula Vigia
Grande

Felipe Carrillo
Puerto
(Chan Santa Cruz)

SIAN KA'AN

BIOSPHERE

RESERVE

Pta. Sta. Rosa

Bahía
del Espíritu
Santo

QUINTANA

ROO

Pta. Herrero

Mosquitero

Los Limones

Cafetal

Placer

307

10

Cayo Norte

Rancho
Encantado
Bacalar

Lago
Bacalar

Bahía
de
San José

Majahual

Banco Chinchorro
(Chinchorro Reef)

Cenote Azul

Maya Ha Dive Resort

Cayo
Lobos

186

Calderitas

Chetumal

Bahía Chetumal

To Escárcega
& the Rio Bec
Ruins

Hotel Tierra Maya
Costa de Cocos
Dive Resort

Xcalak

Caribbean Sea

BELIZE

Airport
Ruins

UNITED STATES

Gulf of
Mexico

MEXICO

BELIZE

Mexico City

PACIFIC
OCEAN

GUATEMALA

EL SALVADOR
HONDURAS

159

claim it's the last virgin reef system in the Caribbean. It's invisible from the ocean side; hence, one of its diving attractions is the **shipwrecks**—at least 30—that decorate the underwater landscape. One is on top of the reef. Divers have counted 40 cannons at one wreck site. On the west side are walls and coral gardens.

The biggest operation making regular trips to the reef is the **Maya-Ha Dive Resort** (✆ 877/443-1600 in the U.S., or 983/831-0065; fax 512/443-2978; www.mayaharesort.com), on the coast between Majahual and Xcalak. Take the road to Xcalak and look for a sign at the turn-off. The resort offers a variety of dive packages, which can include transportation between the hotel and the Cancún airport. It also offers activities for bad-weather days and for non-divers, including tours of ruins. The 18 rooms are large, with large bathrooms and purified tap water. All have air-conditioning and are well lit, thanks to an on-site generator. There are also a few small rental houses on the property. The restaurant serves inventive Mexican *nueva cocina.* There is a pool on site.

Aventuras XTC (✆ 983/831-0461; divextc@pocketmail.com) is the fully equipped dive shop for the hotels in the Xcalak area. It does a lot of dives around the local reefs, which offer some good diving. There's been talk of fixing up a boat to take divers to Chinchorro.

WHERE TO STAY & DINE

Aside from the two places mentioned here, there are six small inns in Xcalak. Americans run most of them, including a four-room property in Xcalak called **Marina Mike's Hotel** (www.xcalak.com).

Costa de Cocos Dive Resort ★★   Lodging here consists of several freestanding cabañas set around a large, attractive sandy beach graced with coconut palms. The cabañas are comfortable and have a lot of cross-ventilation, ceiling fans, hot water, and comfortable beds. They also come with 24-hour electricity generated by wind and solar power and reverse-osmosis purified tap water. Beds are quite comfortable.

Dive equipment is available and included in dive packages; day guests can rent it separately. Watersports equipment for rent includes ocean kayaks. Fly-fishing for bonefish, tarpon, and snook inside Chetumal Bay with experienced English-speaking guides is a popular way to spend the day, as is birding at a sanctuary island. NAUI and PADI resort or open-water certification can be arranged for an additional fee. The hotel recently acquired a 33-foot dive boat and takes divers out to Chinchorro. The main building has a bar and restaurant where guests congregate for an afternoon cocktail. The casual restaurant offers good home-style cooking, usually with a choice of one or two main courses at dinner, sandwiches at lunch, and full breakfast fare. The phone numbers below connect you through an Internet line to an answering machine in Xcalak.

Km 52 Carretera Majahual–Xcalak, Q. Roo. ✆ 800/391-5509 in the U.S., or 206/337-2635 in the U.S. www.costadecocos.com. 16 cabañas. High season $135 double; low season $110 double. Dive rates and packages available; e-mail request. Rates include breakfast and dinner. No credit cards. **Amenities:** Restaurant; bar; watersports equipment; airport transportation; dive shop.

Hotel Tierra Maya   This is a comfortable, modern-style hotel on the beach. Rooms in the two-story building are spacious and designed to have good cross-ventilation. They come with ceiling fans, and some rooms have the option of air-conditioning for an extra charge. All have private balconies or terraces looking out to the sea, hammocks, and bottled purified water. Solar generators provide electricity. Bathrooms are large, and beds are either twins or queens. The owners recently opened a restaurant and can arrange diving, fishing, and snorkeling trips for guests. Guests have Internet access and the use of kayaks and bikes.

Km 54 Carretera Majahual–Xcalak, Q. Roo. © **800/480-4505** in the U.S. or 983/831-0404. www.tierra maya.net. 6 units. High season $85–$95 double; low season $70–$80 double. Rates include continental breakfast. MC, V for advance payments. **Amenities:** Restaurant.

9 Lago Bacalar ⭐⭐⭐

104km (65 miles) SW of Felipe Carrillo Puerto, 37km (23 miles) NW of Chetumal

Bacalar Lake is an elaborate trick played upon the senses. I remember once standing on a pier on the lake and gazing down into perfectly clear water. As I lifted my eyes I could see the blue tint of the Caribbean. Beyond lay a dense tropical forest. A breeze blowing in from the sea smelled of the salt air, and though I knew it to be untrue, I couldn't help but believe that the water I was gazing on was, in fact, an inlet of the sea and not a lake at all; perhaps a well-sheltered lagoon like Xel-Ha. Lakes in tropical lowlands, especially those surrounded by tropical jungle, are always turbid and muddy. How could this one be so clear? The answer is that Bacalar is not fed by surface runoff, but by several *cenotes* that lie beneath its surface. Only in the Yucatán is such a thing possible. It's enchanting.

This is the perfect spot for being bone idle. But there's plenty to do, too. You can explore the jungle, visit some particularly elegant Maya ruins in the nearby Río Bec area, or take in a wonderful museum about the Maya in Chetumal. Given the choice, I would rather stay in Bacalar and visit Chetumal than the reverse. The town of Bacalar is quiet and quaint. There are a few stores and a couple of restaurants. An 18th-century fort with a moat and stout bastions is by the lake. Inside the fort is a small museum (admission is 50¢) that has several artifacts on display. All text is in Spanish.

ORIENTATION Driving south on Highway 307, the town of Bacalar is 1½ hours beyond Felipe Carrillo Puerto, clearly marked by signs. If you're driving north from Chetumal, it takes about a half hour. Buses going south from Cancún and Playa del Carmen stop here, and there are frequent buses from Chetumal.

WHERE TO STAY

Hotel Laguna The Laguna overlooks the lake from a lovely vantage point. All the rooms share the view and have little terraces that make enjoyable sitting areas. The medium-size rooms have ceiling fans, and most come with two double beds. The mattresses in the bungalows aren't good. The bathrooms are simple but have no problem delivering hot water. A restaurant that shares the same view is open from 7am to 9pm. The bar makes a credible margarita. The highest occupancy rates are from July to August and December to January, when you should make a reservation. The hotel is easy to spot from the road; look for the sign about 1km (½ mile) after you pass through the town of Bacalar.

Bulevar Costera de Bacalar 479, 77010 Lago Bacalar, Q. Roo. © **983/834-2206**. Fax 983/834-2205. 34 units. $45 double; $77–$95 bungalow for 5–8 persons. MC, V. **Amenities:** Restaurant; bar; small pool.

Rancho Encantado Cottage Resort ⭐⭐ This beautiful, serene lakeside retreat consists of 12 immaculate white stucco cottages scattered over a shady lawn beside the smooth Lago Bacalar. Each is large and has mahogany louvered windows, a red-tile floor, a dining table and chairs, a living room or sitting area, a porch with chairs, and hammocks strung between trees. Some rooms have cedar ceilings and red-tiled roofs, and others have thatched roofs. All are decorated with folk art and murals inspired by Maya ruins. The newest units are the four waterfront cottages (nos. 9–12). Beds come in different combinations of doubles and twins. Orange, lime, mango, *sapote,* ceiba, banana, palm, and oak trees; wild orchids; and bromeliads on the grounds make great bird shelters, attracting flocks of chattering parrots, turquoise-browed motmots, toucans, and at least 100 more species, many of which are easy to spot outside your room.

The hotel offers almost a dozen excursions. Among them are day trips to the **Río Bec** ruin route, an extended visit to **Calakmul,** outings to the **Majahual Peninsula,** and a riverboat trip to the Maya ruins of **Lamanai,** deep in a Belizian forest. Excursions cost $55 to $115 per person, depending on the length and difficulty of the trip, and several have a three-person minimum. To find the Rancho, look for the hotel's sign on the left about 1.5km (1 mile) before Bacalar.

Km 3 Carretera Felipe Carrillo Puerto–Chetumal, 77000 Chetumal, Q. Roo. ℰ/fax **983/831-0037.** (Reservations: P.O. Box 1256, Taos, NM 87571.) ℰ **800/505-MAYA** in the U.S. Fax 505/751-0972. www.encantado.com. 13 units. Dec–Apr $150–$180 double; May–Nov $100–$120 double. Rates include continental breakfast and dinner. MC, V. **Amenities:** Restaurant; bar; large outdoor whirlpool; watersports equipment; tour desk; massage service. *In room:* Fridge, coffeemaker.

WHERE TO DINE

Besides the restaurants at the hotels discussed above, you may enjoy the **Restaurante Cenote Azul,** a comfortable open-air thatched-roof restaurant on the edge of the beautiful Cenote Azul. Main courses cost $5 to $12. To get to Restaurant Cenote Azul, follow the highway to the south edge of town and turn left at the restaurant's sign; follow the road around to the restaurant. At Rancho Encantado you can swim in Lago Bacalar, and at the Restaurant Cenote you can take a dip in placid Cenote Azul—but without skin lotion of any kind, because it collects in the *cenote.*

10 Chetumal

251km (156 miles) S of Tulum, 37km (23 miles) S of Lago Bacalar

Capital of the state, and the second-largest city (after Cancún), Chetumal (pop. 210,000) is not a tourist destination. The old part of town, down by the river (Río Hondo), has a Caribbean feel, but the rest is unremarkable. Chetumal is the gateway to Belize, to Tikal, and to the Río Bec ruins. If you're going to spend the night here, visit the **Museo de la Cultura Maya** (ℰ **983/832-6838**), especially if you plan to follow the Río Bec ruin route (see below).

ESSENTIALS
GETTING THERE & DEPARTING

BY PLANE **Aviacsa** (ℰ **983/872-7698**) has a direct flight to and from Mexico City. The airport is west of town, just north of the entrance from the highway.

BY CAR It's a little more than 3 hours from Tulum. If you're heading to Belize, you won't be able to take your rental car because the rental companies won't allow it. To get to the ruins of Tikal in Guatemala, you must go through Belize to the border crossing at Ciudad Melchor de Mencos.

BY BUS The main bus station (ℰ **983/832-5110**) is 20 blocks from the town center on Insurgentes at Niños Héroes. Buses go to Cancún, Tulum, Playa del Carmen, Puerto Morelos, Mérida, Campeche, Villahermosa, and Tikal, Guatemala.

To Belize: Buses depart from the Lázaro Cárdenas market (most often called *el mercado nuevo*). Ask for Autobuses Novelo. The company has local service every 45 minutes ($10) and four express buses per day ($14).

VISITOR INFORMATION

The **State Tourism Office** (© 983/835-0860, ext. 1808) is at Calzada del Centenario 622, between Comonfort and Ciricote. Office hours are Monday to Friday from 9am to 3pm.

ORIENTATION

The telephone **area code** is **983.**

All traffic enters the city from the west and feeds onto Avenida **Obregón** into town. Avenida **Héroes** is the main north-south street.

A MUSEUM NOT TO MISS

Museo de la Cultura Maya ★★★   This modern museum unlocks the complex world of the Maya through interactive exhibits and genuine artifacts. Push a button, and an illustrated description appears, explaining the medicinal and domestic uses of plants with their Mayan and scientific names; another exhibit describes the social classes of the Maya by their manners of dress. One of the most fascinating exhibits describes the Maya's ideal of personal beauty and the subsequent need to deform craniums, scar the face and body, and induce cross-eyed vision. An enormous screen flashes images taken from an airplane flying over more than a dozen Maya sites from Mexico to Honduras. Another large television shows the architectural variety of Maya pyramids and how they were probably built. Then a walk on a glass floor takes you over representative ruins in the Maya world. In the center of the museum is the three-story, stylized, sacred ceiba tree, which the Maya believed connected the underworld (Xibalba), Earth, and the heavens. If you can arrange it, see the museum before you tour the Río Bec ruins.

Av. Héroes s/n. © **983/832-6838.** Admission $5. Tues–Thurs 9am–7pm; Fri–Sat 9am–8pm. Between Colón and Gandhi, 8 blocks from Av. Obregón, just past the Holiday Inn.

WHERE TO STAY

Hotel Holiday Inn Puerta Maya   This modern hotel (formerly the Hotel Continental) has the best air-conditioning in town and is only a block from the Museo de la Cultura Maya. Most rooms are medium in size and come with two double beds or one king bed. Bathrooms are roomy and well lit.

Av. Niños Héroes 171, 77000 Chetumal, Q. Roo. © **800/465-4329** in the U.S., or 983/835-0400. Fax 983/832-1676. 85 units. $110 double. AE, MC, V. Free secured parking. From Av. Obregón, turn left on Av. Héroes, go 6 blocks, and look for the hotel on the right. **Amenities:** Restaurant; bar; medium-size pool; room service; laundry. In room: A/C, TV.

Hotel Nachancán   One block from the new market *(el mercado nuevo)* and buses to Belize, this hotel offers plain but comfortable rooms, with one or two double beds. Also a block away is El Buen Gusto, which serves some of the best Yucatecan food in Chetumal. Bathrooms are small, with no counter space, but they offer plenty of hot water (once it finally arrives). A cab to the Museo de la Cultura Maya costs $1.

Calzada Veracruz 379, 77000 Chetumal, Q. Roo. © **983/832-3232.** 20 units. $25 double; $33 suite. No credit cards. Drive the length of Av. Obregón to where it stops at Calzada Veracruz, turn left, and drive 2km (1¼ miles); the hotel will be on the right. **Amenities:** Restaurant; bar. In room: A/C, TV, no phone.

WHERE TO DINE

I can recommend just a few restaurants in Chetumal. If you want to eat in air-conditioned surroundings in a modern, comfortable setting, try **Espress Café & Restaurant,** Calle 22 de Enero 141, corner of Boulevard Bahía (© **983/833-3013**). It serves well-prepared Mexican food, light fare such as sandwiches, and good breakfasts. Open daily from 8am to midnight. For an economical meal with some local atmosphere, try **Restaurante Pantoja,** on the corner of calles Ghandi and 16 de Septiembre (no phone), 2 blocks east of the Museum of Maya Culture. It offers a cheap daily special, good green enchiladas, and such local specialties as *poc chuc.* It's open Monday to Saturday from 7am to 9pm. To sample excellent *antojitos,* the local supper food, go to **El Buen Gusto,** on Calzada Veracruz across from the market (no phone). A Chetumal institution, it serves excellent *salbutes* and *panuchos.* Doors open around 7pm and close around midnight every night.

ONWARD FROM CHETUMAL

From Chetumal you have several choices. The Maya ruins of Lamanai, in Belize, are an easy day trip if you have transportation (not a rental car). You can explore the Río Bec ruin route directly west of the city (see below) by taking Highway 186.

11 The Río Bec Ruin Route

A few miles west of Bacalar and Chetumal begins an area of Maya settlement known to archaeologists as the Río Bec region. A number of ruins stretch from close to Bacalar west into the state of Campeche. These ruins are numerous, intriguing, and dramatic. Their architecture is heavily stylized, with lots of decoration. In recent years, excavation has led to many discoveries. With excavation has come restoration, but the ruins here have not been rebuilt to the same degree as those at Uxmal and Chichén Itzá. However, in some cases, the archaeologists found buildings so well preserved that they needed little restoration.

Nor have these sites been cleared of jungle growth in the same manner as the marquee ruins mentioned above. Trees and vines grow in profusion around the buildings, giving the sites the feel of lost cities. Keep the mosquito repellent handy. In visiting them, you can imagine what John Lloyd Stephens and Catherwood must have felt when they traipsed through the Yucatán in the 19th century. And watch for wildlife; on my last visit I saw several denizens of the tropical forest. The fauna along the entire route is especially rich. You might see a toucan, a grand curassow, or a macaw hanging about the ruins, and orioles, egrets, and several birds of prey are extremely common. Gray fox, wild turkey, *tesquintle* (a bushy-tailed, plant-eating rodent), the raccoon relative coatimundi (with its long tapered snout and tail), and armadillos inhabit the area in abundance. At Calakmul, a family of howler monkeys resides in the trees overlooking the parking area.

THE ROUTE'S STARTING POINT   Halfway between Bacalar and Chetumal is the turn-off for Highway 186 to Escárcega (about 20km/12 miles from either town). It's a major highway and is well marked. This is the same road that leads to Campeche, Palenque, and Villahermosa. There are a couple of gas stations on the route. One is at the town of Xpujil. The Río Bec sites are at varying distances off this highway. You pass through a guard station at the border with Campeche state. The guards might ask you to present your travel papers, or they might just wave you on. Either way, it's no big deal. You can divide your sightseeing into several day trips from Bacalar or Chetumal, or you can spend the night in this area and see more the next day. If you get an early start, you can easily visit a few of the sites mentioned here in a day.

Evidence shows that these ruins, especially Becán, were part of the **trade route** linking the Caribbean coast at Cobá to Edzná and the Gulf coast, and to Lamanai in Belize and beyond. At one time, a great number of cities thrived in this region, and much of the land was dedicated to the intensive cultivation of maize. Today all of this lies hidden under a dense jungle, which blankets the land from horizon to horizon.

I have listed the following sites in east-to-west order, the way you would see them driving from the Caribbean coast. If you decide to tour these ruins, take the time to visit the Museo de la Cultura Maya in Chetumal first. It will lend context to what you see. If you want a guide to show you the area, contact **Luis Téllez** (© **983/832-3496;** www.sacbetravel.com), who lives in Chetumal. The best way to reach him is through the e-mail link on his website. He is an exceptionally well-informed guide, speaks English, and is a good driver. He also knows a lot about local wildlife and guides many tours for birders. For a map of this area, consult the "Yucatán Peninsula" map in chapter 2. Entry to each site is $2 to $4. Informational signs at each building are in Mayan, Spanish, and English. There are few if any refreshments at the ruins, so bring your own water and food. All the principal sites have toilets.

Food and Lodging   Your lodging choices are few. On the upscale side are the Explorean hotel near Kohunlich and the eco-village in Chicanná. Food and lodging of the no-frills sort can be found in the town of Xpujil and near Calakmul.

The **Explorean** (© **888/679-3748;** www.theexplorean.com) is an eco-lodge for adventure travelers who like their comfort. It sits all alone on the crest of a small hill not far from the ruins of Kohunlich. It has a small pool and spa and lovely rooms, and offers guide services and adventure tours (mountain biking, rappelling, kayaking) all as part of an all-inclusive package. The cost is over $500 for two people and, in addition to the tours, includes food and drink. The hotel is a member of the Fiesta Americana chain.

The **Chicanná Eco Village,** Km 144 Carretera Escárcega (© **981/816-2233** in Campeche for reservations), is just beyond the town of Xpujil. It offers 28 nicely furnished rooms distributed among several two-story thatched bungalows. The comfortable rooms have two doubles or a king bed, ceiling fans, a large bathroom, and screened windows. The manicured lawns and flower beds are lovely, with pathways linking the bungalows to each other and to the restaurant and swimming pool. Double rooms go for $110.

In the village of Xpujil (just before the ruins of Xpujil) are three modest hotels and a couple of restaurants. The best food and lodging are at **Restaurant y Hotel Calakmul** (© **983/871-6029**), run by Doña María Cabrera. The hotel

---

⌒Tips   Recommended Reading

For a bit of background reading to help you make the most of your visit, I recommend *A Forest of Kings: The Untold Story of the Ancient Maya,* by Linda Schele and David Freidel (William Morrow, 1990); *The Blood of Kings: Dynasty and Ritual in Maya Art,* by Linda Schele and Mary Ellen Miller (George Braziller, 1968); and *The Maya Cosmos,* by David Freidel and Linda Schele (William Morrow, 1993). *Arqueología Mexicana* magazine devoted its July/August 1995 issue to the Quintana Roo portion of the Río Bec ruin route. Last, though it lacks historic and cultural information and many sites have expanded since it was written, Joyce Kelly's *An Archaeological Guide to Mexico's Yucatán Peninsula* (University of Oklahoma, 1993), is the best companion book to have. For a crash course, focus on the meaning of the jaguar, Xibalba (the underworld), and the earth monster.

has 12 comfortable rooms that go for $40. They have tile floors, private bathrooms with hot water, and good beds. The restaurant is open daily from 6am to midnight. Main courses cost $3 to $8. The chicken cooked in herbs is excellent.

DZIBANCHE AND KINICHNA

The turn-off for this site is 37km (23 miles) from the highway intersection and is well marked. From the turn-off it's another 23km (14 miles) to the ruins. The road has recently been repaired and is in good condition. Dzibanché (or Tzibanché) means "place where they write on wood"—obviously not the original name, which remains unknown. Exploration began here in 1993, and the site opened to the public in late 1994. Scattered over 42 sq. km (26 sq. miles) are several groupings of buildings and plazas; only a small portion is excavated. It dates from the Classic period (A.D. 300–900) and was occupied for around 700 years.

TEMPLES & PLAZAS   Two large adjoining plazas have been cleared. The most important structure yet excavated is called the Temple of the Owl, which is in the main plaza, Plaza Xibalba. Archaeologists found a stairway that descends from the top of the structure deep into the pyramid, ending in a burial chamber. It is closed to visitors. There they uncovered a number of beautiful polychromatic lidded vessels, one of which has an owl painted on the top handle with its wings spreading onto the lid. White owls were messengers of the gods of the underworld in the Maya religion. Also found here were the remains of a sacrificial victim and what appear to be the remains of a Maya queen, which is unique in the archaeology of the Maya.

Opposite the Temple of the Owl is the **Temple of the Cormorant,** named after a polychromed drinking vessel found here depicting the bird. Here, too, archaeologists have found evidence of an interior tomb similar to the one in the Temple of the Owl, but excavations of it have not yet begun. Other magnificently preserved pottery pieces found during excavations include an incense burner with an almost three-dimensional figure of the diving god attached to the outside, and another incense burner with an elaborately dressed representation of the god Itzamná attached.

Situated all by itself is **Structure 6,** a miniature rendition of Teotihuacán's style of *tablero* and *talud* architecture. Each step of the pyramid is made of a sloping surface *(talud)* crowned by a vertical stone facing *(tablero)*. Teotihuacán was near present-day Mexico City, but its influence stretched as far as Guatemala. At the top of the pyramid is a doorway, its wooden lintel still intact after centuries of weathering. This detail gave the site its name. Carved into the wood are date glyphs for the year A.D. 733.

Near the site is another city, **Kinichná** (kee-neech-*nah*). About 2.5km (1½ miles) north, it is reachable only by a rutted road that's impassable during the rainy season. An Olmec-style jade figure was found there. It has a large acropolis with five buildings on three levels, which have been restored and are in good condition, with fragments of the remaining stucco still visible.

KOHUNLICH

Kohunlich (koh-*hoon*-leech), 42km (26 miles) from the turn-off for Highway 186, dates from around A.D. 100 to 900. Turn left off the road, and the entrance is 9km (5½ miles) ahead. From the parking area, you enter the grand, parklike site, crossing a large and shady ceremonial area flanked by four large, conserved pyramidal edifices. Continue walking, and just beyond this grouping you'll come to Kohunlich's famous **Pyramid of the Masks** under a thatched covering. The masks, actually enormous plaster faces, date from around A.D. 500 and are on the facade of the building. Each mask has an elongated face and wears a headdress with a mask on its crest and a mask on the chinpiece, essentially masks within masks. The top one is thought to represent the astral world, while the lower one represents the underworld, suggesting that the wearer of this headdress is among the living and not in either of the other worlds. Note the carving on the pupils, which suggests a solar connection, possibly with the night sun that illuminated the underworld. This may mean that the person had shamanic vision.

It's speculated that masks covered much of the facade of this building, which is built in the Río Bec style, with rounded corners, a false stairway, and a false temple on the top. At least one theory holds that the masks are a composite of several rulers at Kohunlich. Recent excavations of buildings immediately to the left after you enter uncovered two intact pre-Hispanic skeletons and five decapitated heads that were probably used in a ceremonial ritual. To the right after you enter (follow a shady path through the jungle) is another recently excavated plaza. It's thought to have housed priests or rulers, due to the high quality of pottery found there and the fine architecture of the rooms. Scholars believe that Kohunlich became overpopulated, leading to its decline.

XPUJIL

Xpujil (eesh-poo-*heel;* also spelled Xpuhil), meaning either "cattail" or "forest of kapok trees," flourished between A.D. 400 and 900. This is a small site that's easy to get to. Look for a blue sign on the highway pointing to the right. The entrance is just off the highway. After buying a ticket ($3), you have to walk 200 yards to the main structure. Along the path are some *chechén* trees. Don't touch; they are poisonous and will provoke blisters. On the right, you'll see a platform supporting a restored two-story building with a central staircase on the eastern side. Decorating the first floor are the remnants of a decorative molding and two galleries connected by a doorway. About 90m (100 yd.) farther you come to the site's main structure—a rectangular ceremonial platform 2m (6 ft.) high and 52m (173 ft.) long supporting the palace, decorated with three tall towers shaped like miniature versions of the pyramids in Tikal, Guatemala. These towers are purely decorative, with false stairways and temples, too small to serve as such. The effect is beautiful. The main body of the building holds 12 rooms, which are now in ruins.

BECAN ⭐⭐⭐

Becán (beh-*kahn*) is about 7km (4½ miles) beyond Xpujil and is visible on the right side of the highway. Becán means "moat filled by water," and, in fact, it was protected by a moat spanned by seven bridges. The extensive site dates from the early Classic to the late post-Classic (600 B.C.–A.D. 1200) period. Although it was abandoned by A.D. 850, ceramic remains indicate that there may have been a population resurgence between 900 and 1000, and it was still used as a ceremonial site as late as 1200. Becán was an administrative and ceremonial center with political sway over at least seven other cities in the area, including Chicanná, Hormiguero, and Payán.

The first plaza group you see after you enter was the center for grand ceremonies. From the highway, you can see the back of a pyramid (Structure 1) with two temples on top. Beyond and in between the two temples you can see the Temple atop Structure 4, which is opposite Temple 1. When the high priest appeared through the mouth of the earth monster in the center of this temple (which he reached by way of a hidden side stairway that's now partly exposed), he was visible from what is now the highway. It's thought that commoners had to watch ceremonies from outside the ceremonial plaza—thus the site's position was for good viewing purposes. The back of Structure 4 is believed to have been a civic plaza where rulers sat on stone benches while pronouncing judgments. The second plaza group dates from around A.D. 850 and has perfect twin towers on top, where there's a big platform. Under the platform are 10 rooms that are thought to be related to Xibalba (shee-*bahl*-bah), the underworld. Hurricane Isidore damaged them, and they are closed until they can be repaired. Earth monster faces probably covered this building (and appeared on other buildings as well). Remains of at least one ball court have been unearthed. Next to the ball court is a well-preserved figure in an elaborate headdress behind glass. He was excavated not far from where he is now displayed. The markings are well defined, displaying a host of details.

CHICANNA

Slightly over 1.5km (1 mile) beyond Becán, on the left side of the highway, is Chicanná, which means "house of the mouth of snakes." Trees loaded with bromeliads shade the central square surrounded by five buildings. The most outstanding edifice features a monster-mouth doorway and an ornate stone facade with more superimposed masks. As you enter the mouth of the earth monster, note that you are walking on a platform configured as the open jaw of the monster with stone teeth on both sides. Again you find a lovely example of an elongated building with ornamental miniature pyramids on each end.

CALAKMUL ★★★

This area is both a massive Maya archaeological zone, with at least 60 sites, and a 178,699-acre rain forest designated in 1989 as the Calakmul Biosphere Reserve, which includes territory in both Mexico and Guatemala. The best way to see Calakmul is to spend the night at Xpujil or Chicanná and leave early in the morning for Calakmul. If you're the first one to drive down the narrow access road to the ruins (1½ hr. from the highway), you'll see plenty of wildlife.

THE ARCHAEOLOGICAL ZONE   Since 1982, archaeologists have been excavating the ruins of Calakmul, which dates from 100 B.C. to A.D. 900. It's the largest of the area's 60 known sites. Nearly 7,000 buildings have been discovered and mapped. At its zenith, at least 60,000 people may have lived around the site, but by the time of the Spanish Conquest in 1519, there were fewer than 1,000 inhabitants. Visitors arrive at a large plaza filled with a forest of trees. You immediately see several stelae; Calakmul contains more of these than any other site, but they are much more weathered and indistinguishable than the stelae of Palenque or Copán in Honduras. On one of them you can clearly see the work of looters who carefully used some sort of stone-cutting saw to slice off the face of the monument. By Structure 13 is a stele of a woman dating from A.D. 652. She is thought to have been a ruler, which would be exceedingly unusual.

Several structures here are worth checking out; some are built in the Petén style, some in the Río Bec style. Structure 3 must have been the residence of a noble family. Its design is unique and quite lovely; it managed to retain its original form and was never remodeled the way so many other structures were. Offerings of shells, beads, and polychromed tripod pottery were found inside. Structure 2 is the tallest pyramid in the Yucatán, at 54m (178 ft.). From the top

A Driving Caution
Numerous curves in the road make seeing oncoming traffic (what little there is) difficult, and there have been head-on collisions.

of it you can see the outline of the ruins of El Mirador, 48km (30 miles) across the forest in Guatemala. Notice the two stairways that ascend along the sides of the principal face of the pyramid in the upper levels. This has no equivalent in Maya architecture, and when appreciated in conjunction with how the masks break up the space of the front face, you can see just how complex the design was.

Temple 4 charts the line of the sun from June 21, when it falls on the left (north) corner; to September 21 and March 21, when it lines up in the east behind the middle temple on the top of the building; to December 21, when it falls on the right (south) corner. Numerous jade pieces, including spectacular masks, were uncovered here, most of which are on display in the Museo Regional in Campeche. Temple 7 is largely unexcavated except for the top, where in 1984 the most outstanding jade mask yet to be found at Calakmul was uncovered. In *A Forest of Kings,* Linda Schele and David Freidel tell of wars between the Calakmul, Tikal, and Naranjo (the latter 2 in Guatemala), and how Ah-Cacaw, king of Tikal (120km/75 miles S of Calakmul), captured King Jaguar-Paw in A.D. 695 and later Lord Ox-Ha-Te Ixil Ahau, both of Calakmul. The site is open Tuesday to Sunday from 7am to 5pm, but it gets so wet during the rainy season from June to October that it's best not to go.

CALAKMUL BIOSPHERE RESERVE   Set aside in 1989, this is the peninsula's only high-forest *selva,* a rain forest that annually records as much as 5m (16 ft.) of rain. Notice that the canopy of the trees is higher here than in the forest of Quintana Roo. It lies very close to the border with Guatemala, but, of course, there is no way to get there. Among the plants are cactus, epiphytes, and orchids. Endangered animals include the white-lipped peccary, jaguar, and puma. So far, more than 250 species of birds have been recorded. At present, no overnight stay or camping is permitted. If you want a tour of a small part of the forest and you speak Spanish, you can inquire for a guide at one of the two nearby *ejidos.* Some old *chicleros* living there have expert knowledge of flora and fauna and can take you on a couple of trails.

The turn-off on the left for Calakmul is located approximately 232km (145 miles) from the intersection of highways 186 and 307, just before the village of Conhuas. There's a guard station there where you pay $3 to enter. From the turn-off, it's a 1½-hour drive on a paved, but very narrow and somewhat rutted, road that may be difficult during the rainy season, from May to October.

BALAMKU ★★
Balamkú (bah-lahm-*koo*) is a site that should not be missed. A couple of buildings in it were so well preserved that they required almost no reconstruction, just uncovering. Inside one you will find three impressive figures of men sitting in the gaping maws of crocodiles and toads as they descend into the underworld. The whole concept of this building, with its molded stucco facade, is life and death. On the head of each almost-three-dimensional figure are the eyes, nose, and mouth of a jaguar figure, followed by the full face of the human figure, then a neck formed by the eyes and nose of another jaguar, and an Olmec-like face on the stomach, with its neck decorated by a necklace. These figures were saved

in dramatic fashion from looters who managed to get away with a fourth one. Now they are under the protection of a caretaker, who keeps the room under lock and key, but he can be persuaded to open it for visitors. (A tip is appreciated.) If you speak Spanish, you can get the caretaker to explain something of the figures and their complex symbolism. There is also a beautiful courtyard and another set of buildings adjacent to the main group

6

Mérida, Chichén Itzá &
the Maya Interior

Ask most people about the Yucatán, and they think of Cancún, the Caribbean coast, and Chichén Itzá. In fact, there's much more to the Yucatán than just those places. With a little exploring, you'll find a great variety of things to do. One day you can climb a pyramid in the morning and take a dip in the cool, clear water of a *cenote* (natural well) in the afternoon. The next day may find you strolling along a lonely beach or riding in a small boat through mangroves to pay a visit to a colony of pink flamingos, and dancing in the streets of **Mérida** by night. This chapter covers the interior of the Yucatán peninsula, including the famous Maya ruins at **Chichén Itzá** and **Uxmal,** the flamingo sanctuary at **Celestún,** and many less-famous spots that might find special favor with you.

Last year, Hurricane Isadore wreaked havoc with Mérida and the surrounding area, pulling down trees, flooding several areas, and damaging some of the archaeological sights. With the Yucatán's strange hydrology, it took longer than expected for the water levels to recede in some places. I was there 3 months after Isadore and found some of the *cenotes* in the region still flooded. Especially hard hit was the area east of Progreso, where the hurricane made land. Some hotels in that area were destroyed.

EXPLORING THE YUCATAN'S MAYA HEARTLAND

The best way to see the Yucatán is by car. The terrain is flat, there is little traffic, and the main highways are in good shape. If you do drive around the area, you will add one Spanish word to your vocabulary, which through much repetition will stick with you: *topes* (*toh*-pehs), or "speed bumps." *Topes* come in varying shapes and sizes and with varying degrees of warning. Don't let them catch you by surprise. Off the beaten path, the roads are narrow and rough, but hey—we're talking rental cars. Rentals are, in fact, a little pricey compared with those in the U.S. (due perhaps to wear and tear?), but some promotional deals are available, especially in the low season. For more on renting a car, see "By Car," in "Mérida: Gateway to the Maya Heartland," below.

Plenty of buses ply the roads between the major towns and ruins. And plenty of tour buses circulate, too. But buses to the smaller towns and ruins and the haciendas are infrequent or nonexistent. One bus company, Autobuses del Oriente (ADO), controls most of the first-class bus service and does a good job with the major destinations. Second-class buses go to some out-of-the-way places, but they can be slow, they stop a lot, and they are not air-conditioned, which is the key to comfortable bus travel. I will take them when I'm going only a short distance, say around 40 miles. If you don't want to rent a car, a few tour operators take small groups to more remote attractions such as ruins, *cenotes,* and villages.

The Yucatán is *tierra caliente* (the hotlands). Don't travel in this region without a hat, sunblock, mosquito repellent, and water. The coolest weather is from November to February; the hottest is from April to June. From July to October, thundershowers moderate temperatures. More tourists come to the interior during the winter months, but not to the same extent as on the Caribbean coast. The high-season/low-season distinction is less pronounced here.

Should you decide to travel into this part of the world, don't miss **Mérida.** It is, and has been for centuries, the cultural and commercial center of the Yucatán. You won't find a more vibrant tropical city anywhere. Every time I visit, there is some festival or celebration to attend, on top of the nightly performances that the city offers its citizens and visitors. It's also the Yucatán's shopping center, where you can buy the area's specialty items, such as hammocks, Panama hats, and the embroidered native blouses known as *huipiles.* And Mérida makes the perfect base from which to launch a variety of side trips. Here are some of the essential places to visit:

CHICHEN ITZA & VALLADOLID   These destinations are almost midway between Mérida and Cancún. From Mérida it's 2½ hours by car to Chichén on the new toll road, or *autopista.* You can spend a day at the beautifully restored ruins and then stay at one of the nearby hotels—or drive 40km (25 miles) to Valladolid, a quiet, charming colonial town with a pleasant central square. Valladolid features two eerie *cenotes.* The spectacular ruins at Ek Balam are only 40km (25 miles) to the north. Also nearby is the Río Lagartos Nature Reserve, teeming with flamingos and other native birds.

CELESTUN NATIONAL WILDLIFE REFUGE   These flamingo sanctuary wetlands along the Gulf coast contain a unique shallow-water estuary where freshwater from *cenotes* mixes with saltwater, creating the perfect feeding grounds for flamingos. Touring this area by launch is relaxing and rewarding. Only 1½ hours from Mérida, Celestún makes for an easy day trip.

DZIBILCHALTUN   This Maya site, now a national park, is 14km (9 miles) north of Mérida along the road to Progreso. Here you'll find pre-Hispanic ruins, nature trails, a *cenote,* and the Museum of the Maya. You can make this the first stop in a day trip to Progreso and other attractions north of Mérida.

PROGRESO   A modern city and Gulf coast beach escape 34km (21 miles) north of Mérida, Progreso has a wide beach and oceanfront drive that's popular on the weekends and during the summer. The recent arrival of cruise ships might make Progreso even more popular, but with so much beach, you'll easily have a place to yourself. From Progreso you can drive down the coast to **Uaymitún** to see some flamingos and visit the recently excavated ruins of **Xcambó.**

UXMAL   Smaller than Chichén, but architecturally more striking and mysterious, Uxmal is about 81km (50 miles) south of Mérida. You can see it in a day, though it's a good idea to extend that somewhat to see the sound-and-light show and spend the night at one of the hotels by the ruins. Several other nearby sites make up the Puuc route and can be explored the following day. It's also possible, though a bit rushed, to see Uxmal and the other ruins on a 1-day trip by special excursion bus from Mérida.

(Tips Mapping the Region

To check out the region surrounding Mérida, see "The Yucatán Peninsula" map on p. 16.

Tips **The Best Websites for Mérida, Chichén Itzá & the Maya Interior**

- **Maya: Portraits of a People: www.nationalgeographic.com/explorer/ maya/more.html**   A fascinating collection of articles from *National Geographic* and other sources.
- **Yucatán Travel Guide: www.mayayucatan.com**   Yucatán's newly formed Ministry of Tourism maintains this site. It has an update section and good general info on different destinations in the state.
- **Mexico's Yucatán Directory: www.mexonline.com/yucatan.htm**   A nice roundup of vacation rentals, tour operators, and information on the Maya sites. For more information on Mexico's indigenous history, see the links on the pre-Columbian page (www.mexonline. com/precolum.htm).
- **Mysterious Places: Chichén Itzá: www.mysteriousplaces.com/ chichen_itza_page.html**   An illuminating photo tour of Chichén Itzá's temples. See images of the Temple of the Warriors, the Nunnery, and the Observatory, among other ruins.

CAMPECHE   This beautiful, walled colonial city has been so meticulously restored that it's a delight just to stroll down the streets. Campeche is about 3 hours southwest of Mérida in the direction of Palenque. A full day should give you enough time to see its architectural highlights and museums, but there is something about Campeche that makes you want to linger there.

1 Mérida: Gateway to the Maya Heartland ✶✶

1,440km (900 miles) E of Mexico City; 320km (200 miles) W of Cancún

Mérida is the capital of the state of Yucatán and has been the dominant city in the region since the Spanish Conquest. It is a busy city and suffers from the same problems that plague other colonial cities in Mexico—traffic, noise, and the exhaust from buses. Still, it is a fun city and has many admirers, if all of the people who've praised it to me are any measure. Mérida's nightlife is more varied and representative of the region than Cancún's. People here know how to have a good time, and they seem driven to organize concerts, theatrical productions, art exhibits, and such. In recent years the city has been in the midst of a cultural explosion.

ESSENTIALS

GETTING THERE & DEPARTING   **By Plane**   **Aeromexico** (© **999/927-9277** or 999/927-9433; www.aeromexico.com) and **Mexicana** (© **999/924-6633** or 999/924-6910; www.mexicana.com.mx) have nonstop flights to and from Miami. **Continental** (© **999/946-1888** and 999/946-1900; www.continental. com) has nonstop service to and from Houston. Otherwise, you will most likely have to fly through Cancún, Cozumel, or Mexico City. **Mexicana** flies to and from Mexico City. **Aeromexico** flies to and from Cancún and Mexico City. **Aerocaribe** (© **999/928-6786**), a Mexicana affiliate, provides service to and from Cozumel, Cancún, Veracruz, Villahermosa, and points in Central America. **Aviacsa** (© **999/926-9087**) provides service to and from Cancún, Monterrey,

Villahermosa, Tuxtla Gutiérrez, Tapachula, Oaxaca, and Mexico City. Taxis from the airport to the city run $11.

By Ferry   During the winter months (late Nov to late Apr) a car ferry makes weekly trips between the port of Progreso, near Mérida, and Tampa, Florida. The boat is large and offers the amenities of a cruise ship, with lots of entertainment and food. You can book passage one way, round-trip, or as a package, with or without your car. Contact the **Yucatán Express** (© **866/208-4235** in the U. S. or 01-800/514-4235 in Mexico; www.yucatanexpress.com).

By Car   **Highway 180** is the old federal highway *(carretera federal)* between Mérida and Cancún. The trip takes 6 hours, and the road is in good shape; you will pass through many Maya villages. A four-lane divided **toll road** (the *cuota,* or *autopista*) parallels Highway 180 and begins at the town of Kantunil, 56km (35 miles) east of Mérida. By avoiding the tiny villages and their not-so-tiny speed bumps, the autopista cuts 2 hours from the journey between Mérida and Cancún; one-way tolls cost $28. Coming from Cancún (or, for that matter, Valladolid or Chichén Itzá, both of which are en route), Highway 180 enters Mérida by feeding into Calle 65, which passes 1 block south of the main square.

Coming from the south (Campeche or Uxmal), you will enter the city on Avenida Itzáes. To get to the town center, turn right on Calle 59 (the 1st street after the zoo).

A traffic loop or *periférico* encircles Mérida, making it possible to skirt the city. Directional signs into the city are generally good, but going around the city on the loop requires constant vigilance.

By Bus   There are five bus stations in Mérida, two of which offer first-class buses; the other three provide local service to nearby destinations. The larger of the first-class stations, **CAME,** is on Calle 70, between calles 69 and 71 (see "City Layout," below). The ADO bus line and its affiliates operate the station. When you get there, you'll see a row of ticket windows. All but the last couple to the right sell first-class tickets. The first window sells tickets to Palenque and San Cristóbal. The other windows sell tickets to other destinations, including Palenque. The last two windows sell tickets for ADO's deluxe services, ADO-GL and UNO. The former is only slightly better than first class; the latter has superwide roomy seats. Unless it's a long trip, I generally choose the bus that has the most convenient departure time. Tickets can be purchased in advance; just ask the ticket agent for the different options and departure times for the route you need.

The other first-class station is the small **Maya K'iin** used by the bus company Elite. It's at Calle 65 no. 548, between calles 68 and 70.

To and from Cancún: You can pick up a bus at the CAME (almost every hour) or through Elite (5 per day). Both bus lines also pick up passengers at the Fiesta Americana Hotel, across from the Hyatt (12 per day). You can buy a ticket there at the Ticket Bus agency or at the Elite ticket agency. Cancún is 4 hours away; a few buses stop in **Valladolid.**

To and from Chichén Itzá: Three buses per day (2½-hr. trip) depart from the CAME. Also, check out tours operating from the hotels in Mérida if you want to visit in a day.

To and from Playa del Carmen, Tulum, and Chetumal: From the CAME, there are 10 departures per day for Playa del Carmen (5-hr. trip), six for Tulum (6-hr. trip), and eight for Chetumal (7-hr. trip). From Maya K'iin there are three per day to Playa, which stop at the Fiesta Americana.

Casa del Alguacil **7**

Cathedral **2**

El Nuevo Olimpo **6**

Iglesia de Jesús **10**

Iglesia de Santa Lucía **13**

Museo de Arte Contemporáneo **3**

Museo de la Ciudad **9**

Palacio Montejo **4**

Palacio Municipal **5**

Palacio de Gobierno **8**

Palacio Cantón/Museo
    Regional de Antropología **14**

Plaza Mayor **1**

Teatro Peón Contreras **11**

Teatro Ayala **8**

Universidad de Yucatán **12**

To and from Campeche: From the CAME station, there are 36 departures per day. Elite has four departures per day. It's a 2½-hour trip.

To and from Palenque and San Cristóbal de las Casas: There is service to San Cristóbal twice daily from the CAME, and once daily on Elite. To Palenque there are three and one, respectively. There have been reports of minor theft on buses to Palenque. You should do three things: Don't take second-class buses to this destination; check your luggage so that it's stowed in the cargo bay; and put your carry-on in the overhead rack, not on the floor.

The main **second-class bus station** is around the corner from the CAME on Calle 69, between calles 68 and 70.

To and from Uxmal: There are four buses per day. (You can also hook up with a tour to Uxmal through most hotels or any travel agent or tour operator in town.) One bus per day combines Uxmal with the other sites to the south (Kabah, Sayil, Labná, and Xlapak—known as the Puuc route) and does the whole round-trip in a day. It stops for 2 hours at Uxmal and 30 minutes at each of the other sites.

To and from Progreso and Dzibilchaltún: The bus station that serves these destinations is the **Estación Progreso,** Calle 62 no. 524, between calles 65 and 67. The trip to Progreso takes an hour by second-class bus. *Colectivos* to Dzibilchaltún stop beside the San Juan church, south of the main plaza off of Calle 62.

To and from Celestún: The Celestún station is at Calle 71 no. 585 between calles 64 and 66. The trip takes 1½ to 2 hours, depending on how often the bus stops. There are 10 buses per day.

ORIENTATION   Arriving by Plane   Mérida's airport is 13km (8 miles) from the city center on the southwestern outskirts of town, near the entrance to Highway 180. The airport has desks for renting a car, reserving a hotel room, and getting tourist information. Taxi tickets to town ($11) are sold outside the airport doors, under the covered walkway.

VISITOR INFORMATION   There are city tourism offices and state tourism offices, which have different resources; if you can't get the info you're looking for at one, go to the other. The state operates two downtown tourism offices: One is in the **Teatro Peón Contreras,** facing Parque de la Madre (© 999/924-9290); and the other is on the main plaza, in the **Palacio de Gobierno,** immediately to the left as you enter. These offices are open daily from 8am to 9pm. There are also information booths at the airport and the CAME bus station. The city's **visitor information offices** (© 999/928-2020, ext. 133) are on the ground floor of the Ayuntamiento building facing the main square on Calle 62. Look for a glass door under the arcade. Hours are Monday to Saturday from 8am to 8pm and Sunday from 8am to 2pm. At 9:30am every day it offers visitors a free tour of the area around the main square.

Also keep your eye out for the free monthly magazine *Yucatán Today;* it's a good source of info for Mérida and the rest of the region.

CITY LAYOUT   Mérida has the standard layout of towns in the Yucatán: Streets running north-south are even numbers; those running east-west are odd numbers. The numbering begins on the north and the east sides of town, so if you're walking on an odd-numbered street and the even numbers of the cross streets are increasing, then you know that you are heading west; likewise, if you are on an even-numbered street and the odd numbers of the cross streets are increasing, you are going south.

Another useful tip is that address numbers don't tell you anything about what cross street to look for. This is why, in addition to a street number, you will often

⌒ Moments   Festivals & Special Events in Mérida

Many Mexican cities offer weekend concerts in the park and such, but Mérida surpasses them all with performances every day of the week. Unless otherwise indicated, admission to the following is free.

Sunday   Each Sunday from 9am to 9pm, there's a fair called *Mérida en Domingo* (Mérida on Sunday). The main plaza and a section of Calle 60 from El Centro to Parque Santa Lucía close to traffic. Parents come with their children to stroll around and take in the scene. There are booths selling food and drink, along with a lively little flea market and used-book fair, children's art classes, and educational booths. At 11am in front of the Palacio del Gobierno, musicians play everything from jazz to classical and folk music. Also at 11am, the police orchestra performs Yucatecan tunes at the Santa Lucía park. At 11:30am, you'll find bawdy comedy acts at the Parque Hidalgo, on Calle 60 at Calle 59. There's a lull in the mid-afternoon, and then the plaza fills up again as people walk around and visit with friends. Around 7pm in front of the Ayuntamiento, a large band starts playing mambos, rumbas, and cha-cha-chas with great enthusiasm; you may see 1,000 people dancing in the street. Afterward, folk ballet dancers reenact a typical Yucatecan wedding inside.

Monday   *Vaquería Regional,* traditional music and dancing to celebrate the *Vaquerías* feast, was associated originally with the branding of cattle on Yucatecan haciendas. Among the featured performers are dancers with trays of bottles or filled glasses on their heads—a sight to see.

Tuesday   At 9pm in Parque Santiago, Calle 59 at Calle 72, the Municipal Orchestra plays big-band music from the 1940s, both Latin and American.

Wednesday   At 9pm in the Teatro Peón Contreras, Calle 60 at Calle 57, the University of Yucatán Ballet Folklórico presents "Yucatán and Its Roots." Admission is $5.

Thursday   Yucatecan *trova* music (boleros, baladas) and dance are presented at the *Serenata* in Parque Santa Lucía at 9pm.

Friday   At 9pm in the courtyard of the University of Yucatán, Calle 60 at Calle 57, the University of Yucatán Ballet Folklórico performs typical regional dances from the Yucatán.

Saturday   *Noche Mexicana* at the park at the beginning of Paseo de Montejo begins at 9pm. It features several performances of traditional Mexican music and dance. Some of the performers are amateurs who acquit themselves reasonably well; others are professional musicians and dancers who thoroughly know their craft. Food stands sell very good *antojitos,* as well as drinks and ice cream.

see cross streets listed, usually like this: "Calle 60 no. 549 × 71 y 73." The "×" is a multiplication sign—shorthand for the word *por* (meaning "by")—and *y* means "and." So this place would be on Calle 60 between calles 71 and 73.

The town's main square is the busy **Plaza Mayor** (referred to simply as El Centro). It's bordered by calles 60, 62, 61, and 63. Calle 60, which runs in front of the cathedral, is an important street to remember; it connects the main square with several smaller plazas, some theaters and lovely churches, and the University of Yucatán, just to the north. Here, too, you'll find a concentration of handicraft shops, restaurants, and hotels. Around Plaza Mayor are the cathedral, the Palacio de Gobierno (state government building), the Ayuntamiento (town hall), and the Palacio Montejo. The plaza always has a crowd, and it's full on Sunday, when it holds a large street fair. (See "Festivals & Special Events in Mérida," below.) Within a few blocks are several smaller plazas and the bustling market district.

Mérida's most fashionable district is the broad, tree-lined boulevard **Paseo de Montejo** and its surrounding neighborhood. The Paseo de Montejo parallels Calle 60 and begins 7 blocks north and a little east of the main square. There are a number of trendy restaurants, modern hotels, offices of various banks and airlines, and a few clubs here, but the boulevard is mostly known for its stately mansions built during the boom times of the henequén industry. Near where the Paseo intersects Avenida Colón, you'll find the two fanciest hotels in town: the Hyatt and the Fiesta Americana.

GETTING AROUND   **By Car**   In general, reserve your car in advance from the U.S. to get the best weekly rates during high season (Nov–Feb); in low season, I usually do better renting a car once I get to Mérida. The local rental companies are very competitive and have promotional deals that you can get only if you are there. When comparing, make sure that it's apples to apples; ask if the price quote includes the IVA tax and insurance coverage. (Practically everybody offers free mileage.) For tips on saving money on car rentals, see "Getting Around," in chapter 2. Rental cars are generally a little more expensive (unless you find a promotional rate) than in the U.S. By renting for only a day or 2, you can avoid the high cost of parking lots in Mérida. These *estacionamientos* charge one price for the night and double that if you leave your car for the following day. Many hotels offer free parking, but make sure they include daytime parking in the price.

By Taxi   Taxis are easy to come by and much cheaper than in Cancún.

By Bus   City buses are a little tricky to figure out but aren't needed very often because almost everything of interest is within walking distance of the main plaza. Still, it's a bit of a walk from the plaza to the Paseo de Montejo, and you can save yourself some work by taking a bus, minibus, or *pesero* (Volkswagen minivan) that is heading north on Calle 60. Most of these will take you to Paseo de Montejo or drop you off at Plaza Santa Ana, right by the Paseo. The peseros or *combis* (usually painted white) run out in several directions from the main plaza along simple routes. They usually line up along the side streets next to the plaza.

 FAST FACTS: **Mérida**

American Express   The office is at Paseo de Montejo 492 (© **999/942-8200**). It's open for travelers' services weekdays from 9am to 2pm and 4 to 6pm.

Area Code   The telephone area code is 999.

Bookstore   The Librería Dante, Calle 59 between calles 60 and 62 (© **999/ 928-3674**), has a small selection of English-language cultural-history books on Mexico. It's open Monday to Saturday from 8am to 9:30pm, Sunday from 10am to 6pm. There is another Librería Dante on the main plaza in the Nuevo Olimpo.

Business Hours Generally, businesses are open Monday to Saturday from 10am to 2pm and 4 to 8pm.

Climate From November to February, the weather can be pleasantly cool and windy. In other months, it's just hot, especially during the day. Rain can occur any time of year, especially during the rainy season (July–Oct), and usually comes in the form of afternoon tropical showers.

Consulates The **American Consulate** is at Paseo de Montejo 453, at Avenida Colón (✆ **999/925-6219** or **999/925-5011**). Office hours are Monday to Friday from 9am to 1pm. The **British Vice-Consulate** is at Calle 53 no. 498, at Calle 58 (✆ **999/928-6152**). Office hours are weekdays from 9am to 1pm. The vice-consul fields questions about travel to Belize as well as all matters British.

Currency Exchange Most banks in Mérida are a mess to deal with and don't offer outstanding exchange rates to offset the hassle. A *casa de cambio* called **Cambios Portales,** Calle 61 no. 500 (✆ **999/923-8709**), is on the north side of the main plaza in the middle of the block. It's open daily from 8:30am to 8:30pm. There are also many ATMs; one is on the south side of the same plaza.

Hospitals The best hospital is **Centro Médico de las Américas,** Calle 54 no. 365 between 33-A and Avenida Pérez Ponce. The main phone number is ✆ **999/926-2619**; for emergencies, call ✆ **999/927-3199**. You can also call the Cruz Roja (Red Cross) at ✆ **999/924-9813**.

Internet Access There are so many Internet access providers in town that you hardly have to walk more than a couple of blocks to find one.

Pharmacy **Farmacia Yza,** Calle 63 no. 502, between calles 60 and 62 (✆ **999/924-9510**), on the south side of the plaza, is open 24 hours.

Police Mérida has a special body of police to assist tourists. They patrol the downtown area and the Paseo de Montejo, wearing white shirts bearing the words POLICIA TURISTICA. The phone number for both the tourist police and the regular police is ✆ **999/925-2555**.

Post Office The *correo* is near the market at the corner of calles 65 and 56. A branch office is at the airport. Both are open Monday to Friday from 8am to 7pm, Saturday from 9am to noon.

Seasons There are two high seasons for tourism, but they aren't as pronounced as on the coast. One is in July and August, when Mexicans take their vacations, and the other is between November 15 and Easter Sunday, when Canadians and Americans flock to the Yucatán to escape winter weather.

Spanish Classes Maya scholars, Spanish teachers, and archaeologists from the United States are among the students at the **Centro de Idiomas del Sureste,** Calle 14 no. 106 at Calle 25, Col. México, 97000 Mérida, Yuc. (✆ **999/926-1155**; fax 999/926-9020). The school has two locations: in the Colonia México, a northern residential district, and on Calle 66 at Calle 57, downtown. Students live with local families or in hotels; sessions running 2 weeks or longer are available for all levels of proficiency and areas of interest. For brochures and applications, contact Chloe Conaway de Pacheco, Directora.

Telephones There are long-distance phone service centers at the airport and the bus station. In the downtown area is **TelWorld,** Calle 59 no. 495-4 between calles 56 and 58. To use the public phones, buy a **Ladatel** card from just about any newsstand or store. The cards come in a variety of denominations and work for long distance within Mexico and sometimes even abroad. Also see "Telephone/Fax" in "Fast Facts: Mexico," in chapter 2.

EXPLORING MERIDA

Most of Mérida's attractions are within walking distance from the downtown area. To see a larger area of the city, a popular **bus tour** is worth taking. The man who operates these tours has bought a few small buses and given them a fancy paint job, pulled out all the windows, raised the roof several inches, and installed wooden benches so that the buses remind you of the folksy buses of coastal Latin America, known as *chivas* in Colombia and Venezuela or as *guaguas* in other places. You can find these buses on the corner of calles 60 and 55 (next to the church of Santa Lucía) at 10am, 1pm, 4pm, and 7pm. The tour costs $9 per person and lasts 2 hours. Another option for seeing the city is a **horse-drawn carriage.** A 45-minute ride around central Mérida costs $17. You can usually find the carriages beside the cathedral on Calle 61.

EXPLORING PLAZA MAYOR   Downtown Mérida is a great example of a lowland colonial city. The town has a casual, relaxed feel. Buildings lack the severe baroque and neoclassical features that characterize central Mexico; most are finished in stucco and painted light colors. Mérida's gardens add to this relaxed, tropical atmosphere. Gardeners do not strive for control over nature. Here, natural exuberance is the ideal, with plants growing in a wild profusion that disguises human intervention. A perfect example is the courtyard in the Palacio Montejo. Mérida's plazas are a slightly different version of this aesthetic: Unlike the highland plazas, with their carefully sculpted trees, Mérida's squares are typically built around large trees that are left to grow as tall as possible. Hurricane Isidore blew down some of these last year, which has changed the appearance of these plazas as well as the Paseo de Montejo.

Plaza Mayor (often referred to as El Centro) has this sort of informality. Even when there's no orchestrated event in progress, the park is full of people sitting on the benches, talking with friends, or taking a casual stroll. A plaza like this is a great advantage for a big city such as Mérida, giving it a personal feel and a sense of community. Notice the beautiful scale and composition of the major buildings surrounding it. The most prominent of these is the cathedral.

The oldest **cathedral** on the continent, it was built between 1561 and 1598. Much of the stone in the cathedral's walls came from the ruined buildings of Tihó, the former Maya city. The original finish was stucco, and you can see some remnants still clinging to the bare rock. However, people like the way the unfinished walls show the cathedral's age. Notice how the two top levels of the bell towers are built off-center from their bases—an uncommon feature. Inside, decoration is sparse, with altars draped in fabric colorfully embroidered like a Maya woman's shift. The most notable item is a picture of Ah Kukum Tutul Xiú, chief of the Xiú people, visiting the Montejo camp to make peace; it's hanging over the side door on the right.

ACCOMMODATIONS
Casa Mexilio Guest House **7**
Casa San Juan **20**
Fiesta Americana Mérida **1**
Hotel Caribe **16**
Hotel Dolores Alba **19**
Hotel Medio Mundo **5**
Hotel Mucuy **13**
Hyatt Regency Mérida **2**
Maison Lafitte **10**
Posada Toledo **11**

DINING
Alberto's Continental **8**
Café Alameda **12**
Café Amaro **14**
Eladio's **18**
La Casa del Paseo **3**
La Flor de Santiago **6**
Pórtico del Peregrino **9**
Restaurante Kantún **4**
Restaurant Los Almendros **17**
Vito Corleone **15**

To the left of the main altar is a small shrine with a curious figure of Christ that is a replica of one recovered from a burned-out church in the town of Ich-mul. In the 1500s a local artist carved the original figure from a miraculous tree that was hit by lightning and burst into flames—but did not char. The statue later became blistered in the church fire at Ichmul, but it survived. In 1645 it was moved to the cathedral in Mérida, where the locals attached great powers to the figure, naming it *Cristo de las Ampollas* (Christ of the Blisters). It did not, however, survive the sacking of the cathedral in 1915 by revolutionary forces, so another figure, modeled after the original, was made. Take a look in the side chapel (open daily 8–11am and 4:30–7pm), which contains a life-size diorama of the Last Supper. The Mexican Jesus is covered with prayer crosses brought by supplicants asking for intercession.

Next door to the cathedral is the old bishop's palace, now converted into the city's contemporary art museum, **Museo de Arte Contemporáneo Ateneo de Yucatán** (*©* 999/928-3236). The palace was confiscated and rebuilt during the Mexican Revolution in 1915. The museum's entrance faces the cathedral from the recently constructed walkway between the two buildings called the Pasaje de la Revolución. The 17 exhibition rooms display work by contemporary artists, mostly from the Yucatán. (The best known are Fernando García Ponce and Fernando Castro Pacheco, whose works also hang in the government palace described below.) Nine of the rooms hold the museum's permanent collection; the rest are for temporary exhibits. It's open Wednesday to Monday from 10am to 6pm. Admission is $2.50.

Moving clockwise around the plaza, on the south side is the **Palacio Montejo.** Its facade, with heavy decoration around the doorway and windows, is a good example of the Spanish architectural style known as plateresque. But the content of the decoration is very much a New World creation. Conquering the Yucatán was the Montejo family business, begun by the original Francisco Montejo and continued by his son and nephew, both named Francisco Montejo. Construction of the house started in 1542 under the son, Francisco Montejo El Mozo ("The Younger"). Bordering the entrance are politically incorrect figures of conquista-dors standing on the heads of vanquished Indians—borrowed, perhaps, from the pre-Hispanic custom of portraying victorious Maya kings treading on their defeated foes. The posture of the conquistadors and their facial expression of wide-eyed dismay make them less imposing than the Montejos might have wished. A bank now occupies the building, but you can enter the courtyard, view the garden, and see for yourself what a charming residence it must have been for the descendants of the Montejos, who lived here as recently as the 1970s. (Curi-ously enough, not only does Mérida society keep track of who is descended from the Montejos, but it also keeps track of who is descended from the last Maya king, Tutul Xiú.)

In stark contrast to the severity of the cathedral and Casa Montejo is the light, unimposing **Palacio Municipal** (town hall) or Ayuntamiento. The exterior dates from the mid–19th century, an era when a tropicalist aesthetic tinged with romanticism began asserting itself across coastal Latin America. On the second floor, you can see the meeting hall of the city council and enjoy a lovely view of the plaza from the balcony. Next door to the Ayuntamiento is a recently com-pleted building called **El Nuevo Olimpo (The New Olympus).** It took the place of the old Olimpo, which a misguided town council demolished in the 1970s, to the regret of many older Meridanos. The new building tries to incor-porate elements of the original while presenting something new. It holds concert and gallery space, a bookstore, and a lovely courtyard. There is a comfortable cafe under the arches, and a bulletin board at the entrance to the courtyard with postings of upcoming performances.

Cater-corner from the Nuevo Olimpo is the old **Casa del Alguacil (Magistrate's House).** Under its arcades is something of an institution in Mérida: the **Dulcería y Sorbetería Colón,** an ice cream and sweet shop that will appeal to those who prefer less-rich ice creams. A spectacular side doorway on Calle 62 bears viewing, and across the street is the new **Cine Mérida,** with two movie screens showing art films and one stage for live performances. Returning to the main plaza, down a bit from the ice cream store is a **shopping center** of boutiques and convenience food vendors called Pasaje Picheta. At the end of the arcade is the **Palacio de Gobierno,** dating from 1892. Large murals by the Yucatecan artist Fernando Castro Pacheco, executed between 1971 and 1973, decorate the walls of the courtyard. Scenes from Maya and Mexican history abound, and the painting over the stairway depicts the Maya spirit with ears of sacred corn, the "sunbeams of the gods." Nearby is a painting of mustachioed Lázaro Cárdenas, who as president in 1938 expropriated 17 foreign oil companies and was hailed as a Mexican liberator. Upstairs is a long, wide gallery with more of Pacheco's paintings, which achieve their effect by localizing color and imitating the photographic technique of double exposure. The palace is open Monday to Saturday from 8am to 8pm, Sunday from 9am to 5pm. There is a small tourism office to the left as you enter.

Further down Calle 61 is the **Museo de la Ciudad.** It faces the side of the cathedral and occupies the former church of San Juan de Dios. An exhibit outlining the history of Mérida will be of interest to those curious about the city; there is explanatory text in English. Hours are Monday to Friday from 10am to 2pm and 4 to 8pm, Saturday and Sunday from 10am to 2pm. Admission is free.

EXPLORING CALLE 60   Heading north from Plaza Mayor up Calle 60, you'll see many of Mérida's old churches and squares. Several stores along Calle 60 sell gold-filigree jewelry, pottery, clothing, and folk art. A stroll along this street leads to the Parque Santa Ana and continues to the fashionable boulevard Paseo de Montejo and its Museo Regional de Antropología.

The first place of interest is the Teatro Daniel de Ayala, only because it sometimes schedules interesting performances. On the right side of Calle 60 will be a small park called **Parque Cepeda Peraza** (or Parque Hidalgo). Named for 19th-century General Manuel Cepeda Peraza, the *parque* was part of Montejo's original city plan. Small outdoor restaurants front hotels on the parque, making it a popular stopping place at any time of day. Across Calle 59 is the **Iglesia de Jesús,** or *El Tercer Orden* (the Third Order). Built by the Jesuit order in 1618, it has the richest interior of any church in Mérida, making it a favorite spot for weddings. The entire block on which the church stands belonged to the Jesuits, who are known as great educators. The school they left behind after their expulsion became the Universidad de Yucatán.

On the other side of the church is the **Parque de la Madre.** The park contains a modern statue of the Madonna and Child, a copy of the work by Renoir. Beyond the Parque de la Madre and across the pedestrian-only street is the **Teatro Peón Contreras,** an opulent theater designed by Italian architect Enrico Deserti a century ago. The theater is noted for its Carrara marble staircase and frescoed dome. Try to get a peek at it, and look at the performance schedule to see if anything of interest will take place during your stay. National and international performers appear here frequently. In the southwest corner of the theater, facing the Parque de la Madre, is a **tourist information office.** Across Calle 60 is the main building of the **Universidad de Yucatán.** Inside is a flagstone courtyard where the *ballet folklórico* performs on Friday nights.

A block farther north is Parque Santa Lucía. Bordered by an arcade on the north and west sides, this park was where visitors first alighted from the stagecoach. On Sunday, Parque Santa Lucía holds a used-book market, and several evenings a week it hosts popular entertainment. On Thursday nights, performers present Yucatecan songs and poems. Facing the park is the **Iglesia de Santa Lucía** (1575).

Four blocks farther up Calle 60 is Parque Santa Ana; if you turn right, you'll come to the beginning of the Paseo de Montejo in 2 blocks.

EXPLORING THE PASEO DE MONTEJO   The Paseo de Montejo is a broad, tree-lined boulevard that runs north-south starting at Calle 47, 7 blocks north and 2 blocks east of the main square. In the late 19th century, stalwarts of Mérida's upper crust (mostly plantation owners) decided that the city needed something grander than its traditional narrow streets lined by wall-to-wall town houses. They built this monumentally proportioned boulevard and lined it with mansions. Things went sour with the henequén bust, but several of these mansions survive—some in private hands, others as offices, restaurants, or consulates. Today, this is the fashionable part of town, with many fine restaurants, trendy discos, and expensive hotels.

Of the mansions that survived, the most notable is the Palacio Cantón, which now houses the **Museo Regional de Antropología** (★★, or Anthropology Museum (© **999/923-0557**). Designed and built by Enrico Deserti, the architect of the Teatro Peón Contreras, it was constructed between 1909 and 1911, during the last years of the Porfiriato. It was the residence of General Francisco Cantón Rosado, who enjoyed his palace for only 6 years before dying in 1917. For a time the mansion served as the official residence of the state's governor.

Viewing the museum also affords you an opportunity to see some of the surviving interior architecture. The museum's main focus is the pre-Columbian cultures of the peninsula, especially the Maya. Topics include cosmology, history, and culture. Captions for the permanent displays are mostly in Spanish. Starting with fossil mastodon teeth, the exhibits take you through the Yucatán's history, paying special attention to the daily life of its inhabitants.

Exhibits illustrate such strange Maya customs as tying boards to babies' heads to create the oblong shape that they considered beautiful, and filing teeth or perforating them to inset jewels. There are enlarged photos of several archaeological sites and drawings that illustrate the various styles of Maya dwellings. Even if you know only a little Spanish, this is a worthwhile stop, and it provides good background for explorations of Maya sites. The museum is open Tuesday to Saturday from 8am to 8pm, Sunday from 8am to 2pm. Admission is $3.50.

SHOPPING

Mérida is known for **hammocks, guayaberas** (lightweight men's shirts worn untucked), and **Panama hats. Baskets** and **pottery** made in the Yucatán and crafts from all over Mexico are sold cheaply in the **central market.** Mérida is also the place to pick up prepared **achiote,** a pastelike mixture of ground achiote seeds (annatto), oregano, garlic, masa, and other spices used in Yucatecan cuisine. Mixed with sour orange to a soupy consistency, it makes a great marinade, especially for grilled meat and fish. It can be found bottled in this form. It's also the sauce for baked chicken and *cochinita pibil.*

EXPLORING THE MARKET   Mérida's bustling **market district** is a few blocks southeast of the Plaza Mayor. The market and surrounding few blocks make up the commercial center of the city. Hordes of people come here to shop and work. It is by far the most crowded part of town, and the city government is planning on refurbishing the whole area to relieve the traffic congestion, modernize the market building, and add green space. When it will do this is not quite clear, but work may start by 2004. Behind the post office (at calles 65 and 56) is the oldest part of the market, the **Portal de Granos (Grains Arcade),** a row of maroon arches where the grain merchants used to sell their goods. Just east, between calles 56 and 54, is the market building, Mercado Lucas de Gálvez. Inside, chaos seems to reign, but after a short while a certain order emerges. Here you can find anything from fresh fish to flowers to leather goods. In the building directly south of the market, you can find more locally manufactured goods; on the second floor is a crafts market (**Bazaar de Artesanías**). Another crafts market, **Bazaar García Rejón,** lies a block west of the market on Calle 65 between calles 58 and 60.

CRAFTS

Casa de las Artesanías   This store occupies the front rooms of a restored monastery. Here you can find a wide selection of crafts, 90% of which come from the Yucatán. For the most part, the quality of work is higher than elsewhere, but so are the prices. The monastery's back courtyard is used as a gallery, with rotating exhibits on folk and fine arts. It's open Monday to Saturday from 9am to 8pm, Sunday from 9am to 1pm. Calle 63 no. 513 (between calles 64 and 66). ✆ 999/928-6676.

Miniaturas   This fun little store is packed to the rafters with miniatures, a traditional Mexican folk art form that has been evolving in a number of directions, including social and political satire, pop art, and bawdy humor. Alicia Rivero, the owner, collects them from several parts of Mexico and offers plenty of variety, from traditional miniatures, such as dollhouse furniture, to popular cartoon characters and celebrities. The store also sells other forms of folk art such as masks, games, and traditional crafts. Hours are Monday to Saturday from 10am to 8pm. Calle 59 no. 507A-4 (between calles 60 and 62). ✆ 999/928-6503.

Museo de Artes Populares   This isn't a store, but it will be of great interest to crafts collectors. It has been closed for renovations, but should open in late 2003. Exhibits show regional costumes, tools, and crafts from various parts of Mexico. Some of the craftwork displayed here has all but disappeared from present-day Mexico. The collection includes jewelry, folk pottery, baskets, lacquer ware, and woodcarvings. Open Tuesday to Saturday from 8am to 6pm, Sunday from 9am to 2pm. Admission $1.75 adults, 50¢ children under 12. Calle 59 no. 441 (between calles 50 and 48). No phone.

GUAYABERAS

Business suits are hot and uncomfortable in Mérida's soaking humidity, so businessmen, politicians, bankers, and bus drivers alike wear the guayabera, a loose-fitting shirt decorated with narrow tucks, pockets, and sometimes embroidery, worn over the pants rather than tucked in. Mérida is famous as the best place to buy guayaberas, which can go for less than $15 at the market or for more than $50 custom-made by a tailor. A guayabera made of linen can cost about $80. Most are made of cotton, although other materials are available. The traditional color is white.

Most shops display ready-to-wear shirts in several price ranges. Guayabera makers pride themselves on being innovators. I have yet to enter a shirt-maker's shop in Mérida that did not present its own version of the guayabera. When looking at guayaberas, here are a few things to keep in mind: When Yucatecans say *seda,* they mean polyester; *lino* is linen or a linen/polyester combination. Take a close look at the stitching and such details as the way the tucks line up over the pockets; with guayaberas, the details are everything.

Guayaberas Jack   The craftsmanship here is very good, the place has a repu-tation to maintain, and some of the salespeople speak English. Prices are as marked. This will give you a good basis of comparison if you want to hunt for a bargain elsewhere. If the staff does not have the style and color of shirt you want, they will make it for you in about 3 hours. This shop also sells regular shirts and women's blouses. Hours are Monday to Saturday from 10am to 8pm, Sunday from 10am to 2pm. Calle 59 no. 507A (between calles 60 and 62). © 999/928-6002.

HAMMOCKS

Natives across tropical America used hammocks long before the Europeans arrived in the New World. The word comes from the Spanish *hamaca,* which is a borrowing from Taino, a Caribbean Indian language. Hammocks are still in use throughout Latin America and come in a wide variety of forms, but none is so comfortable as the Yucatecan hammock, which is woven with cotton string in a fine mesh. For most of us, of course, the hammock is lawn furniture, something to relax in for an hour or so on a lazy afternoon. But for the vast majority of Yucatecans, hammocks are the equivalent of beds, and they greatly prefer ham-mocks to mattresses. I know a hotel owner who has 150 beds in his establishment but won't sleep on any of them. When he does, he complains of waking up unrested and sore. Many well-to-do Meridanos keep a bed just for show. In hotels that cater to Yucatecans, you will always find hammock hooks in the walls because many Yucatecans travel with their own hammock.

My advice to the hammock buyer: The woven part should be cotton, it should be made with fine string, and the strings should be so numerous that when you get in it and stretch out diagonally (the way you're supposed to sleep in these hammocks), the gaps between the strings remain small. Don't pay attention to the words used to describe the size of a hammock; they have become practically meaningless. Good hammocks don't cost a lot of money ($20–$35). If you want a superior hammock, ask for one made with fine crochet thread *hilo de crochet* (the word *crochet* is also sometimes bandied about, but you can readily see the dif-ference). This should run about $100.

Nothing beats a tryout; the two shops mentioned here will gladly hang a ham-mock for you to test-drive. When it's up, look to see that there are no untied strings. You can also see what street vendors are offering, but you have to know what to look for, or they are likely to take advantage of you.

Hamacas El Aguacate   El Aguacate sells hammocks wholesale and retail. It has the greatest variety and is the place to go for a really fancy or extra-large hammock. A good hammock is the no. 6 in cotton; it runs $33. The store is open Monday to Friday from 8:30am to 7:30pm, Saturday from 8am to 5pm. It's 6 blocks south of the main square. Calle 58 no. 604 (at Calle 73). © 999/928-6429.

Tejidos y Cordeles Nacionales   This place near the municipal market sells only cotton hammocks, priced by weight—a pretty good practice because ham-mock lengths are standard here. The prices are better than at El Aguacate, but quality control isn't as good. My idea of a good hammock weighs about 1½ kilograms and runs about $25. Calle 56 no. 516-B (between calles 63 and 65). © 999/928-5561.

PANAMA HATS

Another useful and popular item is this soft, pliable hat made from the fibers of the *jipijapa* palm in several towns south of Mérida along Highway 180, especially Becal, in the neighboring state of Campeche. The hat makers in these towns work inside caves so that the moist air keeps the palm fibers pliant.

Jipi hats come in various grades determined by the quality (pliability, softness, and fineness) of the fibers and closeness of the weave. The difference in weave is easy to see, as a fine weave improves the shape of a hat. It has more body and regains its shape better. I like two places in particular for Panama hats; if you speak Spanish, you can hear two different takes on buying a hat. Expect to pay between $15 and $80. One store is **El Becaleño,** Calle 65 no. 483, across from the post office. The owner can show you differences in quality and has some very expensive hats. The other store is a short distance away in one of the market buildings: Walk south down Calle 56 past the post office; right before the street ends in the market place, turn left into a passage with hardware stores at the entrance. The fourth or fifth shop is the **Casa de los Jipis.** You can always ask people in the area to point it out to you.

WHERE TO STAY

Mérida is easier on the budget than the resort cities. The stream of visitors is steadier than on the coast, so most hotels no longer use a high-season/low-season rate structure. Still, you are more likely to find promotional rates during low season. Mérida has a new convention center, which attracts large trade shows that can fill a lot of hotels, so it's a good idea to make reservations. The rates quoted here include the 17% tax. When inquiring about prices, always ask if the price quoted includes tax. Most hotels in Mérida offer at least a few air-conditioned rooms, and some also have pools. But many hotels, especially in the inexpensive range, haven't figured out how to provide a comfortable bed. Either the mattresses are bad, or the bottom sheet is too small to tuck in properly. Some hotels here would offer a really good deal if only they would improve their beds. One last thing to note: In Mérida, free parking is a relative concept—for many hotels, free parking means only at night; during the day there may be a charge.

VERY EXPENSIVE

Fiesta Americana Mérida ★★   This six-story hotel on the Paseo de Montejo is built in the grand fin-de-siècle style of the old mansions along the Paseo. Guest rooms are off the cavernous lobby, so all face outward and have views of one or another of the avenues. The rooms are comfortable and large, with furnishings and decorations aiming for, and achieving, innocuousness in light, tropical colors. The floors are tile and the bathrooms large and well equipped. Service is very attentive, better than at the Hyatt. There is a shopping center on the ground floor, below the lobby.

Av. Colón 451, Esq. Paseo Montejo, 92127 Mérida, Yuc. © **800/343-7821** in the U.S. and Canada, or 999/942-1111. Fax 999/942-1112. www.fiestaamericana.com.mx. 350 units. $174 double; $200 executive level; $210 junior suite. AE, DC, MC, V. Free secured parking. **Amenities:** 2 restaurants; bar; medium-size pool; tennis court; health club with saunas, men's steam room, unisex whirlpool, and massage; children's programs; concierge; tour desk; small business center; shopping arcade; 24-hr. room service; babysitting; same-day laundry and dry cleaning; executive-level rooms. *In room:* A/C, TV w/pay movies, Internet connection, minibar, coffeemaker, hair dryer, safe.

Hyatt Regency Mérida ★★   This Hyatt is much like Hyatts elsewhere, wherein lies this hotel's chief asset. The rooms are dependably comfortable and quiet, the quietest in a noisy city. They're carpeted and well furnished, with great bathrooms. In decoration and comfort, I find them superior to those of the Fiesta Americana, but they certainly don't have any local flavor. The Hyatt's facilities, especially its tennis courts and health club, also rank above the Fiesta Americana's. The pool is more attractive and larger, but its location keeps it in the shade for most of the day, and the water never gets a chance to heat up. Rising 17 stories, the Hyatt is not hard to find in Mérida's skyline; it's near the Paseo de Montejo and across Avenida Colón from the Fiesta Americana.

Calle 60 no. 344 (at Av. Colón), 97000 Mérida, Yuc. Ⓒ **800/223-1234** in the U.S. and Canada or 999/942-1234. Fax 999/925-7002. www.merida.regency.hyatt.com. 299 units. $150 standard double; $177 Regency club double. Ask about promotional rates. AE, DC, MC, V. Free guarded parking. **Amenities:** 2 restaurants; 2 bars (1 swim-up, open seasonally); large pool; 2 lighted tennis courts; state-of-the-art health club with men's and women's steam rooms, whirlpool, sauna, and massage; children's activities (seasonal); concierge; tour desk; car rental; business center; shopping arcade; 24-hr. room service; babysitting; same-day laundry and dry cleaning; non-smoking rooms; executive-level rooms. *In room:* A/C, TV, dataport, minibar, hair dryer.

MODERATE

Casa Mexilio Guest House ★★ *(Finds)*   This bed-and-breakfast is unlike any other I know. The owners are geniuses at playing with space in an unexpected and delightful manner. Rooms are at different levels, creating private spaces joined to each other and to rooftop terraces by stairs and catwalks. Most are spacious and airy, furnished and decorated in an engaging mix of new and old, polished and primitive. Five come with air-conditioning. A small pool with a whirlpool and profuse tropical vegetation take up most of the central patio. Breakfasts are great. The hotel is part of the Turquoise Reef Group, a reservation service for inns on Mexico's Caribbean coast. It's 4 blocks west of the plaza. A small bar serves drinks during happy hour, and, weather permitting, you can have your cocktail on one of the rooftop terraces.

Calle 68 no. 495 (between calles 57 and 59), 97000 Mérida, Yuc. Ⓒ **800/538-6802** in the U.S.; Ⓒ/fax 999/928-2505. www.mexicoholiday.com. 9 units. $55–$83 double. Rates include full breakfast. MC, V. **Amenities:** Bar; small pool; whirlpool. *In room:* No phone.

Hotel Caribe   This three-story colonial-style hotel (no elevator) is great for a couple of reasons: Its location at the back of Plaza Hidalgo is both central and quiet, and it has a nice little pool and sun deck on the rooftop with a view of the cathedral. The rooms are moderately comfortable, though they aren't well lit, and have only small windows facing the central courtyard. Thirteen *clase económica* rooms don't have air-conditioning; standard rooms do; and superior rooms (on the top floor) have been remodeled and have safes, hair dryers, larger windows, and quieter air-conditioning. Avoid the rooms on the ground floor. The hotel offers a lot of variety in bedding arrangements, mostly combinations of twins and doubles. Mattresses are often softer than standard. The TVs add little value to the rooms. Nearby parking is free at night but costs extra during the day beginning at 7am. The restaurant serves good Mexican food.

Calle 59 no. 500 (at Calle 60), 97000 Mérida, Yuc. Ⓒ **888/822-6431** in the U.S. and Canada, or 999/924-9022. Fax 999/924-8733. www.hotelcaribe.com.mx. 53 units. $47 *clase económica* double; $54–$70 standard or superior double. AE, MC, V. **Amenities:** Restaurant; bar; small pool; tour desk; room service until 10pm; overnight laundry. *In room:* TV, safe.

Hotel Maison Lafitte ★ *(Value)*   This new 3-story hotel offers modern, attractive rooms with good air-conditioning as well as tropical touches such as wooden louvers over the windows, and light furniture with caned backs and seats. Rooms are medium to large, with medium-size bathrooms that have great showers and good lighting. Most rooms come with either two doubles or a king bed. Rooms are quiet and look out over a pretty little garden with a fountain. A couple of rooms don't have windows. The location is excellent.

Calle 60 no. 472 (between calles 53 and 55), 97000 Mérida, Yuc. © **800/538-6802** in the U.S. and Canada, or 999/928-1243. Fax 999/923-9159. www.maisonlafitte.com.mx. 30 units. $70 double. Rates include full breakfast. AE, MC, V. Free limited secured parking for compact cars. **Amenities:** Restaurant; bar; small outdoor pool; tour desk; car rental; limited room service; in-room massage; same-day laundry and dry cleaning. *In room:* A/C, TV, minibar, hair dryer, safe.

Hotel Medio Mundo ★ *Finds*   This is a quiet courtyard hotel with beautiful rooms and a good location 3 blocks north of the main plaza. The English-speaking owners have invested their money in the right places, going for high quality mattresses, good lighting, quiet air-conditioning units, lots of space, and good bathrooms with strong showers. What they didn't invest in were TVs, which adds to the serenity of the place. Higher prices are for the seven rooms with air-conditioning, but all units have windows with good screens and get ample ventilation. Breakfast is served in one of the two attractive courtyards.

Calle 55 no. 533 (between calles 64 and 66), 97000 Mérida, Yuc. ©/fax **999/924-5472.** www.hotelmedio mundo.com. 10 units. High season $50–$70 double; low season $40–$50 double. Internet specials sometimes available. MC, V. **Amenities:** Small outdoor pool; tour info; in-room massage; same-day laundry; nonsmoking rooms.

INEXPENSIVE

Casa San Juan ★★ *Value*   This B&B, in a colonial house, is loaded with character and provides a good glimpse of the old Mérida that lies behind the colonial facades in the historic district. Guest rooms are beautifully decorated, large, and comfortable. Those in the original house have been modernized but maintain a colonial feel, with 20-foot ceilings and 18-inch-thick walls. The modern rooms in back look out over the rear patio. The lower rate is for the three rooms without air-conditioning (they have ceiling and floor fans). Choice of beds includes one queen-size, one double, or two twins, all with good mattresses and sheets. Breakfast includes fruit or juice, coffee, bread, and homemade preserves. Casa San Juan is 4 blocks south of the main square.

Calle 62 no. 545a (between calles 69 and 71), 97000 Mérida, Yuc. ©/fax **999/986-2937.** www.casasan juan.com. 8 units (7 with private bathroom). $25–$55 double. No credit cards. Rates include continental breakfast. Parking nearby $2. *In room:* No phone.

Hotel Dolores Alba ★★ *Value*   The Dolores Alba offers attractive, comfortable rooms, air-conditioning, a lovely swimming pool, and free parking, all for a great price. The three-story section (with elevator) surrounding the back courtyard offers large rooms with good-sized bathrooms. Beds (either 2 doubles or 1 double and 1 twin) have supportive foam-core mattresses, usually in a combination of one medium firm and one medium soft. All rooms have windows or balconies looking out over the pool. An old mango tree shades the front courtyard. The older rooms in this section are decorated with local crafts and have small bathrooms. The family that owns the Hotel Dolores Alba outside Chichén Itzá manages this hotel; you can make reservations at one hotel for the other. This hotel is 3½ blocks from Plaza Mayor.

Calle 63 no. 464 (between calles 52 and 54), 97000 Mérida, Yuc. © **999/928-5650.** Fax 999/928-3163. www.doloresalba.com. 100 units. $30–$40 double. No credit cards. Free guarded sheltered parking. **Amenities:** Restaurant; pool; tour desk; room service until 10pm; overnight laundry. *In room:* A/C, TV.

Hotel Mucuy   The Mucuy is a simple, quiet, pleasant hotel in a great location. The gracious owners strive to make guests feel welcome, with conveniences such as a communal refrigerator in the lobby and, for a small extra charge, the use of a washer and dryer. Guest rooms are basic; most contain two twin beds (with comfortable mattresses) and some simple furniture. A lovely garden patio with comfortable chairs is the perfect place for sitting and reading. The Mucuy is named for a small dove said to bring good luck to places where it alights.

Calle 57 no. 481 (between calles 56 and 58), 97000 Mérida, Yuc. ℂ **999/928-5193.** Fax 999/923-7801. 24 units. $22 double. No credit cards. **Amenities:** Laundry.

Posada Toledo   This hotel's charm lies in the fact that so much of the original domestic architecture survived the conversion from mansion to hotel. Furniture, decoration, paintings, details of design—from all this, you glean an uncontrived view of the past. As is typical in such old *casonas,* some guest rooms were meant to impress, while others were an expression of simple domesticity—make sure you get one you like. Rooms along the street can be noisy. Two of the grandest rooms, with ornate cornices and woodwork, have been converted into a large suite. Those on the third floor (not originally part of the house) are comfortable and have a rooftop terrace. The hotel has a couple of common rooms and a beautiful courtyard lobby. The location is exceptional.

Calle 58 no. 487 (at Calle 57), 97000 Mérida, Yuc. ℂ **999/923-1690.** Fax 999/923-2256. hptoledo@finred. com.mx. 23 units. $35–$45 double. MC, V. Free parking next door. **Amenities:** Restaurant (breakfast only); tour info. *In room:* A/C, TV.

WHERE TO DINE

The people of Mérida have strong ideas and traditions about food. Certain dishes are always associated with a particular day of the week. In households across the city, Sunday would feel incomplete without *puchero* (a kind of stew). On Monday, at any restaurant that caters to locals, you are sure to find *frijol con puerco.* Likewise, you'll find *potaje* on Thursday; fish, of course, on Friday; and *chocolomo* on Saturday. These dishes are heavy and slow to digest; they are for the midday meal, and not suitable for supper. What's more, Meridanos don't believe that seafood is a healthy supper food. All seafood restaurants in Mérida close by 6pm unless they cater to tourists.

The preferred supper food is turkey (which, by the way, is said to be high in tryptophan, a soporific), and it's best served in the traditional *antojitos—salbutes* and *panuchos.* The best I've eaten were at a well-known restaurant in the village of Kanasín, on the outskirts of Mérida, **La Susana Internacional.** Practically the entire menu is based on turkey, including a delicious soup. The only way to get there is by taxi, but if you are with a fairly large party, it's worth organizing the expedition.

Another thing you may notice about Mérida is the surprising number of Middle Eastern restaurants. The city received a large influx of Lebanese immigrants around 1900. This population has had a strong influence on local society, to the point where Meridanos think of *kibbe* the way Americans think of pizza. Speaking of pizza, if you want to get some to take back to your hotel room, try **Vito Corleone,** on Calle 59 between calles 60 and 62. Its pizzas have a thin crust with a slightly smoky taste from the wood-burning oven.

EXPENSIVE

Alberto's Continental ✦ LEBANESE/YUCATECAN/ITALIAN   There's nothing quite like dining here at night in a softly lit room or on the wonderful old patio framed in Moorish arches. Nothing glitzy; just elegant *mudejar*-patterned tile floors, simple furniture, decoration that's just so, and the gurgling of a fountain creating a romantic mood. I find the prices on the expensive side. For supper, you can choose a sampler plate of four Lebanese favorites, or traditional Yucatecan specialties, such as *pollo pibil* or fish Celestún (bass stuffed with shrimp). You can finish with Turkish coffee.

Calle 64 no. 482 (at Calle 57). © 999/928-5367. Reservations recommended. Main courses $8–$20. AE, MC, V. Daily 1pm–11pm.

El Pórtico del Peregrino ★ REGIONAL/INTERNATIONAL   El Pórtico is a favorite among visitors, who enjoy its charm, comfort, and distinctive Mérida flavor. The interior is a lovely garden with three dining areas—two air-conditioned rooms and a patio. One room is nonsmoking, a rarity in Mexico. The menu offers soups (*sopa de tortilla* and *sopa de lima* are both good), seafood (a platter, or grilled Gulf shrimp), and Yucatecan specialties *(pollo pibil)*. Other favorites include baked eggplant with chicken and cheese, and coconut ice cream topped with Kahlúa. The restaurant is 2 blocks north of the main square.

Calle 57 no. 501 (between calles 60 and 62). © 999/928-6163. Reservations recommended. Main courses $6–$15. AE, MC, V. Daily noon–11pm.

La Casa del Paseo ★★ INTERNATIONAL   Set in one of the mansions on the Paseo de Montejo, this restaurant offers excellent food and service in a lovely setting. You can dine inside or out on a small patio along the Paseo. The cooking is wonderful. Where to begin? Perhaps with *sopa de lima* or artichoke mousse. For main dishes, consider the daily specials. If you want something light, stuffed chicken breast, *pechuga suiza,* is good; for something meatier, try *medallones paseo,* three grilled beef filets, each with a different sauce. Or sample a local specialty, *queso relleno.*

Paseo de Montejo 465 (between Calle 35 and Av. Colón, 2 doors down from the American consulate). © 999/920-0528. Reservations recommended on weekends. Main courses $9–$14. AE, MC, V. Daily 1pm–midnight.

MODERATE

Restaurant Amaro REGIONAL/VEGETARIAN   The menu in this courtyard restaurant offers some interesting vegetarian dishes, such as *crema de calabacitas* (cream of squash soup), apple salad, and avocado pizza. There is also a limited menu of fish and chicken dishes; you might want to try the Yucatecan chicken. The *agua de chaya* (chaya is a leafy vegetable prominent in the Maya diet) is refreshing on a hot afternoon. All desserts are made in-house. The restaurant is a little north of Plaza Mayor.

Calle 59 no. 507 interior 6 (between calles 60 and 62). © 999/928-2451. Main courses $5–$9. MC, V. Mon–Sat 11am–2am.

Restaurante Kantún ★★ (Value) SEAFOOD   This modest little restaurant serves up the freshest seafood for really good prices. The personable owner, the son of a cook, is a conscientious man who is always on the premises. He tells me that he will open late by special arrangement for parties as small as four people. The menu includes excellent *ceviches* and seafood cocktails, and fish cooked in a number of ways. I had the *especial Kantún,* which was lightly battered and stuffed with lobster, crab, and shrimp. The dining room is air-conditioned, the furniture comfortable, and the service attentive.

Calle 45 no. 525-G (between calles 64 and 66). © 999/923-4493. Reservations recommended on Good Friday. Main courses $4–$10. MC, V. Daily noon–6pm.

Restaurant Los Almendros *(Overrated)* YUCATECAN Ask where to eat Yucatecan food, and locals will inevitably suggest this place because of its reputation. After all, this was the first place to offer tourists such Yucatecan specialties as *cochinita pibil, salbutes, panuchos papadzules,* and *poc chuc.* The menu even comes with color photographs to facilitate acquaintance with these strange-sounding dishes. The food is okay and not much of a risk, but you can find better elsewhere. Still, it's a safe place to try Yucatecan food for the first time, and it's such a fixture that the idea of a guidebook that doesn't mention this restaurant is unthinkable. It's 5 blocks east of Calle 60, facing the Parque de la Mejorada.

Calle 50A no. 493. ⓒ **999/928-5459.** Main courses $4–$9, daily special $5–$9. AE, MC, V. Daily 10am–11pm.

INEXPENSIVE

Café Alameda ✪ MIDDLE EASTERN/VEGETARIAN The trappings here are simple and informal (metal tables, plastic chairs), and it's a good place for catching a light meal. The trick is figuring out the Spanish names for popular Middle Eastern dishes. Kibbe is *quebbe bola* (not *quebbe cruda*), hummus is *garbanza,* and shish kebab is *alambre.* I leave it to you to figure out what a spinach pie is called (and it's excellent). Café Alameda is a treat for vegetarians, and the umbrella-shaded tables on the patio are perfect for morning coffee and *mamules* (walnut-filled pastries).

Calle 58 no. 474 (between calles 55 and 57). ⓒ **999/928-3635.** Main courses $2–$4. No credit cards. Daily 7:30am–5:30pm.

Eladio's ✪ YUCATECAN This is where locals come to relax in their off hours, drink very cold beer, and snack or dine on Yucatecan specialties. You have two choices: order a beer and enjoy *una botana* (a small portion that accompanies a drink, in this case usually a Yucatecan dish), or order from the menu. *Cochinita, poc chuc,* and *longaniza asada* are all good. Or try a *panucho* or *salbute* if you're there in the evening. Often there is live music in this open-air restaurant, which is around the corner from Los Almendros, by Parque la Mejorada.

Calle 59 (at Calle 44). ⓒ **999/923-1087.** Main courses $4–$5. MC, V. Daily noon–8pm.

La Flor de Santiago ✪ REGIONAL This is a good place for breakfast, lunch, or supper—particularly supper, because the cooks do a good job with *antojitos* (*panuchos, salbutes,* and *vaporcitos*). They even offer *mucbil pollo;* a traditional food for Day of the Dead, it's much like a *tamal* on the outside, with chicken and a soft center on the inside. The menu includes several sandwiches, *comida corrida,* and a large choice of beverages. Service is excellent, and the dining area is classic, with its high ceiling, plain furniture, and clientele.

Calle 70 no. 478 (between calles 57 and 59). ⓒ **999/928-5591.** Main courses $4–$7; *comida corrida* $3.50. No credit cards. Daily 7am–11pm.

MERIDA AFTER DARK

For nighttime entertainment, see the box, "Festivals & Special Events in Mérida," earlier in this chapter, or check out the theaters noted here.

Teatro Peón Contreras, calles 60 and 57, and **Teatro Ayala,** Calle 60 at Calle 61, feature a wide range of performing artists from Mexico and around the world. **El Nuevo Olimpo,** on the main square, schedules frequent concerts; and **Cine Mérida,** a half block north of the Nuevo Olimpo, has two screens for showing classic and art films, and one live stage.

Mérida's club scene offers everything from ubiquitous rock/disco to some one-of-a-kind spots that are nothing like what you find back home. Most of the discos are in the big hotels or on Paseo de Montejo. For dancing, a small cluster of clubs on Calle 60, around the corner from Santa Lucía, offer live rock and salsa music.

El Trovador Bohemio *Finds* It's hard to overstate the importance of *música de trío* and *trova* in Mexican popular culture. This music, mainly in the form of songs called *boleros,* may have been at its most popular in the 1940s and '50s, but every new Mexican pop music heartthrob feels compelled to release a new version of the classics. I like the originals best, and so do most Mexicans. If you know something of this music and are curious about it, El Trovador gives you a chance to hear how it should be played. And if you understand colloquial Spanish, all the better; the language of boleros is vivid, passionate, and quite Mexican—definitely a unique cultural experience. El Trovador is small and dark, and everything is red. It can be smoky. The best days to go are Thursday, Friday, and Saturday. The club faces the Santa Lucía park. El Trovador is open daily from 9pm to 3am.
Calle 55 no. 504. ℭ 999/923-0385. Cover $2.

Pancho's If you take this place seriously, you won't like it. Pancho's, which serves Tex-Mex and international food, is a parody of a tourist attraction, a place for drinking beer and relaxing. Waiters wear bandoliers and oversized sombreros. Assorted emblems of Mexican identity adorn the walls. Live music in the courtyard begins at 9pm on most nights, 10:30pm on Saturday. The five-piece band, with its large repertoire of cover tunes, is quite good; it cranks out salsa, rock, and jazz. Pancho's is open daily from 6pm to 3am.
Calle 59 no. 509. ℭ 999/923-0942. 2-drink minimum on weekends if you do not order food.

ECOTOURS & ADVENTURE TRIPS
The Yucatán Peninsula has seen a recent explosion of companies that organize nature and adventure tours. One well-established outfit with a great track record is **Ecoturismo Yucatán,** Calle 3 no. 235, Col. Pensiones, 97219 Mérida (ℭ **999/920-2772;** fax 999/925-9047; www.ecoyuc.com). Alfonso and Roberta Escobedo create itineraries to meet just about any special or general interest you may have for going to the Yucatán or southern Mexico. Alfonso has been creating adventure and nature tours for more than a dozen years. Specialties include archaeology, birding, natural history, and kayaking. The company also offers day trips that explore contemporary Maya culture and life in villages in the Yucatán. Package and customized tours are available.

SIDE TRIPS FROM MERIDA
IZAMAL
Izamal is a sleepy town some 81km (50 miles) east of Mérida, an easy day trip by car. You can visit the famous Franciscan convent of San Antonio de Padua and the ruins of four large pyramids that overlook the center of town. One pyramid is partially reconstructed to give the viewer an idea of how they must have appeared before their destruction. Life in Izamal is easygoing in the extreme, as evidenced by the *victorias,* the horse-drawn buggies that serve as taxis here. Even if you come by car, you should make a point of touring the town in one of these.

HACIENDA HOPPING
Another relaxing trip is to one of the former haciendas that dot the countryside around Mérida. In recent years it has become popular practice to restore these decaying haciendas to their former glory and convert them into attractions, restaurants, and even luxury hotels, usually with an ecological bent. One of the fanciest, and the one that gets the most press, is **Hacienda Katanchel** (ℭ **999/920-0997**).

It is also one of the most expensive, offering luxury accommodations, old-world service, a pool, 650 acres of forested land, gardens, gourmet food, and excursions. Other haciendas-turned-hotels include **Hacienda Temozón** and **Hacienda Santa Rosa** (© **999/944-3637**), and **Hacienda Blanca Flor,** in the area of the Puuc route, southeast of Uxmal (© **888/BLANCA-F** in the U.S. or 999/925-9655). **Hacienda Teya** (© **999/928-1885** or 999/988-0800), just outside Mérida, has a lovely restaurant and four guest rooms. For information on **Hacienda Yaxcopoil,** which offers tours of the old buildings and grounds, see "En Route to Uxmal," later in this chapter.

CELESTUN NATIONAL WILDLIFE REFUGE: FLAMINGOS & OTHER WATERFOWL

On the coast west of Mérida is a large area of marshland that has been declared a biopreserve. It is a long, shallow estuary where freshwater mixes with Gulf saltwater, creating a habitat perfect for flamingos and many other species of waterfowl. This estuary (*ría* in Spanish), unlike other estuaries that are fed by rivers or streams, receives fresh water through about 80 *cenotes,* most of which are underwater. It is very shallow (.3–1.2m/1–4 ft. deep) and thickly grown with mangrove, with an open channel .5km (¼ mile) wide and 48km (30 miles) long, sheltered from the open sea by a narrow strip of land. Along this corridor, you can take a launch to see flamingos as they dredge the bottom of the shallows for a species of small crustacean and a particular insect that make up the bulk of their diet.

You can get here by car or bus; it's an easy 90-minute drive. (For information on buses, see "Getting There & Departing: By Bus," earlier in this chapter.) To drive, leave downtown Mérida on Calle 57. Shortly after Santiago Church, Calle 57 ends and there's a dogleg onto Calle 59-A. This crosses Avenida Itzáes, and its name changes to Jacinto Canek; continue until you see signs for Celestún Highway 178. This will take you through Hunucmá, where the road joins Highway 281, which takes you to Celestún. You'll know you have arrived when you get to the bridge.

In the last few years, the state agency CULTUR has come into Celestún and established order where once there was chaos. Immediately to your left after the bridge, you'll find modern facilities with a snack bar, clean bathrooms, and a ticket window. Prices for tours are fixed. A 75-minute tour costs about $45 and can accommodate up to six people. You can join others or hire a boat by yourself. On the tour you'll definitely see some flamingos; you'll also get to see some mangrove close up, and one of the many underwater springs. Please do not urge the boatmen to get any closer to the flamingos than they are allowed to; if pestered too much, the birds will abandon the area for other, less fitting habitat. The ride is quite pleasant—the water is calm, and CULTUR has supplied the boatmen with wide, flat-bottom skiffs that have canopies for shade.

In addition to flamingos, you will probably see frigate birds, pelicans, spoonbills, egrets, sandpipers, and other waterfowl feeding on shallow sandbars at any time of year. At least 15 duck species have been counted, and I once saw an eagle fishing in the waters. Of the 175 bird species that come here, some 99 are permanent residents. Nonbreeding flamingos remain here year-round; the larger group of breeding flamingoes takes off around April to nest on the upper Yucatán Peninsula east of Río Lagartos, returning to Celestún in October.

After the tour, you might want to visit the fishing town of Celestún, which is a little beyond the bridge, on a wide, sandy beach facing the Gulf. It has several seafood restaurants (all very similar). If you want a quiet night away from Mérida, you can stay at one of the local hotels. My favorite is the **Hotel María del Carmen,** Calle 12 no. 111 (© **988/916-2051**), facing the water. The accommodations are simple but comfortable, and all come with small balconies facing the water. Rooms cost $25.

Another option is Eco Paraíso, a big step up from the modest hotels you'll find in Celestún.

Hotel Eco Paraíso Xixim ★★   Eco Paraíso is meant to be a refuge from the modern world. It sits on a deserted 4km (3 mile) stretch of beach that was once part of a coconut plantation. It attracts much the same clientele as the former-haciendas-turned-luxury-hotels, but in some ways it has more going for it (like the beach). Some guests come here for a week of idleness; others use this as a base of operations for visiting the biopreserve and making trips to the Maya ruins in the interior. The hotel offers its own tours to various places. Rooms are quite private; each is a separate bungalow with *palapa* roof. Each comes with two comfortable queen-size beds, a sitting area, ceiling fans, and a private porch with hammocks. On my last visit, the food was very good, and the service was great. What's more, the concept is ecologically friendly in more than name only. The hotel composts waste, and treats and uses wastewater.

Km 10 Antigua Carretera a Sisal, 97367 Celestún, Yuc. © 988/916-2100. Fax 988/916-2111. www.mexonline. com/eco-paraiso.htm. 15 units. High season $192 double; low season $172 double. Rates include 2 meals per person. AE, MC, V. Free parking. **Amenities:** Restaurant; bar; medium-size pool; tour desk. *In room:* Safe.

DZIBILCHALTUN: MAYA RUINS AND MUSEUM

This destination makes for a quick morning trip that will get you back to Mérida in time for a siesta, or it could be part of a longer trip to Progreso, Uaymitún, and Xcambó. It's part of a national park, located 14km (9 miles) north of Mérida along the Progreso road and 4km (3 miles) east of the highway. To get there, take Calle 60 all the way out of town and follow signs for Progreso and Highway 261. Look for the sign for Dzibilchaltún, which also reads UNIVERSIDAD DEL MAYAB; it will point you right. After a few miles you'll see a sign for the entrance to the ruins and the museum. If you don't want to drive, take one of the *colectivos* that line up along Parque San Juan.

Dzibilchaltún was founded about 500 B.C., flourished around A.D. 750, and was in decline long before the coming of the conquistadors. It may have been occupied for almost 100 years after their arrival. Since the ruins were discovered in 1941, more than 8,000 buildings have been mapped. The site covers an area of almost 16 sq. km (10 sq. miles) with a central core of almost 65 acres, but the area of prime interest is limited to the buildings surrounding two plazas next to the *cenote,* and another building, the Temple of the Seven Dolls, connected to these by a *sacbé* (causeway). Dzibilchaltún means "place of the stone writing," and at least 25 stelae have been found, many of them reused in buildings constructed after the original ones were covered or destroyed.

Start at the **Museo del Pueblo Maya,** which is worth seeing. It's open Tuesday to Sunday from 8am to 4pm. Admission is $6. The museum's collection includes artifacts from various sites in the Yucatán. Explanations are printed in bilingual format and are fairly thorough. Objects include a beautiful example of a plumed serpent from Chichén Itzá and a finely designed incense vessel from Palenque. From this general view of the Maya civilization, the museum moves on to exhibit specific artifacts found at the site of Dzibilchaltún, including the rather curious dolls that have given one structure its name. Then there's an exhibit on Maya culture in historical and present times, including a lovely collection of *huipiles,* the woven blouses that Indian women wear. From here a door leads out to the site.

The first thing you come to is the *sacbé* that connects the two areas of interest. To the left is the **Temple of the Seven Dolls.** The temple's doorways line up with the *sacbé* to catch the rising sun at the spring and autumnal equinoxes. To the right are the buildings grouped around the Cenote Xlacah, the sacred well, and a complex of buildings around **Structure 38,** the **Central Group** of temples. The Yucatán State Department of Ecology has added nature trails and published a booklet (in Spanish) of birds and plants seen along the mapped trail.

PROGRESO, UAYMITUN & XCAMBO: GULF COAST CITY, FLAMINGO LOOKOUT & MORE MAYA RUINS

For a beach escape, go to the port of Progreso, Mérida's weekend beach resort. This is where Meridanos have their vacation houses and where they come in large numbers in July and August. At other times the crowds and traffic disappear, and you can enjoy the Gulf waters without fuss. Along the *malecón,* the wide oceanfront drive that extends the length of a sandy beach, you can pull over and enjoy a swim anywhere you like. The water here isn't the blue of the Caribbean, but it is clean. A long pier, or *muelle* (pronounced *mweh*-yeh), extends several miles into the bay to service oceangoing ships. Progreso is also the part-time home of some Americans and Canadians escaping northern winters. A newly established ferry route connects Progreso with Tampa, Florida, from late November to late April (see "Getting There & Departing: By Ferry," earlier in this chapter).

Along or near the *malecón* are several hotels and restaurants, including **Le Saint Bonnet,** at Calle 78 (*©* **969/935-2299**), where locals dine on fresh seafood. It has a large menu with several good dishes; for something very Mexican, I recommend *pescado al ajillo* (fish sautéed with garlic and guajillo chile).

From Mérida, buses to **Progreso** leave the special bus station at Calle 62 no. 524, between calles 65 and 67, every 15 minutes, starting at 5am. The trip takes almost an hour and costs $2.50.

If you have a car, you might want to drive down the coastal road east toward Telchac Puerto. After about 20 minutes, at the right side of the road you'll see a large, solid-looking wooden observation tower for viewing flamingos. It was closed during much of last year due to hurricane damage, but should be open by the time you read this. A sign reads UAYMITUN. The state agency CULTUR constructed the tower, operates it, and provides binoculars free of charge. A few years ago, flamingos from Celestún migrated here and established a colony. Your chances of spotting them are good, and you don't have to pay for a boat.

Twenty minutes farther down this road, there's a turn-off for the road to Dzemul. A few minutes after that, you'll see a sign for **Xcambó** that points to the right. This city is thought to have been a center for maritime trading, and perhaps it made use of some nearby salt flats to produce salt for trade. The central ceremonial center is completely reconstructed, and archaeologists are finding a number of graves.

After viewing these ruins, you can continue on the same road through the small towns of Dzemul and Baca. At Baca, take Highway 176 back to Mérida.

EN ROUTE TO UXMAL

Two routes go to Uxmal, about 81km (50 miles) south of Mérida. The most direct is Highway 261 via Uman and Muna. On the way, you can stop to see Hacienda Yaxcopoil, which is 32km (20 miles) from Mérida. From downtown, take Calle 65 or 69 to Avenida Itzáes and turn left; this feeds onto the highway.

If you have the time and want a more scenic route, try the meandering State Highway 18. This is sometimes known as the Convent Route, but all tourism hype aside, it makes for a good drive and you'll see some really interesting sights. You could make your trip to Uxmal into a loop by going one way and coming back the other, but with so many stops, it would take the better part of 2 days to complete the trip, especially if you want to see the ruins of the Puuc Route. One way to do this would be to take the long route on Highway 18, arriving in Uxmal in time to see the sound-and-light show. Stay overnight in Uxmal and see the ruins early in the morning before returning to Mérida. All the attractions on these routes have the same hours: Churches are open from 10am to 2pm and 4 to 6pm; ruins are open from 8am to 5pm.

HIGHWAY 261: YAXCOPOIL & MUNA   Sixteen kilometers (10 miles) beyond Uman along Highway 261 is **Yaxcopoil** (yash-koh-*poyl*), a fascinating 19th-century hacienda on the right side of the road between Mérida and Uxmal. It's difficult to reach by bus.

This hacienda, dating from 1864, was originally a cattle ranch of more than 23,000 acres. Around 1900, it was converted to henequén production (for the manufacture of rope). Take a half hour to tour the house, factory, outbuildings, and museum. Haciendas were the administrative, commercial, and social centers of vast private domains; they were almost little principalities carved out of the Yucatecan jungle. This hacienda is open Monday to Saturday from 8am to 6pm, Sunday from 9am to 1pm. Admission is $3.50.

Twenty-eight kilometers (17 miles) after Yaxcopoil is the busy little crossroads market town of **Muna** (64km/40 miles from Mérida) where you might run into a traffic slowdown. The typical Yucatecan tricycle taxis are everywhere. Muna offers little for sightseers but may interest those curious about contemporary Maya life. Be sure to stay on Highway 281 as you leave; 16km (10 miles) beyond Muna is Uxmal.

HIGHWAY 18 (THE CONVENT ROUTE): KANASIN, ACANCEH, MAYAPAN & TICUL   Take Calle 63 east to Circuito Colonias and turn right; then make a left at Calle 69, which at that level is a two-way street. This feeds onto Highway 18 to Kanasín (kah-nah-*seen*) and then Acanceh (ah-kahn-*keh*). In **Kanasín,** watch for signs that say "Circulación" or "Desviación." As in many Yucatán towns, you're being redirected to follow a one-way street through the urban area. Go past the market, church, and the main square on your left, and continue straight out of town. (On this route you'll be passing through a lot of small villages without any road signs, so get used to poking your head out the window and saying *"Buenos días, ¿dónde está el camino para . . . ?"* which translates as "Good day, where is the road to . . . ?" This is what I do, and I ask more than one person.)

The next village you come to, at Km 10, is **San Antonio Tehuit,** an old henequén hacienda. At Km 13 is **Tepich,** another hacienda village, with funny little henequén-cart tracks crisscrossing the main road. After Tepich comes **Petectunich** and finally **Acanceh.**

Across the street from and overlooking Acanceh's church is a restored pyramid. On top of this pyramid under a makeshift roof are some recently discovered large stucco figures of Maya deities. The caretaker will guide you up to see the fascinating figures and give you a little explanation (in Spanish). Admission is $3. There are some other ruins a couple of blocks away called **El Palacio de los Estucos.** In 1908, a stucco mural was found here in mint condition. It was left exposed and has deteriorated somewhat. Now it is sheltered, and you can still easily distinguish the painted figures in their original colors.

From Acanceh's main square, turn right (around the statue of a smiling deer) and head for **Tecoh** on a good road. Tecoh's parish church sits on a massive pre-Columbian raised platform—the remains of a ceremonial complex that was sacrificed to build the church. With its rough stone and simple twin towers that are crumbling around the edges, the church looks ancient. Inside are three carved *retablos,* covered in gold leaf and unmistakably Indian in style. In 1998 they were cleaned and refurbished, and are now quite dazzling.

Continuing, shortly after the village of Telchaquillo, a sign on the right side of the road points to the entrance to the ruins of Mayapán.

RUINS OF MAYAPAN

Founded, according to Maya lore, by the man-god Kukulkán (Quetzalcoatl in central Mexico) in about A.D. 1007, Mayapán ranked in importance with Chichén Itzá and Uxmal. It covered at least 4 sq. km (2½ sq. miles). For more than two centuries it was the capital of a Maya confederation of city-states that included Chichén and Uxmal. But before 1200, the rulers of Mayapán ended the confederation by attacking and conquering Chichén and forcing the rulers of Uxmal to live as vassals in Mayapán. Eventually, a successful revolt by the other cities brought down Mayapán, which was abandoned during the mid-1400s.

In the last few years, archaeologists have been busy excavating and rebuilding the city, and work continues. Several buildings bordering the principal plaza have been reconstructed, including one that is similar to El Castillo in Chichén Itzá. The scientists have discovered murals and stucco figures that provide more grist for the mill of conjecture: *atlantes,* skeletal soldiers, macaws, entwined snakes, and a stucco jaguar. This place is definitely worth stopping to see.

The site is open daily from 8am to 5pm. Admission is $2.50. Use of a personal video camera is $4.

FROM MAYAPAN TO TICUL   The road is a good one, but directional signs through the villages are almost nonexistent, so you'll need to stop and ask directions frequently. The streets in these villages are full of children, bicycles, and livestock, so drive carefully and keep an eye out for unmarked *topes.* From Mayapán, continue along Highway 18 to **Tekit** (8km/5 miles). The road narrows, and then you're on to **Mama,** sometimes called Mamita. Stop to see the recently rescued former convent and the church with its lovely facade. Inside are several fascinating *retablos* sculpted in a native form of baroque. During the restoration of these buildings, colonial-age murals and designs were uncovered and restored. Be sure to get a peek at them in the sacristy. From Mama you head to Ticul, a large (for this area) market town with a couple of simple hotels and the original Los Almendros restaurant.

TICUL

Best known for the cottage industry of *huipil* (native blouse) embroidery and for the manufacture of women's dress shoes, Ticul isn't the most exciting stop on the Puuc route, but it's a convenient place to wash up and spend the night. It's also a center for large commercially produced pottery; most of the widely sold sienna-colored pottery painted with Maya designs comes from here. If it's a cloudy, humid day, the potters may not be working (part of the process requires sun drying), but they still welcome visitors to purchase finished pieces.

One place worth a visit is **Arte Maya,** Calle 23 no. 301, Carretera Ticul-Muna (© **997/972-1095;** fax 997/972-0334), owned and operated by Luis

Echeverría and Lourdes Castillo. This shop and gallery produces museum-quality art in alabaster, stone, jade, and ceramics. Much of the work is done as it was in Maya times; soft stone or ceramic is smoothed with the leaf of the siri-cote tree, and colors are derived from plant sources. If you buy something, hang on to the written description of your purchase—the work looks so authentic that U.S. Customs has delayed entry of people carrying it, thinking that they're smuggling real Maya artifacts.

Ticul is only 19km (12 miles) northeast of Uxmal, so thrifty tourists stay here instead of at the more expensive hotels at the ruins. I recommend the **Hotel Plaza,** Calle 23 no. 202, on the town square near the intersection with Calle 26 (© **997/972-0484**). It's a modest hotel, as you would expect in a town of this sort, but it's comfortable and recently remodeled. A double room with air-conditioning costs $30; without air-conditioning, $25. In both cases, there's a 5% charge if you want to pay with a credit card (MC, V). Get an interior room if you're looking for quiet, because Ticul has quite a lively plaza. Once in Ticul, you can do one of two things: head straight for Uxmal via Santa Elena, or loop around the Puuc Route, the long way to Santa Elena. For information on the Puuc route, see "The Puuc Maya Route & Village of Oxkutzcab," below.

FROM TICUL TO UXMAL   Follow the main street (Calle 23) west through town. Turn left at the sign to Santa Elena. It's 16km (10 miles) to Santa Elena; then, at Highway 261, cut back right for about 3km (2 miles) to Uxmal. In Santa Elena, by the side of Highway 261, is a clean restaurant with good food, **El Chac Mool.**

2 The Ruins of Uxmal ⭑⭑⭑

80km (50 miles) SW of Mérida; 19km (12 miles) W of Ticul; 19km (12 miles) S of Muna

One of the highlights of a Yucatán vacation, the ruins of Uxmal (pronounced "oosh-*mahl*")—noted for their rich geometric stone facades—are perhaps the most beautiful on the peninsula. Remains of an agricultural society indicate that the area was occupied possibly as early as 800 B.C. The great building period took place between A.D. 700 and 1000, when the population probably reached 25,000. After 1000, Uxmal fell under the sway of the Xiú princes (who may have come from central Mexico). In the 1440s, the Xiú conquered Mayapán, and not long afterward the age of the Maya ended with the arrival of the Spanish conquistadors.

Close to Uxmal, four other sites—**Sayil, Kabah, Xlapak,** and **Labná**—are worth visiting. With Uxmal, these ruins are collectively known as the **Puuc route,** for the Puuc hills of this part of the Yucatán. See "Seeing Puuc Maya Sites," later in this chapter, if you want to explore these sites.

ESSENTIALS

GETTING THERE & DEPARTING   By Car   Two routes to Uxmal from Mérida, Highway 261 and State Highway 18, are described in "En Route to Uxmal," above. *Note:* There's no gasoline at Uxmal.

By Bus   See "Getting There & Departing" in "Mérida: Gateway to the Maya Heartland," earlier in this chapter for information about bus service between Mérida and Uxmal. To return, wait for the bus on the highway at the entrance to the ruins. To see the sound-and-light show, don't bother with regular buses; sign up with a tour operator in Mérida.

ORIENTATION   Uxmal consists of the archaeological site and its visitor center, five hotels, and a highway restaurant. The visitor center, open daily from

8am to 9pm, has a restaurant (with good coffee); toilets; a first-aid station; shops selling soft drinks, ice cream, film, batteries, and books; and a state-run Casa de Artesanía. There are no phones except at the hotels. Most public buses pick up and let off passengers on the highway at the entrance to the ruins. The site is open daily from 8am to 5pm. Admission to the archaeological site is around $10, which includes admission to the nightly sound-and-light show. Bringing in a video camera costs $4. Parking costs $1. If you're staying the night in Uxmal, it is possible (and I think preferable) to get to the site late in the day and buy a ticket that allows you to see the sound-and-light show that evening and lets you enter the ruins the next morning to explore them before it gets hot. Just make sure that the ticket vendor knows what you intend to do.

Guides at the entrance of Uxmal give tours in a variety of languages and charge $20 for a single person or a group. The guides frown on unrelated individuals joining a group. They'd rather charge you as a solo visitor, but you can ask other English speakers if they'd like to join you in a tour and split the cost. As at other sites, the guides vary in quality but will point out areas and architectural details that you might otherwise miss. You should think of these guided tours as performances—the guides try to be as entertaining as possible and adjust their presentations according to the interests of the visitors.

Included in the price of admission is a 45-minute **sound-and-light show,** staged each evening at 8pm. It's in Spanish, but headsets are available for rent ($3) for listening to the program in several languages. After the impressive show, the chant *"Chaaac, Chaaac"* will echo in your mind for weeks.

A TOUR OF THE RUINS

THE PYRAMID OF THE MAGICIAN   As you enter the ruins, note the *chultún,* or cistern, where Uxmal stored its water. Unlike most of the major Maya sites, Uxmal has no *cenote* to supply fresh water. The city's inhabitants were much more dependent on rainwater, which is why they seem so infatuated with Chaac, the rain god.

Just beyond the *chultún,* the remarkable Pyramid of the Magician (also called Pyramid of the Dwarf) looms majestically on the right. The name comes from a legend about a mystical dwarf who reached adulthood in a single day after being hatched from an egg, and who built this pyramid in one night. Beneath it are five earlier structures, which is a common feature of Maya pyramids; the practice was to build new structures atop old ones at regular intervals. The pyramid is unique because of its rounded sides, height, and steepness, and the doorway on the opposite (west) side near the top. The doorway's heavy ornamentation, a characteristic of the Chenes style, features 12 stylized masks of the rain god Chaac.

Next to the Pyramid of the Magician, to the west, is the Nunnery Quadrangle, and left of it is a partially restored ball court. South of that are several large complexes. The biggest building among them is the Governor's Palace, and behind it lies the massive, largely unrestored Great Pyramid. In the distance is the Dovecote (House of the Doves), a small building with a lacy roof comb that looks like the perfect apartment complex for pigeons. From this vantage point, note how Uxmal is unique among Maya sites for its use of huge terraces constructed to support the buildings; look closely and you'll see that the Governor's Palace is not on a natural hill, but rather on a giant platform of packed earth, as is the nearby Nunnery Quadrangle.

THE NUNNERY QUADRANGLE   The 16th-century Spanish historian Fray Diego López de Cogullado gave the building its name because it resembled a

Uxmal Ruins

To Mérida

North Group
(*Grupo Norte*)

Hotel Hacienda
Uxmal

Northwest Group
(*Grupo Noroeste*)

261 To Puuc Route &
Campeche

Platform of the Stelae
(*Plataforma de las Estelas*)

Columns Group
(*Grupo de las
Columnas*)

Quadrangle of the Nuns
(*Cuadrángulo de las Monjas*)

Villa
Arqueológica
Uxmal

PARKING

Cemetery Group
(*Grupo del Cementerio*)

Pyramid of the Magician
(*Pirámide del Advino*)

Ball Court
(*Juego de Pelota*)

House
of the Doves

House of the Turtles
(*Casa de las Tortugas*)

West Group
(*Grupo Oeste*)

Governor's Palace
(*Palacio del Gobenador*)

South Temple
(*Templo Sur*)

Great Pyramid
(*Gran Pirámide*)

House of the Old Woman
(*Pirámide de la Vieja*)

Information ⓘ

To Chimez Temple ↓

To Temple of the Phallus ↓

0 330 feet
0 100 meters

Spanish convent. Possibly it was a military academy or a training school for princes, who may have lived in the 70-odd rooms. The buildings were constructed at different times: The northern one was first; then the southern, eastern, and western buildings. The western building has the most richly decorated facade, composed of intertwined stone snakes and numerous masks of the hook-nosed rain god Chaac.

The corbeled archway to the south was once the main entrance to the Nunnery complex; as you head toward it out of the quadrangle, look above each doorway in that section for the motif of a Maya cottage, or *nah,* still seen throughout the Yucatán today.

THE BALL COURT   A small ball court is conserved to prevent further decay, but compare it later in your trip to the giant, magnificently restored court at Chichén Itzá.

THE TURTLE HOUSE   Up on the terrace south of the ball court is a little temple decorated with colonnade motif on the facade and a border of turtles. Though it's small and simple, its harmony makes it one of the gems of Uxmal.

THE GOVERNOR'S PALACE   In its size and intricate stonework, this rivals the Temple of the Magician as Uxmal's masterwork—an imposing three-level edifice with a 97m (320 ft.) long mosaic facade done in the Puuc style. Puuc means "hilly country," the name given to the hills nearby and thus to the predominant style of pre-Hispanic architecture found here. Uxmal has many examples of Puuc decoration, characterized by elaborate stonework from door tops to the roofline. Fray Cogullado also gave this building its name. The Governor's Palace may have been just that—the administrative center of the Xiú principality, which included the region around Uxmal. It probably had astrological significance as well. For years, scholars pondered why this building was constructed slightly turned from adjacent buildings. Originally they thought the strange alignment was because of the *sacbé* (ceremonial road) that starts at this building and ends 18km (11 miles) away at the ancient city of Kabah. But recently scholars of archaeoastronomy (a relatively new science that studies the placement of archaeological sites in relation to the stars) discovered that the central doorway, which is larger than the others, is in perfect alignment with Venus.

Before you leave the Governor's Palace, note the elaborately stylized headdress patterned in stone over the central doorway. As you stand back from the building on the east side, note how the 103 stone masks of Chaac undulate across the facade like a serpent and end at the corners, where there are columns of masks.

THE GREAT PYRAMID   A massive, partially restored nine-level structure, it has interesting motifs of birds, probably macaws, on its facade, as well as a huge mask. The view from the top is wonderful.

THE DOVECOTE   This building is remarkable in that roof combs weren't a common feature of temples in the Puuc hills, although you'll see one (of a very different style) on El Mirador at Sayil.

WHERE TO STAY

There are some lovely hotels in Uxmal. If occupancy is low, you might bargain for a room. If you're on a tight budget, consider this a day trip, or stay in nearby Ticul.

Hotel Hacienda Uxmal ★★   One of my favorites, this is also the oldest hotel in Uxmal. Located just up the highway from the ruins, it was built as the archaeology staff headquarters. Rooms are large and airy, exuding an impression of a well-kept yesteryear, with patterned tile floors, heavy furniture, and well-screened windows. Guest rooms surround a handsome central garden courtyard with towering royal palms, a bar, and a pool. Other facilities include a dining room, a gift shop, and a second pool. A guitar trio usually plays on the open patio in the evenings. Checkout time is 1pm, so you can spend the morning at the ruins and take a swim before you hit the road.

Mayaland Resorts, owner of the hotel, also runs the striking **Hotel Lodge at Uxmal,** next door. It has lovely rooms, but the restaurant isn't good, and I like the comforting feel of the older hotel better. Mayaland operates transfer service between the hotel and Mérida for about $30 one-way.

Km 80 Carretera Mérida–Uxmal, 97840 Uxmal, Yuc. (C) **997/976-2011.** (Reservations: Mayaland Resorts, Robalo 30 SM3, 77500 Cancún, Q. Roo; (C) 800/235-4079 in the U.S., or 997/887-0870; fax 997/884-4510.) 80 units. High season $170 double; low season $150 double. AE, MC, V. Free guarded parking. **Amenities:** Restaurant (see "Where to Dine," below); bar; 2 medium-size pools; tour info; room service until 10pm; overnight laundry. *In room:* A/C, TV.

Rancho Uxmal   This modest hotel is an exception to the high prices near Uxmal. Ten rooms have air-conditioning, and all have good screens, hot-water showers, and 24-hour electricity. The restaurant is good; a full meal of *poc chuc,* rice, beans, and tortillas costs about $5, and breakfast is $2.25 to $3. It's a long hike to the ruins from here, but the manager may help you flag down a passing bus or *combi*—or even drive you himself, if he has time. A primitive campground out back offers electrical hookups and use of a shower. The hotel is 4km (2½ miles) north of the ruins on Highway 261.

Km 70 Carretera Mérida–Uxmal, 97840 Uxmal, Yuc. No local phone. (Reservations: Sr. Macario Cach Cabrera, Calle 26 no. 156, Ticul, Yuc., 97860; ℂ 997/949-0526 or 997/923-1576.) 18 units. $30–$35 double; $3 per person campsite. No credit cards. Free guarded parking.

Villas Arqueológicas Uxmal ✿ This hotel is associated with Club Med, but it is just a hotel, not a self-contained vacation village. It offers a beautiful two-story layout around a garden patio and a pool. At guests' disposal are a tennis court, a library, and an audiovisual show on the ruins in English, French, and Spanish. Each of the modern, smallish rooms has two oversized single beds that fit into spaces that are walled on three sides. Very tall people should stay else-where. You can also ask for rates that include half or full board.

Ruinas Uxmal, 97844 Uxmal, Yuc. ℂ 800/258-2633 in the U.S. or 997/976-2018. 43 units. $81 double. Rates include continental breakfast. ½-board (breakfast plus lunch or dinner) $15 per person; full board (3 meals) $30 per person. AE, MC, V. Free guarded parking. **Amenities:** Restaurant; bar; large pool; tennis court. *In room:* A/C.

WHERE TO DINE

Besides the restaurants at the Villa Arqueológicas and the visitor center, there are a few other dining choices.

Café-Bar Nicte-Ha MEXICAN This small restaurant attached to the Hotel Hacienda Uxmal is a lovely place to eat. The food is decent, though prices tend to be high. If you eat here, take full advantage of the experience and spend a few hours by the pool near the cafe: Its use is free to customers. This is a favorite spot for bus tours that fill the place to overcrowding, so come early.

In the Hotel Hacienda Uxmal, Km 80 Carretera Mérida–Uxmal. ℂ 997/976-2011. Main courses $5–$8; fixed-price lunch $9. AE, MC, V. Daily 1–8pm.

Las Palapas MEXICAN/YUCATECAN Five kilometers (3 miles) north of the ruins on the road to Mérida, you'll find this pleasant open-air restaurant with a large *palapa* roof. The amiable owner, María Cristina Choy, charges the lowest prices around. Individual diners can sometimes become lost in the crowd if a busload of tourists arrives, but otherwise the service is fine and the food quite good. There's also a small gift shop with regional crafts and a few books.

Hwy. 261. No phone. Breakfast $3; *comida corrida* (served 1–4pm) $3.75. No credit cards. Daily 9am–6pm.

THE PUUC MAYA ROUTE & VILLAGE OF OXKUTZCAB

South and east of Uxmal are several other Maya cities worth visiting. Though smaller in scale than Uxmal or Chichén Itzá, each contains gems of Maya

---

⟮*Tips* **Seeing Puuc Maya Sites**

All of these sites are currently undergoing excavation and reconstruction, and some buildings may be roped off when you visit. Photographers, take note: You'll find afternoon light the best. The sites are open daily from 8am to 5pm. Admission is $2 to $3 for each site, and $5 for Loltún. Loltún has specific hours for tours—9:30 and 11am, and 12:30, 2, 3, and 4pm—but if the tour guide is there, a generous tip might persuade him to do a tour and not wait for a tour bus. Use of a video camera at any time costs $4; if you're visiting Uxmal in the same day, you pay only once for video permission and present your receipt as proof at each ruin.

architecture. The facade of masks on the Palace of Masks at **Kabah,** the enormous palace at **Sayil,** and the fantastic caverns of **Loltún** may be among the high points of your trip. Also along the way are the **Xlapak** and **Labná ruins** and the pretty village of **Oxkutzcab.**

Kabah is 28km (17 miles) southeast of Uxmal. From there it's only a few miles to Sayil. Xlapak is almost walking distance (through the jungle) from Sayil, and Labná is just a bit farther east. A short drive beyond Labná brings you to the caves of Loltún. Oxkutzcab is at the road's intersection with Highway 184, which you can follow west to Ticul or east all the way to Felipe Carrillo Puerto. If you aren't driving, a daily bus from Mérida goes to all these sites, with the exception of Loltún. (See "By Bus" in "Getting There & Departing," earlier in this chapter.)

PUUC MAYA SITES

KABAH ✪ To reach Kabah from Uxmal, head southwest on Highway 261 to Santa Elena (1km/½ mile), then south to Kabah (13km/8 miles). The ancient city of Kabah lies along both sides of the highway. Turn right into the parking lot.

The most outstanding building at Kabah is the huge **Palace of Masks,** or *Codz Poop* ("rolled-up mat"), named for its decorative motif. You'll notice it first on the right upon a terrace. Its outstanding feature is the Chenes-style facade, completely covered in a repeated pattern of 250 masks of the rain god Chaac, each one with curling remnants of Chaac's elephant-trunk-like nose. There's nothing else like this facade in all of Maya architecture. For years, stone-carved parts of this building lay lined up in the weeds like pieces of a puzzle awaiting the master puzzle-solver to put them into place. Sculptures from this building are in the anthropology museums in Mérida and Mexico City.

Just behind and to the left of the Codz Poop is the **Palace Group** (also called the East Group), with a fine Puuc-style colonnaded facade. Originally it had 32 rooms. On the front are seven doors, two divided by columns, a common feature of Puuc architecture. Across the highway is what was once the **Great Temple.** Past it is a **great arch,** which was much wider at one time and may have been a monumental gate into the city. A *sacbé* linked this arch to a point at Uxmal. Compare this corbeled arch to the one at Labná (see below), which is in much better shape.

SAYIL About 4km (3 miles) south of Kabah is the turn-off (left, or east) to Sayil, Xlapak, Labná, Loltún, and Oxkutzcab. The ruins of **Sayil** ("place of the ants") are 4km (2½ miles) along this road.

Sayil is famous for **El Palacio** ✪✪. This palace of more than 90 rooms is impressive for its size alone. At present it is roped off because of some damage suffered in the last hurricane. Climbing is not permitted. But this is unimportant because what makes it a masterpiece of Maya architecture is the facade, which is best appreciated from the ground. It stretches across three terraced levels, and its rows of columns give it a Minoan appearance. On the second level, notice the upside-down stone figure known to archaeologists as the Diving God, or Descending God, over the doorway; the same motif was used at Tulum several centuries later. The large circular basin on the ground below the palace is an artificial catch basin for a *chultún* (cistern); this region has no natural *cenotes* (wells) to catch rainwater.

In the jungle past El Palacio is **El Mirador,** a small temple with an oddly slotted roof comb. Beyond El Mirador, a crude stele (tall, carved stone) has a phallic idol carved on it in greatly exaggerated proportions. Another cluster of buildings, the Southern Group, is a short distance down a trail that branches off from the one heading to El Mirador.

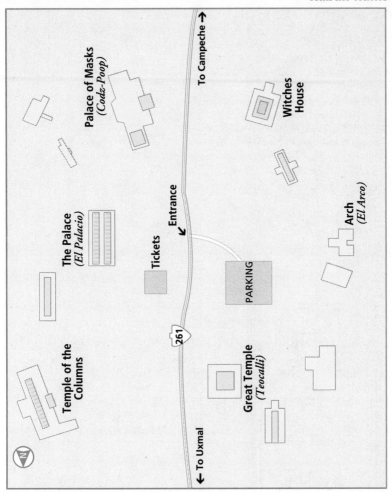

XLAPAK Xlapak (*shla*-pahk) is a small site with one building; it's 5.5km (3½ miles) down the road from Sayil. The Palace at Xlapak bears the masks of the rain god Chaac. You won't miss much if you skip this place.

LABNA Labná, which dates from between A.D. 600 and 900, is 30km (18 miles) from Uxmal and only 3km (2 miles) past Xlapak. Descriptive placards fronting the main buildings are in Spanish, English, and German. The first thing you see on the left as you enter is **El Palacio,** a magnificent Puuc-style building much like the one at Sayil, but in poorer condition. Over a doorway is a large, well-conserved mask of Chaac with eyes, a huge snout nose, and jagged teeth around a small mouth that seems on the verge of speaking. Jutting out on one corner is a highly stylized serpent's mouth from which pops a human head with an unexpectedly serene expression. From the front, you can gaze out to the enormous grassy interior grounds flanked by vestiges of unrestored buildings and jungle.

From El Palacio, you can walk across the interior grounds on a reconstructed *sacbé* leading to Labná's **corbeled arch,** famed for its beauty and for its

Sayil Ruins

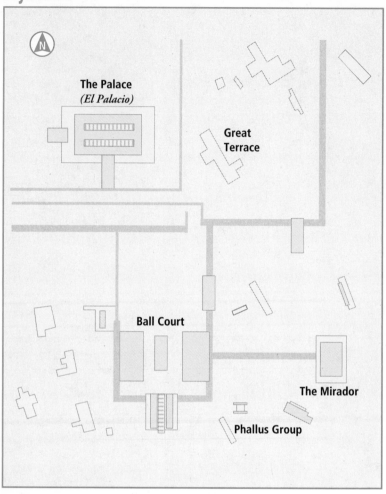

The Palace
(El Palacio)

Great
Terrace

Ball Court

The Mirador

Phallus Group

representation of what many such arches must have looked like at other sites. This one has been extensively restored, although only remnants of the roof comb can be seen. It was once part of a more elaborate structure that is completely gone. Chaac's face is on the corners of one facade, and stylized Maya huts are fashioned in stone above the two small doorways.

You pass through the arch to **El Mirador,** or El Castillo, as the rubble-formed, pyramid-shaped structure is called. Towering on top is a singular room crowned with a roof comb etched against the sky.

There's a snack stand with toilets at the entrance.

LOLTUN   The caverns of Loltún are 31km (19 miles) past Labná on the way to Oxkutzcab, on the left side of the road. These fascinating caves, home of ancient Maya, were also used as a refuge during the War of the Castes (1847–1901). Inside are statuary, wall carvings and paintings, *chultúns* (cisterns), and other signs of Maya habitation. Guides will explain much of what you see. When I was there, the guide spoke English but was a little difficult to understand.

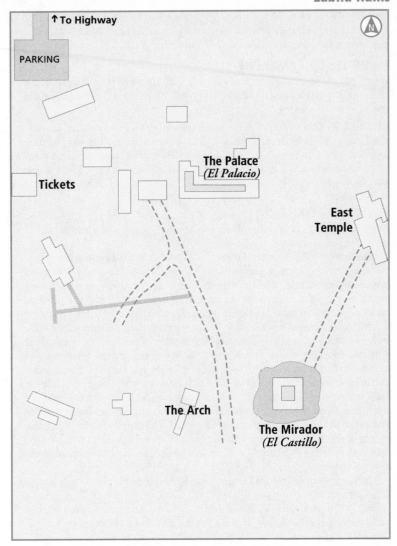

↑ To Highway

PARKING

The Palace
(El Palacio)

Tickets

East Temple

The Arch

The Mirador
(El Castillo)

The admission price includes a 90-minute **tour;** they begin daily at 9:30 and 11am and 12:30, 2, 3 and 4pm. The floor of the cavern can be slippery in places; if you have a flashlight, take it with you. Admission is $5. What you see is quite interesting.

To return to Mérida from Loltún, drive the 7km (4½ miles) to Oxkutzcab. From there, head northwest on Highway 184. It's 19km (12 miles) to Ticul and (turning N onto Hwy. 261 at Muna) 105km (65 miles) to Mérida.

OXKUTZCAB

Oxkutzcab (ohsh-kootz-*kahb*), 11km (7 miles) from Loltún, is the center of the Yucatán's fruit-growing region. Oranges abound. The tidy village of 21,000 centers on a beautiful 16th-century church and the market. **Su Cabaña Suiza** (no phone) is a good restaurant in town. The last week of October and first week of November is the **Orange Festival,** when the village turns exuberant, with a carnival and orange displays in and around the central plaza.

EN ROUTE TO CAMPECHE

From Oxkutzcab, head back 43km (27 miles) to Sayil, and then drive south on Highway 261 to Campeche (126km/78 miles). Along the way are several ruins and caves worth visiting.

CHENES RUINS On the route south, you can detour to see several unexcavated ruined cities in the Chenes style. These visits involve a bit of adventure; pack some food and water. When you get to Hopelchén, take the turn-off for Dzibalchén. When you get to Dzibalchén (42km/26 miles from Hopelchén), ask for directions to Hochob, San Pedro, Dzehkabtún, El Tabasqueño, and Dzibilnocac.

EDZNA From Hopelchén, Highway 261 heads west. After 42km (26 miles), you'll find yourself at the turn-off for the ruins of the city of Edzná, 19km (12 miles) farther south.

Founded probably between 600 and 300 B.C. as a small agricultural settlement, it developed into a major ceremonial center over the next 1,500 years. Archaeologists estimate that building and maintaining such a complex center must have required a population in the tens of thousands. A network of Maya canals once crisscrossed this entire area, making intensive cultivation possible.

The **Great Acropolis** is a unique five-level pyramid with a temple, complete with roof-comb on top. *Edzná* means "house of wry faces," and no doubt there were some of those at one time. Though the buildings at Edzná were mostly in the heavily baroque Chenes, or "well-country," style, no vestige of these distinctive decorative facades remains at Edzná. Several other buildings surround an open central yard. Farther back, new excavations have revealed the **Temple of the Stone Mask,** a structure with several fine stucco masks similar to those of Kohunlich in the Río Bec region near Chetumal. The site takes only 30 minutes or less to see; it may not be worth the price of entry, especially if you've seen many other sites in the Yucatán. (***Note:*** Afternoon light is best for photographing the temple.)

The site is open daily from 8am to 5pm. Admission is $4, plus $4 to use your video camera.

Back on Highway 261, it's 19km (12 miles) to the intersection with Highway 180 and then another 42km (26 miles) to the center of Campeche.

3 Campeche ✸✸

251km (157 miles) SW of Mérida; 376km (235 miles) NE of Villahermosa

Campeche, the capital of the state of the same name, is the most thoroughly restored colonial city in Mexico. It's so well restored that, in some places, you can imagine that you've traveled back in time. The facades of all the houses in the old part of town have been repaired and painted, all electrical and telephone cables have been routed underground, and the streets have been paved to look cobbled. Several Mexican movie companies have taken advantage of the restoration to shoot period films here.

Despite its beauty, not many tourists come to Campeche. Those who do tend to be either on their way to the ruins at Palenque (see chapter 7) or the Río Bec region (see chapter 5), or the kind of travelers who are accidental wanderers

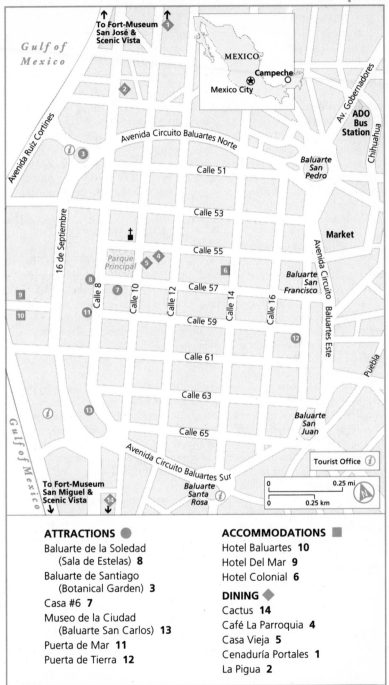

Campeche

ATTRACTIONS ●
Baluarte de la Soledad
  (Sala de Estelas) **8**
Baluarte de Santiago
  (Botanical Garden) **3**
Casa #6 **7**
Museo de la Ciudad
  (Baluarte San Carlos) **13**
Puerta de Mar **11**
Puerta de Tierra **12**

ACCOMMODATIONS ■
Hotel Baluartes **10**
Hotel Del Mar **9**
Hotel Colonial **6**

DINING ◆
Cactus **14**
Café La Parroquia **4**
Casa Vieja **5**
Cenaduría Portales **1**
La Pigua **2**

Bus Travel Warning

There have been some bus holdups on highways in the state of Campeche, though none recently. All occurred at night. The U.S. State Department therefore recommends that you avoid traveling at night.

rather than purposeful sightseers. A couple of things do need to be said: Campeche is not geared to foreign tourism the way Mérida is, so expect less in the way of English translations and such at museums and other sights. Campeche also is a sleepy town with little nightlife.

If you're interested in seeing the ruins and biosphere reserve at Calakmul and the rest of the ruins along the Río Bec route, see the section "The Río Bec Ruin Route," in chapter 5. Calakmul is a large and important site, with the tallest pyramid in the Yucatán peninsula, and if you're going that far, you must stop at Balamkú. From the Campeche side you can get information and contract a tour with one of several tour operators. You might talk with the travel agency at the Hotel Del Mar and arrange an overnight trip with accommodations at its eco-village at Chicanná.

The federal highway that leads to these sights crosses through the Río Bec region and eventually arrives at Chetumal, on Yucatán's southern Caribbean coast. From there you can head up the coast and complete a loop of the peninsula.

Campeche has an interesting history. The first contact between white men and natives occurred in 1517, when Francisco de Córdoba landed here while exploring the coast. Supposedly, it was the first place on the mainland where a Mass was celebrated. Francisco de Montejo the Elder established a settlement here in 1531, but the Indians soon expelled the Spaniards. Finally, Montejo the Younger refounded it in 1540.

For the next century, pirates repeatedly harassed the city. The list of pirates who have attacked Campeche reads like a *Who's Who of Pirating*. On one occasion, several outfits joined forces under the famous Dutch pirate Peg Leg (who most likely was the inspiration for the many fictional 1-legged sailors) and managed to capture the city. And that wasn't the capture of the city. The *Campechanos* grew tired of playing host to pirate parties and erected walls around the city, showing as much industry then as they now show in renovating their historic district. The walls had a number of bastions *(baluartes)* at critical locations. For added security, they constructed two forts, complete with moats and drawbridges, on the hills flanking the city on the north and south sides. There were four entrances to the city, and the two main gates are still intact: the Puerta de Mar (Sea Gate) and the Puerta de Tierra (Land Gate). The pirates never cared to return. Eventually, in the early 1900s, the wall around the city was razed, but the bastions and main gates were left intact, as were the two hilltop fortresses. Most of the bastions and both forts now house museums.

ESSENTIALS

GETTING THERE & DEPARTING   By Plane   Aeromexico (© **981/816-6656** at the airport) flies once daily to and from Mexico City. The **airport** is several miles northeast of the town center, and you'll have to take a taxi into town (about $4).

BY CAR   Highway 180 goes south from Mérida, passing near the basket-making village of Halacho and near Becal, known for its Panama-hat weavers. At Tenabo, take the shortcut (right) to Campeche rather than going farther to the crossroads near Chencoyí. The longer way from Mérida is along Highway 261 past Uxmal. From Uxmal, Highway 261 passes near some interesting ruins (see "En Route to Campeche," above).

When driving in the other direction, toward Celestún and Mérida, use the **Vía Corta** (short route) by going north on Avenida Ruiz Cortines, bearing left to follow the water (this becomes Av. Pedro Sainz de Baranda, but there's no sign). Follow the road as it turns inland to Highway 180, where you turn left (there's a gas station at the intersection). The route takes you through Becal and Halacho. Stores in both villages close between 2 and 4pm.

If you're leaving Campeche for Edzná and Uxmal, go north on either Ruiz Cortines or Gobernadores and turn right on Madero, which becomes **Highway 281.** To Villahermosa, take Ruiz Cortines south; it becomes **Highway 180.**

BY BUS   ADO (② **981/816-2802**) offers a first-class *de paso* bus to Palenque (6 hr.; $15) four times a day and buses to Mérida (2½ hr.; $7) at least every hour from 5:30am to midnight. The ADO **bus station,** on Avenida Gobernadores, is 9 long blocks from Plaza Principal. Turn left out the front door and walk 1 block. Turn right (Calle 49) and go straight for 5 blocks to Calle 8. Turn left here, and Plaza Principal is 3 blocks ahead. Taxis are readily available outside the station.

INFORMATION   The **State of Campeche Office of Tourism** (②/fax **981/ 816-6767**) is in Plaza Moch-Couoh, Avenida Ruiz Cortines s/n, 24000 Campeche. This is in one of the state buildings between the historic center and the shore. There are also information offices in the bastions of Santa Rosa, San Carlos, and Santiago. The tourism office here is better prepared and more helpful than in most other cities, and it hands out good maps. It keeps regular office hours: Monday to Friday from 9am to 2pm and 4 to 7pm.

CITY LAYOUT   The most interesting part of the city is the restored old part, most of which once lay within the walls. Originally, the seaward wall was at the water's edge, but now land has been gained from the sea between the old walls and the coastline. This is where you'll find two of the best hotels in town and most of the state government buildings, which were built in a glaringly modernist style around **Plaza Moch-Couoh:** buildings such as the office tower **Edificio de los Poderes,** or **Palacio de Gobierno**—headquarters for the state of Campeche—and the futuristic **Cámara de Diputados (Chamber of Deputies),** which looks like an enormous square clam.

Campeche's system of street numbering is much like that of other cities in the Yucatán, except that the numbers of the north-south streets increase as you go east instead of the reverse. (See "City Layout" in "Mérida: Gateway to the Maya Heartland," earlier in this chapter.)

GETTING AROUND   Most of the recommended sights, restaurants, and hotels are within walking distance of the old city, except for the two fort-museums. Campeche isn't easy to negotiate by bus; I recommend taxis for anything beyond walking distance. Taxis are inexpensive.

 FAST FACTS: **Campeche**

American Express Local offices are at Calle 59 no. 4 and 5 (② **981/811-1010**), in the Edificio Belmar, a half block toward town from the Hotel Del Mar.

They're open Monday to Friday from 9am to 2pm and 5 to 7pm, and Saturday from 9am to 1pm. This office does not cash traveler's checks.

Area Code The telephone area code is **981**.

ATMs There are more than 10 cash machines in and around the downtown area.

Internet Access There are plenty of these, too. If you don't happen upon any, one called **Multiscomp** is on Calle 16 between calles 53 and 55. It has pretty good machines and is open normal business hours.

Post Office The *correo* is in the Edificio Federal at the corner of Avenida 16 de Septiembre and Calle 53 (✆ **981/816-2134**), near the Baluarte de Santiago; it's open Monday to Saturday from 7:30am to 8pm. The telegraph office is here as well.

EXPLORING CAMPECHE

With beautiful surroundings, friendly people, an easy pace of living, and orderly traffic, Campeche is a lovely city worthy of at least a day on your itinerary. It has some interesting museums, one outstanding restaurant, and several shops worth investigating.

INSIDE THE CITY WALLS

A good place to begin is the pretty *zócalo,* or **Parque Principal,** bounded by calles 55 and 57 running east and west and calles 8 and 10 running north and south. Construction of the church on the north side of the square began in 1650 and was finally completed 1½ centuries later. A pleasant way to see the city is to take the trolley tour *(tranvía)* that leaves three or four times a day from the main plaza; check with one of the tourist information offices for the schedule. This *tranvía* has English-speaking guides.

For a good introduction to the city, stroll into Casa no. 6 (see below), which faces the main plaza opposite the church.

Baluarte de la Soledad   This bastion next to the sea gate houses numerous Maya stelae recovered from around the state. Many are badly worn, but the excellent line drawings beside the stones allow you to appreciate something of their former beauty.

Calle 57 and Calle 8, opposite Plaza Principal. No phone. Admission $2.50. Tues–Sat 9am–8pm; Sun 9am–1pm.

Baluarte de San Carlos/Museo de la Ciudad   This museum features a permanent exhibition of photographs and plans of the city and its history. A model of the city shows how it looked in its glory days and provides a good overview for touring within the city walls. There are several excellent ship models as well.

Circuito Baluartes and Av. Justo Sierra. No phone. Admission $2.50. Tues–Sat 9am–8pm; Sun 9am–1pm.

Baluarte de Santiago   The Jardín Botánico Xmuch'haltun is a jumble of exotic and common plants within the stone walls of this *baluarte.* More than 250 species of plants and trees share what seems like a terribly small courtyard.

Av. 16 de Septiembre and Calle 49. No phone. Free admission. Mon–Fri 9am–8pm; Sat–Sun 9am–1pm.

Casa no. 6 Centro Cultural   In this remodeled colonial house, you'll see some rooms decorated with period furniture and accessories. The patio of mixtilinear arches supported by simple Doric columns is striking. Exhibited in the patio are photos of examples of the city's fine colonial architecture. Several of the photographed buildings have recently been renovated. There is also a small bookstore in back, as well as temporary exhibition space.

Calle 57 no. 6. No phone. Free admission. Daily 9am–9pm.

Puerta de Tierra (Land Gate) At the Land Gate is a small museum displaying portraits of pirates and the city founders. The 1732 French 5-ton cannon in the entryway was found in 1990. On Tuesday, Friday, and Saturday at 8pm, there's a light-and-sound show, as long as 15 or more people have bought tickets. Some shows are in English and some are in Spanish; it depends on the audience. The show is amusing.

Calle 59 at Circuito Baluartes/Av. Gobernadores. No phone. Museum free. Show $2 adults, 50¢ children under 11. Daily 8am–9pm.

OUTSIDE THE WALLS: SCENIC VISTAS

Fuerte–Museo San Miguel ★★ For a good view of the city and a great little museum, take a cab ($2–$3) up to Fuerte–Museo San Miguel. San Miguel is a small fort with a moat and a drawbridge. Built in 1771, it was the most important of the city's defenses. Gen. Santa Anna captured it when he attacked the city in 1842. The museum of the Maya world was renovated in 2000 and is well worth seeing. It groups the artifacts around central issues in Maya culture. In a room devoted to Maya concepts of the afterlife, there's a great burial scene of "Jaguar Claw" with jade masks and jewelry from Maya tombs at Calakmul. Another room explains Maya cosmology, another depicts war, and another explains the gods. There are also exhibits on the history of the fort.

Ruta Escénica s/n. No phone. Admission $2.50. Tues–Sat 9am–7pm; Sun 9am–noon.

Fuerte–Museo San José el Alto San José is higher and has a more sweeping view of Campeche and the coast than Fuerte San Miguel, but it holds only a small exhibit of 16th- and 17th-century weapons and scale miniatures of sailing vessels. This is a nice place for a picnic. Take a cab. On the way, you will pass by an impressive statue of Juárez.

Av. Morazán s/n. No phone. Admission $2.50. Tues–Sun 9am–8pm.

SHOPPING

Casa de Artesanías Tukulná This store run by DIF (a government family assistance agency) occupies a restored mansion. There is an elaborate display of regional arts and crafts in the back. The wares in the showrooms represent everything that is produced in the state. There are quality textiles, clothing, and locally made furniture. Open Monday to Saturday from 9am to 2pm and 5 to 8pm. Calle 10 no. 333 (between calles 59 and 61). © 981/816-9088.

WHERE TO STAY

This wonderful colonial city doesn't have a single good colonial-style hotel or B&B; Campeche is just not that touristy. The most comfortable hotels are outside the historic center; the most economical are inside, and the majority of these don't offer air-conditioning. Those that do are not very attractive or have carpeted rooms, which in Campeche always smell musty. My favorite of these economical hotels, the **Colonial** (not colonial at all), is simple and pretty. The other two listed, the **Baluartes** and the **Del Mar,** are among the nicest hotels in the city and come with the most amenities, such as a swimming pool. They are between the old city walls and the shoreline.

Hotel Baluartes ★ Opposite the Gulf of Mexico and next to the Hotel Del Mar, this was the city's original luxury hotel. All the rooms have been completely refurbished with new tile floors, new furniture, and new mattresses—one king bed or two doubles. Half of the rooms have a Gulf view, and half look toward the city. There's a good restaurant, a coffee shop, a swimming pool, and a bar. You will see the hotel from the sea gate.

Av. 16 de Septiembre no. 128, 24000 Campeche, Camp. ℂ **981/816-3911.** Fax 981/816-2410. baluarte@ campeche.sureste.com. 102 units. $78 double. AE, MC, V. Free parking. **Amenities:** Restaurant; bar; medium-size pool. *In room:* A/C, TV.

Hotel Colonial Despite its name, this hotel doesn't remind me so much of colonial times as it does of the 1940s. The furniture, the fancy tiles, the iron-work—the place is loaded with character. It's also very clean. Rooms come with basic furniture and small bathrooms; they aren't well lit. Four rooms have air-conditioning, and none have televisions, making this the quietest cheap hotel around. The small lobby and inner courtyard are pleasant places to sit and relax. The hotel is inside the walls between calles 55 and 57.

Calle 14 no. 122, 24000 Campeche, Camp. ℂ **981/816-2222.** 30 units. $20 double; $28 double with A/C. No credit cards.

Hotel Del Mar ★ Rooms in this four-story hotel are large, bright, and comfortably furnished. All have balconies that face the Gulf of Mexico. The beds (2 doubles or 1 king) are comfortable. The Del Mar is on the main oceanfront boulevard, between the coast and the city walls. It offers many more services than the Baluartes (see above), but it costs twice as much. You can make a reservation here to stay at the Chicanná eco-village hotel near Calakmul, or you can buy a package that includes guide and transportation. The hotel also offers a tour to Edzná.

Av. Ruiz Cortines 51, 24000 Campeche, Camp. ℂ **981/811-9192** or 981/811-9193. Fax 981/811-1618. margaritamendozamx@yahoo.com.mx. 145 units. $75–$110 double; $125 executive level double. AE, MC, V. Free parking. **Amenities:** 2 restaurants; bar; large pool; gym with sauna; children's playscape; tour desk; car rental; business center; room service until 10pm; babysitting; overnight laundry; executive level. *In room:* A/C, TV.

WHERE TO EAT

Campeche is a fishing town, so seafood predominates. The outstanding restaurant is La Pigua, where I would eat all my afternoon meals. For breakfast, I like one of the traditional eateries such as **La Parroquia.** For a light supper, either get some *antojitos* in the old *barrio* of San Francisco, or have supper above the main plaza at **La Casa Vieja.** If you want a steak, your best bet is **Cactus.**

MODERATE

Cactus STEAKS/MEXICAN If seafood isn't to your taste, try this steak-house; it's a favorite with the locals. The ribeyes are good, as is everything but the *arrachera,* which is the same cut of meat used for fajitas and is very tough.

Av. Malecón Justo Sierra. ℂ **981/811-1453.** Main courses $5–$9. No credit cards. Daily 7am–2am.

Casa Vieja ★ MEXICAN/INTERNATIONAL On a second-story terrace high enough above the main plaza to catch a good breeze and afford a good view of the church, this restaurant has the best location in the city. The food's not bad, either. The *plato cubano* is authentic enough, with pork medallion, black beans and rice, fried plantains, and *yuca con mojo.* For something less starchy, there's steak in mango sauce or shrimp in papaya sauce. The tables are well separated, and the service is good.

Calle 10 no. 319. ℂ **981/811-1311.** Reservations not accepted. Main courses $6–$16. No credit cards. Tues–Sun 9–2am; Mon 5:30pm–2am.

La Pigua ★★★ SEAFOOD   The dining area is an air-conditioned version of the traditional Yucatecan cabin, but with walls of glass looking out on green vegetation. There are not many tables, so by all means, make a reservation. Spanish nautical terms pepper the large menu as the headings for different categories. Sure to be on the menu is fish stuffed with shellfish, which I wholeheartedly recommend. If you're lucky, you might have pompano in a green herb sauce seasoned with *hierba santa*—unbelievable. Other dishes that are sure to please are coconut-battered shrimp with applesauce and *chiles rellenos* with shark. Service is excellent, and the accommodating owner can have your favorite seafood prepared in any style you want.

Av. Miguel Alemán no. 179A. ✆ **981/811-3365**. Reservations recommended. Main courses $7–$13. AE, MC, V. Daily noon–6pm. From Plaza Principal, walk north on Calle 8 for 3 blocks. Cross Av. Circuito by the botanical garden where Calle 8 becomes Miguel Alemán. The restaurant is 1½ blocks farther up, on the right side of the street.

INEXPENSIVE

Cenaduría Portales ★ ANTOJITOS   This is the most traditional of supper places for Campechanos. It's a small restaurant under the stone arches that face the Plaza San Francisco in the *barrio* (neighborhood) of San Francisco. This is the oldest part of town, but it lies outside the walls just to the north. Don't leave without ordering the *horchata* (a sweet drink made of ground almonds and either rice or melon seeds), which is the best I've ever tasted. For food, try the turkey soup, which is wonderful, and the *sincronizadas* (tostadas) and *panuchos*.

Calle 10, Portales San Francisco, no. 86. ✆ **981/811-1491**. Reservations not accepted. Antojitos (small dishes) 40¢–$1.50. No credit cards. Daily 6pm–midnight.

La Parroquia MEXICAN   This popular local hangout has friendly waiters and offers good, inexpensive fare. Here you can enjoy great breakfasts and *colados,* the regional tamales. Selections on the *comida corrida* might include pot roast, meatballs, pork, or fish, with rice or squash, beans, tortillas, and fresh-fruit-flavored water.

Calle 55 no. 9. ✆ **981/816-8086**. Breakfast $2.50–$3, main courses $3–$9; *comida corrida* (served 1–4pm) $3. No credit cards. Daily 24 hr.

4 The Ruins of Chichén Itzá ★★★

179km (112 miles) W of Cancún; 120km (75 miles) E of Mérida

The fabled pyramids and temples of Chichén Itzá (no, it doesn't rhyme with "chicken pizza"; the accents are on the last syllables: chee-*chehn* eet-*zah*) are the Yucatán's best-known ancient monuments. The ruins are plenty hyped, but Chichén is truly worth seeing. Walking among these stone platforms, pyramids, and ball courts gives you an appreciation for this ancient civilization that books cannot convey. The city is built on a scale that evokes a sense of wonder: To fill the plazas during one of the mass rituals that occurred here a millennium ago would have required an enormous number of celebrants. Even today, with the mass flow of tourists through these plazas, the ruins feel empty.

When visiting this old city, remember that much of what is said about the Maya (especially by tour guides, who speak in tones of utter certainty) is merely educated guessing—or just plain guessing. Itzáes established this post-Classic Maya city perhaps sometime during the 9th century A.D. Linda Schele and David Freidel, in *A Forest of Kings* (Morrow, 1990), have cast doubt on the legend of its founding. It says that the Toltec, led by Kukulkán (Quetzalcoatl), came here from the Toltec capital of Tula, in north-central Mexico. Along with Putún Maya coastal traders, they built a magnificent metropolis that combined the Maya Puuc style with Toltec motifs (the feathered serpent, warriors, eagles, and jaguars). Not so, say Schele and Freidel. According to them, readings of Chichén's bas-reliefs and hieroglyphs fail to support that legend and, instead, show that Chichén Itzá was a continuous Maya site influenced by association with the Toltec but not by an invasion. Not all scholars embrace this thinking, so the idea of a Toltec invasion still holds sway.

Though it's possible to make a round-trip from Mérida to Chichén Itzá in a day, it will be a long, tiring, very rushed day. Try to spend at least a night at Chichén Itzá (you will already have paid for the sound-and-light show) or the nearby town of Valladolid. Then you can see the ruins early the next morning when it is cool and before the tour buses arrive.

ESSENTIALS

GETTING THERE & DEPARTING **By Plane** Travel agents in the United States, Cancún, and Cozumel can arrange day trips from Cancún and Cozumel.

By Car Chichén Itzá is on old Highway 180 between Mérida and Cancún. The fastest way to get there from either city is to take the *autopista* (or *cuota*). The toll is $6 from Mérida, $20 from Cancún. The other option is to take Highway 180, which goes right by the ruins. Once you have exited the *autopista,* you will turn onto the road leading to the village of Pisté. After you enter the village, you'll come to Highway 180, where you turn left. Signs point the way. Chichén is 1½ hours from Mérida and 2½ hours from Cancún.

By Bus From Mérida, there are three first-class ADO buses per day, and a couple that go to Valladolid stop here. Also, there are several second-class buses per day. If you want to take a day trip from Mérida, go with a tour company. From Cancún, there are any number of tourist buses, and regular first-class buses leave for Chichén every hour.

AREA LAYOUT The village of **Pisté,** where most hotels and restaurants are located, is about 2.5km (1½ miles) from the ruins of Chichén Itzá. Public buses from Mérida, Cancún, Valladolid, and elsewhere discharge passengers here. A few hotels are at the edge of the ruins, and one, the Hotel Dolores Alba (see "Where to Stay," below), is out of town about 2.5km (1½ miles) from the ruins on the road to Valladolid.

EXPLORING THE RUINS

The site occupies 6.5 sq. km (4 sq. miles), and it takes most of a day to see all the ruins, which are open daily from 8am to 5pm. Service areas are open from 8am to 10pm. Admission is $10, free for children under age 12. A video camera permit costs $4. Parking is extra. *You can use your ticket to re-enter on the same day, but you'll have to pay again for an additional day.* The cost of admission includes the **sound-and-light show,** which is worth seeing. The show, held at 7 or 8pm depending on the season, is in Spanish, but headsets are available for rent ($4.50) in several languages.

The large, modern visitor center, at the main entrance where you pay the admission charge, is beside the parking lot and consists of a museum, an auditorium, a restaurant, a bookstore, and bathrooms. You can see the site on your own or with a licensed guide who speaks English or Spanish. Guides usually wait at the entrance and charge around $40 for one to six people. Although the guides frown on it, there's nothing wrong with approaching a group of people

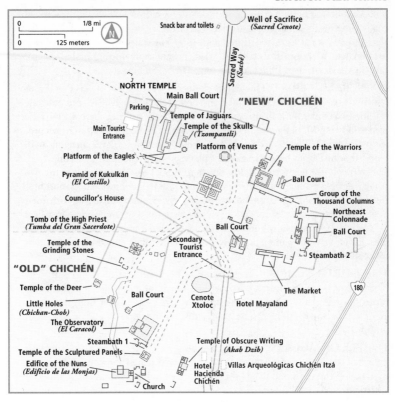

who speak the same language and asking if they want to share a guide. Be wary of the history-spouting guides—some of their information is just plain out-of-date—but the architectural details they point out are enlightening. Chichén Itzá has two parts: the northern (new) zone, which shows distinct Toltec influence, and the southern (old) zone, with mostly Puuc architecture.

EL CASTILLO   As you enter from the tourist center, the magnificent 23m (75 ft.) El Castillo pyramid (also called the Pyramid of Kukulkán) will be straight ahead across a large open area. It was built with the Maya calendar in mind. The four stairways leading up to the central platform each have 91 steps, making a total of 364, which when you add the central platform equals the 365 days of the solar year. On either side of each stairway are nine terraces, which makes 18 on each face of the pyramid, equaling the number of months in the Maya solar calendar. On the facing of these terraces are 52 panels (we don't know how they were decorated), which represent the 52-year cycle when both the solar and religious calendars would become realigned. The pyramid's alignment is such that on the **spring** or **fall equinox** (Mar 21 or Sept 21) a curious event occurs. The setting sun casts the shadow of the terraces onto the ramp of the northern stairway. A diamond pattern is formed, suggestive of the geometric designs on some snakes. Slowly it descends into the earth. The effect is more conceptual than visual, and to view it requires being with a large crowd. It's much better to see the ruins on other days when it's less crowded.

El Castillo was built over an earlier structure. A narrow stairway at the western edge of the north staircase leads inside that structure, where there is a sacrificial altar-throne—a red jaguar encrusted with jade. The stairway is open from 11am to 3pm and is cramped, usually crowded, humid, and uncomfortable. A visit early in the day is best. Photos of the jaguar figure are not allowed.

MAIN BALL COURT (Juego de Pelota) Northwest of El Castillo is Chichén's main ball court, the largest and best preserved anywhere, and only one of nine ball courts built in this city. Carved on both walls of the ball court are scenes showing Maya figures dressed as ball players and decked out in heavy protective padding. The carved scene also shows a headless player kneeling with blood shooting from his neck; another player holding the head looks on.

Players on two teams tried to knock a hard rubber ball through one of the two stone rings placed high on either wall, using only their elbows, knees, and hips (no hands). According to legend, the losing players paid for defeat with their lives. However, some experts say the victors were the only appropriate sacrifices for the gods. One can only guess what the incentive for winning might be in that case. Either way, the game must have been riveting, heightened by the wonderful acoustics of the ball court.

THE NORTH TEMPLE Temples are at both ends of the ball court. The North Temple has sculptured pillars and more sculptures inside, as well as badly ruined murals. The acoustics of the ball court are so good that from the North Temple, a person speaking can be heard clearly at the opposite end, about 136m (450 ft.) away.

TEMPLE OF JAGUARS Near the southeastern corner of the main ball court is a small temple with serpent columns and carved panels showing warriors and jaguars. Up the steps and inside the temple, a mural was found that chronicles a battle in a Maya village.

TEMPLE OF THE SKULLS (Tzompantli) To the right of the ball court is the Temple of the Skulls, an obvious borrowing from the post-Classic cities of central Mexico. Notice the rows of skulls carved into the stone platform. When a sacrificial victim's head was cut off, it was impaled on a pole and displayed in a tidy row with others. Also carved into the stone are pictures of eagles tearing hearts from human victims. The word *Tzompantli* is not Mayan but comes from central Mexico. Reconstruction using scattered fragments may add a level to this platform and change the look of this structure by the time you visit.

PLATFORM OF THE EAGLES Next to the Tzompantli, this small platform has reliefs showing eagles and jaguars clutching human hearts in their talons and claws, as well as a human head emerging from the mouth of a serpent.

PLATFORM OF VENUS East of the Tzompantli and north of El Castillo, near the road to the Sacred Cenote, is the Platform of Venus. In Maya and Toltec lore, a feathered monster or a feathered serpent with a human head in its mouth represented Venus. This is also called the tomb of Chaac-Mool because a Chaac-Mool figure was discovered "buried" within the structure.

SACRED *CENOTE* Follow the dirt road (actually an ancient *sacbé,* or causeway) that heads north from the Platform of Venus; after 5 minutes you'll come to the great natural well that may have given Chichén Itzá (the Well of the Itzáes) its name. This well was used for ceremonial purposes, not for drinking water—according to legend, sacrificial victims were drowned in this pool to honor the rain god Chaac. Anatomical research done early in the 20th century by Ernest A. Hooten showed that bones of both children and adults were found in the well. Judging from Hooten's evidence, they may have been outcasts or diseased or feeble-minded persons.

Edward Thompson, who was the American consul in Mérida and a Harvard professor, purchased the ruins of Chichén early in the 20th century and explored the *cenote* with dredges and divers. His explorations exposed a fortune in gold and jade. Most of the riches wound up in Harvard's Peabody Museum of Archaeology and Ethnology—a matter that continues to disconcert Mexican classicists today. Excavations in the 1960s unearthed more treasure, and studies of the recovered objects detail offerings from throughout the Yucatán and even farther away.

TEMPLE OF THE WARRIORS (Templo de los Guerreros)   Due east of El Castillo is one of the most impressive structures at Chichén: the Temple of the Warriors, named for the carvings of warriors marching along its walls. It's also called the Group of the Thousand Columns for the rows of broken pillars that flank it. During the recent restoration, hundreds more of the columns were rescued from the rubble and put in place, setting off the temple more magnificently than ever. A figure of Chaac-Mool sits at the top of the temple, surrounded by impressive columns carved in relief to look like enormous feathered serpents. South of the temple was a square building that archaeologists called the **Market** *(mercado);* a colonnade surrounds its central court. Beyond the temple and the market in the jungle are mounds of rubble, parts of which are being reconstructed.

The main Mérida–Cancún highway once ran straight through the ruins of Chichén, and though it has been diverted, you can still see the great swath it cut. South and west of the old highway's path are more impressive ruined buildings.

TOMB OF THE HIGH PRIEST (Tumba del Gran Sacerdote)   Past the refreshment stand to the right of the path is the Tomb of the High Priest, which stood atop a natural limestone cave in which skeletons and offerings were found, giving the temple its name.

TEMPLE OF THE GRINDING STONES (Casa de los Metates)   This building, the next one on your right, is named after the concave corn-grinding stones the Maya used.

TEMPLE OF THE DEER (Templo del Venado)   Past Casa de los Metates is this fairly tall though ruined building. The relief of a stag that gave the temple its name is long gone.

LITTLE HOLES (Chichan-Chob)   This next temple has a roof comb with little holes, three masks of the rain god Chaac, three rooms, and a good view of the surrounding structures. It's one of the oldest buildings at Chichén, built in the Puuc style during the Late Classic period.

OBSERVATORY (El Caracol)   Construction of the Observatory, a complex building with a circular tower, was carried out over centuries; the additions and modifications reflected the Maya's careful observation of celestial movements and their need for increasingly exact measurements. Through slits in the tower's walls, astronomers could observe the cardinal directions and the approach of the all-important spring and autumn equinoxes, as well as the summer solstice. The temple's name, which means "snail," comes from a spiral staircase within the structure.

On the east side of El Caracol, a path leads north into the bush to the **Cenote Xtoloc,** a natural limestone well that provided the city's daily water supply. If you see any lizards sunning there, they may well be *xtoloc,* for which this *cenote* is named.

TEMPLE OF PANELS (Templo de los Tableros)   Just south of El Caracol are the ruins of a steam bath *(temazcalli)* and the Temple of Panels, named for the carved panels on top. This temple was once covered by a much larger structure, only traces of which remain.

EDIFICE OF THE NUNS (Edificio de las Monjas)   If you've visited the Puuc sites of Kabah, Sayil, Labná, or Xlapak, the enormous nunnery here will remind you of the palaces at those sites. Built in the Late Classic period, the new edifice was constructed over an older one. Suspecting that this was so, Le Plongeon, an archaeologist working early in the 20th century, put dynamite between the two and blew away part of the exterior, revealing the older structures within. You can still see the results of Le Plongeon's indelicate exploratory methods.

On the east side of the Edifice of the Nuns is an **annex (Anexo Este)** constructed in highly ornate Chenes style with Chaac masks and serpents.

THE CHURCH (La Iglesia)   Next to the annex is one of the oldest buildings at Chichén, the Church. Masks of Chaac decorate two upper stories. Look closely, and you'll see other pagan symbols among the crowd of Chaacs: an armadillo, a crab, a snail, and a tortoise. These represent the Maya gods, called *bacab,* whose job it was to hold up the sky.

TEMPLE OF OBSCURE WRITING (Akab Dzib)   Beloved of travel writers, this temple lies east of the Edifice of the Nuns. Above a door in one of the rooms are some Maya glyphs, which gave the temple its name because the writings have yet to be deciphered. In other rooms, traces of red handprints are still visible. Reconstructed and expanded over the centuries, Akab Dzib may be the oldest building at Chichén.

OLD CHICHEN (Chichén Viejo)   For a look at more of Chichén's oldest buildings, constructed well before the time of Toltec influence, follow signs from the Edifice of the Nuns southwest into the bush to Old Chichén, about 1km (½ mile) away. Be prepared for this trek with long trousers, insect repellent, and a local guide. The attractions here are the **Temple of the First Inscriptions (Templo de los Inscripciones Iniciales),** with the oldest inscriptions discovered at Chichén, and the restored **Temple of the Lintels (Templo de los Dinteles),** a fine Puuc building.

WHERE TO STAY

The expensive hotels in Chichén all occupy beautiful grounds, are close to the ruins, and serve good food. All have toll-free reservations numbers, which I recommend using. Some of these hotels do a lot of business with tour operators—they can be empty one day and full the next. The inexpensive hotels are in the village of Pisté, 2.5km (1½ miles) away. There is little to do in Pisté at night. Another option is to go on to the colonial town of Valladolid, 30 minutes away, but you'll want reservations because a lot of tour-bus companies use the hotels there (see below).

EXPENSIVE

Hacienda Chichén ★★   This is the smallest and most private of the hotels at the ruins. It is also the quietest and the least likely to have bus tour groups. Then a hacienda, it served as the headquarters for the Carnegie Institute's excavations in 1923. Several bungalows were built to house the staff; these have been modernized and are now the guest rooms. Each is simply and comfortably furnished (with a dehumidifier and ceiling fan in addition to A/C) and is a short distance from the others. Each bungalow has a private porch from which you can enjoy the beautiful grounds. Standard rooms come with two twin or two double beds. Suites are larger and have larger bathrooms and double or queen beds. The main building belonged to the hacienda; it houses the terrace restaurant, with dining outside by the pool or inside.

Zona Arqueológica, 97751 Chichén Itzá, Yuc. ©/fax **985/851-0045**. www.yucatanadventure.com.mx. (Reservations: Casa del Balam, Calle 60 no. 488, 97000 Mérida, Yuc. © 800/624-8451 in the U.S., or 999/924-2150; fax 999/924-5011.) 28 units. $130 double; $140 suite. AE, DC, MC, V. Free guarded parking. **Amenities:** Restaurant; bar; large pool. *In room:* A/C, minibar, hair dryer.

Hotel Mayaland ★★ The main doorway frames El Caracol (the observatory) in a stunning view—that's how close this hotel is to the ruins. If there's a drawback, it's that the hotel books large bus tours, but that isn't so bad, because the hotel is on a large piece of property. The long main building is three stories high. The rooms are large, with comfortable beds and large tiled bathrooms. Bungalows, scattered about the rest of the grounds, are built native style, with thatched roofs and stucco walls; they're a good deal larger than the rooms. The grounds are gorgeous, with huge trees and lush foliage—the hotel has had 75 years to get them in shape. Mayaland operates a shuttle service between the hotel and Mérida for about $35 each way.

Zona Arqueológica, 97751 Chichén Itzá, Yuc. © **985/851-0127**. (Reservations: Mayaland Resorts, Robalo 30 SM3, 77500 Cancún, Q. Roo; © 800/235-4079 in the U.S., or 998/887-0870; fax 998/884-4510.) 101 units. High season $150 double, $200 bungalow; 10% low-season discount. AE, MC, V. Free guarded parking. **Amenities:** 2 restaurants; bar; 3 pools; tour desk; room service until 10pm; overnight laundry; babysitting. *In room:* A/C, TV, minibar, coffeemaker, hair dryer.

Villas Arqueológicas Chichén Itzá ★ This lovely hotel is built around a courtyard and a pool. Two massive royal poinciana trees tower above the grounds, and bougainvillea drapes the walls. This chain has similar hotels at Cobá and Uxmal, and is connected with Club Med. The rooms are modern and small but comfortable, unless you're 6 ft. 2 in. or taller—each bed is in a niche, with walls at the head and foot. Most rooms have one double bed and an oversized single bed. You can also book a half- or full-board plan.

Zona Arqueológica, 97751 Chichén Itzá, Yuc. © **800/258-2633** in the U.S. or 985/851-0034 or 985/856-2830. 40 units. $81 double. Rates include continental breakfast. ½-board (breakfast plus lunch or dinner) $15 per person; full board (3 meals) $29 per person. AE, MC, V. Free parking. **Amenities:** Restaurant; bar; large pool; tennis court; tour desk. *In room:* A/C.

MODERATE

Pirámide Inn Less than a mile from the ruins, at the edge of Pisté, this hotel has simple rooms. Most hold two double beds, some three twins or one king. The bathrooms are nice, with counter space and tub/shower combinations. The air-conditioning is quiet and effective. Hot water comes on between 5 and 10am and 5 and 10pm. A well-kept pool and a *temascal* (a native form of steambath) occupy a small part of the landscaped grounds, which include the remains of a Maya wall. Try to get a room in the back. The hotel is right on the highway.

Calle 15 no. 30, 97751 Pisté, Yuc. © **985/851-0115**. Fax 985/851-0114. www.piramideinn.com. 44 units. $47 double. MC, V. **Amenities:** Restaurant; bar; medium-size pool; steam room; room service. *In room:* A/C.

INEXPENSIVE

Hotel Dolores Alba ★ *Value*   This place is of the motel variety, perfect if you come by car. It is a bargain for what you get: two pools (1 really special), *palapas* and hammocks around the place, and large, comfortable rooms. The restaurant serves good meals at moderate prices. The hotel provides free transportation to the ruins and the Caves of Balankanché during visiting hours, though you will have to take a taxi back. The hotel is on the highway 2.5km (1½ miles) east of the ruins (toward Valladolid). You can make reservations here for the Dolores Alba in Mérida.

Km 122 Carretera Mérida–Valladolid, Yuc. ✆ **985/858-1555.** (Reservations: Hotel Dolores Alba, Calle 63 no. 464, 97000 Mérida, Yuc. ✆ 985/928-5650; fax 985/928-3163; www.doloresalba.com.) 40 units. $35 double. No credit cards. Free parking. **Amenities:** Restaurant; bar; 2 pools; room service until midnight; laundry. *In room:* A/C.

WHERE TO DINE

The restaurant in the visitor center at the ruins and the hotel restaurants in Pisté serve reasonably priced meals. Prices jump quite a bit at hotel restaurants near the ruins. In Pisté, however, many places cater to large groups, which descend on them after 1pm.

Cafetería Ruinas INTERNATIONAL   Though it has the monopoly on food at the ruins, this cafeteria actually does a good job with such basic meals as enchiladas, pizza, and baked chicken. It even offers some Yucatecan dishes. Eggs and burgers are cooked to order, and the coffee is very good. You can also get fruit smoothies and vegetarian dishes. Sit outside at the tables farthest from the crowd, and relax.

In the Chichén Itzá visitor center. ✆ **985/851-0111.** Breakfast $4; sandwiches $4–$5; main courses $5–$8. AE, MC, V. Daily 9am–6pm.

Fiesta YUCATECAN/MEXICAN   Though relatively expensive, the food here is dependable and good. You can dine inside or out, but make a point of going for supper or early lunch when the tour buses are gone. The buffet is quite complete, and the menu has many Yucatecan classics. Fiesta is on the west end of town.

Carretera Mérida–Valladolid, Pisté. ✆ **985/851-0038.** Main courses $4–$6; buffet (served 12:30–5pm) $8.50. No credit cards. Daily 7am–9pm.

Restaurant Bar "Poxil" YUCATECAN   A *poxil* is a Maya fruit somewhat akin to a *guanábana*. Although this place doesn't serve them, what is on the simple menu is good, though not gourmet, and the price is right. You will find the Poxil near the west entrance to town on the south side of the street.

Calle 15 no. 52, Pisté. ✆ **985/851-0123.** Main courses $4–$5; breakfast $3. No credit cards. Daily 8am–9pm.

A SIDE TRIP TO THE GRUTA (CAVE) DE BALANKANCHE

The Gruta de Balankanché is 5.5km (3½ miles) from Chichén Itzá on the road to Valladolid and Cancún. Taxis will make the trip and wait. The entire excursion takes about a half hour, but the walk inside is hot and humid. Of the cave tours in the Yucatán, this is the tamest, having good footing and requiring the least amount of walking and climbing. It includes a cheesy and uninformative recorded tour. The highlight is a round chamber with a central column that gives the impression of being a large tree. You come up the same way you go down. The cave became a hideaway during the War of the Castes. You can still see traces of carving and incense burning, as well as an underground stream that served as the sanctuary's water supply. Outside, take time to meander through the botanical gardens, where most of the plants and trees are labeled with their common and scientific names.

The caves are open daily. Admission is $5, free for children 6 to 12. Children under age 6 are not admitted. Use of a video camera costs $4 (free if you've already bought a video permit in Chichén the same day). Tours in English are at 11am and 1 and 3pm, and, in Spanish, at 9am, noon, and 2 and 4pm. Double-check these hours at the main entrance to the Chichén ruins.

5 Valladolid

40km (25 miles) E of Chichén Itzá; 160km (100 miles) SW of Cancún

Valladolid (pronounced "bah-yah-doh-*leed*") is a small, pleasant colonial city halfway between Mérida and Cancún. The people are friendly and informal, and, except for the heat, life is easy. The city's economy is based on commerce and small-scale manufacturing. There is a large *cenote* in the center of town and a couple more 4km (3 miles) down the road to Chichén. A restoration project has reconstructed several rows of colonial housing in the neighborhood surrounding the convent of San Bernardino de Siena. Valladolid can also be the starting point for several interesting side trips (see below).

ESSENTIALS

GETTING THERE & DEPARTING   By Car   From Mérida or Cancún, you have two choices: the toll road *(cuota)* or Highway 180. The **cuota** passes a few miles north of the city; the exit is at the crossing of Highway 295 to Tizimín. **Highway 180** takes significantly longer because it passes through a number of villages (with their requisite speed bumps). Both 180 and 295 lead directly to downtown. Leaving is just as easy: from the main square, Calle 41 turns into 180 east to Cancún; Calle 39 heads to 180 west to Chichén Itzá and Mérida. To take the *cuota* to Mérida or Cancún, take Calle 40 (see "City Layout," below).

By Bus   Expresso de Oriente runs eight first-class buses per day to and from Mérida, nine buses to and from Cancún, three to and from Tulum, and three to and from Playa del Carmen. To secure a seat, you can buy a ticket a day in advance. In addition, first-class buses stop in Valladolid while passing through *(de paso)* on the way to Cancún. To get to Chichén Itzá, you must take a second-class bus, which leaves every hour and sometimes on the half hour. Valladolid has two bus stations, at the corner of calles 39 and 46, and at calles 37 and 54. For all practical purposes, they are interchangeable; buses pass by both stations to pick up passengers. Passengers going first-class to Mérida or Cancún are dropped off at another station (Isleta) on the *autopista*, where they pick up the bus.

VISITOR INFORMATION   At the small **tourism office** in the Palacio Municipal, you can get a map but little else. It's open daily from 10am to 2pm and 4 to 8pm.

CITY LAYOUT   Valladolid has the standard layout for towns in the Yucatán: Streets running north-south are even numbers; those running east-west are odd numbers. The main plaza is bordered by Calle 39 on the north, 41 on the south, 40 on the east, and 42 on the west. The plaza is named Parque Francisco Cantón Rosado, but everyone calls it **El Centro.** Taxis are easy to come by.

EXPLORING VALLADOLID

Before it became Valladolid, the city was a Maya settlement called Zací (zah-*kee*), which means "white hawk." There are two *cenotes* in the area. **Cenote Zací** is at the intersection of calles 39 and 36, in a small park in the middle of town. The walls and part of the roof of the *cenote* have been opened up, and a trail leads down close to the water. Caves, stalactites, and hanging vines contribute to a wild, prehistoric atmosphere. The park has a large *palapa* restaurant that is popular with local residents, plus three traditional Maya dwellings that house a small photograph collection and some historical materials on Valladolid. Admission is $1.50.

Southwest of El Centro is the Franciscan monastery of **San Bernardino de Siena** (1552). Most of the compound was built in the early 1600s; a large underground river is believed to pass under the convent and surrounding neighborhood, which is called Barrio Sisal. "Sisal" is, in this case, a corruption of the Mayan phrase *sis-ha,* meaning "cold water." The barrio has undergone extensive restoration and is a delight to behold.

Valladolid's main square is the social center of town and a thriving market for the prettiest Yucatecan dresses anywhere. On its south side is the principal church, **La Parroquia de San Servacio.** *Vallesoletanos,* as the locals call themselves, believe that almost all cathedrals in Mexico point east, and they cherish a local legend to explain why theirs points north—but don't believe a word of it. On the east side of the plaza is the municipal building, El Ayuntamiento. Be sure to see the four dramatic paintings outlining the history of the peninsula. In particular, note the first panel, featuring a horrified Maya priest as he foresees the arrival of Spanish galleons. On Sunday nights, beneath the stone arches of the Ayuntamiento, the municipal band plays *jaranas* and other traditional music of the region.

SHOPPING

The **Mercado de Artesanías de Valladolid,** at the corner of calles 39 and 44, gives you a good idea of the local merchandise. Perhaps the main handicraft of the town is embroidered Maya dresses, which can be purchased here or from women around the main square. The latter also sell, of all things, Barbie-doll-size Maya dresses! Just ask, *"¿Vestidos para Barbie?"* and out they come. The area around Valladolid is cattle country; locally made leather goods such as sandals *(huaraches)* and bags are plentiful. On the main plaza is a small shop above the municipal bazaar. Another good sandal maker has a shop called **Elio's,** Calle 37 no. 202, between streets 42 and 44 (no phone). An Indian named **Juan Mac** makes *alpargatas,* the traditional sandals of the Maya, in his shop on Calle 39, near the intersection with Calle 38, 1 block from the main plaza, before the store Cielito Lindo. Most of his output is for locals, but he's happy to knock out a pair for visitors.

Tips   **Plan Ahead for a Stay in Valladolid**

Hotels (and restaurants) here are less expensive than the competition in Chichén. But occupancy rates are high, so you should make reservations. If you arrive without reservations and there is no room at either of the hotels I've reviewed below, **Hotel Zací,** Calle 44 between calles 37 and 39 (© **985/856-2167**), is your next-best bet; doubles are $30 without air-conditioning, and $36 with air-conditioning.

Valladolid also produces a highly prized **honey** made from the *tzi-tzi-ché* flower. You can find it and other goods at the **town market,** Calle 32 between calles 35 and 37. The best time to see the market is Sunday morning.

WHERE TO STAY

Hotel El Mesón del Marqués   The Mesón del Marqués is a comfortable, gracious hotel. The first courtyard surrounds a fountain and abounds with hanging plants and bougainvillea. This, the original house, holds a good restaurant (see "Where to Dine," below). In back is another courtyard with plenty of greenery and a pool. Most of the rooms are sheltered from city noise and are large and comfortable. Most have two double beds. The hotel is on the north side of El Centro, opposite the church.

Calle 39 no. 203, 97780 Valladolid, Yuc. ℰ 985/856-3042 or 985/856-2073. Fax 985/856-2280. www.meson delmarques.com. 90 units. $50 double; $60 junior suite. AE. Free secured parking. **Amenities:** Restaurant; bar; pool; room service until 11pm; same-day laundry. *In room:* A/C, TV.

Hotel María de la Luz   The three-story María de la Luz is built around an inner swimming pool. The well-maintained guest rooms have tile floors and bathrooms; three have balconies overlooking the main square. The wide interior space holds a restaurant that is quite comfortable and airy for most of the day— it's a popular place for breakfast. The hotel is on the west side of the main square.

Calle 42 no. 193, 97780 Valladolid, Yuc. ℰ/fax 985/856-2071 or 985/856-2071. www.mariadelaluz.com.mx. 70 units. $30 double. MC, V. Rates include breakfast. Free secured parking. **Amenities:** Restaurant; bar; medium-size pool; tour desk. *In room:* A/C, TV.

WHERE TO DINE

Valladolid is not a center for haute cuisine, but you should try some of the regional specialties. The lowest prices are in the **Bazar Municipal,** a little arcade of shops beside the Hotel El Mesón del Marqués right on the main square.

Hostería del Marqués MEXICAN/YUCATECAN   This is part of the Hotel El Mesón del Marqués, facing the main square. The patio is calm and cool for most of the day. The extensive menu features local specialties. If you are hungry, try the Yucatecan sampler. Any of the enchiladas are good.

Calle 39 no. 203. ℰ 985/856-2073. Breakfast $3–$5; main courses $3.50–$7. AE. Daily 7am–11:30pm.

SIDE TRIPS FROM VALLADOLID
CENOTES DZITNUP & SAMMULA

The **Cenote Dzitnup** (also known as Cenote Xkekén) ⊛, 4km (2½ miles) west of Valladolid off Highway 180, is worth a side trip, especially if you have time for a dip. You can take the bike trail there. Antonio Aguilar, who owns a sporting goods store at Calle 41 no. 225, between calles 48 and 50, rents bikes. Once you get there, you descend a short flight of rather perilous stone steps, and at the bottom, inside a beautiful cavern, is a natural pool of water so clear and blue that it seems plucked from a dream. If you decide to swim, be sure that you don't have creams or other chemicals on your skin—they damage the habitat of the small fish and other organisms living there. Also, no alcohol, food, or smoking is allowed in the cavern. Admission is $2. The *cenote* is open daily from 7am to 7pm. About 100 yards down the road on the opposite side is another recently discovered *cenote,* **Sammulá,** where you can also swim. Admission is $2.

EK BALAM: RECENTLY EXCAVATED MAYA RUINS ⊛⊛⊛

About 18km (11 miles) north of Valladolid, off the highway to Río Lagartos, is the spectacular site at **Ek Balam,** which, owing to a certain ambiguity in Mayan, means either "dark jaguar" or "star jaguar." Relatively unvisited by tourists, the Ek Balam ruins have been undergoing extensive renovation; they are a must-see for travelers who have access to a rental car. Take Calle 40 north out of Valladolid to Highway 295; go 18km (11 miles) to the sign marking the Ek Balam turn-off. Follow a narrow, winding road through a small village. Ek Balam is 13km (8 miles) from the highway; the entrance fee is $2.50, plus $4 for each video camera. The site is open daily from 8am to 5pm.

Built between 100 B.C. and A.D. 1200, the smaller buildings are architecturally unique—especially the large, perfectly restored **Caracol.** The principal buildings in the main group have been reconstructed beautifully. Flanked by two smaller pyramids, the imposing central pyramid is 157m (517 ft.) long and 61m (200 ft.) wide. At more than 30m (100 ft.) high, it is easily taller than the highest pyramids in Chichén Itzá and Uxmal. On the left side of the main stairway, archaeologists have uncovered a large ceremonial doorway of perfectly preserved stucco and stone work. The doorway represents the gaping mouth of the Earth god. Around it are several beautifully detailed human figures. Excavation inside revealed a long chamber filled with Mayan hieroglyphic writing. From the style, it appears that the scribes probably came from Guatemala. So far this chamber is closed to the public. From this script, an epigrapher, Alfonso Lacadena, has found the name of one of the principle kings of the city—Ukit Kan Le'k. He is still working on deciphering the full meaning of the text. If you climb to the top of the pyramid, in the middle distance you can see unrestored ruins looming to the north. To the southeast, you can spot the tallest structures at **Cobá,** 48km (30 miles) away.

Also plainly visible are the **raised causeways** of the Maya—the *sacbé* appear as raised lines in the forest vegetation. More than any of the better-known sites, Ek Balam inspires a sense of mystery and awe at the scale of Maya civilization and the utter ruin to which it came.

RIO LAGARTOS NATURE RESERVE

Some 81km (50 miles) north of Valladolid (40km/25 miles N of Tizimín) on Highway 295 is Río Lagartos, a 118,000-acre refuge established in 1979 to protect the largest nesting population of flamingos in North America. Generally, it's best to see flamingos at the sites near Mérida. According to biologists, flamingos should never be approached when nesting. This said, you may still want to visit the reserve to see natural habitats and many other species of animals and birds.

To get to Río Lagartos, you pass through Tizimín, which is about 30 minutes away. The best place to stay there is **Hotel 49,** Calle 49 373-A (© **986/863-2136**), by the main square. The owner can give you good advice about going to the nature preserve. There is not much to do in Tizimín unless you are there during the first 2 weeks of January, when it holds the largest fair in the Yucatán. The prime fiesta day is January 6.

SEEING THE RIO LAGARTOS REFUGE   Río Lagartos is a small fishing village of around 3,000 people who make their living from the sea and from the occasional tourist who shows up to see the flamingos. Colorfully painted houses face the *malecón* (the oceanfront street), and brightly painted boats dock along the same half-moon-shaped port.

Río Lagartos has a dock area where you can hire a boat to take you to the large flamingo colony for $75, which can be split among up to six people; the trip takes 4 to 6 hours. A shorter trip to a closer colony costs $20.

Although thousands of flamingos nest near here from April to August, the law prohibits visiting their nesting grounds. Flamingos need mud with particular ingredients (including a high salt content) to multiply, and this area's mud does the trick. Flamingos use their bills to suck up the mud, and they have the unique ability to screen the ingredients they need from it. What you see on the boat trip is a mixture of non-nesting flamingos, frigates, pelicans, herons in several colors, and ducks. Don't allow the boatman to frighten the birds into flight for your photographs, or the birds will eventually leave the habitat permanently.

ISLA HOLBOX

A remote island off the farthest eastern point of the Yucatán Peninsula, Holbox (pronounced "hohl-*bosh*") is a half-deserted fishing village, a modest wildlife refuge, and a desert-island getaway for travelers seeking solitude. From Valladolid, take Highway 180 east for 90km (56 miles) toward Cancún; turn north after Nuevo Xcan at the tiny crossroads of El Ideal. Drive nearly 100km (62 miles) north on a poorly maintained state highway to the tiny port of Chiquilá, where you can park your car in a secured parking lot; walk 200 yards to the pier, and haggle over the $20 boat ride 3km (2 miles) to the island. There is a ferry, but it runs only five times per day.

In the late 1840s, Holbox was a refuge for European landowners fleeing Indian mobs during the Caste Wars. Nowadays the village of Holbox is empty when the fishing fleet is out, and only half populated in the best of times. On the beach just beyond the village are a few comfortable *palapa* hotels, which charge $80 to $130 per night and have all the amenities, including a restaurant and a swimming pool. **Villas Delfines** (© **998/884-8606** or 998/874-4014; fax 998/884-6342) is one; **Villas Flamingos** (© **800/538-6802** in the U.S. and Canada) is another. Both of these places offer peace and quiet on a broad, sandy beach. Besides swimming in the Gulf waters, which are a dull green instead of the blue of the Caribbean, you can visit the nearby bird sanctuary that's on the island. Several of the town's residents will be happy to take you on a tour, but this place is more for people who simply want to relax by the seashore.

7

Tabasco & Chiapas

Even though these two states aren't part of the Yucatán, we've included them to present Mexico's **Maya region** in its entirety. Many travelers who go to the Yucatán to see Chichén Itzá and Uxmal also take a side trip to Chiapas to see the famous ruins of Palenque. Some go even farther, all the way to San Cristóbal, to visit the highland Maya.

The terrain and climate of Chiapas and Tabasco differ from what you'll find in the Yucatán. The jungle in Tabasco and the eastern lowlands of Chiapas are more lush and varied. The central highlands of Chiapas are cool and wet, and the mountain air feels refreshing after the stifling heat and humidity of the lowlands. The area has striking mountain vistas, deep canyons, and isolated cloud forests. Getting to the highlands from Palenque is quite easy.

Tabasco is a small, oil-rich state along the Gulf Coast. The capital, **Villahermosa,** has the distinct feel of a boomtown. It was in this coastal region that the Olmec, the mother culture of Mesoamerica, rose to prominence. In Villahermosa, at the Parque–Museo La Venta, you can see some artifacts this culture left to posterity, including its famous megalithic heads.

The two most interesting areas in **Chiapas** are the eastern lowland jungles and the central highlands. In the former lie the famous ruins of **Palenque,** a city that dates to the Classic age of Maya civilization. The ruins look unspeakably old, and the surrounding jungle seems poised to reclaim them if their caretakers ever falter in their duties. Deeper into the interior are the sites of **Yaxchilán** and **Bonampak.** The central highlands are just as dramatic but easier to enjoy. Of particular interest is the colonial city of **San Cristóbal de las Casas** and its surrounding Indian villages. The Indians here cling so tenaciously to their beliefs and traditions that at one time this area was more popular with anthropologists than with tourists.

Ten years ago, Chiapas made international news when the Zapatista Liberation Army launched an armed rebellion and captured San Cristóbal. This forced the Mexican government to recognize the existence of political and economic problems in Chiapas. Negotiations achieved minor results, then stalled. Political violence erupted again in the winter of 1997–1998 with a massacre in Acteal, near San Cristóbal, and sporadic violence occurs in outlying towns from time to time. But no foreigners have been attacked, and no restrictions have been placed on travel to Palenque or the San Cristóbal region. One of the first acts of Mexico's president, Vicente Fox, was to withdraw most of the army from Chiapas and to renew negotiations, which have yet to bear fruit. Social unrest remains latent in the area. This year a small ecotourism lodge outside of Ocosingo owned by an American couple was invaded by the neighboring village. The couple was displaced, and at press time the situation remained unresolved. The U.S. State Department has not issued a travel advisory for the region, but it has put out announcements. Before you go, get the most current information by checking the State Department website, http://travel.state.gov.

EXPLORING TABASCO & CHIAPAS

Airline and bus service to this area has improved vastly in the last few years. Convenient air service connects the Yucatán to Villahermosa and Tuxtla Gutiérrez. Traveling overland, you will likely go through Campeche, which is 5 hours from Palenque and 6 from Villahermosa. Coming from the lower Yucatán, you'll pass through the town of Escárcega. From Palenque it is 4 to 5 hours to San Cristóbal depending on road conditions; from Villahermosa, it's 5 hours. You can see Palenque in a day. A couple of worthwhile side trips would

Map Pointer

For a map of Tabasco and Chiapas, see p. 19.

add a day or 2, and if you plan on going to Bonampak and Yaxchilán (the Maya ruins that border Guatemala), add 2 full days. San Cristóbal and the nearby villages have so much to offer that I consider 4 days the minimum you should spend there.

Note: I suggest that you do your traveling during the day. Reports of highway robberies at night have been rare, but why take the risk?

1 Villahermosa

142km (89 miles) NW of Palenque; 469km (293 miles) SW of Campeche; 160km (100 miles) N of San Cristóbal de las Casas

Villahermosa (pop. 520,000), the capital of the state of Tabasco, is right at the center of Mexico's oil boom—but it's off-center from just about everything else. Oil wealth has transformed this provincial town into a modern city, making it an interesting crossroads for those going overland and a popular port of entry for air travelers.

Prosperity has spurred a number of developments, including a beautiful park containing the **Parque–Museo La Venta;** the CICOM center for Olmec and Maya studies containing the **Museo Regional de Antropología Carlos Pellicer Cámara;** and the pedestrian-only area downtown with a few small galleries and museums. These are the three main areas that a visitor will want to see. Of less interest is the modern office building and shopping development called Tabasco 2000.

Two names that you will likely see and hear are Carlos Pellicer Cámara and Tomás Garrido Canabal. The first was a mid-20th-century Tabascan poet and intellectual. The best known of Mexico's *modernista* poets, he was a fiercely independent thinker. Garrido Canabal, socialist governor of Tabasco in the 1920s and 1930s, tried to turn the conservative, backwater state of Tabasco into a model of socialism. Garrido Canabal supported many socialist causes, but the one that became his passion was anticlericalism. He did such bizarre things as naming his son Lucifer and his farm animals Jesus and the Virgin Mary. He also destroyed or closed many churches in Tabasco, including the cathedral of Villahermosa. Graham Greene provided a fictional depiction of him in *The Power and the Glory.*

ESSENTIALS

GETTING THERE & DEPARTING

BY PLANE Getting to Villahermosa requires going through Mexico City. **Mexicana** (✆ **800/531-7921** or 993/316-3132, or 993/356-0101 at the airport) and **Aeromexico** (✆ **800/237-6639** or 993/312-1528; www.aeromexico.com) both have three flights a day to and from Mexico City. **Aviación de Chiapas (Aviacsa)** (✆ **993/316-5700,** or 993/356-0132 at the airport) flies twice a day to Mexico City and daily to Tapachula. The regional airline **AeroLitoral,** a subsidiary of

Aeromexico (© **800/237-6639** or 993/312-6991), goes through Mexico City with a connection to Veracruz, Tampico, Monterrey, and Houston. **Aerocaribe** (© **800/531-7921** or 993/316-5046), a subsidiary of Mexicana, has flights to several cities in southeast Mexico, including Mérida, Tuxtla Gutiérrez, and Veracruz.

BY CAR   Highway 180 connects Campeche to Villahermosa (7 hr.). Highway 186, which passes by the airport, joins Highway 199 to Palenque and San Cristóbal de las Casas. The road to Palenque is a good one, and the drive takes 2 hours. Between Palenque and San Cristóbal the road enters the mountains and takes 4 to 5 hours. Because of past problems on this highway, it's a good idea to check at the tourism office to see if it's advisable to drive to San Cristóbal. On any of the mountainous roads, road conditions are apt to get worse during the rainy season from May to October.

BY BUS   The first-class **bus station** is at Mina and Merino (© **993/312-8900**), 3 blocks off Highway 180. Fifteen first-class ADO buses leave for Palenque (2½ hr.) between 6am and 7:45pm. There are 22 first-class buses per day to Mexico City (14 hr.) and cities in between. To Campeche there are 12 buses per day (7 hr.); some of these go on to Mérida, or you can transfer. Autotransportes Cristóbal Colón has seven daily buses to Palenque, San Cristóbal de las Casas, and Tuxtla Gutiérrez.

ORIENTATION

ARRIVING   Villahermosa's **airport** is 10km (6½ miles) east of town. Driving in, you'll cross a bridge over the Río Grijalva, then turn left to reach downtown. Taxis to the downtown area cost $14.

From the **bus station,** local buses marked "Mercado–C. Camionera" or simply "Centro" leave frequently for the center of town. Taxis are readily available in front of the station.

Parking downtown can be difficult; it's best to find a parking lot. Use one that's guarded around the clock.

VISITOR INFORMATION   The **State Tourism Office** is in the Tabasco 2000 complex, Paseo Tabasco 1504, SEFICOT Building, Centro Administrativo del Gobierno (© **993/316-5122,** ext. 229); it's on the second floor of the building facing the Liverpool department store. The location is inconvenient for tourists and in most cases not worth a special trip. Office hours are Monday to Friday from 8am to 4pm. There are three information desks: The **airport** desk is staffed daily from 10am to 5pm; another is beside the ticket counter at **Parque–Museo La Venta** (open Tues–Sun 10am–5pm); and the third is at the ADO bus station (Mon–Fri 10am–6pm).

Tips **Road Conditions & Warnings**

The drive between Villahermosa and Chetumal (about 560km/350 miles) can seem interminable if the road is in poor condition. Vast parts of it are quite lonely; the U.S. State Department includes this road on its warning list due to car and bus hijackings. If you take it, one good stopover between the two is Xpujil, 99km (62 miles) west of Chetumal. (See "The Río Bec Ruin Route," in chapter 5.) Another potential stopover is Francisco Escárcega, but only if you're desperate for the lodging—there's little to do there.

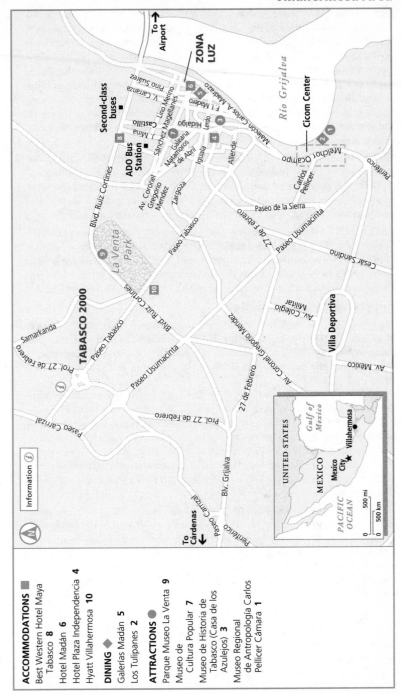

ACCOMMODATIONS ■
Best Western Hotel Maya
Tabasco **8**
Hotel Madán **6**
Hotel Plaza Independencia **4**
Hyatt Villahermosa **10**

DINING ◆
Galerías Madán **5**
Los Tulipanes **2**

ATTRACTIONS ●
Parque Museo La Venta **9**
Museo de
Cultura Popular **7**
Museo de Historia de
Tabasco (Casa de los
Azulejos) **3**
Museo Regional
de Antropología Carlos
Pellicer Cámara **1**

CITY LAYOUT   The downtown area, including the pedestrian-only **Zona Luz,** is on the west bank of the Grijalva River. About 1.5km (1 mile) upstream (south) is **CICOM,** with the large archaeology museum named for the poet Carlos Pellicer Cámara. The **airport** is on the east side of the river. Highway 180 passes the airport and crosses the river just north of downtown, becoming **Bulevar Ruiz Cortines.** To get to the downtown area, turn left onto **Madero** or **Pino Suárez.** By staying on Ruiz Cortines you can reach the city's biggest attraction, the Parque–Museo la Venta. It's well marked. Just beyond that, about 6.5km (4 miles) northwest of downtown, is the intersection with **Paseo Tabasco,** the heart of the modern hotel and shopping district.

GETTING AROUND   All **city buses** converge on Avenida Pino Suárez at the market and are clearly labeled for Tabasco 2000, Parque La Venta, and Centro.

Taxis from the center of town to main sites such as the Parque La Venta are inexpensive. If you're getting around **by car,** you'll be glad to know that Villahermosa's streets are well marked, with arrows clearly designating the direction of traffic.

FAST FACTS   **American Express** is represented by Turismo Nieves, Bulevar Simón Sarlat 202 (© **993/314-1888**); hours are Monday to Friday from 10am to 2pm and 4 to 6pm, Saturday from 10am to 1pm. The telephone **area code** is **993.** There aren't a lot of *casas de cambio,* but you can exchange money at the airport, the hotels, and downtown banks on calles Juárez and Madero. ATMs are plentiful.

EXPLORING VILLAHERMOSA

Major sights in Villahermosa include the **Parque–Museo La Venta,** the **Museo Regional de Antropología Carlos Pellicer Cámara,** and the **History of Tabasco Museum.** You can hit them all in a day. There is also an ecological park called **Yumká** (see below), which is 16km (10 miles) out of town in the direction of the airport.

Stroll about the pedestrian-only Zona Luz, and you'll see a number of outdoor cafes, ice cream shops, and townhouses. Nearby is a small, rather disappointing museum on Tabasco's traditional culture and crafts. You can tour the house of Carlos Pellicer Cámara, the Tabascan poet, art collector, and intellectual who occupied the place in later years with monastic simplicity. You can also walk to the Plaza de Armas to see the Palacio de Gobierno and look out over the Grijalva River; there's a handsome pedestrian bridge with an observation tower that offers a good view.

Museo de Historia de Tabasco (Casa de los Azulejos)   I like this place more for the house than for the exhibits—it is an eye-catcher both outside and inside. *Casa de los Azulejos* means "house of the tiles," and several examples of lovely, intricate tile work are on display. You can see the place, including the exhibits, in less than an hour. The displays mostly include a few antiques and artifacts of Tabasco's history, but it is apparent that not a lot of energy or money went into collecting and displaying them. Most of the descriptive text is in Spanish. The museum is downtown at one end of the pedestrian-only Zona Luz area.

At the corner of 27 de Febrero and Av. Juárez. No phone. Admission $1. Sun–Fri 10am–4pm, Sat 9am–8pm.

Museo Regional de Antropología Carlos Pellicer Cámara ★★   This architecturally bold and attractive museum, on the west bank of the river about 1.5km (1 mile) south of the town center, is well organized and has a great collection. The pre-Hispanic artifacts on display include not only Tabascan finds (Totonac, Zapotec, and Olmec), but also those of other Mexican and Central American cultures.

The first floor contains the auditorium, bookstore, and gift shop. The second floor is devoted to the Olmec. The third floor features artifacts relating to central Mexico, including the Tlatilco and Teotihuacán cultures; the Huasteca culture of Veracruz, San Luis Potosí, and Tampico states; and the cultures of Nayarit state, on the west coast. Photographs and diagrams provide vivid images, but the explanatory signs are mostly in Spanish. Look especially for the figurines that were found in this area and for the colorful Codex (an early book of pictographs).

CICOM Center, Av. Carlos Pellicer Cámara 511. © 993/312-6344. Admission $2. Daily 9am–7:30pm; gift shop Tues–Sun 10am–4pm.

Parque–Museo La Venta ★★   The park and museum occupies a portion of a larger park named after Tomás Garrido Canabal, which includes a lovely lake, a zoo, a natural history museum, and a lot of green space with several walkways frequented by joggers. Once inside the park and museum, a trail leads you from one sculpture to the next. Most of the pieces are massive heads or altars. These can be as tall as 2m (6 ft.) and weigh as much as 40 tons. The faces seem to be half adult, half infant. They have highly stylized mouths with thick fleshy lips that turn down. Known as the "jaguar mouth," this is a principal characteristic of Olmec art. At least 17 heads have been found: 4 at La Venta, 10 at San Lorenzo, and 3 at Tres Zapotes—all Olmec cities on Mexico's east coast. The pieces in this park were taken from La Venta, a major city during the Pre-Classic period (2000 B.C.–A.D. 300). Most were sculpted around 1000 B.C. without the use of metal chisels. The basalt rock used for these heads and altars was transported to La Venta from more than 113km (70 miles) away, which is all the more impressive when you realize that the Olmec had no wheels to move it. The rock was thought to have been brought most of the way by raft. Most of these pieces were first discovered in 1938. Now all that remains at La Venta are some grass-covered mounds that were once earthen pyramids. An exhibition area at the entrance to the park does a good job of illustrating how La Venta was laid out and what archaeologists think the Olmec were like. The Olmec created the first civilization in Mexico and developed several cultural traits that later spread to all subsequent civilizations throughout Mesoamerica. In addition to their monumental works, they carved small exquisite figurines in jade and serpentine, which can be seen in the Museo Regional de Antropología (see below).

As you stroll along, you will see labels identifying many species of local trees, including a grand ceiba tree of special significance to the Olmec and, later, the Maya. A few varieties of local critters scurry about, seemingly unconcerned with the presence of humans or with escaping from the park. Allow at least 2 hours for wandering through the junglelike sanctuary and examining the 3,000-year-old sculpture. And don't forget the mosquito repellent. If you're looking to see more of the local flora and fauna, try the natural history museum next door to the park exit.

Bulevar Ruiz Cortines s/n. © 993/314-1652. Admission $3. Tues–Sun 8am–4pm. Take Paseo Tabasco NE to Hwy. 180 and turn right; it's less than 1.5km (1 mile) farther, on the right.

Yumká   Half safari park, half ecological reserve, Yumká contains native and not-so-native wildlife. Visitors can take a guided tour of indigenous tropical forest, a boat tour of the wetlands ($1 extra for the ride), and a small train ride through grasslands populated with various species of African wildlife. This is a large park; allow at least 2 hours. There's a restaurant on the premises. Yumká is 16km (10 miles) from downtown in the direction of the airport. A minibus provides transportation (ask at the hotel or at a travel agency), or you can take a cab ($9).

Camino Yumká s/n, 86200 Ejido Dos Montes, Tabasco. © 993/356-0107. Admission $4 adults; $2 children under 13. Daily 9am–5pm.

WHERE TO STAY

Hotels are expensive in this boomtown. If you want to stay downtown, you have your choice of modest hotels; if you'd rather stay out by the Parque–Museo La Venta, the Hyatt has the best location.

VERY EXPENSIVE

Hyatt Villahermosa ⭐ A small step below the typical Hyatt, this is still the best hotel in town. The location is great. The rooms are large, quiet, and comfortable. This year they are undergoing a thorough remodeling all the way down to the plumbing and wiring. Work is progressing one floor at a time, to be completed by early 2004. Bathrooms before the remodeling were large with shower-tub combinations. The fifth floor is nonsmoking. A short walk away is the Parque–Museo La Venta. The majority of clients are business travelers.

Av. Juárez 106, 86000 Villahermosa, Tab. © 800/233-1234 in the U.S., or 993/310-1234. Fax 993/315-1963. www.villahermosa.regency.hyatt.com. 207 units. $220 double; $250 Regency Club room; $300 junior suite. AE, DC, MC, V. Free guarded parking. **Amenities:** 2 restaurants; 3 bars (1 with live music; 1 sports bar); large pool, wading pool; 2 tennis courts; small exercise room; concierge; tour desk; car rental; business center; room service until 11:30pm; same-day laundry/dry cleaning; nonsmoking floor; concierge level. *In room:* A/C, TV, dataport, hair dryer, coffeemaker, minibar, safe.

EXPENSIVE

Best Western Hotel Maya Tabasco You can't go wrong with this comfortable and busy four-story hotel, where the service is great. The large, carpeted rooms come with a choice of twin, double, or king beds. Bathrooms are midsize with shower-tubs. Some rooms have individually controlled air-conditioning; others are centrally controlled. It's on the main thoroughfare, making it convenient to the bus station, museums, and downtown.

Bulevar Ruiz Cortines 907, 86000 Villahermosa, Tab. © 800/528-1234 in the U.S. or Canada, or 993/314-4466. Fax 993/312-1097. www.hotelmaya.com.mx. 156 units. $121 double. AE, DC, MC, V. Free parking. **Amenities:** 2 restaurants; 2 bars; large pool; tour desk; free shuttle service to airport and downtown; overnight laundry/dry cleaning. *In room:* A/C, TV, minibar, hair dryer, coffeemaker, safe.

MODERATE

Hotel Plaza Independencia ⭐ *Value* Of the many hotels in this price range, the Plaza Independencia is the best. The guest rooms, on six floors served by an elevator, have rattan furnishings, including small desks, carpeted floors, and bathrooms that are larger than at most hotels in this price range. Some rooms have balconies, and from the top floor you can see the river. It's the only budget hotel with a pool and enclosed parking, and it has laundry service. There's a restaurant and bar off the lobby. It's 2 blocks south of the Plaza de Armas.

Independencia 123, 86000 Villahermosa, Tab. © 993/312-1299 or 993/312-7541. Fax 993/314-4724. www. hotelesplaza.com.mx/independencia. 90 units. $65 double. DC, MC, V. Free parking. **Amenities:** Restaurant; bar; small pool; tour desk; laundry service. *In room:* A/C, TV.

INEXPENSIVE

Hotel Madán The two-story Madán is a convenient downtown hotel within walking distance of the pedestrian-only zone and central-city museums. The cheerful rooms come with two single beds, two doubles, or one double. Beds are a little soft. Rooms in the back are the quietest. The hotel's restaurant serves good food. It's between Reforma and Lerdo de Tejada.

Madero 408, 86000 Villahermosa, Tab. © 993/312-1650. Fax 993/314-3373. 20 units. $47 double. AE, MC, V. Free secured parking. **Amenities:** Restaurant; bar. *In room:* A/C, TV.

WHERE TO DINE
Like other Mexican cities, Villahermosa is beginning to see the arrival of U.S. franchise restaurants, but as chain restaurants go, I prefer the Mexican variety: **Sanborn's,** Av. Ruiz Cortines 1310, near Parque–Museo La Venta (© **993/316-8722**), and **VIPS,** Av. Fco. I. Madero 402, downtown (© **993/312-3237**). Both usually do a good job with traditional dishes such as enchiladas or *antojitos* (supper dishes).

Galerías Madán MEXICAN   Off the lobby of the Hotel Madán, this calm, air-conditioned restaurant serves a *comida corrida* of soup, rice, a main course, vegetables, coffee, and dessert. The *empanadas de carne* (meat pies) are worth a try, and the tamales are just plain good. Another popular dish is *filete a la tampiqueña,* or thin grilled steak served with an enchilada and beans. Large windows look onto the street, and the room has the feel of a hotel coffee shop where downtown shoppers and business types gather. It's between Lerdo de Tejada and Reforma.
Madero 408. © **993/312-1650.** Breakfast $3–$4; *comida corrida* (served 1–4pm) $4; main courses $3–$8. AE, DC, MC, V. Daily 7am–11pm.

Los Tulipanes SEAFOOD/STEAKS/REGIONAL   Popular with the local upper-class crowd, Los Tulipanes offers pricey but good food and excellent service. The staff seems to serve a full house with ease, and, on busy days, a guitar trio strolls and serenades. Because the restaurant is on the Río Grijalva near the Pellicer Museum of Anthropology, you can combine a visit to the museum with lunch here. The staff may bring you a plate of *tostones de plátano*—a mashed banana chip the size of a tortilla. In addition to seafood and steaks, Los Tulipanes serves such Mexican specialties as chiles rellenos, tacos, and *pejelagarto empanadas* (fish empanadas). It has a wonderful buffet on Sunday.
CICOM Center, Periférico Carlos Pellicer Cámara 511. © **993/312-9209** or 993/312-9217. Main courses $7–$13; Sun buffet $12. AE, MC, V. Daily 1–9pm.

A SIDE TRIP TO CHOCOLATE PLANTATIONS & THE RUINS OF COMALCALCO
Eighty kilometers (50 miles) from Villahermosa is **Comalcalco,** the only pyramid site in Mexico made of kilned brick. Your route will take you through Tabasco's cacao-growing country, where you can visit plantations and factories to see the cacao from the pod on the tree to the finished chocolate bars.

You'll need a car to enjoy the cacao touring, but Comalcalco itself is accessible by bus from Villahermosa. ADO runs first-class buses twice daily. From the town of Comalcalco, take a taxi or a VW minivan to the ruins, which are 3km (2 miles) farther. Travel agencies in Villahermosa offer a Comalcalco day trip as well. Generally it leaves at 8am and returns around 5pm.

By car, the fastest route from Villahermosa is Highway 190 west to **Cárdenas,** and then north on Highway 187. Along the road to Cárdenas are numerous banana plantations and roadside stands, where you can buy direct. As you come into Cárdenas, look for the Alteza chocolate factory of the cooperative **Industriador de Cacao de Tabasco (INCATAB).** The shop in front sells boxes of chocolate in all its variations. The big boxes are actually filled with small, wrapped, two-bite bars—which make great gifts and snacks.

Cárdenas is the center of cacao processing, but the fruit itself is grown on plantations in a wide area west of Villahermosa and as far south as Teapa and north to the coast. After you turn right at Cárdenas onto Highway 187, you'll begin passing trees laden with the heavy cacao pod, each full of small beans.

Nineteen kilometers (12 miles) before Comalcalco, in the village of Cunduacán, stop and ask for directions to the **Asociación Agrícola de Productores de Cacao.** It's on the main street, but the sign isn't visible. Mornings from November to April are the best time for a tour, because of the abundance of cacao. Here, the cacao beans are received from the growers and processing begins. First the beans are fermented in huge tubs for a little more than a week, and then they are mechanically dried for 16 hours. A fresh white cacao bean is slightly larger and fatter than a lima bean, but after roasting, it's brown, bitter, and smaller. The roasted beans are sacked and sent to the INCATAB chocolate cooperative in Cárdenas.

Along this route are many mom-and-pop cacao plantations, where families grow and process their own cacao and sell it at local markets and roadside stands rather than to the cooperative. One of these is **Rancho La Pasadita,** 7.5km (4½ miles) before Comalcalco on the right. Look carefully for the sign on the pink-and-blue house (it's a bit obscured) that says CHOCOLATE CASERO LA PASADITA. Here Aura Arellano has 19 acres of cacao trees that she planted in the 1950s. She will gladly take you out back where the trees grow, and if it's bean season (Nov–Apr), you'll more than likely see workers hacking open the football-shaped pods and dumping the contents in big wicker baskets. She ferments her beans the traditional way, in a hollowed-out, canoe-size wooden container. She dries and toasts the beans on a small *comal* (clay pan) over an open fire until they are hard like a nut, after which she grinds them to a powder, mixes it with sugar to cook, and makes it into logs for hot chocolate. She sells them in her living-room storefront. You will see this type of chocolate for sale in shops in Villahermosa.

Comalcalco, 40km (25 miles) from Cárdenas, is a busy agricultural center with an interesting market where you can buy wicker baskets, like those used to ferment cacao, and *pichanchas* (a gourd with multiple holes in it), used to extract flavor from fresh cacao beans for a refreshing drink.

The **ruins of Comalcalco** are about 3km (2 miles) on the same highway past the town; watch for signs to the turn-off on the right. Park in the lot and pay admission at the visitor center by the museum. The museum, with many pre-Hispanic artifacts, is small but interesting and worth the 20 minutes or so it takes to see it. Unfortunately, all the descriptions are in Spanish. It presents a history of the people who lived here, the Putún/Chongal Maya. A rough people, they were traders, spoke fractured Mayan, and were believed to have founded, or at least greatly influenced, Chichén Itzá (for more on Chichén-Itzá, see chapter 6).

The neat, grass-covered site spreads out grandly as you enter, with pyramidal mounds left, right, and straight ahead. *Comalcalco* means "house of the comals" in Nahuatl. A *comal* is a round clay pan used for roasting and making tortillas. All around the grounds you'll see shards of kilned brick that were used to sheath the sides of the pyramidal structures. These bricks were made out of clay mixed with sand and ground oyster shell. Because of the fragile nature of these ruins, there are many NO SUBIR ("no climbing") signs warning visitors against scaling particular structures. Others have paths and arrows pointing to the top. From

Photo Op

The afternoon light at Comalcalco makes for beautiful photographs.

the **palace** there's a fabulous view of the whole site. On the **Acropolis,** under a protective covering, are remains of disappointingly few stucco and plaster masks, though they're in surprisingly good condition. Seeing the ruins takes an hour or so. Admission is $3.50, and the site is open daily from 8am to 5pm.

Tips **An Excellent Website for Chiapas**

The Net Traveler (www.thenettraveler.com) specializes in information about the Yucatán, Quintana Roo (home state of Cancún), and Chiapas, as well as other areas in the old Maya empire. Its information on archaeological sites, as well as on diving in the region's caves and *cenotes,* is especially good.

2 Palenque ★★

142km (89 miles) SE of Villahermosa; 229km (143 miles) NE of San Cristóbal de las Casas

The ruins of Palenque look out over the jungle from a tall ridge that juts out from the base of steep, thickly forested mountains. It is a dramatic sight colored by the mysterious feel of the ruins themselves. The temples here are in the Classic style, with tall, high-pitched roofs crowned with elaborate combs. Inside many are representations in stone and plaster of the rulers and their gods, which give evidence of a cosmology that is—and perhaps will remain—impenetrable to our understanding. This is one of the grand archaeological sites of Mexico.

Eight kilometers (5 miles) from the ruins is the town of Palenque. There you can find lodging and food, as well as make travel arrangements. Transportation between the town and ruins is cheap and convenient.

ESSENTIALS
GETTING THERE & DEPARTING
BY PLANE   There is no regular commercial air service to Palenque.

BY CAR   The 229km (143-mile) trip from San Cristóbal to Palenque takes 5 hours and passes through lush jungle and mountain scenery. Take it easy, though, and watch out for potholes and other hindrances. Highway 186 from Villahermosa is in good condition, and the trip from there should take about 2 hours. You may encounter military roadblocks that involve a cursory inspection of your travel credentials and perhaps your vehicle.

BY BUS   The two first-class bus stations are about a block apart. Both are on Palenque's main street between the main square and the turn-off for the ruins. The smaller company, Transportes Rodolfo Figueroa, offers good first-class service four times a day to and from San Cristóbal (5 hr.) and Tuxtla (6½ hr.). Cristóbal Colón offers service to those destinations and to Campeche (6 per day, 5 hr.), Villahermosa (9 per day, 2 hr.), and Mérida (2 per day, 9 hr.).

ORIENTATION
VISITOR INFORMATION   The **State Tourism Office** (Ⓒ/fax **916/345-0356**) is a block from the main square, where Avenida Juárez intersects Abasolo. The office is open Monday to Saturday from 9am to 9pm, Sunday from 9am to 1pm.

CITY LAYOUT   **Avenida Juárez** is Palenque's main street. At one end of it is the **main plaza;** at the other is the oversize sculpture of the famous Maya head that was discovered here. To the right of the statue is the entrance to the Cañada; to the left is the road to the ruins, and straight ahead past the statue are the airport and the highway to Villahermosa. The distance between the town's main square and the monument is about 1.5km (1 mile).

La Cañada is a restaurant and hotel zone tucked away in a small piece of the forest. Aside from the main plaza area, this is the best location for travelers without cars, because the town is within a few blocks, and the buses that run to the ruins pass right by.

GETTING AROUND The cheapest way to get back and forth from the ruins is on the white **VW buses** that run down Juárez every 10 minutes from 6am to 6pm. The buses pass La Cañada and hotels along the road to the ruins and can be flagged down at any point, but they may not stop if they're full. The cost is 25¢ per person.

FAST FACTS The telephone area code is **916.** As for the **climate,** Palenque's high humidity is downright oppressive in the summer, especially after rain showers. During the winter, the damp air can occasionally be chilly in the evening. Rain gear is important at any time of year. Internet service and ATMs are easily available.

EXPLORING PALENQUE

The reason to come here is the ruins; although you can tour them in a morning, many people savor Palenque for days. There are no must-see sights in town.

PARQUE NACIONAL PALENQUE ★★★

The archaeological site of Palenque underwent several changes in 1994, culminating in the opening of a **museum and visitor center** not far from the entrance to the ruins. The complex includes a large parking lot, a refreshment stand serving snacks and drinks, and several shops.
Though it's not large, the museum is worth the time it takes to see; it's open Tuesday to Sunday from 10am to 5pm and is included in the price of admission. It contains well-chosen and artistically displayed exhibits, including the jade contents of recently excavated tombs. (The museum was robbed in 1996, but most of the jade pieces have been recovered.) Explanatory text in Spanish and English explains the life and times of this magnificent city. New pieces are often added as they are uncovered in ongoing excavations.

> **Out of Order**
>
> King Pacal's crypt is currently closed for restoration and preservation work.

The **main entrance,** about 1km (½ mile) beyond the museum, is at the end of the paved highway. There you'll find a large parking lot, a refreshment stand, a ticket booth, and several shops. Among the vendors selling souvenirs by the parking lot are Lacandón Indians wearing white tunics and hawking bows and arrows.

Admission to the ruins is $4. The fee for using a video camera is $4. Parking at the main entrance and at the visitor center is free. The site and visitor center shops are open daily from 8am to 4:45pm.

TOURING THE RUINS Pottery shards found during the excavations show that people lived in this area as early as 300 B.C. By the Classic period (A.D. 300–900), Palenque was an important ceremonial center. It peaked around A.D. 600 to 700.

When John Stephens visited the site in the 1840s, the ruins that you see today were buried under centuries of accumulated earth and a thick canopy of jungle. The dense jungle surrounding the cleared portion still covers unexcavated temples, which are easily discernible in the forest even to the untrained eye. But be careful not to drift too far from the main paths. In the past there have been a few incidents where solitary tourists venturing into the rain forest were assaulted.

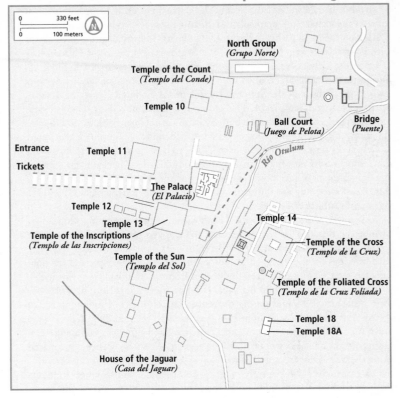

Of all Mexico's ruins, this is the most haunting, because of its majesty; its history, recovered by epigraphers; and its mysterious setting. Scholars have identified the rulers and constructed their family histories, putting visitors on a first-name basis with these ancient people etched in stone. You can read about it in *A Forest of Kings,* by Linda Schele and David Freidel.

As you enter the ruins, the building on your right is the **Temple of the Inscriptions,** named for the great stone hieroglyphic panels found inside. (Most of the panels, which portray the family tree of King Pacal, are in the National Anthropological Museum in Mexico City.) This temple is famous for the crypt of King Pacal deep inside the pyramid, but is closed to the public. The archaeologist Alberto Ruz Lhuller discovered the tomb in the depths of the temple in 1952—an accomplishment many scholars consider one of the great discoveries of the Maya world. In exploratory excavations, Ruz Lhuller found a stairway leading from the temple floor deep into the base of the pyramid. The original builders had carefully concealed the entrance by filling the stairway with stone. After several months of excavation, Ruz Lhuller finally reached King Pacal's crypt, which contained several fascinating objects, including a magnificent carved stone sarcophagus. Ruz Lhuller's own gravesite is opposite the Temple of the Inscriptions, on the left as you enter the park.

Just to your right as you face the Temple of the Inscriptions is **Temple 13,** which is receiving considerable attention from archaeologists. They recently discovered the burial of another richly adorned personage, accompanied in death by an adult female and an adolescent. These remains are still being studied, but some of the artifacts are on display in the museum.

Back on the main pathway, the building directly in front of you is the **Palace,** with its unique tower. The explorer John Stephens camped in the Palace when it was completely covered in vegetation, spending sleepless nights fighting off mosquitoes. A pathway between the Palace and the Temple of the Inscriptions leads to the **Temple of the Sun, the Temple of the Foliated Cross,** the **Temple of the Cross,** and **Temple 14.** This group of temples, now cleared and in various stages of reconstruction, was built by Pacal's son, Chan-Bahlum, who is usually shown on inscriptions with six toes. Chan-Bahlum's plaster mask was found in Temple 14 next to the Temple of the Sun. Archaeologists have begun probing the Temple of the Sun for Chan-Bahlum's tomb. Little remains of this temple's exterior carving. Inside, however, behind a fence, a carving of Chan-Bahlum shows him ascending the throne in A.D. 690. The panels depict Chan-Bahlum's version of his historic link to the throne.

To the left of the Palace is the North Group, also undergoing restoration. Included in this area are the **Ball Court** and the **Temple of the Count,** where Count Waldeck camped in the 19th century. At least three tombs, complete with offerings for the underworld journey, have been found here, and the lineage of at least 12 kings has been deciphered from inscriptions left at this site.

Just past the North Group is a small building (once a museum) now used for storing the artifacts found during the restorations. It is closed to the public. To the right of the building, a stone bridge crosses the river, leading to a pathway down the hillside to the new museum. The rock-lined path descends along a cascading stream on the banks of which grow giant ceiba trees. Benches are placed along the way as rest areas, and some small temples have been reconstructed near the base of the trail. In the early morning and evening, you may hear monkeys crashing through the thick foliage by the path; if you keep noise to a minimum, you may spot wild parrots as well. Walking downhill (by far the best way to go), it will take you about 20 minutes to reach the main highway. The path ends at the paved road across from the museum. The *colectivos* going back to the village will stop here if you wave them down.

WHERE TO STAY

English is spoken in all the expensive hotels and about half of the inexpensive ones. The quoted rates include the 17% tax. High season in Palenque is Easter week, July to August, and December.

MODERATE

Chan-Kah Ruinas ⚓   This hotel is a grouping of comfortable, roomy bungalows that offer privacy and quiet in the surroundings of a tropical forest. Because the town of Palenque isn't particularly worth exploring, you might as well stay here. The grounds are beautifully tended, and there is an inviting pool made to look like a lagoon. A broad stream runs through the property. Some of the bungalows can have a musty smell. The hotel is on the road between the ruins and the town. Christmas prices will be higher than those quoted here, and you may be quoted a higher price if you reserve a room in advance from the United States. The outdoor restaurant and bar serves only passable Mexican food. Room service is pricey.

Km 3 Carretera Las Ruinas, 29960 Palenque, Chi. ✆ **916/345-1100.** Fax 916/345-0820. 83 units. High season $100 double; low season $60–$80 double. MC, V. Free parking. **Amenities:** Restaurant; bar; 2 pools (1 large with natural spring); game room; tour desk; room service until 10pm; laundry. *In room:* A/C.

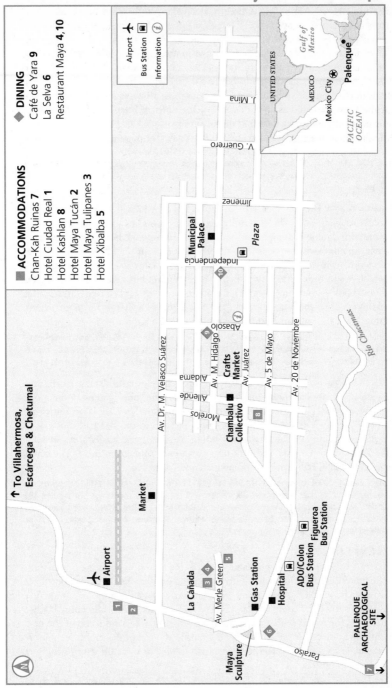

↑ To Villahermosa,
Escárcega & Chetumal

ACCOMMODATIONS
Chan-Kah Ruinas **7**
Hotel Ciudad Real **1**
Hotel Kashlan **8**
Hotel Maya Tucán **2**
Hotel Maya Tulipanes **3**
Hotel Xibalba **5**

◆ **DINING**
Café de Yara **9**
La Selva **6**
Restaurant Maya **4, 10**

Airport ✈
Bus Station ▣
Information ⓘ

Gulf of Mexico
UNITED STATES
MEXICO
Mexico City ✪
Palenque ✪
PACIFIC OCEAN

J. Mina
V. Guerrero
Jimenez
Municipal Palace
Plaza
Independencia
Abasolo
Av. M. Hidalgo
Av. Dr. M. Velasco Suárez
Aldama
Crafts Market
Av. Juárez
Allende
Av. 5 de Mayo
Morelos
Av. 20 de Noviembre
Chambalu Collectivo
Río Chacamax
Market
La Cañada
Av. Merle Green
Gas Station
Hospital
ADO/Colon Bus Station
Figueroa Bus Station
Maya Sculpture
Paraíso
PALENQUE ARCHAEOLOGICAL SITE →
Airport ✈

Hotel Ciudad Real ⭐ This three-story hotel is your best bet for creature comforts and modern convenience. Though in no way fancy, it does the important things right—the rooms are large, quiet, and well lit, with good air-conditioning. They are comfortably, if plainly, furnished in modern style. Suites have a sitting room in addition to a standard room. Most units hold two double beds; some king beds are available. All rooms have a balcony, which in the best case overlooks an attractive garden and pool area. When making a reservation, be sure that the reservation-taker understands that it's for the hotel in Palenque. The hotel is at the edge of town in the direction of the airport.

Carretera a Pakal-Na, Km 1.5, 29960 Palenque, Chi. ℂ **916/345-1343**. (Reservations: ℂ 967/678-4400 in San Cristóbal.) www.ciudadreal.com.mx. 72 units. High season $100 double, $126 suite; low season $95 double, $120 suite. AE, MC, V. Free secured parking. **Amenities:** Restaurant; bar; large pool, baby pool; game room; travel agency, car rental; room service until 11pm, same-day laundry, non-smoking rooms. *In room:* A/C, TV, hair dryer, iron.

Hotel Maya Tucán Get a room in back, and you will have a view of the hotel's natural pond. The cheerfully decorated rooms are adequate in size; they come with double beds and large bathrooms but could use better lighting. Suites are larger and have king beds. The air-conditioner is quiet and gets the job done. Sometimes the hotel operates a discotheque when large tour groups are present (which might bear asking about before checking in), but that won't disturb you if you book a room in back. The grounds are well tended and lush; scarlet macaws kept by the hotel fly about the parking lot. The Maya Tucán is a stone's throw from the Ciudad Real on the highway to the airport.

Carretera-Palenque Km 0.5, 29960 Palenque, Chi. ℂ **916/345-0443**. Fax 916/345-0337. www.hoteles-tucan. com. 56 units. High season $100 double, $120 suite; low season $60 double, $90 suite. MC, V. Free secured parking. **Amenities:** Restaurant; pool; bar; room service until 11pm; overnight laundry. *In room:* A/C, TV, hair dryer.

Hotel Maya Tulipanes The Maya Tulipanes keeps refurbishing rooms and does a good job with upkeep. The best units are the "plus" rooms in the modern wing in back—these are worth the extra money. They are large and come mostly with two double beds, a tile floor, and a medium-size bathroom. Surrounding the hotel is the Cañada, lending tropical-forest shade. You can walk the 2 blocks to the road and pick up a van to the ruins from there. The travel agency operates daily tours to Bonampak and Misol Ha.

Calle Cañada 6, 29960 Palenque, Chi. ℂ **916/345-0201** or 916/345-0258. Fax 916/345-1004. www.maya tulipanes.com.mx. 72 units. High season $89 standard; $95 standard plus. Low season $74 standard; $80 standard plus. Internet specials and promotional rates available. AE, MC, V. Free secured parking. **Amenities:** Restaurant; bar; pool; travel agency; ground transportation to/from Villahermosa airport; room service until 11pm; overnight laundry; nonsmoking rooms. *In room:* A/C, TV.

INEXPENSIVE

Hotel Kashlan This dependable choice is the closest hotel to the bus station. The tidy rooms have interior windows opening onto the hall, marble floors, soft bedspreads, tile bathrooms, small vanities, and luggage racks. Show owner Ada Luz Navarro your Frommer's book, and you'll receive a 20% discount. Higher prices are for rooms with air-conditioning—there are 27, and some of the new units are quite comfortable. The ceiling fans in the rest of the rooms are powerful. The hotel restaurant features vegetarian food. The hotel offers trips to Agua Azul and Misol Ha.

5 de Mayo 105, 29960 Palenque, Chi. ℂ **916/345-0297**. Fax 916/345-0309. kashlan@hotmail.com. 59 units. $23–$50 double. 20% Frommer's discount. Rates include coffee all day. No credit cards. **Amenities:** Restaurant; bar; tour desk; overnight laundry service.

Hotel Xibalba   This small two-story hotel has some fanciful Maya architectural elements that make staying here fun. The medium-size rooms are bright and cheerful, with good air-conditioning. I prefer the upstairs units. The restaurant is pleasant and reliable, and you can arrange a trip to Bonampak or Misol Ha with the hotel management, which owns a long-standing travel agency, Viajes Shivalva (pronounced like Xibalba: "shee-*bahl*-bah"). Take the time to walk down the street to view the full-size replica of the giant stone slab that was the lid to King Pacal's sarcophagus.

Calle Merle Green 9, Col. La Cañada, 29960 Palenque, Chi. ✆ **916/345-0411** or 916/345/0822. Fax 916/345-0392. www.palenquemx.com/shivalva. 14 units. $35 double. MC, V. **Amenities:** Restaurant; bar; travel agency; limited room service; laundry. *In room:* A/C, TV.

WHERE TO DINE

Palenque and, for that matter, the rest of backwater Chiapas, is not for gourmets. Who'd a thunk? But the situation has been improving, and you can get some decent Mexican food. I had an easy time eliminating a number of restaurants that didn't even seem to be keeping up the appearance of serving food.

MODERATE

La Selva ⊛ MEXICAN/INTERNATIONAL   At La Selva (the jungle), you dine under a large, attractive thatched roof beside well-tended gardens. The menu includes seafood, freshwater fish, steaks, and Mexican specialties. The most expensive thing on the menu is *pigua,* freshwater lobster that is caught in the large rivers of southeast Mexico. These can get quite large—the size of small saltwater lobsters. This and the finer cuts of meat have been frozen, but you wouldn't want otherwise in Palenque. I liked fish stuffed with shrimp, and *mole* enchiladas. La Selva is on the highway to the ruins, near the statue of the Maya head.

Km 0.5 Carretera Palenque Ruinas. ✆ **916/345-0363.** Main courses $8–$17. MC, V. Daily 11:30am–11:30pm.

INEXPENSIVE

Café de Yara MEXICAN   A small, modern-style café and restaurant with a comforting, not overly ambitious menu, this is a dependable place for salads, sandwiches, something like *queso fundido* (a melted cheese dish served with tortillas as an appetizer), or a Mexican entree. Try beef or chicken milanesa or chicken with a chile pasilla sauce. The furniture and surroundings are comfortable.

Av. Hidalgo 66 (at Abasolo). ✆ **916/345-0269.** Main courses $4–$7. MC, V. Daily 7am–11pm.

Restaurant Maya ⊛ MEXICAN/STEAKS   A popular place among tourists and locals, Restaurant Maya faces the main plaza on the northwest corner. The dining area is breezy and open. At breakfast there are free refills of strong coffee. I like the *consomé,* a chicken soup with rice and vegetables (be sure to add a little lime juice), or *sopa azteca,* a tortilla soup flavored with a little guajillo chile (add lime juice to this, too). Chicken breast is available in a number of ways that are good, if not terribly original. The plantains fried Mexican style are wonderful. You can also try *tascalate,* a pre-Hispanic drink not commonly seen at restaurants. It is made of water, *masa,* chocolate, and *achiote,* and served room temperature or cold. This restaurant was awarded a national prize for quality and service. There's a branch in the Cañada, called Maya Cañada.

Av. Independencia s/n. ✆ **916/345-0042.** Breakfast $4–$5; main courses $6–$12. AE, MC, V. Daily 7am–11pm.

ROAD TRIPS FROM PALENQUE
SPECTACULAR WATERFALLS AT AGUA AZUL & CASCADA DE MISOL HA

The most popular excursion from Palenque is a day trip to the Misol Ha waterfall and Agua Azul. **Misol Ha** is about 19km (12 miles) from Palenque, just off the Ocosingo road (there's a sign pointing to the right). Visitors can swim in the waters below the falls and scramble up slippery paths to smaller falls beside the large one, which drops about 27m (90 ft.) before spraying its mist on the waters below. There's a small restaurant run by the *ejido* cooperative that owns the site. Entrance costs around $3 per person.

Approximately 38km (24 miles) beyond Misol Ha on the same road are the **Agua Azul waterfalls,** a spectacular series of beautiful cascades tumbling into a wide river. Seeing both is a full day trip. Visitors can picnic and relax (bring something to sprawl on), swim, or clamber over the slippery cascades and go upstream for a look at the jungle encroaching the water. Agua Azul is prettiest after 3 or 4 consecutive dry days; heavy rains can make the water murky. Check with guides or other travelers about the water quality before you decide to go. The cost to enter is around $3.50. Trips can usually be arranged through your hotel, **Viajes Shivalva Tours, Viajes Toniná** (see "Bonampak & Yaxchilán: Ruins & Rugged Adventure," below), or the **Hotel Kashlan.** They cost about $12 per person for the day.

BONAMPAK & YAXCHILAN: RUINS & RUGGED ADVENTURE

Intrepid travelers may want to consider the day trip to the Maya ruins of Bonampak and Yaxchilán. The **ruins of Bonampak,** southeast of Palenque on the Guatemalan border, were discovered in 1946. The site is important for the vivid **murals** of the Maya on the interior walls of one temple. Particularly striking is an impressive battle scene, perhaps the most important painting of pre-Hispanic Mexico. Reproductions of these murals are on view in the Regional Archaeology Museum in Villahermosa.

Several tour companies offer a day trip. The drive to Bonampak is 3 hours. From there you continue by boat to the ruins of Yaxchilán, famous for its highly ornamented buildings. Bring rain gear, boots, a flashlight, and bug repellent. All tours include meals and cost about $50. No matter what agency you sign up with, the hours of departure and return are the same because the vans of the different agencies caravan down and back for safety. You leave at 6am and return at 7pm.

Try **Viajes Na Chan Kan** (© 916/345-2154), at the corner of avenidas Hidalgo and Jiménez, across from the main square, or **Viajes Shivalva,** Calle Merle Green 1 (© 916/345-0411; fax 916/345-0392). A branch of Viajes Shivalva (© 916/345-0822) is a block from the *zócalo* (main plaza) at the corner of Juárez and Abasolo, across the hall from the State Tourism Office. It's open Monday to Saturday from 9am to 9pm.

3 San Cristóbal de las Casas ⟨★⟩

229km (143 miles) SW of Palenque; 80km (50 miles) E of Tuxtla Gutiérrez; 74km (46 miles) NW of Comitán; 166km (104 miles) NW of Cuauhtémoc; 451km (282 miles) E of Oaxaca

San Cristóbal is a colonial town of white stucco walls and red-tile roofs, of cobblestone streets and narrow sidewalks, of graceful arcades and open plazas. It lies in a lush valley nearly 2,121m (7,000 ft.) high. The city owes part of its name to the 16th-century cleric Fray Bartolomé de las Casas, who was the town's first

San Cristóbal de las Casas

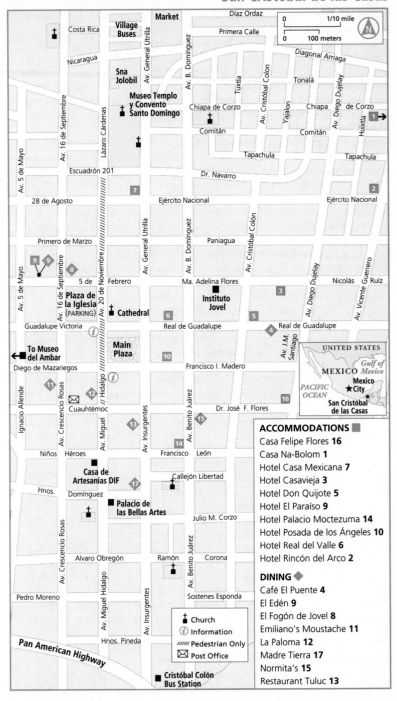

ACCOMMODATIONS ■
Casa Felipe Flores **16**
Casa Na-Bolom **1**
Hotel Casa Mexicana **7**
Hotel Casavieja **3**
Hotel Don Quijote **5**
Hotel El Paraíso **9**
Hotel Palacio Moctezuma **14**
Hotel Posada de los Ángeles **10**
Hotel Real del Valle **6**
Hotel Rincón del Arco **2**

DINING ◆
Café El Puente **4**
El Edén **9**
El Fogón de Jovel **8**
Emiliano's Moustache **11**
La Paloma **12**
Madre Tierra **17**
Normita's **15**
Restaurant Tuluc **13**

✝ Church
ⓘ Information
///// Pedestrian Only
✉ Post Office

bishop and spent the rest of his life waging a political campaign to protect the indigenous peoples of the Americas.

Surrounding the city are many villages of Mayan-speaking Indians who display great variety in their language, dress, and customs, making this area one of the most fascinating in Mexico. San Cristóbal is the principal market town for these Indians, and their point of contact with the outside world. Most of them trek down from the surrounding mountains to sell goods and perform errands; some even live in San Cristóbal because they have been expelled from their villages for religious reasons.

Probably the most visible among the local indigenous groups are the **Chamula.** The men wear baggy thigh-length trousers and white or black *sarapes,* while the women wear blue *rebozos,* gathered white blouses with embroidered trim, and black wool wraparound skirts.

Another local Indian group is the **Zinacantecan,** whose men dress in light-pink overshirts with colorful trim and tassels and, sometimes, short pants. Hat ribbons (now a rare sight) are tied on married men, while ribbons dangle loosely from the hats of bachelors and community leaders. Zinacantecan women wear beautiful, brightly colored woven shawls and black wool skirts. You may also see **Tenejapa** men clad in knee-length black tunics and flat straw hats, and Tenejapa women dressed in beautiful reddish and rust-colored huipiles. Women of all groups go barefoot, while men wear handmade sandals or cowboy boots.

Several Indian villages lie within reach of San Cristóbal by road: **Chamula,** with its weavers and highly unorthodox church; **Zinacantán,** whose residents practice their own syncretic religion; **Tenejapa, San Andrés,** and **Magdalena,** known for brocaded textiles; **Amatenango del Valle,** a town of potters; and **Aguacatenango,** known for embroidery. Most of these "villages" consist of little more than a church and the municipal government building, with homes scattered for miles around and a general gathering only for church and market days (usually Sun).

Evangelical Protestant missionaries have converted large numbers of indigenous peoples, and some villages expel new converts from their homelands; in Chamula, for example, as many as 30,000 people have been cast out. Many of these people, *los expulsados* ("the expelled ones"), have taken up residence in new villages on the outskirts of San Cristóbal de las Casas. They still wear traditional dress. Other villages, such as Tenejapa, allow the Protestant church to exist and villagers to attend it without prejudice.

Although the influx of outsiders is nothing new, and in the last 20 years has been increasing, it hasn't created in most Indians a desire to adopt mainstream customs and dress. It's interesting to note that the communities closest to San Cristóbal are the most resistant to change. The greatest threat to the cultures in this area comes not from tourism but from the action of large market forces, population pressures, environmental damage, and poverty. The Indians aren't interested in acting or looking like the foreigners they see. They may steal glances or even stare at tourists, but mainly they pay little attention to outsiders, except as potential buyers for handicrafts.

You'll hear the word *ladino* here; it refers to non-Indian Mexicans. It may be used derogatorily or descriptively, depending on who is using the term and how.

Other local lingo you should know about includes *Jovel,* San Cristóbal's original name, used often by businesses, and *coleto,* meaning someone or something from San Cristóbal. You'll see signs for tamales coletos, coleto bread, and coleto breakfast.

ESSENTIALS
GETTING THERE & DEPARTING
BY PLANE   San Cristóbal has a new airport. **AeroMar** (© **967/674-3014** or 967/674-3003) operates daily flights to and from Mexico City, but these flights are subject to cancellation on short notice.

BY CAR   From Tuxtla Gutiérrez (see later in this chapter), the 1½-hour trip winds through beautiful mountain country. From Palenque, the road is just as beautiful (if longer—5 hr.), and it provides jungle scenery, but portions of it may be heavily potholed or obstructed during rainy season. Check with the local state tourism office before driving.

BY TAXI   Taxis from Tuxtla Gutiérrez to San Cristóbal cost around $50. Another way to travel to and from Tuxtla is by *combi*. The Volkswagen vans, which can get extremely crowded, make the run every 15 to 30 minutes and cost $3. They can be found just off the highway by the bus station. You'll have to ask someone to point them out to you because there isn't a sign.

BY BUS   The two bus stations in town are directly across the Pan American Highway from each other. The smaller one belongs to Transportes Rodolfo Figueroa, which provides first-class service to and from Tuxtla (every 40 min.) and Palenque (4 buses per day, with a stop in Ocosingo—cheaper than the competition). For other destinations, go to the large station run by ADO and its

  The Zapatista Uprising & Lingering Tensions

In January 1994, Indians from this area rebelled against the *ladino*-led towns and Mexican government over health care, education, land distribution, and representative government. Their organization, the **Zapatista Liberation Army,** known as EZLN (Ejército Zapatista de Liberación Nacional), and its leader, Subcomandante Marcos, have become emblematic of the problems Mexico has with social justice. Since the revolt, discussions between government officials and the leadership of the EZLN have stalled. Progress has been made, but the principal issues remain unresolved, and tension remains. In 1997 and 1998 there were more killings, but these have been attributed to local political division rather than the tension between Zapatistas and the national government. We may never know the truth.

When in San Cristóbal, you'll see little evidence of social tension. There might be a political demonstration or perhaps a strike; you will see some political graffiti here and there, and, of course, you'll find little Subcomandante Marcos dolls, replete with black ski masks, offered for sale by street vendors (a hot-selling item, by the way). Locals don't seem concerned, and tourists are showing up in substantial numbers.

One of the first actions that Vicente Fox took on assuming the presidency of Mexico was to withdraw most of the military forces from the region and offer an olive branch to the Zapatistas. But direct talks between Zapatistas and members of the national legislature ended in stalemate. Before traveling to Chiapas, check your news sources and see if the State Department has issued any advisories: **http://travel.state.gov.**

affiliates, Altos, Cristóbal Colón, and Maya de Oro. This company offers service to and from Tuxtla (12 buses per day), Palenque (almost every hr.), and several other destinations: Mérida (2 buses per day), Villahermosa (2 buses per day), Oaxaca (2 buses per day), and Puerto Escondido (2 buses per day). To buy a bus ticket without going down to the station, go to the **Ticket Bus** agency, Av. Belisario Domínguez 8 (© **967/678-0291**). Hours are Monday to Saturday from 9am to 2pm and 4pm to 7pm, Sunday from 9am to 5pm.

ORIENTATION

ARRIVING   To get to the main plaza if you're arriving by car from Oaxaca and Tuxtla, turn left on **Avenida Insurgentes** (there's a traffic light); if you're coming from Palenque and Ocosingo, turn right. From the bus station, the main plaza is 9 blocks north up Avenida Insurgentes (a 10-min. walk, slightly uphill). Cabs are cheap and plentiful.

VISITOR INFORMATION   The **State Tourism Office** is just off the southwest corner of the main plaza, at Avenida Hidalgo 1-B (© **967/678-6570**); it's open Monday to Friday from 8am to 8pm, Saturday from 9am to 8pm, and Sunday from 9am to 2pm. The **Municipal Tourism Office** (©/fax **967/678-0665**) is in the town hall, west of the main square. Hours are Monday to Saturday from 9am to 8pm. Check the bulletin board here for apartments, shared rides, cultural events, and local tours. Both offices are helpful, but the state office is open an hour later and is better staffed.

CITY LAYOUT   San Cristóbal is laid out on a grid; the main north-south axis is **Insurgentes/Utrilla,** and the east-west axis is **Mazariegos/Madero.** All streets change names when they cross either of these streets. The *zócalo* (main plaza) lies where they intersect. **Real de Guadalupe** seems to have become a principal street for tourism-related businesses. The market is 7 blocks north of the *zócalo* along Utrilla.

Take note that this town has at least three streets named Domínguez and two streets named Flores. There's Hermanos Domínguez, Belisario Domínguez, and Pantaleón Domínguez, and María Adelina Flores and Dr. José Flores.

GETTING AROUND   Most of the sights and shopping in San Cristóbal are within walking distance of the plaza.

Urbano **buses** (minibuses) take passengers between town and the residential neighborhoods. All buses pass by the market and central plaza on their way through town. Utrilla and Avenida 16 de Septiembre are the two main arteries; all buses use the market area as the last stop. Any bus on Utrilla will take you to the market.

Colectivos (minibuses) to outlying villages depart from the public market at Avenida Utrilla. Buses late in the day are usually very crowded. Always check to see when the last or next-to-last bus returns from wherever you're going, and then take the one before that—those last buses sometimes don't materialize, and you might be stranded. I speak from experience!

Rental cars come in handy for trips to the outlying villages and may be worth the expense when shared by a group, but keep in mind that insurance is invalid on unpaved roads. Try **Optima Car Rental,** Av. Mazariegos 39 (© **967/674-5409**). Office hours are daily from 9am to 1pm and 5 to 8pm. You'll save money by arranging the rental from your home country; otherwise, a day's rental with insurance will cost around $60 for a VW Beetle with manual transmission, the cheapest car available.

Bikes are another option for getting around the city; a day's rental is about $8. **Los Pingüinos,** Av. Ecuador 4-B (© **967/678-0202;** pinguinosmex@yahoo.com), offers bike tours to a few out-of-town locations. Tours in the valley around San Cristóbal last 4 to 6 hours and cost $20 to $25. It's open daily from 10am to 2:30pm and 4 to 7pm.

 FAST FACTS: **San Cristóbal de las Casas**

Area Code The telephone area code is **967.**

Books **Living Maya,** by Walter Morris, with photography by Jeffrey Fox, is the best book to read to understand the culture, art, and traditions surrounding San Cristóbal de las Casas, as well as the unsolved social, economic, and political problems that gave rise to the 1994 Chiapas Indian uprising. *The People of the Bat: Mayan Tales and Dreams from Zinacantán,* by Robert M. Laughlin, is a priceless collection of beliefs from that village near San Cristóbal. Another good book with a completely different view of today's Maya is *The Heart of the Sky,* by Peter Canby, who traveled among the Maya to chronicle their struggles (and wrote his book before the Zapatista uprising).

Bookstore For the best selection of new and used books and reading material in English, go to **La Pared,** Av. Hidalgo 2 (© **967/678-6367**). The owner, Dana Gay Burton, also sells postcards and T-shirts, and is a fanatic about amber.

Bulletin Boards Because San Cristóbal is a cultural crossroads for travelers from all over the world, several places maintain bulletin boards with information on Spanish classes, local specialty tours, rooms or houses to rent, rides needed, and so on. These include boards at the **Tourism Office, Café El Puente, Madre Tierra,** and **Casa Na-Bolom.**

Climate San Cristóbal can be chilly when the sun isn't out, especially during the winter. It's 7,200 feet above sea level. Most hotels are not heated, although some have fireplaces. There is always a possibility of rain, but I would avoid going to San Cristóbal from late August to late October, during the height of the rainy season.

Currency Exchange There are at least five *casas de cambio* on Real de Guadalupe near the main square, and a couple under the colonnade facing the square. Most are open until 8pm, and some are open Sunday. There are also a number of ATMs.

Doctor The only doctor worth seeing is **Dr. Roberto Lobato,** Av. Belisario Domínguez 17, at Calle Flavio A. Paniagua (© **967/678-7777**). Don't be unsettled by the fact that his office is next door to Funerales Canober.

Internet Access **The Cyberc@fe** (© **967/678-7488**) is in the little concourse that cuts through the block just east of the main square. Look for the entrance on Real de Guadalupe or Francisco Madero. It is one of the largest Internet cafes I have seen in Mexico, with several well-connected machines and a few other toys.

Parking If your hotel does not have parking, use the underground public lot *(estacionamiento)* in front of the cathedral, just off the main square on 16 de Septiembre. Entry is from Calle 5 de Febrero.

Population San Cristóbal has 132,000 residents.

Post Office The *correo* is at Crescencio Rosas and Cuauhtémoc, a block south and west of the main square. It's open Monday to Friday from 8am to 7pm, Saturday from 9am to 1pm.

Spanish Classes The **Instituto Jovel,** María Adelina Flores 21 (Apdo. Postal 62), 29250 San Cristóbal de las Casas, Chi. (©/fax **967/678-4069**), gets higher marks for its Spanish courses than the competition. It also offers courses in weaving and cooking. The **Centro Bilingüe,** at the Centro Cultural El Puente, Real de Guadalupe 55, 29250 San Cristóbal de las Casas, Chi. (© **800/303-4983** in the U.S., or ©/fax 967/678-3723), offers classes in Spanish. Both schools can arrange home stays for their students.

Telephone The best price for long-distance telephone calls and faxing is at **La Pared** bookstore (see "Bookstore," above) at Av. Hidalgo 2, across the street from the State Tourism Office.

EXPLORING SAN CRISTOBAL

With its beautiful scenery, clean air, and mountain hikes, San Cristóbal draws many visitors. However, the town's biggest attraction is its colorful, centuries-old indigenous culture. The Chiapanecan Maya, attired in their unique native garb, can be seen anywhere in San Cristóbal, but most travelers take at least one trip to the outlying villages to get a close-up of Maya life. Don't neglect to meander through the San Cristóbal market. It's behind the Santo Domingo church (see "Attractions in Town," below) and is open almost every day, but never on Sunday. You can witness scenes of everyday local life, plus some that aren't so everyday.

ATTRACTIONS IN TOWN

Casa Na-Bolom ★★   If you're interested in the anthropology of the region, you'll want to visit this house museum. Stay here, if you can. The house, built as a seminary in 1891, became the headquarters of anthropologists Frans and Trudy Blom in 1951, and the gathering place of outsiders interested in studying the region. Frans Blom led many early archaeological studies in Mexico, and Trudy was noted for her photographs of the Lacandón Indians and her efforts to save them and their forest homeland. A room at Na-Bolom contains a selection of her Lacandón photographs, and postcards of the photographs are on sale in the gift shop (daily 9am–2pm and 3–7pm). A tour of the home covers the displays of pre-Hispanic artifacts collected by Frans Blom; the cozy library, with its numerous volumes about the region and the Maya (weekdays 10am–2pm); and the gardens Trudy Blom started for the ongoing reforestation of the Lacandón jungle. The tour ends with a showing of *La Reina de la Selva,* an excellent 50-minute film on the Bloms, the Lacandón, and Na-Bolom. Trudy Blom died in 1993, but Na-Bolom continues to operate as a nonprofit public trust.

The 12 guest rooms, named for surrounding villages, are decorated with local objects and textiles. All rooms have fireplaces and private bathrooms. Prices for rooms (including breakfast) are $44 single, $55 double.

Even if you're not a guest here, you can come for a meal, usually a delicious assortment of vegetarian and other dishes. Just be sure to make a reservation at least 2½ hours in advance, and be on time. The colorful dining room has one large table, and the eclectic mix of travelers sometimes makes for interesting conversation. Breakfast costs $4; lunch and dinner cost $7 each. Dinner is

---

(*Tips* **Photography Warning**

Photographers should be cautious about when, where, and at whom or what they point their cameras. In San Cristóbal, taking a photograph of even a chile pepper can be a risky undertaking; locals just do not like having people take pictures. Especially in the San Cristóbal market, people who think they or their possessions are being photographed may angrily pelt photographers with whatever object is at hand—rocks or rotten fruit. Be respectful and ask first. Young handicraft vendors will sometimes offer to be photographed for money.

Nearby villages have strict rules about photography. Villages around San Cristóbal, especially Chamula and Zinacantán, require visitors to go to the municipal building upon arrival and sign an agreement (written in Spanish) not to take photographs. The penalty for disobeying these regulations is stiff: confiscation of your camera and perhaps even a lengthy stay in jail. And they mean it!

---

served at 7:30pm. Following breakfast (8–10am), a guide not affiliated with the house offers tours to San Juan Chamula and Zinacantán (see "The Nearby Maya Villages & Countryside," later in this chapter).

Av. Vicente Guerrero 3, 29200 San Cristóbal de las Casas, Chi. (967/678-1418. Fax 967/678-5586. Group tour and film $3. Tours Tues–Sun 11:30am and 4:30pm. Leave the square on Real de Guadalupe, walk 4 blocks to Av. Vicente Guerrero, and turn left; Na-Bolom is 5½ blocks up Guerrero.

Catedral   San Cristóbal's main cathedral was built in the 1500s. It has little of interest inside besides a lovely, uncommon beam ceiling and a carved wooden pulpit.

Calle 20 de Noviembre at Guadalupe Victoria. No phone. Free admission. Daily 7am–6pm.

Museo del Ambar 🌟   If you've been in this town any time at all, you know what a big deal amber is here. Chiapas is the third-largest producer of amber in the world, and many experts prefer its amber for its colors and clarity. A couple of stores tried calling themselves museums but they didn't fool anybody. Now a real museum moves methodically through all the issues surrounding amber— mining, shaping, the differences between real and fake amber, variations of the mineral you'll find in different parts of the world. It's interesting, it's cheap, and you get to see the restored area of the old convent it occupies. There are a couple of beautiful pieces of worked amber that are on permanent loan. Make sure you see them. In mid-August, the museum holds a contest for local artisans who work amber. Check it out.

Exconvento de la Merced, Diego de Mazariegos s/n. (967/678-9716. Admission $1. Tues–Sun 10am–2pm; 4–7pm.

Museo Templo y Convento Santo Domingo   Inside the front door of the carved-stone plateresque facade, there's a beautiful gilded wooden altarpiece built in 1560, walls with saints, and gilt-framed paintings. Attached to the church is the former Convent of Santo Domingo, which houses a small museum about San Cristóbal and Chiapas. The museum has changing exhibits and often shows cultural films. It's 5 blocks north of the zócalo, in the market area.

Av. 20 de Noviembre. (967/678-1609. Church admission free; museum admission $2. Museum Tues–Sun 10am–5pm.

> ⌒ **Moments** Special Events in & near San Cristóbal
>
> In nearby Chamula, **Carnaval,** the big annual festival that takes place in the days before Lent, is a fascinating mingling of the Christian pre-Lenten ceremonies and the ancient Maya celebration of the 5 "lost days" at the end of the 360-day Maya agricultural cycle. Around noon on Shrove Tuesday, groups of village elders run across patches of burning grass as a purification rite. Macho residents then run through the streets with a bull. During Carnaval, roads close in town, and buses drop visitors at the outskirts.
>
> During this time, nearby villages (except Zinacantán) also have celebrations, although perhaps not as dramatic. Visiting these villages, especially on the Sunday before Lent, will round out your impression of Carnaval in all its regional varieties. In Tenejapa, the celebration continues during the Thursday market after Ash Wednesday.
>
> During Easter and the week after, for the annual **Feria de Primavera (Spring Festival),** San Cristóbal is ablaze with lights and excitement and gets hordes of visitors. Activities include carnival rides, food stalls, handicraft shops, parades, and band concerts. Hotel rooms are scarce and more expensive.
>
> Another spectacle is staged from July 22 to 25, during the annual **Fiesta de San Cristóbal,** honoring the town's patron saint. The steps up to the San Cristóbal church are lit with torches at night. Pilgrimages to the church begin several days earlier, and on the 24th, there's an all-night vigil.
>
> For the **Día de Guadalupe,** on December 12, honoring Mexico's patron saint, the streets are gaily decorated, and food stalls line the streets leading to the church on a hill where she is honored.

Palacio de las Bellas Artes   Be sure to check out this building if you are interested in the arts. It periodically hosts dance events, art shows, and other performances. The schedule of events is usually posted on the door if the Bellas Artes is not open. There's a public library next door. Around the corner, the Centro Cultural holds a number of concerts and other performances; check the posters on the door to see what's scheduled.

Av. Hidalgo, 4 blocks S of the plaza. No phone.

Templo de San Cristóbal   For the best view of San Cristóbal, climb the seemingly endless steps to this church and *mirador* (lookout point). A visit here requires stamina. By the way, there are 22 more churches in town, some of which also demand strenuous climbs.

At the very end of Calle Hermanos Domínguez.

HORSEBACK RIDING

The **Casa de Huéspedes Margarita,** Real de Guadalupe 34, and **Hotel Real del Valle** (see "Where to Stay," later in this chapter) can arrange horseback rides for around $15 for a day, including a guide. Reserve your steed at least a day in advance. A horseback-riding excursion might go to San Juan Chamula, to nearby caves, or just up into the hills.

THE NEARBY MAYA VILLAGES & COUNTRYSIDE

The Indian communities around San Cristóbal are fascinating worlds unto themselves. If you are unfamiliar with these indigenous cultures, you will understand and appreciate more of what you see by visiting them with a guide, at least for your first foray out into the villages. Guides are acquainted with members of the communities and are viewed with less suspicion than newcomers. These communities have their own laws and customs—and visitors' ignorance is no excuse. Entering these communities is tantamount to leaving Mexico, and if something happens, the state and federal authorities will not intervene except in case of a serious crime.

The best guided trips are the locally grown ones. Three operators go to the neighboring villages in small groups. They all charge the same price ($10 per person), use minivans for transportation, and speak English. They do, however, have their own interpretations and focus.

Pepe leaves from **Casa Na-Bolom** (see "Attractions in Town," above) for daily trips to San Juan Chamula and Zinacantán at 10am, returning to San Cristóbal between 2 and 3pm. Pepe looks at cultural continuities, community relationships, and, of course, religion.

Mercedes Hernández Gómez, a very opinionated *mestiza* woman, leads a tour from the main plaza at 9am. She always carries an umbrella by which you can identify her. Mercedes, a largely self-trained ethnographer, is informed about the history and folkways of the villages, and her opinions make for a good tour. Lately, clients have reported that she's been behaving erratically and dictatorially, and has offended a few of those she has taken on tour.

Alex and **Raúl** can be found in front of the cathedral between 9:15 and 9:30am. They are quite personable and get along well with the Indians in the communities. They focus on cultural values and their expression in social behavior, which provides a glimpse of the details and the texture of life in these communities (and, of course, they talk about religion). Their tour is very good.

For excursions farther afield, see "Road Trips from San Cristóbal," later in this chapter. Also, the above-mentioned guides (especially Alex and Raúl) can be persuaded to go to other communities besides Chamula and Zinacantán; talk to them.

CHAMULA & ZINACANTAN A side trip to the village of San Juan Chamula will really get you into the spirit of life around San Cristóbal. Sunday, when the market is in full swing, is the best day to go for shopping; other days, when you'll be less impeded by eager children selling their crafts, are better for seeing the village and church.

The village, 8km (5 miles) northeast of San Cristóbal, has a large church, a plaza, and a municipal building. Each year, a new group of citizens is chosen to live in the municipal center as caretakers of the saints, settlers of disputes, and enforcers of village rules. As in other nearby villages, on Sunday local leaders wear their leadership costumes, including beautifully woven straw hats loaded with colorful ribbons befitting their high position. They solemnly sit together in a long line somewhere around the central square. Chamula is typical of other villages in that men are often away working in the "hotlands," harvesting coffee or cacao, while women stay home to tend the sheep, the children, the cornfields, and the fires. It's almost always the women's and children's work to gather firewood, and you see them along roadsides bent under the weight.

Don't leave Chamula without seeing the **church interior.** As you step from bright sunlight into the candlelit interior, you feel as if you've been transported to another country. Pine needles scattered amid a sea of lighted candles cover the tile floor. Saints line the walls, and before them people are often kneeling and praying aloud while passing around bottles of Pepsi-Cola. Shamans are often on hand, passing eggs over sick people or using live or dead chickens in a curing ritual. The statues of saints are similar to those you might see in any Mexican Catholic church, but beyond sharing the same name, they mean something completely different to the Chamulas. Visitors can walk carefully through the church to see the saints or stand quietly in the background and observe.

Carnaval, which takes place just before Lent, is the big annual festival. The Chamulas are not a wealthy people, but the women are the region's best wool weavers, producing finished pieces for themselves and for other villages.

In Zinacantán, a wealthier village than Chamula, you must sign a rigid form promising *not to take any photographs* before you see the two side-by-side sanctuaries. Once permission is granted and you have paid a small fee, an escort will usually show you the church, or you may be allowed to see it on your own. Floors may be covered in pine needles here, too, and the rooms are brightly sunlit. The experience is an altogether different one from that of Chamula.

AMATENANGO DEL VALLE About an hour's ride south of San Cristóbal is Amatenango, a town known mostly for its **women potters.** You'll see their work in San Cristóbal—small animals, jars, and large water jugs—but in the village, you can visit the potters in their homes. Just walk down the dirt streets. Villagers will lean over the walls of family compounds and invite you in to select from their inventory. You may even see them firing the pieces under piles of wood in the open courtyard or painting them with color derived from rusty iron water. The women wear beautiful red-and-yellow *huipils,* but if you want to take a photograph, you'll have to pay.

To get here, take a *colectivo* from the market in San Cristóbal. Before it lets you off, be sure to ask about the return-trip schedule.

AGUACATENANGO This village 16km (10 miles) south of Amatenango is known for its **embroidery.** If you've visited San Cristóbal's shops, you'll recognize the white-on-white and black-on-black floral patterns on dresses and blouses for sale. The locals' own regional blouses, however, are quite different.

TENEJAPA The **weavers** of Tenejapa, 28km (17 miles) from San Cristóbal, make some of the most beautiful and expensive work you'll see in the region. The best time to visit is on market day (Sun and Thurs, though Sun is better). The weavers of Tenejapa taught the weavers of San Andrés and Magdalena—which accounts for the similarity in their designs and colors. To get to Tenejapa, try to find a *colectivo* in the very last row by the market, or hire a taxi. On Tenejapa's main street, several stores sell locally woven regional clothing, and you can bargain for the price.

THE HUITEPEC CLOUD FOREST **Pronatura,** Av. Benito Juárez 11-B (© **967/678-5000**), a private, nonprofit, ecological organization, offers environmentally sensitive tours of the cloud forest. The forest is a haven for **migratory birds,** and more than 100 bird species and 600 plant species have been discovered here. Guided tours run from 9am to noon Tuesday to Sunday. They cost $25 per group of up to eight people. Make reservations a day in advance. To reach the reserve on your own, drive on the road to Chamula; the turn-off is at Km 3.5. The reserve is open Tuesday to Sunday from 9am to 4pm.

SHOPPING

Many Indian villages near San Cristóbal are noted for **weaving, embroidery, brocade work, leather,** and **pottery,** making the area one of the best in the country for shopping. You'll see beautiful woolen shawls, indigo-dyed skirts, colorful native shirts, and magnificently woven *huipils,* all of which often come in vivid geometric patterns. Working in leather, the craftspeople are artisans of the highest caliber. Tie-dyed *jaspe* from Guatemala comes in bolts and is made into clothing. The town is also known for **amber,** sold in several shops and at La Pared bookstore (see "Bookstore" in "Fast Facts," earlier in this chapter). Shops line the streets leading to the market. Calle Real de Guadalupe has more shops than any other street.

CRAFTS

Casa de Artesanías   This fine showroom is in one of the city's old houses. Here you'll find such quality products as lined woolen vests and jackets, pillow covers, amber jewelry, and more. In back, a fine little museum shows costumes worn by villagers who live near San Cristóbal. It's open Tuesday to Saturday from 9am to 2pm and 5 to 8pm. Niños Héroes at Hidalgo. © 967/678-1180.

Central Market   The market buildings and the surrounding streets offer just about anything you need. The market in San Cristóbal is open every morning except Sunday (when each village has its own local market), and you'll probably enjoy observing the sellers as much as the things they sell. See "Photography Warning," earlier, regarding picture-taking here. The *mercado* is north of the Santo Domingo church, about 7 blocks from the *zócalo.* Av. Utrilla. No phone.

El Encuentro   You should find some of your best bargains here—at a minimum, you'll think that the price is fair. The shop carries many regional ritual items, such as new and used men's ceremonial hats, false saints, and iron rooftop adornments, plus many *huipils* and other textiles. It's open Monday to Saturday from 9am to 8pm. Calle Real de Guadalupe 63-A (between Diego Dujelay and Vicente Guerrero). © 967/678-3698.

La Alborada, Centro Desarrollo Comunitario DIF   At this government-sponsored school, young men and women from surrounding villages come to learn how to hook Persian-style rugs, weave fabric on foot looms, sew, make furniture, construct a house, cook, make leather shoes and bags, forge iron, and grow vegetables and trees for reforestation. Probably the most interesting crafts for the general tourist are the rugs and woven goods. Artisans from Temoaya in Mexico state learned rug making from Persians, who came to teach this skill in the 1970s. The Temoaya artisans, in turn, traveled to San Cristóbal to teach the craft to area students, who have taught others. The beautiful rug designs come from brocaded and woven designs used to decorate regional costumes. Visitors should stop at the entrance and ask for an escort. You can visit the various areas and see students at work, or go straight to the weavers. A small outlet at the entrance sells newly loomed fabric by the meter, leather bags, rugs, and baskets made at another school in the highlands. La Alborada is in a far southern suburb of the city off the highway to Comitán, to the right. To get there, take a cab. The school may be closed; midmorning is the likeliest time to find it open. Barrio María Auxiliadora. No phone.

La Galería   This lovely gallery beneath a cafe shows the work of well-known national and international painters. Also for sale are paintings and greeting cards by Kiki, the owner, a German artist who has found her niche in San Cristóbal. There are some Oaxacan rugs and pottery, plus unusual silver jewelry. It's open daily from 10am to 9pm. In the evenings, the bar opens and a jazz band plays from 9 to 10pm; afterward, another band plays Latin dance music. Hidalgo 3. © 967/678-1547.

Taller Leñateros   Paper making isn't all they do here, but it's executed with enough creativity and diversity of materials to warrant mention on that alone. This shop and workshop is a cooperative effort by six women: five Maya Indians and one American. They also make paper creations, silk screens, woodcuts, and binding, and they've put all those talents together to produce their own magazine, which has garnered quite a bit of attention in Mexico City. This shop is open Monday to Friday from 8:30am to 8pm, Saturday from 8:30am to 6pm; if you want to see paper being made, show up before 4pm. Flavio A. Paniagua 54. ℂ **967/678-5174.**

TEXTILES

Kun Kun SC   The name means "little by little." This cooperative society to aid local native artisans sells mostly ceramic tiles, weavings, and pottery. The weavings are made of locally produced wool that has been spun, dyed, and woven by members. Kun Kun holds workshops for artisans on such things as working with floor looms, which you can watch at the store. The tiles are wonderful. Also, if you're interested, ask about classes in using a backstrap loom. The workshop and store are open Monday to Saturday from 9am to 3pm. Another store, at Real de Guadalupe 55, closer to the plaza, stays open until 8pm. Real de Mexicanos 21. ℂ **967/678-1417.**

Plaza de Santo Domingo   The plazas around this church and the nearby Templo de Caridad fill with women in native garb selling their wares. Here you'll find women from Chamula weaving belts or embroidering, surrounded by piles of loomed woolen textiles from their village. Their inventory includes Guatemalan shawls, belts, and bags. There are also some excellent buys on Chiapanecan-made wool vests, jackets, rugs, and shawls, similar to those at Sna Jolobil (described below), if you take the time to look and bargain. Vendors arrive between 9 and 10am and begin to leave around 3pm. Av. Utrilla. No phone.

Sna Jolobil   Meaning "weaver's house" in Mayan, this place is in the former convent (monastery) of Santo Domingo, next to the Templo de Santo Domingo. Groups of Tzotzil and Tzeltal craftspeople operate the cooperative store, which has about 3,000 members who contribute products, help run the store, and share in the moderate profits. Their works are simply beautiful; prices are high, as is the quality. Be sure to take a look. It's open Monday to Saturday from 9am to 2pm and 4 to 6pm; credit cards are accepted. Calzada Lázaro Cárdenas 42 (Plaza Santo Domingo, between Navarro and Nicaragua). ℂ **967/678-2646.**

Unión Regional de Artesanías de los Altos   Also known as J'pas Joloviletic, this cooperative of weavers is smaller than Sna Jolobil (described above) and not as sophisticated in its approach to potential shoppers. It sells blouses, textiles, pillow covers, vests, sashes, napkins, baskets, and purses. It's near the market and worth looking around. Open Monday to Saturday from 9am to 2pm and 4 to 7pm, Sunday from 9am to 1pm. Av. Utrilla 43. ℂ **967/678-2848.**

WHERE TO STAY

Among the most interesting places to stay in San Cristóbal is the seminary-turned-hotel-museum **Casa Na-Bolom;** see "Attractions in Town," earlier in this chapter, for details.

Hotels in San Cristóbal are inexpensive by comparison with most of Mexico. You can do pretty well for $20 to $30 per night per double. Rates listed here include taxes. High season is Easter week, July, August, and December.

EXPENSIVE

Casa Felipe Flores ★★   This beautifully restored colonial house is the perfect setting for getting the feel of San Cristóbal. The patios and common rooms are relaxing and comfortable, and their architectural details are so very *coleto*. The guest rooms are nicely furnished and full of character. And they are warm in winter. The owners, Nancy and David Orr, are gracious people who enjoy sharing their appreciation and knowledge of Chiapas and the Maya. Their cook serves up righteous breakfasts.

Calle Dr. Felipe Flores 36, 29230 San Cristóbal de las Casas, Chi. ℂ/fax **967/678-3996**. www.felipeflores.com. 5 units. High season $77–$92 double. Rates include full breakfast. 10% service charge. No credit cards. **Amenities:** Tour info; laundry; library.

Hotel Casa Mexicana ★   Created from a large mansion, this beautiful hotel with a colonial-style courtyard offers comfortable lodging. Rooms, courtyards, the restaurant, and the lobby are decorated in modern-traditional Mexican style, with warm tones of yellow and red. The rooms are carpeted and come with two double beds or one king. They have good lighting, electric heaters, and spacious bathrooms. Guests are welcome to use the sauna, and inexpensive massages can be arranged. The hotel handles a lot of large tour groups; it can be quiet and peaceful one day and full and bustling the next. There is a new addition to the hotel across the street, but I like the doubles in the original section better. This hotel is 3 blocks north of the main plaza.

28 de Agosto 1 (at Utrilla), 29200 San Cristóbal de las Casas, Chi. ℂ **967/678-1348** or 967/678-0698. Fax 967/678-2627. www.hotelcasamexicana.com. 55 units. High season $80 double, $130 junior suite, $160 suite; low season $75 double, $120 junior suite, $130 suite. AE, MC, V. Free secure parking 1½ blocks away. **Amenities:** Restaurant; bar; sauna; tour info; room service until 10pm; massage; babysitting; overnight laundry. *In room:* TV, hair dryer on request.

MODERATE

Hotel Casavieja ★   The Casavieja is aptly named: It has a charming old feel that is San Cristóbal to a "T." Originally built in 1740, it has undergone restoration and new construction faithful to the original design in essentials such as wood-beam ceilings. One nod toward modernity is carpeted floors, a welcome feature on cold mornings. The rooms also come with electric heaters. Bathrooms vary, depending on what section of the hotel you're in, but all are adequate. The hotel's restaurant, Doña Rita, faces the interior courtyard, with tables on the patio and inside, and offers good food at reasonable prices. I recommend the *molcajete de pollo* (chicken and vegetables baked in a volcanic stone mortar). The hotel is 3½ blocks northeast of the plaza.

María Adelina Flores 27 (between Cristóbal Colón and Diego Dujelay), 29200 San Cristóbal de las Casas, Chi. ℂ/fax **967/678-6868** or 967/678-0385. www.casavieja.com.mx. 39 units. $60 double. AE, MC, V. Free parking. **Amenities:** Restaurant; bar; room service until 10:30pm; same-day laundry. *In room:* TV.

Hotel El Paraíso   For the independent traveler, this is a safe haven from the busloads of tour groups that can upset the atmosphere and service at other hotels. Rooms are small but beautifully decorated. They have comfortable beds with soft patchwork bedspreads and reading lights; some rooms even have a ladder to a loft holding a second bed. Bathrooms are small, too, but the plumbing is good. The entire hotel is decorated in terra cotta and blue, with beautiful wooden columns and beams supporting the roof. The hotel's restaurant, El Edén (see "Where to Dine," below) may be the best in town.

Av. 5 de Febrero 19, 29200 San Cristóbal de las Casas, Chi. ℂ **967/678-0085** or 967/678-5382. Fax 967/678-5168. www.hotelposadaparaiso.com. 14 units. $53 double. AE, MC, V. **Amenities:** Restaurant; bar; tour info; room service until 11pm; overnight laundry. *In room:* TV.

Hotel Rincón del Arco   This well-run hotel has comfortable rooms at a good price. The original section of the former colonial-era home surrounds a small interior patio and dates from 1650. Rooms in this part are spacious, with tall ceilings and carpet over hardwood floors. The adjacent new section looks out across a grass yard to the mountains and the valley. These rooms are nicely furnished, and the thick bedspreads come from the family factory, which you can visit next door. Some rooms have small balconies; all have fireplaces. There's a restaurant just behind the lobby. The only downside is that it's a bit of a walk from the main plaza (8 blocks NE).

Ejército Nacional 66 (at Av. Vicente Guerrero), 29220 San Cristóbal de las Casas, Chi. © **967/678-1313.** Fax 967/678-1568. hotel_rincon@hotmail.com. 50 units. $62 double. MC, V. Free parking. **Amenities:** Restaurant; room service; laundry. *In room:* TV.

INEXPENSIVE

Hotel Don Quijote   Rooms in this three-story hotel (no elevator) are small but quiet, cheerful, carpeted, and well lit. All have two double beds with reading lamps over them, tiled bathrooms, and plenty of hot water. The TVs actually carry English channels (uncommon for hotels in this price range). There's complimentary coffee in the mornings, and Internet access. It's 2½ blocks east of the plaza.

Cristóbal Colón 7 (near Real de Guadalupe), 29200 San Cristóbal de las Casas, Chi. © **967/678-0920.** Fax 967/678-0346. 24 units. $25 double. MC, V. Free secure parking 1 block away. *In room:* TV.

Hotel Palacio de Moctezuma   This three-story hotel is more open and lush with greenery than other hotels in this price range. Fresh-cut flowers tucked around tile fountains are its hallmark. The rooms have carpeting and modern tiled showers; many are quite large but, alas, can be cold in winter. The restaurant looks out on the interior courtyard. On the third floor is a solarium with comfortable tables and chairs and great city views. The hotel is 3½ blocks southeast of the main plaza.

Juárez 16 (at León), 29200 San Cristóbal de las Casas, Chi. © **967/678-0352** or 967/678-1142. Fax 967/678-1536. 42 units. $25 double. No credit cards. Free limited parking. **Amenities:** Restaurant. *In room:* TV, no phone.

Hotel Posada de los Angeles   This well-managed hotel offers good service and tidy rooms and public areas. Guest rooms come with either a single and a double bed or two double beds, and the well-kept bathrooms are modern; windows open onto a pretty courtyard with a fountain. The rooftop sun deck is a great siesta spot. Make sure that your reservation is for Posada de los Angeles.

Calle Francisco Madero 17, 29200 San Cristóbal de las Casas, Chi. © **967/678-1173** or 967/678-4371. Fax 967/678-2581. hmansion@sancristobal.podernet.com.mx. 20 units. $40 double. AE, MC, V. *In room:* TV.

Hotel Real del Valle   The Real del Valle is just off the main plaza. The 24 recently added rooms in the back three-story section have new bathrooms, big closets, and tile floors. In addition to a rooftop solarium, you'll find a small cafeteria and an upstairs dining room with a double fireplace.

Real de Guadalupe 14, 29200 San Cristóbal de las Casas, Chi. © **967/678-0680.** Fax 967/678-3955. hrvalle@mundomaya.com.mx. 36 units. $27–$32 double. No credit cards. **Amenities:** Restaurant; same-day laundry. *In room:* TV, no phone.

WHERE TO DINE

San Cristóbal is not known for its cuisine, but you can eat well at several restaurants. **El Fogón de Jovel** (see review below) is the place to try typical Chiapanecan fare. Some interesting local dishes include tamales, *butifarra* (a type of sausage), and *pox* (pronounced "posh"—the local firewater). For baked goods, try the **Panadería La Hojaldra,** Mazariegos and 5 de Mayo (© **967/678-4286**). It's open daily from 8am to 9:30pm. In addition to the restaurants listed below, consider making reservations for dinner at Casa Na-Bolom (see "Attractions in Town," earlier in this chapter).

MODERATE

El Edén ★★ INTERNATIONAL   This is a small, quiet restaurant where it is obvious that somebody who enjoys the taste of good food prepares the meals; just about anything except Swiss rarebit is good. The meats are especially tender, and the margaritas are especially dangerous (one is all it takes). Specialties include Swiss cheese fondue for two, Edén salad, and brochette. This is where locals go for a splurge. It's 2 blocks from the main plaza.

In the Hotel El Paraíso, Av. 5 de Febrero 19. © 967/678-5382. Breakfast $5; main courses $6–$15. AE, MC, V. Daily 8am–9pm.

El Fogón de Jovel CHIAPANECAN   The waiters here wear local costumes, and Guatemalan and Chiapanecan prints and folk art hang on the walls. The menu, which is available in English, explains each dish and regional drink. A basket of warm handmade tortillas with six filling condiments arrives before the meal. Among the specialties are corn soup, *mole chiapaneco,* pork or chicken *adobado* in a chile sauce, and *pipián,* a dish of savory chile-and-tomato sauce served over chicken. For a unique dessert, try the *changleta,* which is half of a sweetened, baked *chayote.* Cooking classes for small groups can be arranged, but make reservations well in advance. The restaurant is a block northwest of the plaza.

16 de Septiembre 11 (at Guadalupe Victoria/Real de Guadalupe). © 967/678-1153. Main courses $4–$9. No credit cards. Daily 12:30–10pm.

Madre Tierra INTERNATIONAL/VEGETARIAN   For vegetarians and meateaters alike, Madre Tierra is a good place for a cappuccino and pastry or an entire meal. The *comida corrida* is very filling; or try the chicken curry, lasagna, and fresh salads. The bakery specializes in whole-wheat breads, pastries, pizza by the slice, quiche, grains, granola, and dried fruit. The restaurant is in an old mansion with wood-plank floors, long windows looking onto the street, and tables covered in colorful Guatemalan *jaspe.* Madre Tierra is 3½ blocks south of the plaza.

Av. Insurgentes 19. © 967/678-4297. Main courses $4–$8; *comida corrida* (served after noon) $6. No credit cards. Restaurant daily 8am–9:45pm; bakery Mon–Sat 9am–8pm, Sun 9am–2pm.

La Paloma INTERNATIONAL/MEXICAN   La Paloma is San Cristóbal's newest, hippest restaurant and bar. I particularly like it in the evening, when the lighting shows off the modern design to best advantage. The menu has a lot of the classic Mexican dishes. For starters, I enjoyed the quesadillas cooked Mexico City style (small fried packets of *masa* stuffed with a variety of fillings). Don't make my mistake of trying to share them with your dinner companion; it will only lead to a quarrel over the last one. The *tampiqueña* (steak with an enchilada, guacamole, beans, and rice) is a good bet for a main course if you're hungry. Less ambitious appetites might go for the chicken in peanut sauce. Avoid the profiteroles.

Hidalgo 3. © 967/678-1547. Main courses $6–$12, MC, V. Daily 9am–11pm.

INEXPENSIVE

Café el Puente ★ MEXICAN/AMERICAN   El Puente is more than a cafe; it's a center for cultural activities where tourists and locals can converse, take Spanish classes, arrange a homestay, leave a message on the bulletin board, and send and receive faxes. Movies are presented nightly in a back courtyard and meeting room. The front courtyard holds a pleasant cafe, the kind of place where a Brandenburg concerto accompanies waffles for breakfast, and sub sandwiches or brown rice and vegetables for lunch. There is Mexican fare as well. The long bulletin board is well worth checking out if you're looking for a ride, a place to stay, or information on out-of-the-way destinations. It's 2½ blocks east of the plaza.

Real de Guadalupe 55 (between Diego Dujelay and Cristóbal Colón). No phone. Breakfast $2–$3; main courses $3–$7. No credit cards. Mon–Sat 8am–11pm, Sun 3–11pm.

Emiliano's Moustache *Finds* MEXICAN/TACOS   Like any right-thinking tourist, I initially avoided this place on account of its unpromising name and some cartoonlike *charro* (cowboy) figures by the door. But a conversation with some local folk tickled my sense of irony, and I overcame my prejudice. Sure enough, the place was crowded with *coletos* enjoying the restaurant's highly popular *comida corrida* and delicious tacos, and there wasn't a foreigner in sight. The daily menu is posted by the door; if it isn't appealing, you can choose from a menu of taco plates (a mixture of fillings cooked together and served with tortillas and a variety of hot sauces).

Crescencio Rosas 7. © 967/678-7246. Main courses $3–$6; *comida corrida* $3.50. No credit cards. Daily 8am–midnight.

Normita's MEXICAN   Normita's is famous for its *pozole*, a hearty chicken and hominy soup to which you add a variety of things. It also offers cheap, dependable, short-order Mexican mainstays. It's an informal "people's" restaurant; the open kitchen takes up one corner of the room, and tables sit in front of a large paper mural of a fall forest scene from some faraway place. It's 2 blocks southeast of the plaza.

Av. Juárez 6 (at Dr. José Flores). No phone. Breakfast $2–$2.50; *comida corrida* (served 1:30–7pm) $4; *pozole* $3; tacos $1. No credit cards. Daily 7am–11pm.

Restaurant Tuluc *Value* MEXICAN/INTERNATIONAL   A real bargain here is the popular *comida corrida*—it's delicious and filling. Tuluc also has that rarest of rarities in Mexico: a nonsmoking section. Other popular items are sandwiches and enchiladas. The house specialty is *filete Tuluc,* a beef filet wrapped around spinach and cheese served with fried potatoes and green beans; while not the best cut of meat, it's certainly priced right. The Chiapaneco breakfast is a filling quartet of juice, toast, two Chiapanecan tamales, and your choice of tea, coffee, cappuccino, or hot chocolate. Tuluc is 1½ blocks south of the plaza.

Av. Insurgentes 5 (between Cuauhtémoc and Francisco León). © 967/678-2090. Breakfast $2–$3; main courses $4–$5; *comida corrida* (served 2–4pm) $3.75. No credit cards. Daily 7am–10pm.

COFFEEHOUSES

Because Chiapas-grown coffee is highly regarded, it's natural to find a proliferation of coffeehouses here. Most are concealed in the nooks and crannies of San Cristóbal's side streets. Try **Café La Selva,** Crescencio Rosas 9 (© **967/678-7244**), for coffee served in all its varieties and brewed from organic beans. It's well known for its baked goods, and open daily from 9am to 11pm. A more traditional-style cafe, where locals meet to talk over the day's news, is **Café San Cristóbal,** Cuauhtémoc 1 (© **967/678-3861**). It's open Monday to Saturday from 9am to 10pm, Sunday from 9am to 9pm.

SAN CRISTOBAL AFTER DARK

San Cristóbal is blessed with a variety of species of nightlife, both resident and migratory. There is a lot of live music, which is surprisingly good and varied. The bars and restaurants are cheap—none charges a cover, and only one imposes a minimum. And they are easy to get to: You can hit all the places mentioned here without setting foot in a cab. Weekends are best, but on any night you'll find something going on.

You can start at **El Cocodrilo** (© **967/678-0871**), on the main plaza in the Hotel Santa Clara. It gets going the earliest, with a variety of live acts playing original arrangements of cover tunes—nothing with an edge. The music shuts down by 11pm for the sake of hotel guests. If you want to continue the mellow tone, walk down Real de Guadalupe to no. 34—when I've been there, **La Margarita** (no phone) has had some good guitarists playing Latin jazz and flamenco. The setting is casual, cozy, and softly lit. If you want to dance, you have two choices, both on Francisco Madero: **Las Velas** (© **967/678-7584**) at no. 14, and **Latino's** (© **967/ 678-2083**), across the way and down a bit at no. 23. Las Velas usually attracts a younger crowd, while people of all ages go to Latino's. Both have Latin music— salsa, merengue, and such. Sometimes it's live, sometimes canned.

4 Road Trips from San Cristóbal

For excursions to nearby villages, see "The Nearby Maya Villages & Country-side," earlier in this chapter; for destinations farther away, there are several local travel agencies. I recommend **ATC Travel and Tours,** Calle 5 de Febrero 15, at the corner of 16 de Septiembre (© **967/678-2550;** fax 967/678-3145), across from El Fogón restaurant. The agency has bilingual guides and reliable vehicles. ATC regional tours focus on birds and orchids, textiles, hiking, and camping.

Strangely, the cost of the trip includes a driver but does not necessarily include either a bilingual guide or guided information of any kind. You pay extra for those services, so when checking prices, be sure to flesh out the details.

RUINS OF TONINA ✦

Two hours from San Cristóbal is the impressive Maya city of Toniná (the name translates as "house of rocks"), 14km (9 miles) east of Ocosingo, midway between San Cristóbal and Palenque. The site dates from the Classic period and covers an area of at least 14km (9 sq. miles). Excavation and restoration have been relatively recent; otherwise, Toniná would be much more famous. If a Maya site can be called a sleeper, Toniná is it. Extensive excavations are under way here during the dry season.

As early as A.D. 350, Toniná emerged as a separate dynastic center of the Maya. It enjoys the distinction of having the last recorded date yet found (A.D. 909) on a small stone monument. The date marks the end of the Classic period. Another stone, dated A.D. 711, shows King Kan-Xul of Palenque (the younger brother of Chan-Bahlum and the son of King Pacal) as a royal prisoner of Ton-iná, with his hands tied but still wearing his royal headdress. Recently a huge stucco panel was unearthed picturing the Lord of Death holding Kan-Xul's head, confirming long-held suspicions that the king died at Toniná.

At the moment there are no signs to guide visitors through the site, so you're on your own. The caretaker can also show you around (in Spanish), after which a tip is appreciated. A typical guided tour to Toniná should include the services of a bilingual driver, a tour of the site, lunch, and a swim in the river. From November to February, you'll see thousands of swallows swarming near the ruins.

Near the ruins is a lodge called **Rancho Esmeralda,** which was invaded by residents of a neighboring village. Until the situation is resolved, the hotel is not functioning.

PALENQUE, BONAMPAK & YAXCHILAN

For information on these destinations, see the section on Palenque, earlier in this chapter.

CHINCULTIC RUINS, COMITAN & MONTEBELLO NATIONAL PARK

Almost 161km (100 miles) southeast of San Cristóbal, near the border with Guatemala, is the **Chincultic** archaeological site and Montebello National Park, with **16 multicolored lakes** and exuberant pine-forest vegetation. Seventy-four kilometers (46 miles) from San Cristóbal is **Comitán,** a pretty hillside town of 40,000 inhabitants known for its flower cultivation and a sugar cane–based liquor called *comitecho*. It's also the last big town along the Pan-American Highway before the Guatemalan border.

The Chincultic ruins, a late Classic site, have barely been excavated, but the main **acropolis,** high up against a cliff, is magnificent to see from below and is worth the walk up for the view. After passing through the gate, you'll see the trail ahead; it passes ruins on both sides. More unexcavated tree-covered ruins flank steep stairs leading up the mountain to the acropolis. From there, you can gaze upon distant Montebello lakes and miles of cornfields and forest. The paved road to the lakes passes six lakes, all different colors and sizes, ringed by cool pine forests; most have parking lots and lookouts. The paved road ends at a small restaurant. The lakes are best seen on a sunny day, when their famous brilliant colors are optimal.

Most travel agencies in San Cristóbal offer a daylong trip that includes the lakes, the ruins, lunch in Comitán, and a stop in the pottery-making village of Amatenango del Valle. If you're driving, follow Highway 190 south from San Cristóbal through the pretty village of Teopisca and then through Comitán; turn left at La Trinitaria, where there's a sign to the lakes. After the Trinitaria turnoff and before you reach the lakes, there's a sign pointing left down a narrow dirt road to the Chincultic ruins.

5 Tuxtla Gutiérrez

82km (51 miles) W of San Cristóbal; 277km (173 miles) S of Villahermosa; 242km (151 miles) NW of Ciudad Cuauhtémoc on the Guatemalan border

Tuxtla Gutiérrez (altitude 557m/1,838 ft.) is the boomtown capital of Chiapas. Coffee is the basis of the region's economy, along with recent oil discoveries. Tuxtla (pop. 300,000) is a business town; there are some attractive parts, but nothing to keep you here more than a day. For tourists, it's mainly a way station en route to San Cristóbal or Villahermosa. The main attraction in town is the zoo; the main attraction nearby is the magnificent Sumidero Canyon, which should not be missed.

ESSENTIALS

GETTING THERE & DEPARTING

BY PLANE Aviación de Chiapas, or **Aviacsa** (© **961/612-6880** or 961/612-8081) can get you to several cities in Mexico, but all flights go through Mexico City—even flights to Cancún, Chetumal, Mérida, Guatemala City, Villahermosa, and Oaxaca. **Aerocaribe,** a subsidiary of Mexicana (© **961/612-0020** or 961/612-5402), has five nonstop flights a day to and from Mexico City, with connections to all major cities, and nonstop service to Oaxaca and Villahermosa, Tapachula (on the Guatemalan border), and Veracruz.

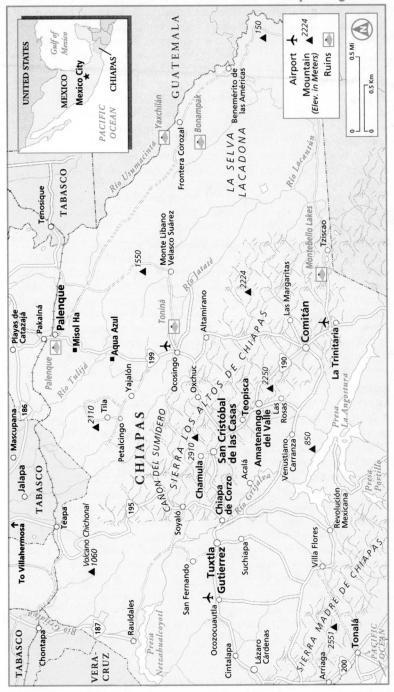

Due to its peculiar weather, Tuxtla has two airports: **Terán** and **Llano San Juan.** The airlines use one for half the year (Oct–Apr) and the other for the rest—although occasionally the schedule flip-flops. Be sure to double-check which airport you're departing from, and allow enough time to get there. The Terán airport is 8km (5 miles) from town; the Llano San Juan airport is 18km (11 miles). There is taxi and minivan service from both airports.

BY CAR   From Oaxaca you enter Tuxtla by Highway 190. From Villahermosa, or Palenque and San Cristóbal, you'll enter at the opposite end of town on the same highway from the east. In both cases, you'll arrive at the large main square at the center of town, La Plaza Cívica (see "City Layout," below).

From Tuxtla to Villahermosa, take Highway 190 east past the town of Chiapa de Corzo; soon you'll see a sign for Highway 195 north to Villahermosa. To San Cristóbal and Palenque, take Highway 190 east. The road from Tuxtla to San Cristóbal and Palenque is beautiful but tortuous. It's in good repair to San Cristóbal, but there may be bad spots between San Cristóbal and Palenque. The trip from Tuxtla to Villahermosa takes 8 hours by car; the scenery is beautiful.

BY BUS   The first-class bus station ((C) **961/612-2624**) is at the corner of streets 2 Norte and 2 Poniente (see "City Layout," below). All bus lines serving this station and the deluxe section across the street (Uno, Maya de Oro, Cristóbal Colón, Servicios Altos) belong to the same parent company, ADO. The main station sells tickets for all buses. All buses are air-conditioned and have bathrooms. There are two levels of first class; the first-class *económico* has less legroom. Then there's deluxe, which features a few extras: slightly better seats, better movies, and free coffee and soda. There are buses every half hour to San Cristóbal, eight buses a day to Villahermosa, three or four buses a day to Oaxaca, and five to Palenque. There's usually no need to buy a ticket ahead of time, except during holidays.

ORIENTATION

ARRIVING   The Llano San Juan airport is off Highway 190 west of town, about 40 minutes away; the Terán airport is off the same highway going east of town, about 15 minutes away. A *colectivo* (minivan) is much cheaper than a taxi if you can find one; they leave as soon as they are full. The ADO/Cristóbal Colón bus terminal is downtown.

VISITOR INFORMATION   The **Tourist Office** ((C) **01-800/280-3500** in Mexico, or 961/613-4499) is in the Secretaría de Fomento Económico building, formerly the Plaza de las Instituciones, on Avenida Central/Bulevar Domínguez, near the Hotel Bonampak Tuxtla. It's on the first floor of the plaza and is open Monday to Friday from 8am to 9pm. The staff at the information booth in front of the office can answer most questions. There are also information booths at the **international airport** (staffed when flights are due) and at the **zoo** (open Tues–Sun 9am–3pm and 6–9pm).

CITY LAYOUT   Tuxtla is laid out on a grid. The main street, **Avenida Central,** is the east-west axis and is the artery through town for Highway 190. In the west it is called **Bulevar Belisario Domínguez,** and in the east it becomes **Bulevar Angel Albino Corzo. Calle Central** is the north-south axis. The rest of the streets have names that include one number and two directions. This tells you how to get to the street. For example, to find the street 5 Norte Poniente (5 North West), you walk 5 blocks north from the center of town and turn west (which is left). To find 3 Oriente Sur, you walk 3 blocks east from the main square and turn south. When people indicate intersections, they can shorten the names because it's redundant. The bus station is at the corner of 2 Norte and 2 Poniente.

GETTING AROUND **Buses** to all parts of the city converge upon the Plaza Cívica along Calle Central. **Taxi** fares are higher here than in other regions.

FAST FACTS The local **American Express** representative is Viajes Marabasco, Plaza Bonampak, Loc. 4, Col. Moctezuma, near the tourist office (② **961/612-6998;** fax 961/612-4053). Office hours are Monday to Friday from 9am to 1:30pm and 3:30 to 6:30pm. The **telephone area code** is **961.** If you need medical help, the best **clinic** in town is Sanatorio Rojas, Calle 2 Sur Poniente 1847 (② **961/611-2079** or 961/612-5414).

TUXTLA'S MUSEUM & ZOO

Most travelers simply pass through Tuxtla on their way to San Cristóbal or Oaxaca. The excellent zoo and the Sumidero Canyon are the top sights, and you might also visit the Parque Madero and its anthropology museum.

Calzada de los Hombres Ilustres Tuxtla's cultural highlights cluster in this area, also referred to as the Parque Madero. The park also holds the **Regional Museum of Anthropology,** a botanical garden, a children's area, and the city theater. The museum features exhibits on the lifestyles of the people of Chiapas and some artifacts from the state's archaeological sites. In one short stop you can learn about Chiapas's past civilizations, its flora, and its present-day accomplishments. It also has a FONART (government crafts) shop and cafeteria.

11 Norte Oriente at 5 Oriente Norte. Park and botanical garden free. Museum $3.50; free on Sun. Museum Tues–Sun 9am–4pm; botanical garden daily 8:30am–5pm; children's area Tues–Sun 8am–8pm. The park is 15 blocks NW of the main plaza; catch a *colectivo* along Av. Central, or walk about 15 min. east along 5 Oriente Norte.

Miguel Alvarez del Toro Zoo (ZOOMAT) ⚇ Located in the forest called El Zapotal, ZOOMAT is one of the best zoos in Mexico. The collection of animals and birds indigenous to this area gives the visitor a tangible sense of what the wilds of Chiapas are like. The zoo keeps jaguars, howler monkeys, owls, and many more exotic animals in roomy cages that replicate their home terrain; the whole zoo is so deeply buried in vegetation that you can almost pretend you're in a natural habitat. Unlike at other zoos I've visited, the animals are almost always on view; many will come to the fence if you make a kissing noise.

Bulevar Samuel León Brinois, SE of downtown. No phone. Free admission; donations solicited. Tues–Sun 9am–5:30pm. The zoo is about 8km (5 miles) SE of downtown; catch a bus along Av. Central and at the Calzada.

SHOPPING

The government-operated **Casa de las Artesanías,** Bulevar Domínguez 2035 (② **961/612-2275**), is a shop and gallery. The two stories of rooms feature a fine, extensive collection of crafts grouped by region and type from throughout the state of Chiapas. It's open Monday to Saturday from 10am to 8pm.

WHERE TO STAY

As Tuxtla booms, the center of the hotel industry has moved out of town, west to Highway 190. As you come in from the airport, you'll notice the new motel-style hotels, such as the **Hotel Flamboyán, Palace Inn, Hotel Laganja,** and **La Hacienda.** All of these are more expensive than those listed here, which are in the heart of town.

Gran Hotel Humberto *Value* This older 10-story hotel is your best budget bet in Tuxtla. It's comfortable enough, with well-kept furnishings that appear to date from the 1950s. However, it isn't always an oasis of peace and quiet, especially on weekends, when church bells compete with the ninth-floor nightclub for the dubious honor of Noisiest Distraction. The location is ideal—it's in the center of town a half block from the Plaza Cívica restaurants and the Mexicana airline office, and 1½ blocks from the Cristóbal Colón bus station.

Av. Central 180, 29000 Tuxtla Gutiérrez, Chi. ℭ **961/612-2080.** Fax 961/612-9771. 112 units. $52 double. AE, MC, V. Free parking. **Amenities:** Restaurant; bar. *In room:* A/C, TV.

Hotel Bonampak Tuxtla   This large, sprawling hotel has a swimming pool, a tennis court, a travel agency, a boutique, a coffee shop, and a nice restaurant. The rooms facing the street are noisy, even with the air-conditioning on, but the interior rooms are blissfully quiet. The hotel's coffee shop, one of the best in town, is often packed with locals and tourists. The extensive menu includes an economical *comida corrida.* It's on the outskirts of downtown, where Avenida 14 de Septiembre becomes Bulevar Domínguez.

Bulevar Domínguez 180, 29030 Tuxtla Gutiérrez, Chi. ℭ **961/613-2050.** 70 units. $74 double. AE, MC, V. Free secured parking. **Amenities:** Restaurant; bar; pool; travel agency; boutique; room service until midnight; laundry. *In room:* A/C, TV.

Hotel Esponda   In a city where inexpensive rooms are hard to come by, the nondescript five-story Esponda is a good choice. The brown, green, and yellow decor is a bit unsettling, but the rooms are satisfactory—they have one, two, or three double beds; showers (without doors or curtains); big closets; and powerful ceiling fans, but no air-conditioning. The hotel is 1 block from the Plaza Cívica, near the Cristóbal Colón bus station.

1 Poniente Norte 142, 29030 Tuxtla Gutiérrez, Chi. ℭ **961/612-0080.** Fax 961/612-9771. 50 units. $26 double. AE, MC, V. Free parking.

WHERE TO DINE

Tuxtla's main plaza, the **Plaza Cívica** (Av. Central at 1 Poniente), is actually two plazas separated by Avenida Central. Numerous restaurants, many of which serve customers outdoors under umbrella-shaded tables, border the plaza. The restaurants change names with frequency, so I won't recommend one over another. Just stroll the area and pick one that looks interesting, clean, and reasonably priced.

Las Pichanchas ⭐ *(Finds)* MEXICAN   No trip to Tuxtla Gutiérrez is complete without a meal at this colorfully decorated restaurant devoted to the regional food and drink of Chiapas. Inverted *pichanchas* (pots full of holes used to make *nixtamal masa* dough) hang on posts as lanterns. For a sampler plate, try the *platón de carnes frías* (cold meat platter, which includes local sausages, ham, cheese, and tortillas) or the *platón de botana regional* (a variety of hot tidbits). The cold meat platter and the especially tasty *butifarra* (sausage) both will feed two or three people nicely. Chiapan tamales are tastier and larger than those you may have eaten elsewhere, so I heartily recommend that you try them at least once.

Av. Central Oriente 837. ℭ **961/612-5351.** Tamales $1–$2; main courses $5–$8. AE, DC, MC, V. Daily noon–midnight (live marimba music 2:30–5:30pm and 8:30–11:30pm; patio dinner show Tues–Sun at 9pm). Closed Jan 1 and the 2 days following Easter. From the Hotel Humberto in the center of town, walk 6–8 blocks S; you'll find the restaurant on the left.

ROAD TRIPS FROM TUXTLA GUTIERREZ: CHIAPA DE CORZO & THE SUMIDERO CANYON

The small town of **Chiapa de Corzo** is just off the highway to San Cristóbal, 13km (8 miles) from Tuxtla Gutiérrez. It's a 30-minute bus ride from the main square (buses leave every 15 min. in the morning and every 30 min. in the afternoon), or a 10- to 15-minute ride by *colectivo*—they leave every 10 minutes from the stand at the corner of 3 Oriente and 3 Sur and cost about $1.

Chiapa de Corzo has a small **museum** on the main square dedicated to the city's lacquer industry; an interesting church; a colonial fountain; and a small **pyramid,** somewhat restored and visible from the road. In the museum, you can often see women learning the regional craft of lacquer painting, and mask makers sometimes give carving demonstrations and lessons.

From this town you can embark on a spectacular trip to the **Canyon of El Sumidero** ★★. Boat rides through the canyon leave from the docks in Chiapa de Corzo when there are enough people (6–8). Cost per person is about $10. This is the best way to see the canyon. However, you can tour the canyon from the top by negotiating a ride along the canyon rim; the cost is around $50 for five people for a 2-hour ride. The easiest thing to do if you're coming from Tuxtla is to hire a taxi, but you might get a better deal in a van tour that agencies in town sometimes offer. Ask around when you arrive to see if such tours are available.

Appendix A:
The Yucatán in Depth

The Yucatán peninsula is a land unlike anywhere else on Earth. To begin with, it has a unique geology. The entire peninsula is a flat slab of limestone that millions of years ago absorbed the force of a giant meteor (the same one blamed for killing off the dinosaurs). The impact sent shock waves through the brittle limestone, fracturing it throughout, creating an immense network of fissures that drain all rainwater away from the surface. When driving through northern and central Yucatán, you don't see any rivers, lakes, or watercourses. The vast subterranean basin, which stretches for miles across the peninsula, is invisible but for the area's many *cenotes*—sinkholes or natural wells that exist nowhere else. Many are perfectly round vertical shafts that look like nothing else in nature (such as the Grand Cenote at Chichén Itzá); others retain a partial roof, often perforated by tree roots—quiet, dark, and cool, they are the opposite of the warm, brightly lit outside world. To the Maya, they were sacred passageways to the underworld.

Those curious people, the Maya, are another fascinating part of this land. The ancients left behind elegant and mysterious ruins that, despite all that we now know, seem to defy interpretation. Almost every year, archaeological excavation leads to the discovery of more ruins, adding to a growing picture of an urban civilization that thrived in an area where only scantily populated jungle now exists. What can we make of such a civilization? What value do we accord the Maya among the other lost civilizations of the ancient world? Even this is unclear, but the art and architecture they left behind are stunning expressions of a rich and complex worldview.

Then there was the arrival of the Spaniards, in the early 1500s—an event that in hindsight seems almost apocalyptic. Military conquest and old-world diseases decimated the native population. A new social order predicated on a starkly different religion rose in place of the old one. Through all of this, the Maya held on to their language but lost most of the living memory of their pre-Hispanic ways. What they retained they cloaked in the language of myth and legend, and, with this, formed a rough synthesis of old and new. They selectively appropriated elements of the new religion that could help make sense of the world, and this process continues today in the many Maya communities that have native churches.

For these reasons and more, the Yucatán is a curious place; it may beckon you with its turquoise-blue waters and tropical Caribbean climate, but what will ultimately hold your attention is the unique character of the land and its people. There is no other place like it.

1 The Land & Its People

SOCIAL MORES   American and English travelers have often observed that Mexicans have a different conception of time, that life in Mexico obeys slower rhythms. This is true, and yet few observers go on to explain what the consequences of this are for the visitor to Mexico. This is a shame, because an imperfect appreciation of the difference causes a good deal of misunderstanding between tourists and locals.

Mexican acquaintances have asked me why Americans grin all the time. At first, I wasn't sure what to make of the question, and only gradually came to appreciate what was at issue. As the pace of life for Americans, Canadians, and others has quickened, they have come to skip some of the niceties of social interaction. When walking into a store, many Americans simply smile at a clerk and launch right into a question or request. The smile, in effect, replaces the greeting. In Mexico, it doesn't work that way. Mexicans misinterpret this American manner of greeting. After all, a smile when there is no context can be ambiguous; it can convey amusement, smugness, or superiority.

One of the most important pieces of advice I can offer travelers is this: Always give a proper greeting when addressing Mexicans. Don't try to abbreviate social intercourse. Mexican culture places a higher value on proper social form than on saving time. A Mexican must at least say *"¡Buenos días!"* or a quick *"¿Qué pasó?"* (or its equivalent), even to total strangers—a show of proper respect. When an individual meets a group of people, he will greet each person separately, which can take quite a while. For us, the polite thing would be to keep our interruption to a minimum and give a general greeting to all.

Mexicans, like most people, will consciously or subconsciously make quick judgments about individuals they meet. Most divide the world into the well raised and cultured *(bien educado),* and the poorly raised *(mal educado).* Unfortunately, many visitors are reluctant to try out their Spanish, preferring to keep exchanges to a minimum. Don't do this. To be categorized as a foreigner isn't a big deal. What's important in Mexico is to be categorized as one of the cultured foreigners and not one of the barbarians.

TODAY'S MAYA CULTURE & PEOPLE   As with lowlanders elsewhere in Mexico, Yucatecans are warm and friendly, and they show little reserve. Entering into conversation with them could not be easier. In the peninsula's interior, you might find people who are unexpectedly reticent, but most likely these are Maya Indians who aren't comfortable speaking Spanish. It may come as a surprise that you don't have to leave Cancún to meet the Maya; thousands come from the interior to work at hotels and restaurants in Cancún, and many can switch easily among Spanish, English, and Yukatek, the local Mayan language. More than 350,000 Maya living in the Yucatán's three states speak Yukatek, and most, especially men, speak Spanish, too.

Completely different are the estimated one million **Tabascan** and **Chiapan Maya,** who speak four different Mayan languages with dozens of dialects. The Maya groups around San Cristóbal de las Casas generally choose not to embrace outside cultures, preferring to live in small mountain hamlets and meeting only for ceremonies and market days. Their cloud-forest homeland in Chiapas is cold—in contrast to the predominant heat in the lowland regions of Tabasco

---

Impressions

. . . *we both learned that the Maya are not just a people of the past. Today, they live in their millions in Mexico, Guatemala, Belize, and western Honduras, still speaking one of the 35 Mayan languages as their native tongue. They continue to cultivate their fields and commune with their living world in spite of the fact that they are encapsulated within a larger modern civilization whose vision of reality is often alien to their own.*
    —Linda Schele and David Freidel, *A Forest of Kings* (1990)

and the Yucatán Peninsula. They, too, live much as their ancestors did, but with beliefs distinct from their peninsular relatives.

THE YUCATAN'S GEOGRAPHY   The Yucatán is edged by the dull aquamarine Gulf of Mexico on the west and north, and the clear cerulean blue Caribbean Sea on the east. The peninsula covers almost 134,400 sq. km (84,000 sq. miles), with nearly 1,600km (1,000 miles) of shoreline. Most terrain is porous limestone, with thin soil supporting a primarily low, scrubby jungle. There are almost no surface rivers; instead, rainwater filters through the limestone into underground rivers.

The only sense of height comes from the hills along the western shores of Campeche, rising inland to the border with Yucatán state. These are the Puuc Hills, less than 300m (1,000 ft.) high at their highest. The highways undulate a bit as you go inland, and south of Ticul there's a rise in the highway that provides a marvelous view of the "valley" and the misty Puuc hills lining the horizon.

NATURAL LIFE & PROTECTED AREAS   The Yucatán state's nature preserves include the 118,000-acre **Río Lagartos Wildlife Refuge** north of Valladolid—where you'll find North America's largest flock of nesting flamingos—and the 14,000-plus acre **Celestún Wildlife Refuge,** which harbors most of the flamingos during non-nesting season. The state also has incorporated nature trails into the archaeological site of **Dzibilchaltún,** north of Mérida.

In 1989, the Campeche state set aside 178,699 acres in the **Calakmul Biosphere Reserve** that it shares with Guatemala. The area includes the ruins of Calakmul, as well as acres of thick jungle.

Quintana Roo's protected areas are some of the region's most beautiful, wild, and important. In 1986, the state ambitiously set aside the 1.3 million–acre **Sian Ka'an Biosphere Reserve,** conserving a significant part of the coast in the face of development south of Tulum. **Isla Contoy,** also in Quintana Roo, off the coast of Isla Mujeres and Cancún, is a beautiful island refuge for hundreds of birds, turtles, plants, and other wildlife. And in 1990, the 150-acre **Jardín Botánico,** south of Puerto Morelos, opened to the public. Along with the Botanical Garden at Cozumel's Chankanaab Lagoon, it gives visitors an idea of the biological importance of Yucatán's lengthy shoreline: Four of Mexico's eight marine turtle species—loggerhead, green, hawksbill, and leatherback—nest on Quintana Roo's shores, and more than 600 species of birds, reptiles, and mammals have been counted.

2 A Look at the Past

PRE-HISPANIC CIVILIZATIONS

The earliest "Mexicans" were Stone Age hunter-gatherers coming from the north, descendants of a race that had crossed the Bering Strait and reached North America around 12000 B.C. They arrived in what is now Mexico by 10000 B.C. Sometime between 5200 and 1500 B.C., in what is known as the **Archaic period,** they began practicing agriculture and domesticating animals.

Dateline

- 10,000–1500 B.C. Archaic period: Hunting and gathering; later, the dawn of agriculture: domestication of chiles, corn, beans, avocado, amaranth, and pumpkin. Mortars and pestles in use. Stone bowls and jars, obsidian knives, and open-weave basketry developed.
- 1500 B.C.–A.D. 300 Pre-Classic period: Olmec culture develops large-scale

continues

THE PRE-CLASSIC PERIOD
(1500 B.C.–A.D. 300) Eventually, agriculture improved to the point that it could provide enough food to support large communities and enough surplus to free some of the population from agricultural work. A civilization emerged that we call the **Olmec**—an enigmatic people who settled the lower Gulf Coast in what is now Tabasco and Veracruz. Anthropologists regard them as the mother culture of Mesoamerica because they established a pattern for later civilizations in a wide area stretching from northern Mexico into Central America. The Olmec developed the basic calendar used throughout the region, established principles of urban layout and architecture, and originated the cult of the jaguar and the sacredness of jade. They may also have bequeathed the sacred ritual of "the ball game"—a universal element of Mesoamerican culture.

One intriguing feature of the Olmec was the carving of colossal stone heads. We still don't know what purposes these heads served, but they were immense projects; the basalt from which they were sculpted was mined miles inland and transported to the coast, probably by river rafts. The heads share a rounded, baby-faced look, marked by a peculiar, high-arched lip—a "jaguar mouth"—that is an identifying mark of Olmec sculpture.

The Maya civilization began developing in the pre-Classic period, around 500 B.C. Our understanding of this period is only sketchy, but Olmec influences are apparent everywhere. The Maya perfected the Olmec calendar and, somewhere along the way, developed their ornate system of hieroglyphic writing and their early architecture. Two other civilizations also began their rise to prominence around this time: the people of Teotihuacán, just north of present-day

settlements and irrigation methods. Cities develop for the first time. Olmec influence spreads over other cultures in the Gulf Coast, central and southern Mexico, Central America, the lower Mexican Pacific Coast, and the Yucatán. Several cities in central and southern Mexico begin the construction of large ceremonial centers and pyramids. The Maya develop several city-states in Chiapas and Central America.

- **1000–900 B.C.** Olmec San Lorenzo center is destroyed; they begin anew at La Venta.
- **600 B.C.** La Venta Olmec cultural zenith.
- **A.D. 300–900** Classic period: Broad influence of Teotihuacán culture and the establishment there of a truly cosmopolitan urbanism. Satellite settlements spring up across central Mexico and as far away as Guatemala. Trade and cultural interchange with the Maya and the Zapotec flourish. The Maya perfect the calendar and improve astronomical calculations. They build grandiose cities at Palenque, Calakmul, and Cobá, and in Central America.
- **683** Maya King Pacal is buried in an elaborate tomb below the Palace of the Inscriptions at Palenque.
- **800** Bonampak battle/victory mural is painted.
- **900** Post-Classic period begins: More emphasis is placed on warfare in central Mexico. The Toltec culture emerges at Tula and replaces Teotihuacán as the dominant city of central Mexico. Toltec influence spreads to the Yucatán, forming the culture of the Itzaés, who become the rulers of Chichén Itzá.
- **909** This is the date on a small monument at Toniná (near San Cristóbal de las Casas), the last Long Count date yet discovered, symbolizing the end of the Classic Maya era.
- **1156–1230** Tula, the Toltec capital, is abandoned.
- **1325–1470** Aztec capital Tenochtitlán is founded; Aztecs begin military campaigns in the Valley of Mexico and

continues

Mexico City, and the Zapotec of Monte Albán, in the valley of Oaxaca.

THE CLASSIC PERIOD (A.D. 300–900)

The flourishing of these three civilizations marks the boundaries of this period—the heyday of pre-Columbian Mesoamerican artistic and cultural achievements. These include the pyramids and palaces in Teotihuacán; the ceremonial center of Monte Albán; and the stelae and temples of Palenque, Bonampak, and the Tikal site in Guatemala. Beyond their achievements in art and architecture, the Maya made significant discoveries in science, including the use of the zero in mathematics and a complex calendar with which the priests could predict eclipses and the movements of the stars for centuries to come.

The inhabitants of **Teotihuacán** (100 B.C.–A.D. 700—near present-day Mexico City) built a city that, at its zenith, is thought to have had 100,000 or more inhabitants covering 14 sq. km (9 sq. miles). It was a well-organized city, built on a grid with streams channeled to follow the city's plan. Different social classes, such as artisans and merchants, were assigned to specific neighborhoods. Teotihuacán exerted tremendous influence as far away as Guatemala and the Yucatán Peninsula. Its feathered serpent god, later known as **Quetzalcoatl,** became part of the pantheon of many succeeding cultures, including the Toltecs, who brought the cult to the Yucatán where the god became known as Kukulkán. The ruling classes were industrious, literate, and cosmopolitan. The beautiful sculpture and ceramics of Teotihuacán display a highly stylized and refined aesthetic whose influences can be seen clearly in objects of Maya and Zapotec origin. Around the 7th century, the city was abandoned for unknown reasons. Who these people were and where they went remains a mystery.

then thrust farther out, subjugating the civilizations of the Gulf Coast and southern Mexico.

- **1516** Gold found on Cozumel during aborted Spanish expedition of Yucatán Peninsula arouses interest of Spanish governor in Cuba, who sends Juan de Grijalva on an expedition, followed by another, led by Hernán Cortez.

- **1518** Spaniards first visit what is today Campeche.

- **1519** Conquest of Mexico begins: Hernán Cortez and troops make their way along Mexican coast to present-day Veracruz.

- **1521** Conquest is complete after Aztec defeat at Tlatelolco.

- **1521–24** Cortez organizes Spanish empire in Mexico and begins building Mexico City on the ruins of Tenochtitlán.

- **1524–35** Cortez is removed from power, and royal council governs New Spain.

- **1526** King of Spain permits Francisco Montejo to colonize the Yucatán.

- **1535–1821** Viceregal period: 61 viceroys appointed by King of Spain govern Mexico. Control of much of the land ends up in the hands of the church and the politically powerful. A governor who reports to the king rather than to viceroys leads the Yucatán.

- **1542** Mérida is established as capital of Yucatán Peninsula.

- **1546** The Maya rebel and take control of the peninsula.

- **1559** French and Spanish pirates attack Campeche.

- **1562** Friar Diego de Landa destroys 5,000 Mayan religious stone figures and burns 27 hieroglyphic painted manuscripts at Maní, Yucatán. Maya, believed to be secretly practicing pre-Hispanic beliefs, endure widespread torture and death.

- **1810–21** War of Independence: Miguel Hidalgo starts movement for Mexico's independence from Spain but is executed within a year; leadership and goals change during the war years, but Agustín de Iturbide outlines a compromise between monarchy and republic.

continues

THE POST-CLASSIC PERIOD (A.D. 900–1521)

Warfare became a more conspicuous activity of the civilizations that flourished in this period. Social development was impressive but not as cosmopolitan as the Maya, Teotihuacán, and Zapotec societies. In central Mexico, a people known as the **Toltec** established their capital at Tula in the 10th century. They were originally one of the barbarous hordes of Indians that periodically migrated from the north. At some stage in their development, the Toltec were influenced by remnants of Teotihuacán culture and adopted the feathered serpent Quetzalcoatl as their god. They also revered a god known as **Tezcatlipoca,** or "smoking mirror," who later became a god of the Aztecs. The Toltec maintained a large military class divided into orders symbolized by animals. At its height, Tula may have had 40,000 people, and it spread its influence across Mesoamerica. By the 13th century, however, the Toltec had exhausted themselves, probably in civil wars and in battles with the invaders from the north.

During this period, the Maya built beautiful cities near the Yucatán's Puuc hills. The regional architecture, called **Puuc style,** is characterized by elaborate exterior stonework appearing above door frames and extending to the roofline. Examples of this architecture, such as the Codz Poop at Kabah and the palaces at Uxmal, Sayil, and Labná, are beautiful and quite impressive. Associated with the cities of the Puuc region was Chichén Itzá, ruled by the Itzaés. This metropolis evidences strong Toltec influences in its architectural style as well as the cult of the plumed-serpent god, Kukulkán.

The precise nature of this Toltec influence is a subject of debate. But there is an intriguing myth in central Mexico that tells how Quetzalcoatl quarrels with Tezcatlipoca and through trickery is shamed by his rival

- **1822** First Empire: Iturbide ascends throne as Emperor of Mexico, loses power after a year, and loses life in an attempt to reclaim throne.
- **1824–64** Early Republic period, characterized by almost perpetual civil war between federalists and centralists, conservatives and liberals, culminating in the victory of the liberals under Juárez.
- **1864–67** Second Empire: The French invade Mexico in the name of Maximilian of Austria, who is appointed Emperor of Mexico. Juárez and liberal government retreat to the north and wage war with the French forces. The French finally abandon Mexico and leave Maximilian to be defeated and executed by the Mexicans.
- **1847–66** War of the Castes in the Yucatán: Poverty and hunger cause the Maya to revolt and gain control of half of the peninsula before being defeated by army. Strife lasts well into the 20th century.
- **1872–76** Juárez dies, and political struggles ensue for the presidency.
- **1877–1911** Porfiriato: Porfirio Díaz, president/dictator of Mexico for 33 years, leads country to modernization by encouraging foreign investment in mines, oil, and railroads. Mexico witnesses the development of a modern economy and a growing disparity between rich and poor. Social conditions, especially in rural areas, become desperate.
- **1911–17** Mexican Revolution: Francisco Madero drafts revolutionary plan. Díaz resigns. Leaders jockey for power during period of great violence, national upheaval, and tremendous loss of life.
- **1917–40** Reconstruction: Present constitution of Mexico is signed; land and education reforms are initiated and labor unions strengthened; Mexico expropriates oil companies and railroads. Pancho Villa, Zapata, and presidents Obregón and Carranza are assassinated.
- **1940** Mexico enters period of political stability and makes tremendous economic progress. Quality of life improves, although problems of corruption, inflation, national health,

continues

into leaving Tula, the capital of the Toltec empire. He leaves heading eastward towards the morning star, vowing someday to return. In the language of myth, this could be a shorthand telling of an actual civil war between two factions in Tula, each led by the priesthood of a particular god. Could the losing faction have migrated to the Yucatán and formed the ruling class of Chichén Itzá? Perhaps. We do know for certain that this myth of the eventual return of Quetzalcoatl became, in the hands of the Spanish, a powerful weapon of conquest.

THE CONQUEST

In 1517, the first Spaniards arrived in Mexico and skirmished with Maya Indians off the coast of the Yucatán Peninsula. One of the fledgling expe-

and unresolved land and agricultural issues continue.

- 1974 Quintana Roo achieves statehood and Cancún opens to tourism.
- 1994–97 Mexico, Canada, and the United States sign the North American Free Trade Agreement (NAFTA). An Indian uprising in Chiapas sparks countrywide protests over government policies concerning land distribution, bank loans, health, education, and voting and human rights.
- 1999 The governor of Quintana Roo goes into hiding after accusations of corruption and ties to drug money.
- 2000 Mexico elects Vicente Fox of the PAN party president.
- 2002 The PAN party wins the governorship of the Yucatán.
- 2003 Yucatán tourism recovers after the drop in the 2001–2002 season.

ditions ended in a shipwreck, leaving several Spaniards stranded as prisoners of the Maya. The Spanish sent out another expedition, under the command of **Hernán Cortez,** which landed on Cozumel in February 1519. Cortez inquired about the gold and riches of the interior, and the coastal Maya were happy to describe the wealth and splendor of the Aztec empire in central Mexico. Cortez promptly disobeyed all orders of his superior, the governor of Cuba, and sailed to the mainland.

Cortez arrived when the Aztec empire was at the height of its wealth and power. **Moctezuma II** ruled over the central and southern highlands and extracted tribute from lowland peoples. His greatest temples were literally plated with gold and encrusted with the blood of sacrificial captives. Moctezuma was a fool, a mystic, and something of a coward. Despite his wealth and military power, he dithered in his capital at Tenochtitlán, sending messengers with gifts and suggestions that Cortez leave. Meanwhile, Cortez blustered and negotiated his way into the highlands, always cloaking his real intentions. Moctezuma, terrified, convinced himself that Cortez was in fact the god Quetzalcoatl making his long-awaited return. By the time the Spaniards arrived in the Aztec capital, Cortez had gained some ascendancy over the lesser Indian states that were resentful tributaries to the Aztec. In November 1519, Cortez confronted Moctezuma and took him hostage in an effort to leverage control of the empire.

In the middle of Cortez's dangerous game of manipulation, another Spanish expedition arrived with orders to end Cortez's authority over the mission. Cortez hastened to meet the rival's force and persuade them to join his own. In the meantime, the Aztec chased the garrison out of Tenochtitlán, and either they or the Spaniards killed Moctezuma. For the next year and a half, Cortez laid siege to Tenochtitlán, with the help of rival Indians and a decimating epidemic of smallpox, to which the Indians had no resistance. In the end, the Aztec capital fell, and when it did, all of central Mexico lay at the feet of the conquistadors.

The Spanish Conquest started as a pirate expedition by Cortez and his men, unauthorized by the Spanish crown or its governor in Cuba. The Spanish king legitimized Cortez following his victory over the Aztec and ordered the forced conversion to Christianity of this new colony, to be called **New Spain.** Guatemala and Honduras were explored and conquered, and by 1540, the territory of New Spain included possessions from Vancouver to Panama. In the 2 centuries that followed, Franciscan and Augustinian friars converted millions of Indians to Christianity, and the Spanish lords built huge feudal estates on which the Indian farmers were little more than serfs. The silver and gold that Cortez looted made Spain the richest country in Europe.

THE COLONIAL PERIOD

Hernán Cortez set about building a new city upon the ruins of the old Aztec capital. To do this he collected from the Indians the tributes once paid to the Aztec emperor, much of it rendered in labor. This arrangement, in one form or another, became the basis for the construction of the new colony. But diseases brought by the Spaniards devastated the native population over the next century and drastically reduced the pool of labor.

Over the 3 centuries of the colonial period, Spain became rich from New World gold and silver, chiseled out by Indian labor. The colonial elite built lavish homes in Mexico City and in the countryside. They filled their homes with ornate furniture, had many servants, and adorned themselves in imported velvets, satins, and jewels.

A new class system developed. Those born in Spain considered themselves superior to the *criollos* (Spaniards born in Mexico). Those of other races and the *castas* (mixtures of Spanish and Indian, Spanish and African, or Indian and African) occupied the bottom rungs of society. It took great cunning to stay a step ahead of the avaricious Crown, which demanded increasing taxes and contributions from its fabled foreign conquests. Still, wealthy colonists prospered enough to develop an extravagant society.

However, discontent with the mother country simmered for years. In 1808, Napoléon invaded Spain and crowned his brother Joseph king in place of Charles IV. To many in Mexico, allegiance to France was out of the question; discontent reached the level of revolt.

INDEPENDENCE

The rebellion began in 1810, when **Father Miguel Hidalgo** gave the *grito,* a cry for independence, from his church in the town of Dolores, Guanajuato. The uprising soon became a full-fledged revolution, as Hidalgo and Ignacio Allende gathered an "army" of citizens and threatened Mexico City. Although Hidalgo ultimately failed and was executed, he is honored as "the Father of Mexican Independence." Another priest, José María Morelos, kept the revolt alive with several successful campaigns through 1815, when he, too, was captured and executed.

After the death of Morelos, prospects for independence were rather dim until the Spanish king who replaced Joseph Bonaparte decided to make social reforms in the colonies, which convinced the conservative powers in Mexico that they didn't need Spain after all. With their tacit approval, Agustín de Iturbide, then commander of royalist forces, changed sides and declared Mexico independent and himself emperor. Before long, however, internal dissension brought about the fall of the emperor, and Mexico was proclaimed a republic.

Political instability engulfed the young republic, which ran through a dizzying succession of presidents and dictators as struggles between federalists and centralists, and conservatives and liberals, divided the country. Moreover, Mexico waged a disastrous war with the United States and lost half its territory. A central figure was **Antonio López de Santa Anna,** who assumed the leadership of his country no fewer than 11 times. He probably holds the record for frequency of exile; by 1855 he was finally left without a political comeback and ended his days in Venezuela.

Political instability persisted, and the conservative forces, with some encouragement from Napoléon III, hit upon the idea of inviting in a Hapsburg to regain control. They found a willing volunteer in Archduke Maximilian of Austria, who accepted the position of Mexican emperor with the support of French troops. The rag-tag Mexican forces defeated the modern, well-equipped French force in a battle near Puebla (now celebrated annually as **Cinco de Mayo**). A second attempt was more successful, and Ferdinand Maximilian Joseph of Hapsburg became emperor. After 3 years of civil war, the French were finally induced to abandon the emperor's cause; Maximilian was captured and executed by a firing squad near Querétaro in 1867. His adversary and successor (as president of Mexico) was **Benito Juárez,** a Zapotec Indian lawyer and one of the great heroes of Mexican history. Juárez did his best to unify and strengthen his country before dying of a heart attack in 1872; his impact on Mexico's future was profound, and his plans and visions bore fruit for decades.

THE PORFIRIATO & THE REVOLUTION

A few years after Juárez's death, one of his generals, **Porfirio Díaz,** assumed power in a coup. He ruled Mexico from 1877 to 1911, a period now called the "Porfiriato." He stayed in power through repressive measures and by courting the favor of powerful nations. Generous in his dealings with foreign investors, Díaz became, in the eyes of most Mexicans, the archetypal *entreguista* (one who sells out his country for private gain). With foreign investment came the concentration of great wealth in few hands, and social conditions worsened.

In 1910, Francisco Madero called for an armed rebellion that became the **Mexican Revolution** ("La Revolución" in Mexico; the revolution against Spain is the "Guerra de Independencia"). Díaz was sent into exile; while in London, he became a celebrity at the age of 81, when he jumped into the Thames to save a drowning boy. He is buried in Paris. Madero became president, but **Victoriano Huerta** promptly betrayed and executed him. Those who had answered Madero's call responded again—the great peasant hero **Emiliano Zapata** in the south, and the seemingly invincible **Pancho Villa** in the central north, flanked by Alvaro Obregón and Venustiano Carranza. They eventually put Huerta to flight and began hashing out a new constitution.

For the next few years, the revolutionaries Carranza, Obregón, and Villa fought among themselves; Zapata did not seek national power, though he fought tenaciously for land for the peasants. Carranza, who was president at the time, betrayed and assassinated Zapata. Obregón finally consolidated power and probably had Carranza assassinated. He, in turn, was assassinated when he tried to break one of the tenets of the Revolution—no reelection. His successor, Plutarco Elias Calles, installed one puppet president after another, until **Lázaro Cárdenas** severed the puppeteer's strings and banished him to exile.

Until Cárdenas's election in 1934, the outcome of the Revolution remained in doubt. Cárdenas changed all that. He implemented massive redistribution of land and nationalized the oil industry. He instituted many reforms and gave shape to the ruling political party (now the **Partido Revolucionario Institucional,** or PRI) by bringing a broad representation of Mexican society under its banner and establishing mechanisms for consensus building. Most Mexicans practically canonize Cárdenas.

MODERN MEXICO

The presidents who followed were noted more for graft than for leadership. The party's base narrowed as many of the reform-minded elements were marginalized. Economic progress, a lot of it in the form of large development projects, became the PRI's main basis for legitimacy. In 1968, the government violently repressed a democratic student movement. Though the PRI maintained its grip on power, it lost all semblance of being a progressive party. In 1985, a devastating **earthquake in Mexico City** brought down many of the government's new, supposedly earthquake-proof buildings, exposing shoddy construction and the widespread government corruption that fostered it. There was heavy criticism, too, of the government's handling of the relief efforts. In 1994, a political and military **uprising in Chiapas** focused world attention on Mexico's great social problems. A new political force, the Zapatista National Liberation Army (EZLN, for Ejército Zapatista de Liberación Nacional), has skillfully publicized the plight of the peasant in today's Mexico.

In the years that followed, opposition political parties grew in power and legitimacy. Facing pressure and scrutiny from national and international organizations, and widespread public discontent, the PRI had to concede defeat in state and congressional elections throughout the '90s. Elements of the PRI pushed for, and achieved, reforms from within and greater political openness. This led to deep divisions between party activists, rancorous campaigns for party leadership, and even political assassination. The party began choosing its candidates through primaries instead of by appointment. But in the presidential elections of 2000, Vicente Fox of the opposition party PAN won by a landslide. In hindsight, there was no way that the PRI could have won in a fair election. For most Mexicans, a government under the PRI was all that they had ever known. Many voted for Fox just to see whether the PRI would let go of power. It did, and the transition ran smoothly thanks in large part to the outgoing president, Ernesto Zedillo, who was one of the PRI's reformers. Since then Mexico has sailed into the uncharted waters of coalition politics, with three main parties, PRI, PAN, and PRD. To their credit, the sailing has been much smoother than many observers predicted. But the real test will be weathering the economic slowdown that accompanied the downturn in the U.S. economy, and in carrying out the next presidential elections, in 2006.

3 Art & Architecture 101

Mexico's artistic and architectural legacy reaches back more than 3,000 years. Until the conquest of Mexico in A.D. 1521, art, architecture, politics, and religion were intertwined. Although the European conquest influenced the style and subject of Mexican art, this continuity remained throughout the colonial period.

PRE-HISPANIC FORMS

Mexico's **pyramids** were truncated platforms crowned with a temple. Many sites have circular buildings, such as El Caracol at Chichén Itzá, usually called the observatory and dedicated to the god of the wind. El Castillo at Chichén Itzá has 365 steps—one for every day of the year. The Temple of the Magicians at Uxmal has beautifully rounded and sloping sides. Evidence of building one pyramidal structure on top of another, a widely accepted practice, has been found throughout Mesoamerica.

Architects of many Toltec, Aztec, and Teotihuacán edifices alternated sloping panels *(talud)* with vertical panels *(tablero)*. Elements of this style occasionally show up in the Yucatán. Dzibanché, a newly excavated site near Lago Bacalar, in southern Quintana Roo state, has at least one temple with this characteristic. The true arch was unknown in Mesoamerica, but the Maya made use of the corbelled arch—a method of stacking stones that allows each successive stone to be cantilevered out a little farther than the one below it, until the two sides meet at the top, forming an inverted V.

The Olmec, considered the parent culture of Mesoamerica, built pyramids of earth. Unfortunately, little remains to tell us what their buildings looked like. The Olmec, however, left an enormous sculptural legacy, from small, intricately carved pieces of jade to 40-ton carved basalt rock heads.

Throughout Mexico, carved stone and mural art on pyramids served a religious and historic function rather than an ornamental one. **Hieroglyphs,** picture symbols etched on stone or painted on walls or pottery, functioned as the written language of the ancient peoples, particularly the Maya. By deciphering the glyphs, scholars allow the ancients to speak again, providing us with specific names to attach to rulers and their families, and demystifying the great dynastic histories of the Maya. For more on this, read *A Forest of Kings* (1990), by Linda Schele and David Freidel, and *Blood of Kings* (1986), by Linda Schele and Mary Ellen Miller. Good hieroglyphic examples appear in the site museum at Palenque.

Carving important historic figures on freestanding stone slabs, or **stelae,** was a common Maya commemorative device. Several are in place at Cobá; Calakmul has the most, and good examples are on display in the Museum of Anthropology in Mexico City and the archaeology museum in Villahermosa. **Pottery** played an important role, and different indigenous groups are distinguished by their different use of color and style. The Maya painted pottery with scenes from daily and historic life.

Pre-Hispanic cultures left a number of fantastic painted **murals,** some of which are remarkably preserved, such as those at Bonampak and Cacaxtla. Amazing stone murals or mosaics, using thousands of pieces of fitted stone to form figures of warriors, snakes, or geometric designs, decorate the pyramid facades at Uxmal and Chichén Itzá.

SPANISH INFLUENCE

With the arrival of the Spaniards, new forms of architecture came to Mexico. Many sites that were occupied by indigenous groups at the time of the conquest were razed, and in their place appeared Catholic churches, public buildings, and palaces for conquerors and the king's bureaucrats. In the Yucatán, churches at Izamal, Calkani, Santa Elena, and Muná rest atop former pyramidal structures. Indian artisans, who formerly worked on pyramidal structures, were recruited to build the new buildings, often guided by drawings of European buildings. Frequently left on their own, the indigenous artisans implanted traditional symbolism in the new buildings: a plaster angel swaddled in feathers, reminiscent of the god Quetzalcoatl, and the face of an ancient god surrounded by corn leaves. They used pre-Hispanic calendar counts—the 13 steps to heaven or the nine levels of the underworld—to determine how many florets to carve around the church doorway.

To convert the native populations, New World Spanish priests and architects altered their normal ways of teaching and building. Often before the church was built, an open-air atrium was constructed to accommodate large numbers of parishioners for services. *Posas* (shelters) at the four corners of churchyards were another architectural technique unique to Mexico, again to accommodate crowds. Because of the language barrier between the Spanish and the natives, church adornment became more explicit. Biblical tales came to life in frescoes splashed across church walls. Christian symbolism in stone supplanted that of pre-Hispanic ideas as the natives tried to make sense of it all. Baroque became even more baroque in Mexico and was dubbed **churrigueresque** or **ultrabaroque.** Exuberant and complicated, it combines Gothic, baroque, and plateresque elements.

Almost every village in the Yucatán Peninsula has the remains of **missions, monasteries, convents,** and **parish churches.** Many were built in the 16th century following the early arrival of Franciscan friars. Examples include the Mission of San Bernardino de Sisal in Valladolid; the fine altarpiece at Teabo; the folk-art *retablo* (altarpiece) at Calkani; the large church and convent at Mani with its retablos and limestone crucifix; the facade, altar, and central *retablo* of the church at Oxkutzcab; the 16-bell belfry at Ytholin; the baroque facade and altarpiece at Maxcanu; the cathedral at Mérida; the vast atrium and church at Izamal; and the baroque *retablo* and murals at Tabi.

When Porfirio Díaz became president in the late 19th century, the nation's art and architecture experienced another infusion of European sensibility. Díaz idolized Europe, and he commissioned a number of striking European-style public buildings, including many opera houses. He provided European scholarships to promising young artists who later returned to Mexico to produce Mexican subject paintings using techniques learned abroad.

THE ADVENT OF MEXICAN MURALISM

As the Mexican Revolution ripped the country apart between 1911 and 1917, a new social and cultural Mexico was born. In 1923, Minister of Education José Vasconcelos was charged with educating the illiterate masses. As one means of reaching people, he invited **Diego Rivera** and several other budding artists to paint Mexican history on the walls of the Ministry of Education building and the National Preparatory School in Mexico City. Thus began the tradition of painting murals in public buildings, which you will find in towns and cities throughout Mexico and the Yucatán.

4 Religion, Myth & Folklore

Mexico is predominantly Roman Catholic, a religion introduced by the Spaniards during the Conquest of Mexico. Despite its preponderance, the Catholic faith in many places in Mexico (Chiapas and Oaxaca, for example) has pre-Hispanic undercurrents. You need only visit the *curandero* section of a Mexican market (where you can purchase copal, an incense agreeable to the gods; rustic beeswax candles, a traditional offering; the native species of tobacco used to ward off evil; and so on), or attend a village festivity featuring pre-Hispanic dancers, to understand that supernatural beliefs often run parallel with Christian ones.

Mexico's complicated mythological heritage from pre-Hispanic religion is full of images derived from nature—the wind, jaguars, eagles, snakes, flowers, and more—all intertwined with elaborate mythological stories to explain the universe, climate, seasons, and geography. Most groups believed in an underworld (not a hell), usually containing nine levels, and a heaven of 13 levels—which is why the numbers 9 and 13 are so mythologically significant. The solar calendar count of 365 days and the ceremonial calendar of 260 days are significant as well. How one died determined one's resting place after death: in the underworld (*Xibalba* to the Maya), in heaven, or at one of the four cardinal points. For example, men who died in battle or women who died in childbirth went straight to the sun. Everyone else first had to make a journey through the underworld.

Gods & Goddesses

Each of the ancient cultures had its gods and goddesses, and while the names might not have crossed cultures, their characteristics or purposes often did. Chaac, the hook-nosed rain god of the Maya, was Tlaloc, the squat rain god of the Aztecs; Quetzalcoatl, the plumed-serpent god/man of the Toltecs, became Kukulkán of the Maya. The tales of the powers and creation of these deities make up Mexico's rich mythology. Sorting out the pre-Hispanic pantheon and beliefs in ancient Mexico can become an all-consuming study (the Maya alone had 166 deities), so here's a list of some of the most important gods:

Chaac   Maya rain god.

Ehécatl   Wind god whose temple is usually round; another aspect of Quetzalcoatl.

Itzamná   Maya god above all, who invented corn, cacao, and writing and reading.

Ixchel   Maya goddess of water, weaving, and childbirth.

Kinich Ahau   Maya sun god.

Kukulkán   Quetzalcoatl's name in the Yucatán.

Ometeotl   God/goddess, all-powerful creator of the universe, and ruler of heaven, earth, and the underworld.

Quetzalcoatl   A mortal who took on legendary characteristics as a god (or vice versa). When he left Tula in shame after a night of succumbing to temptations, he promised to return. He reappeared in the Yucatán. He is also symbolized as Venus, the moving star, and Ehécatl, the wind god. Quetzalcoatl is credited with giving the Maya cacao (chocolate) and teaching them how to grow it, harvest it, roast it, and turn it into a drink with ceremonial and magical properties.

Tlaloc   Aztec rain god.

5 Food & Drink

Authentic Mexican food differs quite dramatically from what is frequently served in the United States under that name. For many travelers, Mexico will be new and exciting culinary territory. Even grizzled veterans will be pleasantly surprised by the wide variation in specialties and traditions offered from region to region.

Despite regional differences, some generalizations can be made. Mexican food usually isn't pepper-hot when it arrives at the table (though many dishes must have a certain amount of piquancy, and some home cooking can be very spicy, depending on a family's or chef's tastes). Chiles and sauces add piquant flavor after the food is served; you'll never see a table in Mexico without one or both of these condiments. Mexicans don't drown their cooking in cheese and sour cream, a la Tex-Mex, and they use a great variety of ingredients. But the basis of Mexican food is simple—tortillas, beans, chiles, squash, and tomatoes—the same as it was centuries ago, before the Europeans arrived.

THE BASICS

TORTILLAS   Traditional tortillas are made from corn that's boiled in water and lime, and then ground into *masa* (a grainy dough), patted and pressed into thin cakes, and cooked on a hot griddle known as a *comal*. In many households, the tortilla takes the place of fork and spoon; Mexicans merely tear them into wedge-shaped pieces, which they use to scoop up their food. Restaurants often serve bread rather than tortillas because it's easier, but you can always ask for tortillas. A more recent invention from northern Mexico is the flour tortilla, which is seen less frequently in the rest of Mexico.

ENCHILADAS   The tortilla is the basis of several Mexican dishes, but the most famous of these is the enchilada. The original name for this dish would have been *tortilla enchilada,* which simply means a tortilla dipped in a chile sauce. In like manner, there's the *entomatada* (tortilla dipped in a tomato sauce) and the *enfrijolada* (a bean sauce). The enchilada began as a very simple dish: A tortilla is dipped in chile sauce (usually with ancho chile) and then into very hot oil, and then is quickly folded or rolled on a plate and sprinkled with chopped onions and a little *queso cotija* (crumbly white cheese) and served with a few fried potatoes and carrots. You can get this basic enchilada in food stands across the country. I love them, and if you come across them in your travels, give them a try. In restaurants you get the more elaborate enchilada, with different fillings of cheese, chicken, pork, or even seafood, and sometimes in a casserole.

TACOS   A taco is anything folded or rolled into a tortilla, and sometimes a double tortilla. The tortilla can be served either soft or fried. *Flautas* and *quesadillas* are species of tacos. For Mexicans, the taco is the quintessential fast food, and the taco stand *(taquería)*—a ubiquitous sight—is a great place to get a filling meal. See the section "Eating Out: Restaurants, *Taquerías* & Tipping," later in this chapter for information on taquerías.

FRIJOLES   An invisible "bean line" divides Mexico: It starts at the Gulf Coast in the southern part of the state of Tamaulipas and moves inland through the eastern quarter of San Luis Potosí and most of the state of Hidalgo, then goes straight through Mexico City and Morelos and into Guerrero, where it curves slightly westward to the Pacific. To the north and west of this line, the pink bean known as the *flor de mayo* is the staple food; to the south and east, including all of the Yucatán, the standard is the black bean.

In private households, beans are served at least once a day and, among the working class and peasantry, with every meal, if the family can afford it. Mexicans almost always prepare beans with a minimum of condiments—usually just a little onion and garlic and perhaps a pinch of herbs. Beans are meant to be a contrast to the heavily spiced dishes. Sometimes they are served at the end of a meal with a little Mexican-style sour cream.

Mexicans often fry leftover beans and serve them on the side as *frijoles refritos.* "Refritos" is usually translated as refried, but this is a misnomer—the beans are fried only once. The prefix "re" actually means "well" (as in thoroughly).

TAMALES   You make a tamal by mixing corn masa with a little lard, adding one of several fillings—meats flavored with chiles (or no filling at all)—then wrapping it in a corn husk or in the leaf of a banana or other plant, and finally steaming it. Every region in Mexico has its own traditional way of making tamales. In some places, a single tamal can be big enough to feed a family, while in others they are barely 3 inches long and an inch thick.

CHILES   Many kinds of chile peppers exist, and Mexicans call each of them by one name when they're fresh and another when they're dried. Some are blazing hot with only a mild flavor; some are mild but have a rich, complex flavor. They can be pickled, smoked, stuffed, stewed, chopped, and used in an endless variety of dishes.

MEALTIME

MORNING   The morning meal, known as *el desayuno,* can be something light, such as coffee and sweet bread, or something more substantial: eggs, beans, tortillas, bread, fruit, and juice. It can be eaten early or late and is always a sure bet in Mexico. The variety and sweetness of the fruits is remarkable, and you can't go wrong with Mexican egg dishes.

MIDAFTERNOON   The main meal of the day, known as *la comida,* is eaten between 2 and 4pm. Stores and businesses close, and most people go home to eat and perhaps take a short afternoon siesta before going about their business. The first course is the *sopa,* which can be either soup *(caldo)* or rice *(sopa de arroz)* or both; then comes the main course, which ideally is a meat or fish dish prepared in some kind of sauce and served with beans, followed by dessert.

EVENING   Between 8 and 10pm, most Mexicans have a light meal called *la cena.* If eaten at home, it is something like a sandwich, bread and jam, or perhaps a couple of tacos made from some of the day's leftovers. At restaurants, the most common thing to eat is *antojitos* (literally, "little cravings"), a general label for light fare. Antojitos include tostadas, tamales, tacos, and simple enchiladas, and are big hits with travelers. Large restaurants offer complete meals as well. In the Yucatán, antojitos include *papadzules* (a species of enchilada filled with hard-boiled egg), *sincronizadas* (small tostadas), and *panuchos* (fried tortillas filled with bean paste and topped with *cochinita pibil* and marinated onions).

EATING OUT: RESTAURANTS, *TAQUERIAS* & TIPPING

First of all, I feel compelled to debunk the prevailing myth that the cheapest place to eat in Mexico is in the market. Actually, this is almost never the case. You can usually find better food at a better price without going more than 2 blocks out of your way. Why? Food stalls in the marketplace pay high rents, they have a near-captive clientele of market vendors and truckers, and they get a lot of business from many Mexicans for whom eating in the market is a traditional way of confirming their culture.

   What's Cooking in the Yucatán

Yucatecan cooking is the most distinct of the many kinds of regional cooking, probably because the Maya and Caribbean cultural traditions influenced it. Yucatecans are great fans of achiote (or *annatto,* a red seed pod from a tree that grows in the Caribbean area), which is the basic ingredient for perhaps its most famous dish, *cochinita pibil* (pork wrapped in banana leaves, pit-baked, and served with a *pibil* sauce of achiote, sour orange, and spices). And good seafood is readily available. Many of the most common Mexican dishes are given a different name and a different twist here. Waiters are happy to explain what's what. With a couple of meals under your belt, you'll feel like a native.

On the other side of the spectrum, avoid eating at those inviting sidewalk restaurants that you see beneath the stone archways that border the main plazas. These places usually cater to tourists and don't need to count on getting any return business. But they are great for getting a coffee or beer.

Most nonresort towns have one or two restaurants (sometimes one is a coffee shop) that are social centers for a large group of established patrons. These establishments over time become virtual institutions, and change comes very slowly. The food is usually good standard fare, cooked as it was 20 years ago; the decor is simple. The patrons have known each other and the staff for years, and the *charla* (banter), gestures, and greetings are friendly, open, and unaffected. If you're curious about Mexican culture, eating and observing the goings-on is fun.

During your trip, you're going to see many *taquerías* (**taco joints).** These are generally small places with a counter or a few tables set around the cooking area; you get to see exactly how the cooks make their tacos before deciding whether to order. Most tacos come with a little chopped onion and cilantro, but not tomato and lettuce. Find one that seems popular with the locals and where the cook performs with brio (a good sign of pride in the product). Sometimes there will be a woman making the tortillas right there (or working the masa into *gorditas, sopes,* or *panuchos* if these are also served). You will never see men doing this—this is perhaps the strictest gender division in Mexican society. Men do all other cooking and kitchen tasks, and work with prepared tortillas, but they will never be found working masa.

For the main meal of the day, many restaurants offer a multicourse blue-plate special called **comida corrida** or **menú del día.** This is the least expensive way to get a full dinner. In Mexico, you need to ask for your check; it is generally considered inhospitable to present a check to someone who hasn't requested it. If you're in a hurry to get somewhere, ask for the check when your food arrives.

Tips are about the same as in the United States. You'll sometimes find a 15% **value-added tax** on restaurant meals, which shows up on the bill as "IVA." This is a boon to arithmetically challenged tippers, saving them from undue exertion.

To summon the waiter, wave or raise your hand, but don't motion with your index finger, which is a demeaning gesture that may even cause the waiter to ignore you. Or if it's the check you want, you can motion to the waiter from across the room using the universal pretend-you're-writing gesture.

Most restaurants do not have **nonsmoking sections;** when they do, we mention it in the reviews. But Mexico's wonderful climate allows for many open-air restaurants, usually set inside a courtyard of a colonial house, or in rooms with tall ceilings and plenty of open windows.

DRINKS

All over Mexico you'll find shops selling *jugos* (**juices**) and *liquados* (**smoothies**) made from several kinds of tropical fruit. They're excellent and refreshing; while traveling, I take full advantage of them. You'll also come across *aguas frescas*— water flavored with hibiscus, melon, tamarind, or lime. Soft drinks come in more flavors than in any other country I know. Pepsi and Coca-Cola taste the way they did in the United States years ago, before the makers started adding corn syrup. The coffee is generally good, and **hot chocolate** is a traditional drink, as is *atole*—a hot, corn-based beverage that can be sweet or bitter.

Of course, Mexico has a proud and lucrative **beer**-brewing tradition. A lesser-known brewed beverage is *pulque,* a pre-Hispanic drink: the fermented juice of a few species of maguey or agave. Mostly you find it for sale in *pulquerías* in central

Mexico. It is an acquired taste, and not every gringo acquires it. **Mezcal** and **tequila** also come from the agave. Tequila is a variety of mezcal produced from the *A. tequilana* species of agave in and around the area of Tequila, in the state of Jalisco. Mezcal comes from various parts of Mexico and from different varieties of agave. The distilling process is usually much less sophisticated than that of tequila, and, with its stronger smell and taste, mezcal is much more easily detected on the drinker's breath. In some places such as Oaxaca, it comes with a worm in the bottle; you are supposed to eat the worm after polishing off the mezcal. But for those teetotalers out there who are interested in just the worm, I have good news—you can find these worms for sale in Mexican markets when in season. *¡Salud!*

Appendix B:
Useful Terms & Phrases

USING THE TELEPHONES

All phone numbers listed in this book have a total of 10 digits—a two- or three-digit area code plus the telephone number. Local numbers in Mexico City, Guadalajara, and Monterrey have eight digits; everywhere else, local numbers have seven digits.

To call long distance within Mexico, dial the national long-distance code **01** before dialing the area code and then the number. Mexico's area codes *(claves)* are listed in the front of telephone directories. Area codes are listed before all phone numbers in this book. For long-distance dialing, you will often see the term "LADA," which is the automatic long-distance service offered by Telmex, Mexico's former telephone monopoly and its largest phone company. To make a person-to-person or collect call inside Mexico, dial ✆ **020.** You can also call 020 to request the correct area codes for the number and place you are calling.

To make a long-distance call to the United States or Canada, dial **001,** then the area code and seven-digit number. For international long-distance numbers in Europe, Africa, and Asia, dial **00,** then the country code, the city code, and the number. To make a person-to-person or collect call to a number outside Mexico, to obtain other international dialing codes, or for further assistance, dial ✆ **090.**

For additional details on making calls in Mexico and to Mexico, see chapter 2 and the inside front cover of this book.

POSTAL GLOSSARY
Airmail   **Correo Aéreo**
Customs   **Aduana**
General delivery   **Lista de correos**
Insurance (insured mail)   **Seguro (correo asegurado)**
Mailbox   **Buzón**
Money order   **Giro postal**
Parcel   **Paquete**
Post office   **Oficina de correos**
Post office box (abbreviation)   **Apdo. Postal**
Postal service   **Correos**
Registered mail   **Registrado**
Rubber stamp   **Sello**
Special delivery, express   **Entrega inmediata**
Stamp   **Estampilla** or **timbre**

2 Basic Vocabulary

Most Mexicans are very patient with foreigners who try to speak their language; it helps a lot to know a few basic phrases. I've included simple phrases for expressing basic needs, followed by some common menu items.

ENGLISH-SPANISH PHRASES

English	Spanish	Pronunciation
Good day	**Buen día**	bwehn *dee*-ah
Good morning	**Buenos días**	*bweh*-nohss *dee*-ahss
How are you?	**¿Cómo está?**	*koh*-moh ehss-*tah?*
Very well	**Muy bien**	mwee byehn
Thank you	**Gracias**	*grah*-syahss
You're welcome	**De nada**	deh *nah*-dah
Good-bye	**Adiós**	ah-*dyohss*
Please	**Por favor**	pohr fah-*vohr*
Yes	**Sí**	see
No	**No**	noh
Excuse me	**Perdóneme**	pehr-*doh*-neh-meh
Give me	**Déme**	*deh*-meh
Where is . . . ?	**¿Dónde está . . . ?**	*dohn*-deh ehss-*tah?*
the station	**la estación**	lah ehss-tah-*syohn*
a hotel	**un hotel**	oon oh-*tehl*
a gas station	**una gasolinera**	*oo*-nah gah-soh-lee-*neh*-rah
a restaurant	**un restaurante**	oon res-tow-*rahn*-teh
the toilet	**el baño**	el *bah*-nyoh
a good doctor	**un buen médico**	oon bwehn *meh*-dee-coh
the road to . . .	**el camino a/hacia . . .**	el cah-*mee*-noh ah/*ah*-syah
To the right	**A la derecha**	ah lah deh-*reh*-chah
To the left	**A la izquierda**	ah lah ees-*kyehr*-dah
Straight ahead	**Derecho**	deh-*reh*-choh
I would like	**Quisiera**	key-*syeh*-rah
I want	**Quiero**	*kyeh*-roh
to eat	**comer**	koh-*mehr*
a room	**una habitación**	*oo*-nah ah-bee-tah-*syohn*
Do you have . . . ?	**¿Tiene usted . . . ?**	tyeh-neh oo-*sted?*
a book	**un libro**	oon *lee*-broh
a dictionary	**un diccionario**	oon deek-syow-*nah*-ryo
How much is it?	**¿Cuánto cuesta?**	*kwahn*-toh *kwehss*-tah?
When?	**¿Cuándo?**	*kwahn*-doh?
What?	**¿Qué?**	keh?
There is (Is there . . . ?)	**(¿)Hay (. . . ?)**	eye?
What is there?	**¿Qué hay?**	keh eye?
Yesterday	**Ayer**	ah-*yer*
Today	**Hoy**	oy
Tomorrow	**Mañana**	mah-*nyah*-nah
Good	**Bueno**	*bweh*-noh
Bad	**Malo**	*mah*-loh
Better (best)	**(Lo) Mejor**	(loh) meh-*hohr*
More	**Más**	mahs
Less	**Menos**	*meh*-nohss

English	Spanish	Pronunciation
No smoking	**Se prohibe fumar**	seh proh-*ee*-beh foo-*mahr*
Postcard	**Tarjeta postal**	tar-*heh*-ta pohs-*tahl*
Insect repellent	**Repelente contra insectos**	reh-peh-*lehn*-te *cohn*-trah een-*sehk*-tos

MORE USEFUL PHRASES

English	Spanish	Pronunciation
Do you speak English?	**¿Habla usted inglés?**	*ah*-blah oo-*sted* een-*glays*?
Is there anyone here who speaks English?	**¿Hay alguien aquí que hable inglés?**	eye *ahl*-gyehn ah-*kee* keh *ah*-bleh een-*glehs*?
I speak a little Spanish.	**Hablo un poco de español.**	*ah*-bloh oon *poh*-koh deh ehss-pah-*nyohl*
I don't understand Spanish very well.	**No (lo) entiendo muy bien el español.**	noh (loh) ehn-*tyehn*-doh mwee byehn el ehss-pah-*nyohl*
The meal is good.	**Me gusta la comida.**	meh *goo*-stah lah koh-*mee*-dah
What time is it?	**¿Qué hora es?**	keh *oh*-rah ehss?
May I see your menu?	**¿Puedo ver el menú (la carta)?**	*pueh*-do vehr el meh-*noo* (lah *car*-tah)?
The check, please.	**La cuenta, por favor.**	lah *quehn*-tah pohr fa-*vorh*
What do I owe you?	**¿Cuánto le debo?**	*kwahn*-toh leh *deh*-boh?
What did you say?	**¿Mande?** (formal)	*mahn*-deh?
	¿Cómo? (informal)	*koh*-moh?
I want (to see) . . .	**Quiero (ver) . . .**	*kyeh*-roh (vehr) . . .
a room	**un cuarto** or	oon *kwar*-toh,
	una habitación	*oo*-nah ah-bee-tah-*syohn*
for two persons	**para dos personas**	*pah*-rah dohss pehr-*soh*-nahs
with (without) bathroom	**con (sin) baño.**	kohn (seen) *bah*-nyoh
We are staying here	**Nos quedamos aquí**	nohs keh-*dah*-mohss ah-*kee*
only	**solamente**	soh-lah-*mehn*-teh
one night	**una noche**	*oo*-nah *noh*-cheh
one week	**una semana**	*oo*-nah seh-*mah*-nah
We are leaving tomorrow	**Partimos (Salimos) mañana**	pahr-*tee*-mohss (sah-*lee*-mohss) mah-*nyah*-nah
Do you accept traveler's checks?	**¿Acepta usted cheques de viajero?**	Ah-*sayp*-tah oo-*sted* *chay*-kays day bee-ah-*hehr*-oh?
Is there a laundromat? near here?	**¿Hay una lavandería? cerca de aquí?**	eye *oo*-nah lah-*vahn*-deh-*ree*-ah *sehr*-kah deh ah-*kee*
Please send these clothes to the laundry	**Hágame el favor de mandar esta ropa a la lavandería.**	*ah*-gah-meh el fah-*vohr* deh mahn-*dahr* *ehss*-tah *roh*-pah a lah lah-*vahn*-deh-*ree*-ah

NUMBERS

1	**uno** (*ooh*-noh)		7	**siete** (*syeh*-teh)
2	**dos** (dohss)		8	**ocho** (*oh*-choh)
3	**tres** (trehss)		9	**nueve** (*nweh*-beh)
4	**cuatro** (*kwah*-troh)		10	**diez** (dyess)
5	**cinco** (*seen*-koh)		11	**once** (*ohn*-seh)
6	**seis** (sayss)		12	**doce** (*doh*-seh)

13	**trece** (*treh*-seh)		50	**cincuenta** (seen-*kwen*-tah)
14	**catorce** (kah-*tohr*-seh)		60	**sesenta** (seh-*sehn*-tah)
15	**quince** (*keen*-seh)		70	**setenta** (seh-*tehn*-tah)
16	**dieciseis** (dyess-ee-*sayss*)		80	**ochenta** (oh-*chehn*-tah)
17	**diecisiete** (dyess-ee-*syeh*-teh)		90	**noventa** (noh-*behn*-tah)
18	**dieciocho** (dyess-ee-*oh*-choh)		100	**cien** (syehn)
19	**diecinueve** (dyess-ee-*nweh*-beh)		200	**doscientos** (doh-*syehn*-tohs)
20	**veinte** (*bayn*-teh)		500	**quinientos** (kee-*nyehn*-tohs)
30	**treinta** (*trayn*-tah)		1,000	**mil** (meel)
40	**cuarenta** (kwah-*ren*-tah)			

TRANSPORTATION TERMS

English	Spanish	Pronunciation
Airport	**Aeropuerto**	ah-eh-roh-*pwehr*-toh
Flight	**Vuelo**	*bweh*-loh
Rental car	**Arrendadora de autos**	ah-rehn-da-doh-rah deh ow-tohs
Bus	**Autobús**	ow-toh-*boos*
Bus or truck	**Camión**	ka-*myohn*
Lane	**Carril**	kah-*reel*
Nonstop	**Directo**	dee-*rehk*-toh
Baggage (claim area)	**Equipajes**	eh-kee-*pah*-hehss
Intercity	**Foraneo**	foh-rah-*neh*-oh
Luggage storage area	**Guarda equipaje**	gwar-dah eh-kee-*pah*-heh
Arrival gates	**Llegadas**	yeh-*gah*-dahss
Originates at this station	**Local**	loh-*kahl*
Originates elsewhere	**De paso**	deh *pah*-soh
Stops if seats available	**Para si hay lugares**	*pah*-rah see eye loo-*gah*-rehs
First class	**Primera**	pree-*meh*-rah
Second class	**Segunda**	seh-*goon*-dah
Nonstop	**Sin escala**	seen ess-*kah*-lah
Baggage claim area	**Recibo de equipajes**	reh-see-boh deh eh-kee-*pah*-hehss
Waiting room	**Sala de espera**	*sah*-lah deh ehss-*peh*-rah
Toilets	**Sanitarios**	sah-nee-*tah*-ryohss
Ticket window	**Taquilla**	tah-*kee*-yah

3 Menu Glossary

Achiote   Small red seed of the *annatto* tree.

Achiote preparado   A Yucatecan prepared paste made of ground *achiote*, wheat and corn flour, cumin, cinnamon, salt, onion, garlic, and oregano.

Agua fresca   Fruit-flavored water, usually watermelon, cantaloupe, chia seed with lemon, hibiscus flour, rice, or ground melon-seed mixture.

Antojito   Typical Mexican supper foods, usually made with *masa* or tortillas and having a filling or topping such as sausage, cheese, beans, and onions; includes such things as *tacos, tostadas, sopes,* and *garnachas.*

Atole   A thick, lightly sweet, hot drink made with finely ground corn and usually flavored with vanilla, pecan, strawberry, pineapple, or chocolate.

Botana   An appetizer.

Buñuelos   Round, thin, deep-fried crispy fritters dipped in sugar.

Carnitas   Pork deep-cooked (not fried) in lard, and then simmered and served with corn tortillas for tacos.

Ceviche   Fresh raw seafood marinated in fresh lime juice and garnished with chopped tomatoes, onions, chiles, and sometimes cilantro.

Chayote   A vegetable pear or mirliton, a type of spiny squash boiled and served as an accompaniment to meat dishes.

Chiles en nogada   Poblano peppers stuffed with a mixture of ground pork and beef, spices, fruits, raisins, and almonds. Can be served either warm—fried in a light batter—or cold, sans the batter. Either way it is then covered in walnut-and-cream sauce.

Chiles rellenos   Usually poblano peppers stuffed with cheese or spicy ground meat with raisins, rolled in a batter, and fried.

Churro   Tube-shaped, breadlike fritter, dipped in sugar and sometimes filled with *cajeta* (milk-based caramel) or chocolate.

Cochinita pibil   Pork wrapped in banana leaves, pit-baked in a *pibil* sauce of *achiote,* sour orange, and spices; common in the Yucatán.

Enchilada   A tortilla dipped in sauce, usually filled with chicken or white cheese, and sometimes topped with *mole* (*enchiladas rojas* or *de mole*), or with tomato sauce and sour cream (*enchiladas suizas*—Swiss enchiladas), or covered in a green sauce *(enchiladas verdes),* or topped with onions, sour cream, and guacamole *(enchiladas potosinas).*

Escabeche   A lightly pickled sauce used in Yucatecan chicken stew.

Frijoles refritos   Pinto beans mashed and cooked with lard.

Garnachas   A thickish small circle of fried *masa* with pinched sides, topped with pork or chicken, onions, and avocado, or sometimes chopped potatoes and tomatoes, typical as a *botana* in Veracruz and Yucatán.

Gorditas   Thick, fried corn tortillas, slit and stuffed with choice of cheese, beans, beef, chicken, with or without lettuce, tomato, and onion garnish.

Horchata   Refreshing drink made of ground rice or melon seeds, ground almonds, cinnamon, and lightly sweetened.

Huevos mexicanos   Scrambled eggs with chopped onions, hot green peppers, and tomatoes.

Huitlacoche   Sometimes spelled "cuitlacoche." A mushroom-flavored black fungus that appears on corn in the rainy season; considered a delicacy.

Manchamantel   Translated, means "tablecloth stainer." A stew of chicken or pork with chiles, tomatoes, pineapple, bananas, and jícama.

Masa   Ground corn soaked in lime; the basis for tamales, corn tortillas, and soups.

Mixiote   Rabbit, lamb, or chicken cooked in a mild chile sauce (usually chile *ancho* or *pasilla*), and then wrapped like a tamal and steamed. It is generally served with tortillas for tacos, with traditional garnishes of pickled onions, hot sauce, chopped cilantro, and lime wedges.

Pan de muerto   Sweet bread made around the Days of the Dead (Nov 1–2), in the form of mummies or dolls, or round with bone designs.

Pan dulce   Lightly sweetened bread in many configurations, usually served at breakfast or bought in any bakery.

Papadzules   Tortillas stuffed with hard-boiled eggs and seeds (pumpkin or sunflower) in a tomato sauce.

Pibil   Pit-baked pork or chicken in a sauce of tomato, onion, mild red pepper, cilantro, and vinegar.

Pipián   A sauce made with ground pumpkin seeds, nuts, and mild peppers.

Poc chuc   Slices of pork with onion marinated in a tangy sour orange sauce and charcoal-broiled; a Yucatecan specialty.

Pulque   A drink made of fermented juice of the maguey plant; best in the state of Hidalgo and around Mexico City.

Quesadilla   Corn or flour tortillas stuffed with melted white cheese and lightly fried.

Queso relleno   "Stuffed cheese," a mild yellow cheese stuffed with minced meat and spices; a Yucatecan specialty.

Rompope   Delicious Mexican eggnog, invented in Puebla, made with eggs, vanilla, sugar, and rum.

Salsa verde   An uncooked sauce using the green tomatillo and puréed with spicy or mild hot peppers, onions, garlic, and cilantro; on tables countrywide.

Sopa de flor de calabaza   A soup made of chopped squash or pumpkin blossoms.

Sopa de lima   A tangy soup made with chicken broth and accented with fresh lime; popular in Yucatán.

Sopa de tortilla   A traditional chicken broth–based soup, seasoned with chiles, tomatoes, onion, and garlic, served with crispy fried strips of corn tortillas.

Sopa tlalpeña (or *caldo tlapeño*)   A hearty soup made with chunks of chicken, chopped carrots, zucchini, corn, onions, garlic, and cilantro.

Sopa tlaxcalteca   A hearty tomato-based soup filled with cooked nopal cactus, cheese, cream, and avocado, with crispy tortilla strips floating on top.

Sope   Pronounced "*soh*-peh." An *antojito* similar to a *garnacha,* except spread with refried beans and topped with crumbled cheese and onions.

Tacos al pastor   Thin slices of flavored pork roasted on a revolving cylinder dripping with onion slices and juice of fresh pineapple slices. Served in small corn tortillas, topped with chopped onion and cilantro.

Tamal   Incorrectly called a tamale (*tamal* singular, *tamales* plural). A meat or sweet filling rolled with fresh *masa,* wrapped in a corn husk or banana leaf, and steamed.

Tikin xic   Also seen on menus as "tik-n-xic" and "tikik chick." Charbroiled fish brushed with *achiote* sauce.

Torta   A sandwich, usually on *bolillo* bread, typically with sliced avocado, onions, tomatoes, with a choice of meat and often cheese.

Xtabentun   Pronounced "shtah-behn-*toon.*" A Yucatecan liquor made of fermented honey and flavored with anise. It comes *seco* (dry) or *crema* (sweet).

Zacahuil   Pork leg tamal, packed in thick *masa,* wrapped in banana leaves, and pit-baked, sometimes pot-made with tomato and *masa;* a specialty of mid- to upper Veracruz.

Index

See also Accommodations and Restaurant indexes, below.

Frommer's
Portable Guides
Complete Guides for the
Short-Term Traveler

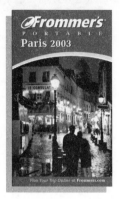

Great Trips Like Great Days Begin with a Plan

FranklinCovey and Frommer's Bring You *Frommer's Favorite Places*® Planner

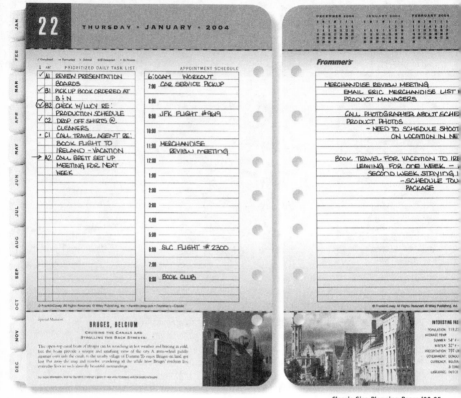

Classic Size Planning Pages $39.95

The planning experts at FranklinCovey have teamed up with the travel experts at Frommer's. The result is a full-year travel-themed planner filled with rich images and travel tips covering fifty-two of Frommer's Favorite Places.

- Each week will make you an expert about an intriguing corner of the world
- New facts and tips every day
- Beautiful, full-color photos of some of the most beautiful places on earth
- Proven planning tools from FranklinCovey for keeping track of tasks, appointments, notes, address/phone numbers, and more

Save 15%

when you purchase Frommer's Favorite Places travel-themed planner and a binder.

Order today before your next big trip.

www.franklincovey.com/frommers
Enter promo code 12252 at checkout for discount. Offer expires June 1, 2005.

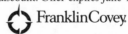

Frommer's is a trademark of Arthur Frommer.

FROMMER'S® COMPLETE TRAVEL GUIDES

Alaska
Alaska Cruises & Ports of Call
Amsterdam
Argentina & Chile
Arizona
Atlanta
Australia
Austria
Bahamas
Barcelona, Madrid & Seville
Beijing
Belgium, Holland & Luxembourg
Bermuda
Boston
Brazil
British Columbia & the Canadian Rockies
Brussels & Bruges
Budapest & the Best of Hungary
California
Canada
Cancún, Cozumel & the Yucatán
Cape Cod, Nantucket & Martha's Vineyard
Caribbean
Caribbean Cruises & Ports of Call
Caribbean Ports of Call
Carolinas & Georgia
Chicago
China
Colorado
Costa Rica
Cuba
Denmark
Denver, Boulder & Colorado Springs
England
Europe
European Cruises & Ports of Call

Florida
France
Germany
Great Britain
Greece
Greek Islands
Hawaii
Hong Kong
Honolulu, Waikiki & Oahu
Ireland
Israel
Italy
Jamaica
Japan
Las Vegas
London
Los Angeles
Maryland & Delaware
Maui
Mexico
Montana & Wyoming
Montréal & Québec City
Munich & the Bavarian Alps
Nashville & Memphis
New England
New Mexico
New Orleans
New York City
New Zealand
Northern Italy
Norway
Nova Scotia, New Brunswick & Prince Edward Island
Oregon
Paris
Peru
Philadelphia & the Amish Country
Portugal

Prague & the Best of the Czech Republic
Provence & the Riviera
Puerto Rico
Rome
San Antonio & Austin
San Diego
San Francisco
Santa Fe, Taos & Albuquerque
Scandinavia
Scotland
Seattle & Portland
Shanghai
Sicily
Singapore & Malaysia
South Africa
South America
South Florida
South Pacific
Southeast Asia
Spain
Sweden
Switzerland
Texas
Thailand
Tokyo
Toronto
Tuscany & Umbria
USA
Utah
Vancouver & Victoria
Vermont, New Hampshire & Maine
Vienna & the Danube Valley
Virgin Islands
Virginia
Walt Disney World® & Orlando
Washington, D.C.
Washington State

FROMMER'S® DOLLAR-A-DAY GUIDES

Australia from $50 a Day
California from $70 a Day
England from $75 a Day
Europe from $70 a Day
Florida from $70 a Day
Hawaii from $80 a Day

Ireland from $60 a Day
Italy from $70 a Day
London from $85 a Day
New York from $90 a Day
Paris from $80 a Day

San Francisco from $70 a Day
Washington, D.C. from $80 a Day
Portable London from $85 a Day
Portable New York City from $90 a Day

FROMMER'S® PORTABLE GUIDES

Acapulco, Ixtapa & Zihuatanejo
Amsterdam
Aruba
Australia's Great Barrier Reef
Bahamas
Berlin
Big Island of Hawaii
Boston
California Wine Country
Cancún
Cayman Islands
Charleston
Chicago
Disneyland®
Dublin
Florence

Frankfurt
Hong Kong
Houston
Las Vegas
Las Vegas for Non-Gamblers
London
Los Angeles
Los Cabos & Baja
Maine Coast
Maui
Miami
Nantucket & Martha's Vineyard
New Orleans
New York City
Paris
Phoenix & Scottsdale

Portland
Puerto Rico
Puerto Vallarta, Manzanillo & Guadalajara
Rio de Janeiro
San Diego
San Francisco
Savannah
Seattle
Sydney
Tampa & St. Petersburg
Vancouver
Venice
Virgin Islands
Washington, D.C.

FROMMER'S® NATIONAL PARK GUIDES

Banff & Jasper
Family Vacations in the National Parks

Grand Canyon
National Parks of the American West
Rocky Mountain

Yellowstone & Grand Teton
Yosemite & Sequoia/Kings Canyon
Zion & Bryce Canyon

FROMMER'S® MEMORABLE WALKS

Chicago	New York	San Francisco
London	Paris	

FROMMER'S® WITH KIDS GUIDES

Chicago	Ottawa	Vancouver
Las Vegas	San Francisco	Washington, D.C.
New York City	Toronto	

SUZY GERSHMAN'S BORN TO SHOP GUIDES

Born to Shop: France	Born to Shop: Italy	Born to Shop: New York
Born to Shop: Hong Kong, Shanghai & Beijing	Born to Shop: London	Born to Shop: Paris

FROMMER'S® IRREVERENT GUIDES

Amsterdam	Los Angeles	San Francisco
Boston	Manhattan	Seattle & Portland
Chicago	New Orleans	Vancouver
Las Vegas	Paris	Walt Disney World®
London	Rome	Washington, D.C.

FROMMER'S® BEST-LOVED DRIVING TOURS

Britain	Germany	Northern Italy
California	Ireland	Scotland
Florida	Italy	Spain
France	New England	Tuscany & Umbria

HANGING OUT™ GUIDES

Hanging Out in England	Hanging Out in France	Hanging Out in Italy
Hanging Out in Europe	Hanging Out in Ireland	Hanging Out in Spain

THE UNOFFICIAL GUIDES®

Bed & Breakfasts and Country Inns in:	Southwest & South Central Plains	Mexio's Best Beach Resorts
California	U.S.A.	Mid-Atlantic with Kids
Great Lakes States	Beyond Disney	Mini Las Vegas
Mid-Atlantic	Branson, Missouri	Mini-Mickey
New England	California with Kids	New England & New York with Kids
Northwest	Central Italy	
Rockies	Chicago	New Orleans
Southeast	Cruises	New York City
Southwest	Disneyland®	Paris
Best RV & Tent Campgrounds in:	Florida with Kids	San Francisco
California & the West	Golf Vacations in the Eastern U.S.	Skiing & Snowboarding in the West
Florida & the Southeast	Great Smoky & Blue Ridge Region	Southeast with Kids
Great Lakes States	Inside Disney	Walt Disney World®
Mid-Atlantic	Hawaii	Walt Disney World® for Grown-ups
Northeast	Las Vegas	Walt Disney World® with Kids
Northwest & Central Plains	London	Washington, D.C.
	Maui	World's Best Diving Vacations

SPECIAL-INTEREST TITLES

Frommer's Adventure Guide to Australia & New Zealand
Frommer's Adventure Guide to Central America
Frommer's Adventure Guide to India & Pakistan
Frommer's Adventure Guide to South America
Frommer's Adventure Guide to Southeast Asia
Frommer's Adventure Guide to Southern Africa
Frommer's Britain's Best Bed & Breakfasts and Country Inns
Frommer's Caribbean Hideaways
Frommer's Exploring America by RV
Frommer's Fly Safe, Fly Smart

Frommer's France's Best Bed & Breakfasts and Country Inns
Frommer's Gay & Lesbian Europe
Frommer's Italy's Best Bed & Breakfasts and Country Inns
Frommer's Road Atlas Britain
Frommer's Road Atlas Europe
Frommer's Road Atlas France
The New York Times' Guide to Unforgettable Weekends
Places Rated Almanac
Retirement Places Rated
Rome Past & Present